Lady Outlaw
becoming
UNTAMED

TIFFANY SPARKS

Full Moon Publishing, LLC
Glade Spring, VA
Fullmoonpublishingllc.com

ISBN: 978-1-946232-19-9

DEDICATION

This collection of forty years of my life history
is dedicated to:
First and Foremost My Children
Grace, J.J., Faith
You are my heart and soul,
My pride and joy,
My sunrise and sunset,
My reason for living and breathing,
My whole world.
Being your mother has been the greatest
blessing and honor of my lifetime.
And Secondly
To all of my descendants, whether we meet or not
in this lifetime or the next..
I leave this behind as a testament of who I was,
so you will know where you came from.
All My Love Always,
Tiffany Beth Sparks

CONTENTS

A Black Sheep Is Born

It's hard to know where to start when you're telling the story of your life. I had considered writing a book several times in the past, but the dilemma of not knowing where to begin always deterred me. The obvious starting point is at the very beginning, but that's just a drop in the bucket of the grand scheme of things for me. And at the same time, the most relevant part. So I will start there. I also struggled with trying to decide which parts of my life to include. I am just going to tell it all; the good, the bad, and the ugly. The truth as I know it. My mother was fourteen years old when she married my father who was 19 at the time. She had my sister Haley at the age of 15, and I came along when she was sixteen years old. (Which thinking about that now takes on a whole new meaning for me since my youngest daughter is sixteen, and I can't imagine her being a mother at that age. I still see her as my baby girl.)

Anyways, it was not an ideal situation. Just based on the above circumstances alone, my entry into the world came about during an inopportune time frame where my parents were basically teenagers. Kids raising kids. My mom and dad were both born and raised in West Virginia, where generations of both sides of my family came from. I made my official debut in the small town of Somerset, Kentucky on Friday, April 11, 1980, at 7:17 p.m. I weighed 7 pounds and 7 ounces. (Mama has always said I was an ugly baby. Her description is that I looked like an Ethiopian with eyes that were way too big for my head.) My mother was going to name me Tiffany Elizabeth, but my great grandfather said that was too long a name, so she shortened it to Tiffany Beth. She had chosen my first name based on the Tiffany & Co. jewelry store.

My daddy was working as a travelling contractor at the time of my birth, for a company run by his sister JoAnn, so Kentucky was home base for us for a few years. Now going back several generations, some of my ancestors on my dad's side once lived in Pike County, Kentucky. My great x3 grandfather, Bandy Bill Mullens Senior, managed to get the entire family banned from the state of Kentucky on the grounds of having an affair with a Cherokee woman who turned out to be my great x3 grandmother. But that type of relations between a white man and Native American was apparently against Kentucky law in that day and age. So that is how and why that side of my family ended up migrating to West Virginia. But leave it to me to be born in the one state my people were banished from.

My first memories began at the age of two. I remember one thing specifically—the house we lived in at the time. More or less, the feel of the house. But I also remember the layout of it and the way it looked. It had been an old two-story house that was eventually converted into two townhouses. I remember feeling very uneasy in the bedroom Haley and I shared on the second floor. But I was mostly afraid of the living room, which I could see through the vent in the floor in between our two beds. When I became older my mother told me of that house being haunted. She would have jewelry disappear, then show up somewhere else. The light on her makeup mirror would turn on and off. The living room door would frequently open by itself. My dad would smell strong perfume on the stairway every time he came up and down. One of the previous occupants had told mom that the house was haunted by an old lady who died there, and said they had once seen her walking down the hallway past the bathroom. Finally, one night while my dad was at work, my mom heard footsteps approaching her bed, then they stopped at the end of her bed. She took us kids that night and left, never went back. Dad returned the next day and packed our belongings to move to an apartment complex.

The only thing I remember from the apartment, are two of the epic messes Haley and I made. One of which we poured out an entire bottle of chocolate syrup onto the white carpet in the living room, in front of the television. We ate the chocolate off the floor while we watched cartoons. And the second one was a massive scale mess we made in the kitchen in the middle of the night. Haley and I climbed up on the countertops, got all of the canisters down, and poured every one of them out onto the tile floor. We dumped sugar, flour and coffee grounds into a big pile. Then we ran our little yellow bulldozers and dump trucks through it all, creating roadways and construction sites all over the kitchen. Daddy took a picture of that grand disaster. Also, at two years old, my mother and father separated and divorced. And so the shuffling began. The term "it takes a village", well that definitely applies to my upbringing because I was raised by a village.

Initially, after the divorce, my sister and I stayed in Kentucky with our father, while our mother went to Florida to live with her parents and get her feet on the ground as an 18-year-old divorced mother of two with a GED and no work experience. Dad tried to take care of us, but with his travelling work schedule and lack of cooking skills, he felt he wasn't succeeding adequately as a single father. So he took us to our Aunt JoAnn in Somerset for a short period, making her our temporary caregiver. She treated us as her own and bought us pretty dresses and patent leather shoes. We were well taken care of by her. At some point, it was decided that the best place for us girls would be our grandparents' farm in Canvas, West Virginia. So Daddy packed us up and delivered us to the doorstep of his parents' home, on the farm where he was raised. Which turned out to be the best-case scenario in our increasingly unstable circumstances. And honestly, Haley and I both agree that looking back on our lives, this was the best time of our entire childhoods.

There have been variations of stories, depending on the teller, as to the timeline of how long we lived with Grandma and Grandpa Sparks. I will tell it as I recall. Their farm was situated in the midst of a bigger cattle farm, tucked up against the mountainside. You crossed two cattle guards on the gravel road to get to it. That second cattle guard was the gateway to Heaven on Earth for me. And there it was in all its glory. A lush green three-acre lawn meticulously manicured. A narrow walkway behind a row of cedar trees leading up to a small whitewashed farmhouse. Up behind the house sat a row of mature apple trees and behind that a huge garden. Just over the hillside from the garden were the barn, the water spring, and berry patch with blueberries, strawberries, raspberries and blackberries. There was a small cabin, a root cellar and a carport close to the house. Although it was small and modest, Grandpa kept the entire place immaculate. And as a child, it seemed like paradise to me. Life on the farm was the epitome of "the good old days". Grandma and Grandpa were up there in age and were never wealthy. They had always been hard workers and earned everything they ever had. But as a psychologist once said to my big sister, "Where everyone else got it wrong, they got it right." Our days there flowed with rhythm like a familiar melody. Starting and ending on the same notes, with a chorus of innocence and carefree bliss in between. We were safe, happy and most importantly, we knew we were loved.

In the early mornings, Grandma would fix our breakfast of Coco Wheats and toast with her homemade strawberry jam... while Grandpa would feed the fire of the cast iron wood burning stove with kindling and old newspapers. That stove, was in my opinion, the heart of the home. Grandpa would pull his ladder backed chair with basket weaved seat up to the stove, and I would climb up on his lap with my ragged blanket and bare feet. He would sing the old-time mountain songs, Old Dan Tucker and Groundhog Gravy, to the tune of the fire crackling in that old stove.

The afternoons consisted of fetching water from the spring, filling our galvanized tin buckets with berries, helping in the garden, climbing the apple trees, riding our little red Radio Flyer wagon down the hillside, and walking down the gravel road to the general store in order to pay a few coins in exchange for a brown paper sack filled to the brim with candy that we would eat all the way back home.

Grandma always fixed a feast in midday, which they called dinner back then. She would have the entire dining table filled with a variety of meats, all sorts of canned vegetables from the garden, fresh fruits, mashed potatoes and gravy, homemade biscuits and cornbread, as well as a few desserts of angel food cake and pound cake. Then supper at night was the leftovers from dinner. She was the best cook I've ever known, and folks would come from all over to dine at her table. She always seemed to be happiest when she was feeding family and visitors. If there is one place I could go back in time and revisit it would be my granny's kitchen.

After supper, Grandma would make us homemade popcorn and Neapolitan ice cream cones. Haley and I would play dress up in grandma's long silk nightgowns, her old lady shades of lipstick, strands of pearls, clip-on earrings and conservative high heels. I would climb up on the back of the couch and comb Grandpa's white hair while he dozed off between tobacco spits of his Red Man pouch chew, into a big tin Folger's coffee can he kept on the floor beside the couch. On one occasion he fell fast asleep and I accidentally got Grandma's round bristled brush so tangled up in his hair that she had to get the scissors and cut his hair to get it out. He slept through the whole ordeal. If he ever noticed he was missing a big patch of his hair after that, he never let on or said a word about it. At nightfall, it was bath time, pajama time, story-time, then bedtime. Everything was like clockwork. As was common in the older days, Grandma and Grandpa slept in different bedrooms. Theirs were on opposite sides of the living room. And since it had been determined early on that Grandma claimed Haley and Grandpa claimed me as their individual favorites, we slept accordingly. However one night, I fell asleep with Haley in Grandma's room as she was reading us bedtime stories. I awoke in the middle of the night and started making way across the living room to Grandpa's room where I normally slept. And I was stopped in my tracks by a ghost that materialized right before me. Now I was really too young to even know what a ghost was at the time, barely four years old. But I knew that whatever it was, wasn't supposed to be there. And it frightened me. I can only describe it as a tall white glow of light in the form of a man. I ran back to Grandma's room, turned on the light and told what I saw. Nobody believed me. To this day, that occurrence has been a very vivid memory for me. Not something that scares me, just something I remember well.

Grandpa Sparks was a 6'3" tall, slender man. Very serious, hard worker, and the most particular man I have ever known. Everything had to be a certain way according to him. He was especially intent on the fact that you did not ever sit or lie on a made bed unless you were sick or sleeping, or dying. The only time he ever gave me a whipping was the one and only time I ever sat on his made bed. A rule I have since then carried on and have always enforced in my own household. Grandpa could lighten up his serious nature at times though, like for instance when we would ride to Sunday church or to town, he would tap his foot on the gas pedal of his white Lincoln Town Car to the happy beat of whatever hymn he was singing at the time, giving us all an unintentional slight case of whiplash and motion sickness. From what I have been told though, he had become more gentle with age. When he was bringing up his six children he was known to have a bad temper. I never saw that side of him. I would describe him as constant, and deliberate.

Grandma Edith, on the other hand, stood 4'11". But she was like a small package of spitfire and dynamite. She was sweet and sassy. Bossy and sentimental. Strong and soft. She was the hardest working woman I have ever known. She would toil from sun up to sundown, cooking, cleaning, doing the wash, sewing, mending, ironing, working in the garden, canning and baking, churning butter and making lye soap. She never stopped or even slowed down. She was a master storyteller and a good writer, she loved poetry and photographs. Grandma was basically everything I thought a woman should be. And as a wife and mother, I have always strived to fashion myself into what I saw her as through my eyes, a role model of how a traditional homemaker should conduct herself. Grandma was creative and thrifty, she could take nothing and turn it into something.

Of my grandmother's six children, she had been the most protective of my dad. There were several years difference between her first four children and her last two. Dad was the second to last in order and her youngest of two sons. She had been out chopping firewood for the winter when she was 7 months pregnant with him. A piece of wood flew up from the axe and hit her in the stomach, causing her to go into early labor with him. When he was born on November 16th, 1958 he only weighed 3 pounds. The doctors told Grandma he wouldn't make it. She took him home and kept him on her chest all through that harsh winter. He survived, and grew to be a big strong man. But because of his frail entry into the world, she always coddled him more than the others. He was her baby. As I stated before, Grandma claimed Haley and Grandpa claimed me. So if we wanted our way about something she and I would use this to our advantage. For example; one time at the dinner table with Grandpa's mother Lizzy present (who was even more serious than he was). I hadn't finished my plate of food, but I asked Grandpa if I could be excused. Of course, he granted my request. Then Haley immediately tried to follow suit, and was scolded by Grandpa and made to sit there although Grandma quickly stated otherwise. Haley looked at him and said in a matter of fact way, "Grandma said I don't have to you mean old asshole." To that end, Haley dismissed herself and stern Lizzy sat there having a good laugh about it. Alas, and so we had carried on this happy and content existence with our grandparents on the farm, day in and day out, through the changing of several seasons.

Until one winter night, in the front sunroom of the house where we had just decorated our Christmas tree, we saw headlights coming up the long gravel road. It was our mother, returning from Florida to collect us. And just like that, our days of living on the farm came to an abrupt and sudden halt. Grandma told us later on that Grandpa stood in the doorway and cried as he watched the taillights fade out of sight. I remember looking behind me from the backseat of Mama's car and seeing the glow of the Christmas lights through the windows of the house, on the tree we had just moments before adorned together as a happy family.

And so the next chapter of my life began. I was four years old when Mama came back. Mom's parents had also come back to West Virginia from Florida. (There is an ongoing curse between these two states for my mother's side of the family which I will explain later.) We lived all together with mom, her younger sister, and our maternal grandparents for a while in the town of Summersville, WV where Mom was raised. Then mom got an apartment for her and us girls. We settled into new routines. Going to a babysitter while Mom worked driving a 7UP route truck for the warehouse owned by her father. Visiting the farm in Canvas on the weekends. And Daddy would come there to see us. Our lives took on a new normal during this time. And meanwhile, Haley and I began our school years. Mom got engaged to an old school flame of hers while we were at the apartment. He was ill-tempered and all I remember of him from then was him mistreating my mother, and in more blatant terms, I recalled him hitting her. In one particular episode of my introduction to Domestic Violence 101, I witnessed him hurting her. Although I was young and not completely aware of what I had seen, I instinctively knew that it wasn't right. And so I asked her, "Mommy are you okay?" She replied (in a voice trying to choke back tears), "Yes honey, we were just playing a game." Low and behold, they split up and she met someone new. They were soon married in a small civil ceremony, and when I was five years old we moved to central Florida.

Relocating is always difficult, but especially when you are going from one state to another that is so drastically different from anything you've ever known. I went from the Appalachian mountain region to the flat swampland of Florida. Something I never grew accustomed to. Everything changed. I had a new stepdad, new school, new surroundings and new environment. As a child you don't have a say so in these matters, so what do you do? You just roll with the changes against your will.

Again a new normal takes effect. Days turn into weeks, then months, then years. When I was six years old, I experienced the first worst year of my life. That June 8th on what would have been my parents' eighth wedding anniversary, my Grandpa Sparks passed away from a heart attack. He had worked on the farm's cistern that morning, put his Sunday clothes on for church, sat down on the same couch where I used to brush his hair, and quietly left this world behind.

Then on December 3rd, my daddy died. I had spoken with him for the last time over the phone from my Aunt Brenda's in Louisiana a few nights before his accident, and he asked us, girls, what we wanted for Christmas. He was travelling through Indiana on his way back home to Somerset and was severely injured in an auto accident involving a deer. He lay in a coma for three days before he was taken off of life support, and passed away. His pregnant wife was with him in the wreck, and he was hauling a construction trailer behind his truck, with the Christmas presents he had just bought for me and Haley. These were my first experiences with death. Losing my grandfather hit me hard. I was his favorite, and he was mine. But I couldn't believe that I would never see him again. I couldn't understand the concept and finality of death. And I didn't have a chance to see for myself or to say goodbye because no one took me to his funeral. But then standing at my father's funeral six months later, I suddenly did understand in the abstract way that a child does. I was given a single white rose to lay in his open casket, and when I placed it on his chest, I went to hold his hand. When I felt his big cold hand with my tiny warm hand, I knew. But I could never make peace with it. I cannot even now, even after being through the many hells of my life and the many deaths of my loved ones. I will never really understand.

After his funeral, Haley and I opened the presents he had gotten us. And visited with his wife, who was six months pregnant with our little sister, Marci. That was the closest encounter I would have of my baby sister until she was eleven years old.

My father was a good man. Everyone who knew him still speaks of the fact that he was just a special person; and how no one else will ever be like Mark Sparks. What I remember most of him was his quiet gentle nature, the way his eyes twinkled when he smiled, and the way I felt so safe when he would hold me in his strong arms. But he was much more than even that. He was an adventurer, a lover of life, a nature enthusiast, a kind and compassionate human being, a photographer and an incredibly talented artist. He started drawing at the age of three, and never finished till the end of his life at the age of 28. He did wood burnings, charcoal drawings, pen and ink sketches, paintings. It was just in him, part of him, he had to create artwork. It came as natural to him as breathing air. And I thank God for his art because that is all I have left of him. But it is something and everything to me. Over the years different family members have given me pieces of his art that he had given to them while he was living because they knew I would treasure and protect them as long as I live. The walls of my home are filled with my daddy's work, whatever came from his mind and heart onto a surface. It is priceless to me. I was, always have been, and still am the type of girl who needs her daddy. I'm a tomboy and I like to fish and play in the dirt. I needed him to teach me to throw a ball and shoot a gun. How to drive a car and change a tire. And a million other things in between all that. His absence is one of the most key elements of struggle I have had to deal with almost all of my life. He would have been my best friend, my hero. I needed him here to protect me and he was taken away. Taken too soon. Not just from me but from everyone who loved him. I don't think I was ever right with the world after that year, 1986 changed who I was, and who I would become. I was already a quiet child, introverted, extremely observant, independent and stubborn by nature. But I withdrew from people even more once I realized they wouldn't always be around, that death could take them away from me.

We had something that resembled a traditional family system with my mom and stepdad. We moved from one apartment to another, and finally to a brick ranch style house on 1 ¼ acres that they purchased in Lakeland, Florida. They went to work, we went to school, and we did family activities on the weekends. But summer was what I looked forward to. Because I knew that was the season when my Grandpa Venable (Peepaw) would take me to the mountains of West Virginia. And as soon as those mountains came into view, I knew I was home. It was the only place that ever felt like home.

Since my dad died, Peepaw was the man who stepped up and took on the role as a father figure to me and my sister. His own dad was killed in action during a WWII battle in France when he was only three-years-old. So he knew from experience what it meant to lose and miss your father. And I think with his compassion for us girls in that regard, an overall sense of duty came over him in a way that he knew he was the only real chance we had for a protector, guardian, and teacher that only a father can be to his children. And so, he became the man who raised us.

If it wasn't for him we wouldn't have been able to go back to the farm to spend the summers with Grandma Sparks. And going back to the farm was crucial to us. It was the place of our best childhood memories, a glimpse of the time before this cruel world taught us about death and sadness. It was our lighthouse in the storms of life, a beacon in the dark. And Grandma needed us as much as we needed to return to that happy place because we were all she had left of her beloved son. Peepaw knew that, and he would have gone to the ends of the earth to make that connection possible for all of us. He was the bridge that linked us.

After Grandpa Sparks passed, Grandma was basically stranded on an island at the farm, as she never in her life learned to operate a vehicle. So without him there to maintain the grounds, and with no means of transportation, she was overwhelmed and isolated on top of being still devastated by the loss of her husband and son. When I was eleven years old, Grandma sold the farm. And so came the end of an era. That piece of my soul became lost to me forever. But it has long since been a familiar song like a lullaby that I have replayed in my mind frequently. My stepdad at the time did try to fulfill a paternal role. And I finally accepted him as that. He made an effort to take us fishing, taught us how to use tools, mow the lawn, do chores around the house and gave us lessons on responsibility and common sense. He got us our first dog, took us to amusement parks, bowling and to the movies, put a swimming pool in the back yard and had cookouts. He was present for birthdays and holidays, father-daughter dances and vacations. Things were okay for a while. Mom had settled into a Susie-Homemaker typical mom life getting us involved in activities, doing homeroom mother type stuff, helping with school projects, etc. Mama always made birthdays and holidays so special. She would throw us extravagant parties. And she made every occasion and season so magical. She's fun to be around and has been a cool mom as long as I can remember.

It actually felt like a normal existence. We even bestowed the honor upon our stepdad of calling him "Dad", years after our own father had passed. But after getting used to that dynamic, fast forward to 1992, when I was twelve years old my mom and stepdad got a divorce. A man who had been in my life for seven years was suddenly gone. And the illusion of a happy home life was shattered yet again. This taught me for the second time the difficult lesson that not only does death have the power to take your loved ones from you, but divorce can do the same thing in a different way. Throughout my life, to this point, the only constant person who was always with me was my sister Haley. She remained the one common thread that weaved throughout the entirety of the patchwork quilt that was our childhood. This was also the first realization I had that I was beginning to develop abandonment issues. This is the time in my life when I first decided to just not give a damn. Which basically translated into me disguising my pain by wearing the mask of a tough loner/badass. From then on I would use this as a coping mechanism. I had already been typecast as the black sheep of the family. I was always more like Dad's side of the Sparks and Haley was always more like Mom's side. It's just the way things were. It wasn't a bad thing. It happened to be predetermined by the hereditary order of hierarchy. But I accepted it at this point, being off to myself and separated from the rest of the herd. I even embraced it.

So far, aside from typical sibling rivalry fights I had gotten into with my sister, and trying to steal candy from a gumball machine at a bowling alley; I had only done one intentionally bad thing up to date. In the first grade, I was picked on daily by a red-haired boy, until one day I had enough. I nonchalantly made my way up to the pencil sharpener and sharpened a fine tip on my #2 pencil. I went back to my desk and waited for him to pick on me again. Well, when he did, my temper flared and I drew that pencil back like it was a sword and stabbed him in the hand as hard as I could, breaking that sharp #2 lead off under his skin. My teacher Ms. Betty Daniels, I'll never forget her, bless her heart (a big black woman who looked like Aunt Jemima) took me in front of the entire class and whooped my scrawny white ass with a yardstick. And I don't mean she paddled me lightly, oh no. She wore my ass out. I stood there bent over with an audience of classmates and took my whipping, knowing full well that I deserved it for what I had done. But that red-haired boy never picked on me again.

Anyways, after the divorce, I found myself at a turning point because I was starting to catch a glimpse of the dirty hand life intended to deal me. So out with the sweet innocent good girl, and in with the trouble-making don't-give-a-damn bad girl. Why not? Life has already knocked me down a few times. Might as well get up and fight back. And so I stood on the verge of breaking bad.

Rebel On The Run

I have always had a rebel streak, it was born into me. It runs through my veins like a genetic code, and I could never get rid of it even if I wanted to. But I never really wanted to. If someone tells me not to do something, I will do it just for the sake of showing myself that I'm my own boss. At times in my life, this has laid more dormant than others, like a volcano predicted to erupt. But when that rebel streak starts running its course, even I can't stop it. It's like a river that has to make its way to the sea in order to break free of its boundaries.

Thus far, my formative childhood years had been littered with chaos and tragedy. Reaching adolescence is challenging in even the most stable of circumstances. But as a girl about to make the transition towards womanhood, well I was just having a hell of a time. And I have always been the type that went all or nothing. Go big or go home. So when I found myself not characteristically turning inward for meditation during a time of struggle, but instead acting outward in a teenage sized temper tantrum; I didn't just take baby steps, I dove headfirst off the deep end and made a giant splash. Kinda like the saying, "if you can't beat 'em, join 'em." If turmoil was going to keep rearing its ugly head at me, I was gonna create some turbulence of my own.

After Mom's second divorce, she sunk into what I refer to as her 'dark period'. We had gone from a sense of normalcy to a time of uncertainty. During her dark period, Mom spent much of her time literally in the dark, sitting in her favorite blue upholstered wing back chair with a bottle of red wine and probably a box of tissues, along with a pack of Capri Light 120 cigarettes. She was going back to the drawing board, re-evaluating her past decisions, contemplating her newfound situation, and carefully calculating which move to make next on the big proverbial chessboard of life.

At this interval, I want to speak of my mother's character. Mama was raised in a middle to upper-class Christian home. Although she had somewhat of a gypsy lifestyle, moving from West Virginia to Florida and back again several times. (My mother's maternal grandmother was the one who first started what would become a family curse for all of her descendants.) But suffice it to say my mom had a good and decent childhood. And although she wound up in extenuating circumstances at the age of 14, her parents were supportive. I think that is what made all the difference in influencing the type of mother she turned out to be.

Mom was never a conventional mother. At times she was sort of like a big sister because she was so young when she had us. And other times she was more of a friend. At present-day she is one of my best friends. But growing up, she was always transparent and honest with us girls and made a point to frequently preach against teen pregnancy, with a strong emphasis on birth control. Seemed like the birds and the bees were a daily topic in our household. She wouldn't have changed having us girls. But she had seen firsthand the many struggles and hardships associated with teen mom life. She didn't want us to have to learn that lesson the hard way.

My mother was never rich, but she worked her ass off. She was never highly educated, but she taught us everything she knew. She had been depleted of love herself, but she always gave us all the affection she could spare. She may not have won a mother-of-the-year

award, but she damn sure gave it hell and did her best by us. Mama tried. And she holds my enduring respect and honor just based on that.

I saw that she was suffering alone in her dark period, and the compassionate side of me wanted to comfort her. She was going through something that had her corralled into her own personal hell, and no matter what attempts I made, I couldn't break through to her. So I turned to the dark side myself. What happened next was a series of rebellious acts that I committed. I started off by skipping school here and there. Then fell into the wrong crowd. Next, I tested my luck with sneaking out of the house at night. I had this part down to an art. I knew exactly which doors made what noise, and how to open them with just the right momentum to keep them quiet. It was like I was rehearsing for a prison break. I got so good at it, in fact, that I never got caught. The funny thing is when I would sneak out at night I wasn't even doing anything worth writing home about, I was just wandering the neighborhood alone, with no sense of direction, contemplating my life. But the more I got away with, the more addicted I got to pushing my limits even further.

To make myself fit more into the role of the little badass I was pretending to be, I thought to myself, hmm, I've got to project the image I'm trying to portray. So I stole a pack of my mom's Capri cigarettes from the carton she kept in the freezer. I proceeded to hide in my closet with them, lit one up, and about choked to death on my ignorance of how to inhale smoke. No one teaches you these things. I wish that the first trial and error of smoking had been enough to keep me from ever wanting to light up another one. But that has been a battle I have fought off and on from that day forward.

Next on my bad girl checklist was alcohol. My stepdad had built a custom made bar and it was located in the dining room. It stayed after he left. I had mixed his drinks when he was still around, he taught me how to. A whiskey glass, four ice cubes, a third of Crown, and the rest Pepsi. (He worked for Pepsi Cola so Coca Cola was strictly prohibited under his roof. We even had a Pepsi machine on our back porch). But he was gone now so we could have Coke if we damn well pleased. I used to sneak and get my favorite drink of Cherry Coke from the 7-Eleven station down the road and enjoy a cold one while he was away at work. Now I could have as many as I wanted whenever I wanted. Since he was out the door, so were his rules. But that's beside the point. Anyways, I had my first taste of liquor behind that bar.

At school, I was usually perceived as being stuck up. But I truly wasn't. I've never thought I was better than anyone else. And I have practiced the policy as long as I can remember of treating the janitor like I treat the CEO. I was just always shy and quiet. But that was mistaken by my classmates as something else entirely.

I was in middle school at the time, and since I wasn't fitting in well with the cliques that kids sort themselves into like herds of cattle; I tended to gravitate towards the underdogs. The loners and the unwanted. The misfits and the outcasts. We shared that in common. I identified with them. To this day I seek out individuals who exhibit characteristics of not being normal. I've always thought "normal" (if there's any such thing) is boring. And the typecast people who fit into this category of being different or unique, sad or lost; those have always been my friends. My tribe. I can spot one in a crowd from a mile away.

Skipping school became more frequent throughout the seventh grade. Towards the end of that school year, it became more evident that I was disliked by my peers. Walking home from school one day I was confronted by a girl I had been friends with. She started yelling at me, then to my surprise she bitch-slapped me. I didn't even know what it was about but I stood there stunned like a deer in the headlights. I couldn't even react. I walked away making a vow to myself that no one else would ever hit me without getting hit in return. Then another girl that had been my friend before, accused me of trying to steal her boyfriend. I didn't even know who her boyfriend was and had no interest in dating at the time. She told another group of girls this lie. Next thing I knew I was in the school parking lot at the end of the school day, and here she came at me with a catfight. As I vowed to myself before… once she struck the first time, I went back at her with everything I had. Then the other girls jumped in, about a dozen of them. I ended up on the asphalt, with someone jumping up and down on my head. I passed out. At that point, someone must have broken up the fight. After that, I was walking home and I felt so dizzy. I blacked out and hit the ground. Next thing I remember is waking up in the back of an ambulance. I was hospitalized with a severe concussion.

I was out of school due to my head injury for about a month. Cards and letters with well wishes from students and teachers poured in daily. When I recovered I went back to school, suddenly everyone was nice to me. But I was put on a 3-day suspension from school as my punishment handed down by the principal, and also summoned to a court hearing by law for the fight. And although I was the only one hospitalized, I was found guilty and sentenced with one month of community service. I was given the choice between trash pick-up and volunteering at a nursing home. I chose the latter because I had always held a soft spot in my heart for the elderly. And I rather enjoyed my month with the old folks, I became attached to some of them and was kinda sad to leave when I had served my sentence.

By the time I was in the eighth grade, I began to unravel downhill at a much faster rate. I started hanging out with an even rougher and rowdier crowd. Next thing I knew I was trying street drugs. Not anything hardcore by today's standards, just the usual gateway drugs of marijuana and speed. But that's bad enough and I'm ashamed to even admit that now. I wish I could say that I had never tried any drugs. I have seen how they can destroy lives and I have been very much against the use of them my entire adult life. Although the lesser of those evils I grant is marijuana and being a natural plant I can understand why people use it for its medicinal properties.

Somehow I managed to skip pretty much my entire eighth-grade year. Doing nothing but wasting time. This was my daily format: skip school, go hang out with my older friends who weren't even school age, play cards, drink screwdrivers, and smoke Swishier Sweet filtered cigars. I fancied myself as a gangster. If I had known then just how precious time is I would have stopped myself in my tracks and snapped out of the mess I was making of my life. But grown-up Tiff can't go back and tell teenage Tiff what to do. No one could tell me what to do cause I was out of control. At the time I had no self-worth and was convinced I held no value for anyone else. So nothing anyone said to persuade me otherwise mattered to me.

At this point, Mama had already emerged from her dark period and was working full time at a respectable job. So she was having a hard time keeping track of me and my whereabouts. This was back in the dark ages before cellphones when if you didn't want to be found, there was no way for anyone to get a hold of you. I hate to say but I knowingly took advantage of the fact that she was now a busy working single mom, still trying to get her own shit back together. Those facts allowed me to come and go as I pleased, and I used that as a free ticket to misbehave. But the moments when she did catch up to me, we began having full-on mother/daughter blowouts.

Don't get me wrong, it wasn't tragic every second of every day. There were moments in between all this mass chaos where the three of us, (me, Mom, & Haley) all got along and I think we even found it rather nice at times having just all females in the house. We could have girl time, have pool parties, watch chick flicks, do whatever girls do when there is no man around to rule the roost. Plus my mom's

little sister, my Aunt Vicki, spent a lot of time with us then so it was sometimes just like we were all sisters.

My sister was the golden child. She had turned out so far to be someone that Mama could be proud of, doing well in school and involved in social activities. And it was evident that she had more in common with Mom than I did. Our mother came from a family of musicians and singers. (My favorite memories of her are all the times she would sit and play her guitar, and sing. There is always something so comforting about hearing your own mother's voice.) Haley inherited her musical talent, so Mom nurtured that and made sure Haley had the opportunities necessary to expand that talent. And personality-wise they were more alike. So their relationship was in good standing. Everyone was so proud of Haley. I was proud of Haley too. I always looked up to my big sister, I still do now as an adult. She has been successful in everything she's ever done and I have admired her for that. She is beautiful, talented and kind, smart and funny. For all of my life, she has been my guardian angel on earth. She has always watched out for me and let me know that I'm not alone in this big world. After all, everything we had been through up to this point had been shared experiences. There were only 14 months age difference between us, but as my big sister, she tried to take care of me. Even when I was a baby in my crib if I would start crying she would bring me a glass of milk and one slice of bread with peanut butter on it and place them in the crib with me. She was always protective of me. And I wanted to be just like her.

But meanwhile, I'm like hey look at me over here in the naughty corner! I was waving the black sheep flag. The odd one out. I had no talents that I was aware of, I wasn't special or gifted. I was just merely existing, and wreaking havoc every which way I turned. I know now looking back that it wasn't because of anything anyone else had done. Or even because life had already let me down so many times. I had singled myself out and had brought about my own self-destruction. I was subconsciously pushing people away and distancing myself further and further because I was so afraid to lose anyone else. So my relationship with my mother suffered severely, and we clashed on every possible level.

This led to a more serious turn of events. I was riding in Mom's car with her, going down the road near our house. We got into a big argument in which case she was yelling and I was crying. I opened the car door, then took off like a bat out of hell. And I ran away from home for the first time. I didn't know where I was going or what I would do when I got there. I just ran. This was the prison break I had been rehearsing for.

I ended up cutting through the woods and came out in the neighborhood where my best friend at the time lived. Her name was Ann. Somehow I then influenced her to be my accomplice in crime. So off we went headed as far to the edge of town as we could get. There was an old abandoned blue Italianate style house I knew of there, and if I recall correctly we hitched a ride to it. Once we got there and explored every room, it was like okay now what do we do? It was starting to get dark, we had no food or water, no electricity. This was quickly starting to seem like the makings of a bad idea. We went into the tower section of the Italianate house, sat together in a windowsill amid the graffitied walls.. and since we had nothing better to do, we came up with the bright idea to carve each other's initials into our hands with broken glass, and as if that wasn't enough we also proceeded to brand ourselves with those stupid smiley face scars made with a hot lighter. Brilliant huh? I suppose we thought of it then as some sort of ritualistic sisterhood pact. I still have Ann's initials on my left hand, and we are still friends. We started to get scared once the sun had completely set outside of that big abandoned spooky house on the edge of town. And I don't recall how we got back to our respective houses, but somehow we managed to go back home. Yep, big bad teenager that I was, I wound up tucking tail and doing the walk of shame right back through the front door. I remember hoping Mama would have something for dinner as I made way back through that door since I had been a poor starving runaway for the day. (And Mom wasn't exactly a good cook at the time. In fact, I'm convinced the woman tried to poison me with Hamburger Helper and Kool-Aid back in the day.) But even Mama's bad cooking sounded pretty good that night. I didn't get in as much trouble as I thought I would for running away that time, and Mama did feed me when I got home. Mom had whipped us girls with a wooden spoon when we were little (she especially broke many a wooden spoon on Haley's ass because, of the two of us, I was the most well behaved when we were younger). But I was too big for that now, so I was wondering what my punishment would be. I had already been grounded and gotten my land-line phone plus my black & white tv taken out of my bedroom for the previous trouble I had been in. She had also forced me to sit in the boring clinic where she worked on a few different occasions, as punishment for skipping school. So what else could she do? Well, she was more concerned than mad. But she did call for backup from her parents who lived on the other side of town because that particular stunt I pulled made her realize she couldn't handle me on her own. And I think she knew at that point that it was more of a cry for help than anything else.

Mom had always taken guidance from her mother and father especially since becoming a parent herself at such a young age, and she was very wise to do so. Meemaw and Peepaw had been like a second set of surrogate parents to me and my sister and we had spent much of our time with them since our initial move to Florida, as they had also returned there from West Virginia. Truth be told they actually seemed more like our real parents.. with me, Haley, Mom, and Aunt Vicki seeming more like sisters. They had been our support system since day one of our lives. And with good reason. When Mama went to them at 14 years old and revealed to them that she was pregnant, they guided her through that. They were there every step of the way and never turned their backs on her or us girls. (Mom said to me just the other day when I was discussing this book with her), even though it was a very hard time and they all felt devastated when they first got the news that their little girl was pregnant, as soon as Haley arrived and they all saw her and held her... and then I came along and they welcomed me, she said, "I would never take back having you girls and neither would they." She said, "You girls were the light of my dad's life."

Going back to what I said in the first chapter, Peepaw was the man who raised us. He first accepted that role after the death of our father, then when our stepdad left us he extra stepped up to the plate. He knew we needed him then more than ever. I could write an entire book just based on my Peepaw. He was larger than life and the most incredible man I have ever known. I respected him more than I have respected any one human as long as I have lived. I just can't say enough about my grandfather, he was everything. If we were a tribe, he was our Chief. Our leader. The top of the totem pole. He was a devoted man of God, first and foremost. I guarantee no one has ever said more prayers for me than he did. His family was everything to him. He had a presence about him that commanded instant and pure regard and respect. He didn't speak unless he really had something meaningful to say. And if he did have something to say, it was important, and you knew to be quiet and listen. His wisdom and advice was invaluable.

The truth resonated from him as clear as a bell. He never minced words and you always knew and remembered exactly what he said word for word. He is the only person whose guidance I have ever truly and thoroughly trusted. He is the only man I have ever completely respected. He stood for everything that was good and only for what was right. No one, as long as I live, will ever hold a candle to him or measure up to the man that he was. He was many things during his life, a master of all trades. He was an Army veteran, a talented singer, a brilliant guitar player, a pro-level golfer, a fisherman, a flight instructor and a pilot, among many other things. He was an expert travelling man. He taught me how to travel, he drove a car like he flew a plane (and I still to this day implement his techniques into every road trip I take). He taught all us girls how to ride a bike, how to fish, how to read a roadmap, how to wash a vehicle, how to play guitar. He taught us how to pray. He taught us countless lessons on every subject under the sun. If we needed an answer to a question, he always had the right one. He was unwavering and as steady as a rock. He was our foundation.

He was a living legend in my eyes. Peepaw had a very humble beginning being raised in the Coal Fields of West Virginia. But he had worked his way up and risen to a place of high standing. He had been a dirt track racer, a foreman in the coal mines, the owner of a 7-UP plant, and more. He was taught by Johnny Cash's brother Tommy how to play guitar, in the attic of a castle when they were stationed in the Army together in Germany during the late 1950s. He was highly respected in his career as a pilot. He was a private flight instructor and taught many celebrities how to fly private planes. He gave flying lessons to Christopher Reeve (Superman) and taught Sam Walton how to fly a Lear jet, along with many others. He and Dennis Quaid became golfing buddies. Peepaw had his own private plane that he used to take us up in. He would even let me co-pilot when it was just him and I. There was nothing better than being up in the clouds with my Peepaw... I always felt so safe with him navigating through the sky. It was the closest thing to being in Heaven, like floating on the wings of an angel. He was a pretty big deal. The biggest deal to me. But he never let on like he was. He remained humble all his life.

Peepaw had the most kind and gentle hazel eyes. You could tell by looking into his eyes that he had seen some hard times. But if you ever saw the look of disappointment in those eyes, they made you feel like you were the most shameful low-life human being on the planet. He wouldn't get mad at you if you'd done something wrong. He would just give you that look of disappointment and that was enough, you would know right away that you had let him down. It was the worst punishment I've ever known. Letting Peepaw down was unacceptable. I have only had the misfortune of seeing that look in his eyes directed at me a total of three times in my life. And this occasion was the first time. He and Meemaw had come to the rescue of Mama, and they sat me down. It was like being in a confessional at Catholic church, with Peepaw standing in as the priest. I felt an immediate need to repent my sins and ask for forgiveness. But in my headstrong attitude at the time, I also felt like they only knew Mom's side of the story. And they couldn't possibly understand mine. So I didn't even bother trying to give explanations or excuses. I just bowed my head in shame and listened to what my mother and grandparents had to say.

I was already going so fast on my downhill slide out of control, that the force of gravity was too strong to turn back now. Although I had listened that night to my elders, I let their words of wisdom go through one ear and out the other. And I carried on single-handedly creating my own path of destruction, like a tornado ripping through the landscape. And I had no means to clean up the mess I had made in the aftermath. So I did the only thing I seemed to be good at, I kept making that mess bigger and bigger. I continued cooking up a grand recipe for disaster. I had all the ingredients together that I had gathered so far… cigarettes, alcohol, drugs, sneaking out, school skipping, running away. The dark place I was in just kept getting darker. It got to the point where I didn't even want to let the light in. I didn't want to matter to anyone, or laugh, or be happy. I felt like I didn't deserve to be happy. I had disappointed my family and felt like I had nothing else to lose. I just wanted to disappear.

At fourteen years old and towards the end of my eighth-grade year (that I had almost completely skipped out on), I was still up to no good. Not only had my mother and grandparents tried to straighten me out, but now the school I was supposed to be attending started getting more heavily involved in my truancy. Which led to even more trouble on the home front. I just couldn't take the fighting and animosity anymore or the sight of the devastation I had caused. But instead of getting off of my highway to hell and trying to get back on the right track, I bolted again. This was to be my big runaway and I planned to never return. I left and started walking and walking and walking. I walked so far I didn't even know what town I was in when I stopped. I had no real plan or script to go off of for this prison break. I was just shooting off the hip, aiming blindly. I ended up in a swampland forest, full of Spanish Moss and Cyprus trees. I found an abandoned campsite with an old rusty lounge chair. I unfolded it and set it up, that became my bed. It was the year of the locusts and the one profound thing I remember from my time in that forest was the deafening sound of them. It was driving me crazy.

Like my first escape, I hadn't prepared at all for this runaway. I had no basic necessities.. blanket, food, or drink. After 48 hours of hiding out in the forest in the humid Florida heat, I was beginning to feel delirious. I was hungry, thirsty and had been cold at night. So the third morning, I started aimlessly wandering out of the forest and tried to find some sort of civilization. I came to a two-lane highway and started trekking down it. Seemed like I walked for miles before I finally found a house. I was so desperate at this point that I went to the house and knocked on the door, hoping the occupant could help me. No answer. So I added to my list of crimes and broke in. I had never before considered breaking and entering or stealing. I had been self-destructing, I had no intentions of doing any harm to anyone else besides myself. But there I was, rummaging through someone else's house, through their personal belongings. Hoping they wouldn't walk in and catch me. And then stealing was also checked off of my naughty list. It was a man's house so I found no female clothes. My own clothes were filthy from being in the forest for two days and all the sweating I had done in walking such far distances. So I stole a set of man clothes, t-shirt, boxer shorts, pants, and socks. I stripped off my dirty clothes, took a quick shower and put on the stolen outfit. Then I scavenged his kitchen for any food or beverage items I could find. I stuffed all my findings along with my dirty laundry into a grocery sack. Then tried to tidy any messes I had made. And out the door I went. I continued walking down that highway not even knowing which way I was headed. I have never had a good sense of direction anyways. The longer I walked, the more lost I felt. I started feeling so hopeless that I broke down crying and began to panic. What had I done? I was feeling guilty for the act of burglary I had just committed. Now I was no more than a damn thief and a criminal. How did I end up here?

For the first time since I had bolted, I began to feel remorseful for what my mother and family must be going through. I had been gone for two days and two nights. They had no idea where I was. I could be dead or in jail for all they knew. Then I started to picture them calling every hospital and police station in town. And as much as I wanted to just go back home, I became scared of what kind of trouble I would be in this time. I knew I wouldn't get away with it. So maybe I should never go back. The more thoughts that ran through my head, the more confused I was becoming. The feeling of complete and utter despair took over me. I didn't know what to do. It felt like the end of the world. I suddenly didn't feel like a big tough badass anymore. I was vulnerable and defeated. My mask fell off and I stood there in those stolen clothes but stripped down of my fraudulent facade. Exposed for what I really was, a sad, lonely, lost little girl.

I finally came upon a landmark that looked familiar, but in my dazed state, it took me a minute to recognize where I was. When it dawned on me, I breathed a sigh of relief. I was back to a point where I knew I could find my way home. And after breaking down and shedding my thick skin, I wanted nothing more than to go home. No matter the consequences. It hit me like a ton of bricks that I owed it to my family to put their minds at peace. So I quickened my pace and began my homeward bound journey. The sun was starting to set on that third day of my runaway, and I still had a ways to go. I was so tired and distraught. I was coming upon the neighborhood where my best friend Ann lived, so I decided to go to her house and use her phone to call my mom or see if her mom would drive me the rest of the way home.

As soon as I reached her street, I was stopped in my tracks by the blue lights of a police car. Instantly my mind raced to "I'm going to be arrested for my breaking and entering from this morning." Then I realized that my mother had in fact called the police station. They had been patrolling all possible locations my mom thought I could be since my disappearance. And of course, Ann's neighborhood was one of the areas they were covering. And they had a full description of me given to them by my family. The officer got out of his squad car, handcuffed me, read me my rights and put me in the backseat.

Lost And Found

It was only a few miles from the location where I was arrested to my home. But that ride in the backseat of a cop car felt like a hundred miles. After lecturing me about the dangers of running away from home, the policeman informed me that I wasn't going to jail like I initially assumed, but instead he was taking me home. The officer was on his radio the whole time calling in codes to report the missing girl found. I was mostly relieved that I was being delivered back to safety after my harrowing ordeal. But the closer we got the more nervous I became. I had no idea what I was going to walk into this time, or how I would be received. Would they be happy to see me? Would they hug me and cry tears of joy upon my safe return? Or would I be in the biggest trouble of my life? One thing was certain, it couldn't get much worse than being arrested and at least I wasn't on my way to the penitentiary.

We pulled into the driveway, and I was escorted to the door. The policeman knocked and Mama answered. She knew we were on the way since it had been radioed in and she was immediately notified. Once inside, there were discussions between her and the officer. There was no hugging or crying. No emotions. It was just very serious and tense. Mom had already called Peepaw for backup before we arrived and he was in route from the other side of town. The officer waited until my grandfather got there before he left. It was clear that my mother didn't trust me or feel safe to be left alone with me. I really did feel like a criminal then. Once the police were out of the picture, I was told by Mom in no uncertain terms that I was no longer welcome in her home. She was visibly shaken and upset, but she held her ground and stood firm. She was not able to deal with me anymore. I had pushed her past her breaking point and she was done. I truly and literally had reached the point of no return. She had tried everything else and exhausted all other options. Now she was going to resort to the only tool in a parents' arsenal that she had left to use, the method of tough love. I left her no choice.

Peepaw and I didn't speak on the 45-minute long drive to his house. But he had that pitiful look of disappointment in his eyes the whole ride. I didn't just disappoint him this time though, I had broken his heart. How could I? How dare I? I felt more ashamed knowing that I had hurt him than I did about any of the other bad things I had done in my life. It was killing what was left of me to know I had done this to the man who would have never in a million years let me down. To the man who I revered, admired and respected above all. To the man who had so graciously and selflessly raised me as his own even though he didn't have to. The man who prayed for me daily and loved me beyond measure. When we got to my grandparents' house, Meemaw was waiting for me on their screened-in patio out back. I wasn't at all prepared for what would happen next.

Meemaw had been raised in an upper-class home. She was the only child of wealthy parents who had gained their fortunes from their parents who were Coal Barons and Presidents of the Coca-Cola company in her hometown of Beckley, West Virginia. Her family at one time basically owned the town of Beckley. She was brought up in mansions with maids. Living a grand and interesting lifestyle. But she's never acted uppity or entitled. She has always been humble and meek. In my opinion, she is the most fascinating member of my family because my other three grandparents had come from more simple roots of farming, timbering and coal mining. But Meemaw is different. As much as I respect the backgrounds of my other family members and their hard-working blue-collar status, she stands out in contrast as a queen among peasants in my mind.

My grandmother as I know her is perfect in every way. She was then, is now, and has always been the classiest lady I know. Always strikingly beautiful and feminine. She never ages. Her own mother was a beauty too. Meemaw was the picture of an all American wife and mother throughout my childhood. She was always cooking, cleaning, baking, sewing…whistling or humming a pretty tune all the while, with a smile on her face. She always had a look of pure devotion in her beautiful brown eyes for her family. It was obvious that she loved being a wife, mother and grandmother. That she felt special and important because she had family to tend to and take care of. It made her happy to go out of her way to do something nice for us. Growing up she always supplied us with coloring books and crayons, paper dolls, a pitcher of homemade sweet tea, desserts and goodies. She had a computer before anyone even knew what a computer was and let us play games on it when we would visit. She was always ahead of her time, modern but still traditional. She is a devout and faithful Christian. She is kind and gentle. She is conservative and holds high moral values. She has always had impeccable etiquette and remarkable taste. An avid reader. Extremely intelligent and knowledgeable on every subject. Talented in many ways. She is genuine and courteous. Graceful and stylish. She has every admirable attribute a woman can have. Meemaw is an impressive woman. And I have always thought of her as another mother rather than as a grandmother. As she sat at the table on the patio that evening, she was pleasant as always, but I could tell she had something to say to me. In her gentle way, instead of scolding me like I deserved, she began to speak as I had never heard her speak before. And what she said came as a complete surprise to me. My Meemaw who could do no wrong and who I thought of as the most innocent lady that ever was, told me of a troubled past she had when she was young, that I never knew or could have ever even imagined existed. What? Some of the stories she told raised my eyebrows and about knocked me out of my seat. I was so taken back by it I didn't know what to say, or what to think, or how to react.

All these things she had kept from me before, she was now telling me; it was her way of reaching me a lifeline and something to grab onto because she knew I was drowning. She was relating to me and letting me know that she had been down a similar path to the one I was on and she understood. But she overcame it and survived. In that moment, for the first time since I had unraveled my life, I had a glimmer of hope. Because if she could arise from the depths of despair and become the incredible woman that she is, maybe I could find it within me to do the same. Maybe all wasn't truly lost. It never dawned on me that she had any sort of difficult journey to endure. I just always thought she was perfect and had been born that way and was always like that. This opened up my eyes to the fact that maybe it's not too late for me. Maybe I still had a chance. Maybe I could still salvage the good in me and turn this sinking ship back to shore and actually make something worthwhile of myself someday. Meemaw gave me a light at the end of the tunnel. She saved me.

The following days allowed me to begin the decompression process of releasing all the horrific acts I had committed and the negative feelings I had built up. It was almost like an exorcism, ridding myself of these demons that had corrupted my very soul. I slept it off at first, then began to emerge from the shadows I had been hiding behind. The walls I had fabricated around myself started to slowly come down, one brick at a time. It was the equivalent of being put into rehab. I was instantly free of all the physical addictions I had been abusing myself with.. the cigarettes, alcohol, drugs, etc. And that, in turn, allowed me to start letting go of the emotional baggage I had been dragging around with me and little by little I started laying my burdens down. I still had a very long way to go, but I was in a safe and peaceful place that fostered an atmosphere of affirmation and positive re-enforcement. I spent about a month and a half living with my grandparents. I was on my road to recovery.

I had been a bad person and I had done bad things. I was a monster. I wasn't the sweet innocent little girl they knew before my rebellion. I didn't deserve their forgiveness or compassion. But they gave it freely anyways. They didn't treat me like I was a bad person or a criminal. They treated me the same as they always had, with kindness and dignity. Like I was special and important. That is what made the biggest difference, that's what I needed the most. It's what snapped me out of the daze I was in and brought me back around to remembering the original version of myself.

I began to see the good in life again for the first time in a long time, smiling, laughing, breathing fresh air, listening to birds sing, looking at the sunset, watching a storm roll in, having heart-to-heart talks with Meemaw and Peepaw, taking evening walks with them and their dog Scruffy, enjoying a good meal and a glass of sweet tea. The little things that I had forgotten could make you feel alive and content. But most importantly, spending quality time together as a family. I look back on those days with them and have such fondness and profound appreciation for the help they gave me and the love they surrounded me with.

Along with working on my emotional stability, I was also given complete medical evaluations for a clean bill of health. I got braces and glasses too. I had transformed into full-on "Nerd Tiff" and I even welcomed the change because I wanted a new identity since I was releasing myself of the bad girl persona. Next on the agenda, was what to do about school. It was May now and the conclusion had been drawn as to the fact that I had completely flunked 8th grade. So Mama, Meemaw, and Peepaw came up with a solution for everything that entailed not only getting me back on the right track but also keeping me there, which is the most important part when you have been on the ups and downs of a roller coaster ride to hell and back. And so it was unanimously decided that I was to attend an all-girls boarding school for troubled teens.

They could have taken me without warning, kicking and screaming. It was that kind of place. But they had the decency to forewarn me of my fate. And I agreed to it because I knew just as well as they did that it was a chance to redeem myself. (Well, I also agreed to it because it was on a farm). So on June 27, 1994, my family all loaded up in Peepaw's van. And we headed for the location of Lithia, Florida which was about an hour southwest of Lakeland. My destination was a place called "Stepping Stone Farm". I had seen a brochure of it that sort of sold me on the idea, but other than that I didn't really know much about where I was headed. I was nervous and excited. A new adventure awaited. A new chapter.

We pulled into the dirt road driveway of the place and found the main building. It looked more like a compound than a farm, at first glance. It was basically a glorified juvenile detention center, minus the tall outer walls lined with barbed wire. I got out of the van and Peepaw got my suitcase. My mother signed some paperwork and we were briefed separately. I was told I wouldn't see my family for a year, and could only speak to them once a month over the phone. Then it was time to say our goodbyes. I hugged each one, Mom, Haley, Vicki, Meemaw and Peepaw. Told them I loved them, then bid them farewell. The place had seemed decent enough while my family was there, but watching Peep's van along with my family fading off into the distance, gave me a sudden and intense feeling of desolate solitude. I was completely among strangers in a strange place. It had turned from a Hallmark movie moment of hugs and I love you's into an episode of Naked and Afraid, with an SPCA commercial in between. I had been abandoned again.

Immediately I was informed of all the rules. This was a Christian based and military-style institution and all protocols were strictly enforced. You had 15 minutes to eat in the chow hall, and you must clean your plate and eat everything every time. You had 5 minutes to take a shower, except for on Saturday when you were issued a razor and given 10 minutes in order to shave. You were to make your bed to specifications with hospital corners. A strict dress code. No makeup. No jewelry. No secular music. Supervised interaction with the other girls. Early wake up calls and lights out time at night. There were designated chores that rotated on a bi-weekly basis. And so on, and so on. I may not have been dragged in there kicking and screaming, (like I witnessed of other girls the same day I was admitted and many times after), but I was kicking and screaming on the inside. That rebel streak in me was trying to rise to the surface again. I had to fight like hell to keep it at bay. Thoughts of another more elaborate prison break quickly raced to my mind. But my actions for the past 2+ years all led me to where I had landed myself. I had to suck it up and face the music. This was my last resort. I was shown to my "Cottage" assigned a "House Mother", a roommate/"Big Sister", and a bed in our shared room. All the cottages had 4 bedrooms, one master room for the poor soul in charge of babysitting us brats and three more with 2 beds each. So I'm stuck in this bunkhouse with a bunch of other disturbed teens. I've never gotten along very well with girls in general. I have mostly had guy friends because they are less drama and like the outdoor things that I do. But now I was locked up with an entire nut house full of hormonal girls. Bad girls like me in an all-girl prison camp. I just knew these other punk-ass psychopaths were going to make my life a mortal hell for the next year. I hated everything and everyone on that first day. I was hating life altogether. All the progress of self-improvement I had made over the past six weeks just seemed wasted now. All for nothing. Dammit. It looked way more appealing and pleasant on the brochure. False advertising, I was sure of it. It was like all us girls had big question marks over our heads. Like we were all inmates looking at one another and wondering what each criminal had done to get thrown into the big house. Now mind you I wasn't "Gangster Tiff" anymore, I was now "Nerd Tiff", so I didn't exactly look the part. Just based on that and the fact I was the new girl, I had an extra big question mark over my head. I have never liked change, even if I know it's for the best. In this case, I had no choice but to adjust accordingly even though I wanted to buck the system. After a few weeks, I finally fell into the routines and protocols of daily life there. And once I started getting to know the other girls, I realized they were my kind of people...the outcasts and misfits, the ones I had always been drawn to. And so I accepted them and they accepted me in return. They became my sisters.

We basically ran the place as far as work goes. Depending on which chore rotation you were on, you either had kitchen duty, dining hall duty, house duty, laundry duty or animal duty. (There were more but I can't remember all of them now.) I didn't particularly like any of the ones I had been assigned to so far. It was a big place to run and all of them required hard work. I was waiting for my turn on a specific one. The one I knew I would like. When I finally got to take my turn on animal duty, that's when I decided that I liked this place and made my peace with being there. For the first time in my life, I knew with one hundred percent certainty exactly what I was good at and where my true talents lied. There were horses, cattle, pigs, goats, sheep, chickens, dogs and cats. Throughout my life, to this point, I always loved animals, and always felt like I could communicate better with them than I could with humans. Like they understood me better than my own species.

At home, I had my Golden Retriever dog Trudy, the one my stepdad got me when I was seven years old. She was just a puppy when we picked her up, and I rode in the back of our pickup truck all the way home with her, sharing my McDonalds Happy Meal together. She had been my best friend since the moment I first saw her. And for Christmas one year when I was nine years old, I got my beagle pup, Chutney. Those dogs and two cats that I had were my everything. I had also collected all manner of birds, rodents, frogs, fish, etc. during my childhood and they had been my friends too.

The farm was in the middle of nowhere and sat on a large tract of land. It was part swamp-like setting with the Alafia River running through it, Cyprus trees, Spanish moss, grapevines, palmetto bushes and palm trees...and the other part flatland farm fields with fences and dirt roads. It was a beautiful place in its own Floridian way. And I was happy to be in the country. Whoever was on animal duty was the first one up of the morning. Before the sun even made an appearance. And the mornings there were especially magical once the sun began to rise and shine through the Spanish moss, with fog and steam floating above the ground, before the Florida heat and humidity set in.

Although I had been around livestock before on my grandparents' farm in Canvas, and my Aunt Alta's farm in Braxton County, WV, this was my first time ever actually tending to livestock. I was up and out the door of the cottage at 5am. I followed the dirt pathway to the kitchen where I fetched two 5 gallon slop buckets. Then wound my way through the pathways that led to the animal housing. I emptied the slop buckets, threw hay, scattered grain into feed troughs, filled all the water troughs and gathered eggs. It also entailed shoveling manure, re-placing old bedding with fresh, mucking horse stalls and raking cattle pens. I swear I had a smile on my face the whole time. All the while greeting each animal by name and talking to them like they spoke my language. I took great pride in taking care of my furry and feathered friends. I even found that I was good at using farm tools, wheelbarrows, shovels, rakes, etc. I liked getting my hands dirty. I repeated my rounds again each evening. I loved every second of it. It was the highlight of my every day. I decided I would let this place be my home after all. When my first two weeks of animal duty were up, I found myself back on kitchen duty, and then the next duty, and the next one after that. It felt like I had lost my sense of purpose. By this time we had all started to school. We had a little one-room schoolhouse, and there were varied grade levels amongst us girls. So we all worked at our own pace with a teacher to oversee our individual curriculums. Based on my failure of eighth grade, I was actually completing 8th and 9th grades simultaneously during my one year there. So I just tried to focus on my studies. Aside from school and chores and schedules at the farm, we also went to church every Sunday and had field trips to different places. I had so many experiences there that it's impossible to include them all in one chapter.

My time finally came back around to take another turn on animal duty. Most of the other girls hated it because they didn't want to get up so early or get dirty. I couldn't wait! This time I did such a good job in my duties, that the lady in charge of the animals on the farm, Ms. Jayne, took notice. And so she pulled some strings and animal duty became my full-time job on the farm from then on. Now I could be happy all the time. Now my life had meaning. I was worth something. And as if that wasn't enough, I also got chosen by Ms. Jayne to have my own steer calf to raise and show for the big Strawberry Festival in central Florida. This to me, was the highest honor. And only a few select girls were chosen at the farm each year for this 4-H project. You had to have good grades in school and a good conduct record to be eligible. I had both and felt proud of myself for that. And I had always wanted my own cow. Several times I had asked my mom to get me one so I could have it as a pet in the back yard. She never granted this request. But now someone else was going to make my dream come true.

Our tennis coach at the farm was a big Cattle Baron. I got to take a field trip to his ranch and see his vast pastures filled with his Brahman breed herds. Soon after, he came hauling a livestock trailer behind his truck, and my calf was unloaded into one of the cattle pens. There he was, my largest baby I ever had. A beautiful red Brahman steer. It was love at first sight. I named him Stanley Estil, (Stanley after my dad's brother and the Estil part was my Peepaw's middle name). I instantly knew that this calf would become my whole world. I spent every free waking moment I could with him. Feeding him, bathing him, brushing him, petting him, talking and singing songs to him. I made sure his living quarters were always perfectly clean and comfortable for him. I got him a shiny cowbell and he wore it proudly. I would take him on walks with a halter and lead rope outside of his pen. He would have followed me anywhere even without being harnessed. Stanley loved me as much as I loved him. He would lick me on the face constantly with a big slobbery kiss. I would lay down with him, nestled on his soft belly between his four legs with my head on his shoulder, listening as he would chew his cud. Sometimes he would stretch out beside me and we would just snuggle. Or I would sit on his back like he was a horse. And my favorite chicken, Tina Turner (a silky hen with a funky hairdo) would hitch rides on his back frequently. He knew the sound of my walk and he would start mooing happily as loud as he could every time he would hear me approaching. And as I would walk away to leave, his moo sounded more like a sad cry of farewell. I would yell, "Goodbye Stanley, I love you," over and over till I got out of hearing distance from him.

I had been forewarned when I was chosen to have my own calf, that the 4-H project included raising, showing, and then auctioning off the steer. But somehow in the midst of my happy day to day life with Stanley over the past several months, and my immense love for him… I had let this one aspect escape me. The cruel and cold fact that I was virtually raising him to go to market; I just swept it under the rug and pretended it didn't exist. Maybe they would see how much I loved him and let me keep him forever as my own. This was my biggest wish. Certainly, in some fortunate turn of fate, my wish could be granted. Just this once and I would never ask for anything again.

The time came for the big Strawberry Festival. I faced it with dread. (Other than the fact that my family was to attend and I was looking forward to seeing them since I had only seen them twice during that year… once at Christmas when I got to go home on short leave, and the other time at a Family Day pot luck dinner hosted on the farm.) But aside from that, the more quickly the event approached, the more I felt my heart breaking in two. I was going to have to tell my Stanley goodbye for the last time.

When Stanley and I first arrived at the Strawberry Festival, it felt like a happy occasion. My family visited with us and bought gifts for me and Stanley from the festival vendors. A wood-carved sign with his name engraved, for him and a plush cow pillow, for me. (I still have both). During the livestock exhibit, Stanley was a big hit. The spectators had seen me snuggling with my 2,000 pound Brahman bull in the cow pens for the first two days. Then on the third day, it was showtime. He was all shined up and slicked down. I had spent all day grooming him. He looked like a million dollars with his show sheen and hoof polish. Stanley kissed me on the face all the way around the arena. The crowd went wild when they saw this petite little girl with a giant-sized baby, side by side. Everyone could see how inseparable we were.

The way these livestock shows work is during the show, bidders are present in the audience. When the bids are placed afterwards, the cattle are auctioned off. The steers are then tagged, loaded onto big livestock trailers, delivered to market, slaughtered, packaged, and sent to their final bidder. We live in a cruel fucking world.

The show was over, and I thought I would have more time to say my final farewells to my baby, my best friend. But it was all very rushed and chaotic. I was hugging his big neck and soaking his soft shiny red coat with my tears. Kissing him on his cheek and telling him how much I loved him and what a good boy he was. Then we were quickly separated and the last thing I saw of Stanley was him being corralled onto a semi-truck with a cattle prod. He was so distressed because the more he tried to break away from the other steers and come back to his girl, the more they laid the cattle prod to him. He was crying his farewell cry. Then he was gone. Just as quickly as he had come into my life and changed my whole world, he was gone. I would never see him again. My heart was shattered into a million pieces, and I lost another part of my soul that day. I didn't see any way to ever recover from this blow that had knocked me to the ground. I was beyond heartbroken. I was devastated to the core. I am crying now as I write this and recall my dear Stanley. To this day, I still miss him. I keep his cowbell on a shelf in my house. When I got back to the farm after the show, I was given a report from the USDA pertaining to the grade of beef from my steer. I spent many hours laying on the ground in Stanley's empty pen, (where we used to snuggle). Sobbing uncontrollably and asking God why. Why did I always have to lose the ones I love? I didn't understand, and I still don't. I never will.

My one year at the farm was coming to an end and suddenly it was June 27th, 1995. The place that I had initially hated, had in fact, become my home. I didn't want to leave and return to my mother's home, it had become a distant memory, faded by all the changes that had occurred within me. Sending me to the farm was the best thing Mama ever did for me. But it was time to say goodbye to the girls who had become my sisters, the faculty who had become my family, and the animals who had been my friends. I wrote an entire book about all the animals there throughout my stay. One of my dad's sisters, my Aunt Violet, later typed those stories up for me and I still have them. At present day I continue to keep in touch with many of the people I knew from the farm, including the head mistress, Ms. Cynthia, who is one of the classiest ladies I have ever known. She is one of the women who taught me how a true lady should conduct herself with poise and manners. Among the skills and lessons that I learned there, I still practice many of them on a daily basis. In one year's time, I was back on track. Stepping Stone Farm changed the course of the rest of my life. It saved me from my own self-destruction. Also, during my time at the farm, I became saved by the grace of God and baptized. I found the Lord and gained my eternal salvation. So all was not lost.

Shifting Gears

I returned home from the farm in Lithia, back to my mother's house in Lakeland. I felt like an alien in a foreign universe after being gone for so long. Step one, I had to get re-acquainted with my family because reform school had quite literally reformed me. It was as if I had walked through a revolving door and by the time that door came around full circle, my identity had also done a complete 360. Everyone else was still the same like time had stood still, but I wasn't the same person that left a year ago. So I had to re-introduce myself to them. There was one distinct difference on the home-front though. Remember the guy my mom was engaged to in the first chapter? The one who mistreated her? Yeah, well he was back in the picture for an encore presentation. And he was living in our house. But more on that later.

Step two, what was I to do with myself now? I had no desire to go back to my old ways, and I had to move forward from my farm days, so I was faced with the task of reinventing a new life for myself, a new strategy. What could I concoct with all the gathered experiences and knowledge I had accumulated so far? I had some ideas but still had some figuring to do on that one. Step three was a physical transformation. I'm not gonna lie, after perfecting such a rather homely character as "Nerd Tiff" for so long, I was ready to emerge from that and become more fashion-forward and feminine. And I was evolving into womanhood now at the age of fifteen. I had been a scrawny awkward looking girl historically, but I was currently starting to take shape and form.

Plus I just had a broader sense of who I was along with a better sense of self-esteem now. And I wanted to project that. The first order of business was to ditch the braces and glasses. Straight teeth and contacts made a huge improvement alone. My face looked completely different, gave me something to work with. Next, I finished off my makeover with cosmetics and a new wardrobe. Ta-da! "Cowgirl Tiff" on the scene.

I had never been referred to as beautiful before, other than by my family who probably just said so to be nice. Mama always said I would look pretty even wearing a potato sack. But as my appearance was altered almost immediately, I noticed compliments starting to come at me left and right. I didn't see myself as beautiful, but it was reassuring for me to hear that from others and made me feel more confident when I would see my own reflection in the mirror. It started to change my perception of myself. Remember, Mama also always said I had been an ugly baby (I have pictures to prove it, she was right). But now I was transforming from an ugly duckling into a swan. Or, well, at least a better looking duck. I was enrolled in a private Catholic high school for 10th grade, Santa Fe. Complete with pleated plaid schoolgirl uniforms, knee-high socks and theology class. I have to say looking back now, that those kids were the worst group of students I ever had the displeasure of attending school with. Holy Hellions they were. My inmate sisters back on the farm seemed like angels in comparison to these filthy rich, self-righteous, pompous ass, thug-like, inglorious bastards. So I really had to walk a fine line to keep from being corrupted by them and ultimately derailing myself back off track. Also, keep in mind that since my religious revelation, I honestly intended to maintain a carefully calibrated moral compass.

My sophomore year was also the first instance in which guys started to take notice of me. And to be honest, after being at an all-girls school for a year on lockdown, I was beginning to take notice of them too. I never made very many friends at Santa Fe.. [refer to the above description]. But I did make one good girlfriend, Amy. One good guy friend, Jesse. And I had one boyfriend while I was there. His name is not worth mentioning, he was a total ass-hat. Jesse and I hit it off right away as buddies. And he lived on a horse ranch in the hick town of Kathleen, which ultimately became my regular stomping grounds during my high school years. I wound up spending most of my weekends on the ranch with him, riding horses and learning how to throw a rope. And that led to me finding the key to reinvent my new life (which I had still been trying to figure out from step two). Florida is not all Disney and beaches. There is some pure country in the central region amidst the cow pastures and orange groves. And being a country girl at heart, that's what I sought out.

In my duration at Stepping Stone Farm, my passion and obsession for horses was born. That's where I discovered that my spirit animal was, undeniably, a horse. It's where I learned how to saddle up and ride, how to work with horses. And also, where I had my first riding accident. My very first time on a horse's back, they had me mount up on a 23-year-old Morgan gelding named Cheyenne. Since he was way up there in age, I underestimated his get-up-and-go. And I had no clue yet as to the maneuvers of operating a horse. So off we went through the middle of a swamp at full speed gallop, and I was trying so hard just to stay on top of the horse that I became totally oblivious to my surroundings. Suddenly a grapevine reached down from out of nowhere and grabbed a hold of my neck. It hit me with such brute force that the back of my head literally touched the horse's ass, with me still in the saddle. Luckily, good ole Cheyenne came to a sliding halt then, or I may not have lived to tell the tale. Funny thing is, my voice was hoarse for days from that horse wreck. I had bruises around my neck for a month afterward, looked like I had either tried to hang myself or someone had strangled me. After that scary rodeo ride, I hesitated initially, but then I caught a second wind and got more brave. I took several other horses for a test drive around the farm till I finally got the hang of it. And I was hooked.

All this tied in with my newfound friend Jesse. He made it possible for me to have the outlet in which to plug in my ever-expanding horse obsession. And so that became my new life and my new identity. Everything horse related… rodeos, horse shows, trail rides, lasso ropes, saddles, bridles, reins, spurs, cowboy hats, belt buckles, wranglers and boots. I ended up working extensively with one horse in particular on Jesse's ranch, a strawberry roan

Tennessee Walker stallion named El Dorado's Gold. He and I became partners, competing on the show circuit in the Western Pleasure division, and we usually placed well.

During this time I also began working with horses who had been physically abused in the past or were psychologically unstable for various reasons. I had become a good rider and felt that I had a gift communicating with horses in a way that seemed to settle them down from their flightiness. Some of these distraught horses would react well to my therapy sessions with them, becoming docile and submissive. But some of them sadly were too far gone. And I experienced every possible horse wreck known to man. I was bucked, thrown, kicked, rolled over, ran into trees, drug on the ground with my foot caught in the stirrup. You name it, I did it all. But I was young and dumb at the time, so I just kept picking myself up and getting back in the saddle for another go-round. I grew tougher by the day. Life had taught me so far, what doesn't kill you makes you stronger. So I applied this lesson to every aspect of life, including wild horses.

I was doing everything I could to stay away from home. Haley was also busy and rarely home. She had been accepted into a highly accredited performing arts high school for her musical talents and was actively involved in stage theater productions as well. Since my mom had gotten back with her old flame, he had completely taken over the house while I was away at boarding school. My dog Trudy, who had always been an inside dog, had been kicked outside. He also talked Mom into letting him remove my bedroom door from its hinges so they could spy on me. (Apparently, I was still labeled as a "bad kid" even though I had turned my life around). And everything else had to be his way when he said. Besides, all I had to base my opinions of him on, were the bad memories from the past. So I was never fond of him just on those grounds alone. When I was 15, Mama married him, and he became our second stepdad. So we had no choice but to deal with him when we were home.

Before that school year ended, I also had acquired my driver's license and my first car (a hideous grey 1986 Plymouth Horizon), which had belonged to my new stepdad. Once I had wheels I assumed the next logical step was to get a job so I could pay for gas, and fund my horse hobbies. So that summer, I got my first job at a Lone Star Steakhouse & Saloon, where I was a hostess, and had to perform country line dances in the aisles between dinner booths with peanut shells all over the floor. Even though it was ugly as sin, I went everywhere in that Horizon. Doing eighty miles an hour. It was my first real taste of freedom. Open road, radio up, windows down, the wind blowing through my hair. I got addicted to it like a drug. Unfortunately, that summer I also revisited the bad habit of smoking. A choice I regret to this day. It was how I coped with what was happening at home… road trips and cigarettes.

My new stepdad wasn't lashing out at Mom like I remembered from my early childhood. He was now directing his bad temper towards me. I was the target. He never bothered my sister. I think he chose me because I was the more strong-willed of the two of us, and I would put up a fight in self-defense. He would also use the car he had given me as leverage. Hold it over my head every chance he got. For example, one night I was coming home from working at Lone Star, and someone sideswiped my car and ran me off the road. I was still shaken up over it by the time I got home. When I told him what had happened, he picked my car keys up off the kitchen counter and launched them at me, hit me in the face with them. Then he took them back and confiscated the car. I didn't like that stupid car anyway. Although he ended up giving it back to me later.

I didn't want to return back to Santa Fe, I didn't fit in well there although I remained friends with Amy and Jesse. But for my Junior and Senior years, I ended up enrolling at Lakeland Senior High School, which was on the same campus as the performing arts school that my sister attended. I was heavily involved with the FFA and the Ag Department during both my years there and agriculture was my course of study. I had a pet pig named Jackson that resided in the school barnyard at the ag department, along with my blue ribbon prize-winning rooster named Henry that I showed at county fairs. I would take that rooster on outings in my car to the Beverage Castle drive-thru convenience store, where I would buy some junk food to share with him and Jackson.

I continued my activities with horses and the rodeo circuit outside of school. I also worked two jobs through the remainder of my school years, one at a restaurant called Texas Cattle Company, and the other as an assistant at a Veterinarian clinic. I kept my head to the grindstone constantly, just waiting for adulthood and my grand finale prison break from home. I had a good handle on who I was at this time and began to make plans pertaining to my future. I knew I wanted to work within the agriculture industry. Plus I had wanted to be a farmer since the time I was a little girl on my grandparents' farm. So after taking a field trip with the Future Farmers of America to attend an expo at an agricultural college in Georgia, I aligned my goals and set my path towards that.

During my junior year, I met who would become my next best friend, Jennie. We worked together at the Texas Cattle Company. And through her, I also met my first real boyfriend, David. They both lived in the town of Kathleen like Jesse. Pretty much everyone I associated with in my high school years was from that area. It was all about bonfires, dirt roads, pickup trucks and tailgate parties, Boone's Farm Strawberry Hill, mud bogging, country music, and of course horses.

One night, Jennie came home with me late after we got off of work. She fell asleep while we were watching the movie Brave Heart on the tv in the living room. And here comes my stepdad like a zombie in his underwear to get a midnight snack out the fridge. He instantly barked at me to turn the volume down, (which wasn't very loud to begin with), then he stood over my shoulder and watched me do as he said (the little volume lines going down as I pushed the button on the remote control). He repeated himself with the same demand, and at the same time, smacked me hard upside the back of my head. He had already provoked my bad temper too many times before this. So as soon as he struck me this time, all hell broke loose. I got up, turned around like I was possessed, and went full-on psychotic; I mean lunatic crazy. I went at him like a mad woman with everything I had. He ended up overpowering me and threw me up against a wall, punching me repeatedly and knocking a framed picture off the wall.

The struggle started in the living room and ended up in the dining room. He had never seen Jennie asleep on the couch under a blanket, didn't even know she was there. Of course, she woke up while the whole dramatic scene was unfolding. I had a witness. The entire household was awakened by the ordeal. And Haley (being my lifelong protector and bodyguard) quickly rushed to my rescue, demanding that Mom kick him out of the house. She did that night but he was back the very next day. Mom had no choice but to let him back in, she was pregnant at the time, carrying his unborn son. And she had gone to a lot of trouble to make that possible. After I was born, she had her tubes tied, thinking she would never want to have any more children. But when she was reunited with him, they decided they wanted to start a family together... upon which she had gone through major surgery to reverse her tubal ligation. He was like a miracle baby. So what else could she do but allow the father of her child to return home?

After that night, I began to spend even more time away from the house. That summer I continued to work both my jobs, and the rest of my time was spent with my boyfriend David. He was my support system. Plus I was young and in love. We would ride the backroads, go catfishing on the rivers, wild boar hunting in the swamps, take getaways to his family's fishing camp on a lake and to a cabin they owned in Georgia. I started staying the night at his house on a regular basis. He was older than me, 21 at the time but he still lived with his mother. She allowed me to stay since he had relayed my home-life situation to her. And I, in turn, cleaned their house daily.

My baby brother was born that June 8th, so Mama was busy with him and didn't object much to my frequent absence. I would really only go home to see my brother Andrew. I loved him instantly and he was my little buddy from day one. I took care of him anytime my mom and stepdad were gone. Fed him, changed his diapers, rocked him to sleep. And occasionally took him for a ride in my car to settle him down. I was happy to babysit him.

I was still active in conducting my work with the wild horses. David knew of one that especially needed help, she was located in the Green Swamp, a vast expanse of swampland off of Highway 471 in another county. We arrived at the location and I scoped the Palomino mare out, trying to get a gauge on the extent of her bad behavior and tendencies. I could tell she was way worse off than any of the other abused or neglected horses I had worked with before. But I saddled up anyways and climbed aboard. One of the biggest mistakes I've ever made.

I cautiously proceeded to gently give her the back-up command, and she went ape shit. Completely flipped out. She reared up as high as she could, with so much horsepower that she ended up falling straight backwards and directly on top of me. I only weighed about 98 pounds at the time. But there I was, on the hard ground with a nearly two thousand pound animal on top of me. The saddle horn pressed into my chest directly over my heart. I thought for sure I was a goner. I blacked out momentarily, and when I came to I couldn't breathe. I thought my back was broken and I had been paralyzed. I couldn't feel any part of my body. I could see my life flashing before my eyes like a slideshow, accompanied by a kaleidoscope of blurry lights and colors. I just knew I was about to see the bright white light of Heaven and enter those pearly gates. I was waiting for it.

David and the owner of the horse got my feet loose of the stirrups and hastily got the mare off and away from me. She was fine. After what seemed like forever, I started breathing again, but I still couldn't move. Being out in the middle of nowhere as we were, there was no way to call for an ambulance. So David picked me up off the ground, carried me to his truck, and laid me down on the seat. He drove me home and informed my parents that I needed to go to the hospital. It was late at night and I didn't want to be a bother to anyone, so I just had him carry me in and put me to bed. I tried to just sleep it off and wait to see what my condition would be the following morning.

The next day, when Mama saw how bad of shape I was in, she made me go to the hospital to be evaluated. They took a million x-rays, so many in fact, that they said I needed to be careful for the rest of my life to make sure I didn't have too many more because of the amount radiation I was exposed to that day. I wasn't paralyzed, and miraculously I didn't even have any broken bones or internal injuries. I was just severely banged up and the impact from the weight of the horse had caused damage to my back.. bulging disks, pinched nerves, and sciatica (on top of the scoliosis I already had). They put me on a heavy dose of pain meds and sent me home. It took me months to heal from the accident, and I had a bruise in the perfect shape of a saddle horn right over my heart for a long time.

I didn't know if I could ever ride again after that. It instilled a fear of horses into me that I never had before. I had always respected their size and strength, but after my near-death experience, I was truly afraid of them. I wasn't sure if I could ever get over that, even with my great love for horses. And I never fully recovered from my injuries. From that day on, I have endured excruciating chronic back pain, every second of every day. My spine and hips were permanently damaged. And this fact has since hindered me in every imaginable way and kept me from leading a normal fully functioning life. I still live with a daily reminder of that single bad decision. I pay for it constantly.

At the end of that summer, Peepaw took me for our annual trip to my beloved West Virginia mountains. He and Meemaw had relocated back up there again. These trips were our tradition. Those hills meant the same thing to Peepaw as they did to me. We shared that in common, it was our bond. Where the other half of our people felt more at home in the flatland of Florida, Peep and I were mountain folk through and through. He had seen all the progress I had made since my return from Stepping Stone, and he was proud of me. We were in good standing with one another. He always had his travelling van prepared for a trip, and would stock up on all my favorite items when I would travel with him... Cherry Coke, salt & vinegar potato chips and a Butterfinger candy bar. That's how I rolled (and still do) on road trips. We would sing along to the radio the whole time, and catch up on life and current events. He was the best travelling buddy of all time. This trip was special though because Peepaw was buying me my very own vehicle. One that would actually be mine and no one would ever hold over my head. He knew that I would be heading off to college as soon as I graduated. He also knew of the trouble I had dealt with over the Plymouth Horizon. (Once I even had to call a damn taxi cab to take me to work when the Horizon was confiscated for no good reason). But Peepaw was about to come to my rescue and save the day.

We made it to Summersville, WV to a family-owned dealership where he purchased a navy blue 1987 Jeep Cherokee 2 door 4WD 6-cylinder SUV for me. It had been a previous Department of Natural Resources vehicle for the state of WV, so it was well taken care of before I was the owner of it. He got her all washed up, waxed and polished. I got an upgrade! It wasn't brand new, but it was brand new to me. It was one of the nicest gifts anyone has ever given me. I was so proud and happy. Peepaw did me a solid! We took it on a test drive around town and I felt like the king of the road. Then I drove myself to Braxton County to visit with Dad's side of the family. I stayed with Grandma Sparks at her house on the Elk River for a few days, along with my Aunt Violet. After that, I stopped back in to visit with Meemaw and Peepaw awhile longer. Meem fed me and prepared for me step by step directions from WV to FL, then packed me a to-go satchel of goodies for my trip. Peepaw gave me gas money, driving advice, and a new toolbox filled with tools he had bought for me. They prayed over me for my safety. We said our goodbyes, and they sent me on my way Southbound to what was my first ever long haul solo road trip. I thoroughly enjoyed every mile of it in my new Jeep Cherokee.

Back in Florida, I was 17, and it was time to start my senior year of high school. I steered clear of home other than going there occasionally to see Mama, my little brother Andrew who I completely adored, and my loyal dog Trudy (my beagle dog Chutney had died while we were all out of town at Mom's wedding two years before). But I never stayed long. There was almost always a hostile environment there… fighting, yelling, slamming doors, throwing things, etc. Tension filled the air in that house. I swore I would never live like that when I had my own home and family someday. I would make a happy and peaceful home for myself.

Haley had moved away to attend the performing arts college of New World in Miami, where she majored in Musical Theater and Opera. So with her gone, I had no one there to take up for me. And by this time my mother's sister Vicki had a baby too, (my cousin Tyler) so the two of them were always busy spending time together raising their boys. Mama barely seemed to notice when I came and went. She knew I was alright so she didn't have to worry about me. I was still dating David and I had moved in with him pretty much on a full-time basis. He had given me a female Cur pup that I named Whiskey, and she lived with us too. I was in a good place mentally and emotionally, although I was still in a great deal of physical pain from my horse accident. But I was stable.

That spring, something I had been waiting for since I was six years old, finally happened. I was contacted by my father's second wife (also named Lori like my mom). She informed me that she and Marci would be at Daytona Beach for spring break, and invited me to come there and meet my baby sister. Marci was eleven years old at the time, and I had never even seen her, other than in photographs. I had always felt the absence of my little sister. She was a part of Dad, a link to me that existed out there somewhere in the big world, that I had lost all connection to. But I always thought about her and wondered where she was and how she was doing. It is most definitely possible to miss someone you've never even met. I can attest to that. I missed her every day.

The time came when I was to finally be reunited with Marci, the closest I would get to her since her mother had been pregnant with her at our father's funeral. When I first saw her there on the Atlantic Ocean, a thousand emotions poured over me like waves crashing to the shore. I probably startled her, by the way, I went charging at her like a bull in a China shop. I couldn't get to her fast enough. I had waited for what seemed like an eternity for this moment. It meant everything to me. We spent the day on the beach.. talking, laughing, riding four-wheelers through the sand. It was everything I had hoped for. Me and my baby sister, catching up on lost time. The only thing that could have made our reunion any better, is if Haley had been there with us. But I felt like all was right with the world that day. Like the last piece of an incomplete puzzle had been put into its rightful place. And I felt Daddy smiling down on us, like a ray of sunshine.

May rolled around and I had made it through my senior year. I applied for the only college I ever wanted to go to, Abraham Baldwin Agricultural College and was accepted. I had maintained good grades throughout high school. I ended up graduating at the top of my class with high honors, a sash full of awards, and a 4.0 GPA. I went to the bank and withdrew all the money I had saved up from my jobs. Mama took me up to Georgia to enroll for college and tour the campus. I felt like I was handed a clean slate, to write whatever happy ending I wanted to. In spite of all the hardships I'd been through, I had my shit together and my life was pretty well under control. I was ready to spread my wings and fly. As an 18-year-old adult, I was prepared to set sail. I tied up all my loose ends. David helped me load up my Jeep with everything I owned. I bid farewell to Mama, Andrew, Trudy and Whiskey shed a few tears, then headed off Northbound on the road towards my bright future. Leaving Florida and my life there behind for a new life in Georgia. And I never even looked back behind me in my rear-view mirror. David rode ahead of me in his truck, and I followed.

He was going to help me unpack and settle into my dorm room on the college campus. It was right at a four-hour drive from Lakeland, FL to Tifton, GA. On I-75 in the left lane, doing 80 mph with back-to-back traffic on all sides... my front right tire had a big blowout. I was forced to pull it off the left-hand side of the Interstate into the median. David never even noticed that I was no longer behind him. So there I was, stranded. I had to take all my carefully packed belongings out of the Jeep and set them on the side of the road, so I could get to the spare tire. Next, I had to lay on the right side of my vehicle to change the tire, with traffic rushing past way too close for comfort. Then reloaded my cargo. Good thing Peepaw taught me how to change my own tire. David had made it all the way to Tifton before he realized I wasn't trailing him. Just my luck.. great way to start a new endeavor.

Long story short, I settled into the dormitory as well as my new role as a college student at Abraham Baldwin Agricultural College in Tifton, GA. I majored in Animal Science and Livestock Health. I made a ton of friends there, instantly. They were all my kinda people. I even played Quarterback on the girls' football team, the "Beechnut Bunnies". The school had a 4 to 1 male to female student body ratio. So if you were a girl there, you had like a hundred guys chasing after you. But I turned all the ones who chased me into my buddies and stayed true to David. Until eventually we drifted apart from the 300 miles distance between us. We have remained friends to this day though.

I got a full-time job working on the college campus farm. I was first in charge of the swine unit, then I managed the cattle unit. Also, I learned how to operate heavy equipment... bulldozers, backhoes, front end loaders, dump trucks, combines, and a dozen makes and models of tractors. I had a ball running all that machinery in the clay dirt and cotton fields of South Georgia. (As a young child I would select die cast construction toys over a Barbie Doll any day, and run them through the dirt for hours). Now it was full scale and real life, and I loved it. Plus I was really good at it. I also worked for ABAC's official rodeo team, making my rounds on the circuit and hauling their 30 foot stock trailer. I was issued an old Dodge dually crew cab pickup truck to use for my farm use and rodeo jobs.

Socially, there was way too much fun to be had. I see why so many students flunk out of college. It is one big nonstop party. I tried to be responsible for the most part, but I also liked to let my hair down and have a good time. I made my rounds to the big field parties, to the house parties, and to a little dive bar in downtown Tifton where I sang karaoke on the weekends. I came to be known by the owner there as the "Singing Cowgirl". I never inherited the musical talents passed down through my family. I could usually carry a decent tune, but I was no professional. Hell, it was karaoke though, so it's alright if you suck. Also, one of my best friends, Oren Hayes, was the college radio station DJ. He would let me in after hours and put me live on air to sing "Coal Miner's Daughter"... or a drunk version of it anyways. Then like every proper college student rite of passage, we ended our late nights with a trip to the local Waffle House.

Part 2

After a few months of living in the dorms, I decided to rent a place on the outskirts of town. A newly manufactured doublewide with a big yard, so I could bring my dogs up from Florida to live with me. Trudy and Whiskey were so happy when I loaded them up in the Jeep and took them to our new home. It was a nice place, and I chose a few of my good girlfriends to be my roommates there. About that time I met one of the male students from the Forestry Department. We were at the same party but I'd never seen him before that night. He just marched right up to me, out of the blue, and started kissing me with no warning. Needless to say, we became an instant item. His name was Chapel, and I quickly fell in love with him. He was very handsome and a true Southern Georgian Gentleman. I was thoroughly content during that time. I had made a good life for myself in Tift County, Georgia. I felt settled, assured that I was exactly where I was supposed to be. It was the happiest I had ever been in my life. I had everything going for me... perfect job, perfect school, perfect boyfriend, perfect setting. I had a five-year structured plan to finish school, start my career as a state department of agriculture inspector, then get married and have babies. It was a solid plan. I believed that nothing could stand in my way or stop me from attaining my dreams, and nothing could possibly go wrong.

Meanwhile back in Florida my mom, stepdad and brother were about to relocate back to West Virginia. By the time winter rolled around, they had officially made the move. So I had no place left to go home to in Florida. Peepaw had written to me every week while I was in college.. and enclosed a $50 bill in each letter, to make sure I had enough to eat and was taken care of. He was really the only member of my family I kept in regular contact with during my time in Georgia. He was always amused by the fact, and would say out loud, "Tiff lives in Tifton, in Tift County." He had even come to Tifton to see me on a couple occasions. And treated me out to dine at restaurants while he was there to visit. He liked the place I had rented. I could tell he was genuinely pleased with the progress I had made as a grown-up so far. He called me a few weeks before Christmas and relayed that he wished for me to come to West Virginia for my two-week break. He didn't want me to be alone during the holidays. But he insisted that he would drive down and pick me up, and I would ride home with him. He was worried I would get caught in a snowstorm and be on dangerous roadways if I travelled alone. So I agreed. Peepaw came right on schedule as he had promised. (He was always very punctual and kept as strict a travel schedule on the road as he did as a pilot in the sky). He had some minor mechanical issues with his van. (That was the first instance I had ever seen a cell phone, he was one of the first people to get one. It was the size of a brick, with a spiral cord attached that plugged into the cigarette adapter on the dash). He called Meemaw to let her know we were a little behind schedule.

We finally made it to West Virginia where I would spend my holiday break with family. It was a snowy winter. A welcome change of weather and scenery from the flat land and Georgia heat I had grown accustomed to. I was happy to be back in my mountains. I spent time with Peepaw, just me and him one grey skied day, at my grandparents' house on Oak Street in Summersville. I had put down cigarettes for a while (since I always worked in barns around hay), and traded them for Red Man Golden Blend pouch tobacco, (shameful and unladylike, I know). But I recall that day asking Peep if he minded me taking a chew, to which he replied, "Nah, go ahead," and brought me a spittoon. Then he cranked some Willie Nelson up on the stereo, and we danced around the living room. We had such a lovely time. He was the greatest man on Earth.

On New Year's Day 1999, I went to visit some family on my stepdad's side. I had known most of them nearly all my life... and I felt as though they were extended family. I was at my cousin's house and we were just having a low key evening. When in walked a gorgeous man that caught my eye. I had actually met him before at my mom's wedding back in '95 when he showed up as the date of the very cousin I was currently hanging out with. But we had only met in passing, through a brief introduction. And I paid little mind to him then.

I had zero intention of having a winter break fling. I had a boyfriend that I was happy with back in Georgia. I wanted to be faithful to him. I thought Chapel might even be "The One". This is what was going through my mind as I caught myself being captivated by the stranger that just walked through the door. But here is this good looking Marine Corps soldier, in on leave from Camp Pendleton, California. His name was Jason. He had a dark tan, light hair, a barbed wire tattoo and the prettiest green eyes I had ever seen. He was hard to resist. And he took a liking to me because I was a southern country girl. Sparks flew, chemistry flowed and an intense flame was ignited.

We spent the rest of my time in WV together, inseparable for five days straight.. riding around in his green '73 Oldsmobile Cutlass Supreme. He was a Summersville native and even took me home to introduce me to his parents. He also took me to meet his grandfather and grandmother. And I introduced him to all my family. It seemed to get serious instantly. But I had firmly made up my mind that I would forget all about him when it was time for me to leave and go back to college. My mother walked into my cousin's house, one of the days we spent together, and saw him with his arm around me. Mama took one look at him and said, "Who are you?" To which he replied, "I'm Trouble."

Domesticated

Back down in the land of the Georgia pines and peaches, it was time for "College Girl Tiff" to start the second semester at ABAC. I was ready to clear my mind and refocus on my life there after being away for two weeks on winter holiday. I was looking forward to getting back to work and starting the next school session. I especially couldn't wait to see Chapel. Although I felt extremely guilty for going astray on him, I wanted to make things right. I wanted to be his girl, and forget all about the Marine soldier. Besides, I knew my brief romance with Jason was just that.. he lived clear on the other side of the country in California, a place I had never even been to. I knew for a fact that I would never see Jason again.

Everything resumed as normal for the most part. But it seemed as though Chapel had also encountered a winter break fling of his own because he just became so distant after that. Things were not the same with him. The intimacy we had shared before felt more forced now. I finally asked him directly what the deal was, to which he somewhat admitted to reconnecting with an ex-fiancé while he had been home to his family's ranch. After that conversation, our relationship just gradually faded into a thing of the past. I went on about my daily business anyways. Hoping Chapel would come back around and we would get back together. We never did. And I found myself thinking more and more about the soldier in California. I had his phone number, so I called him one day. We started talking over the phone on a regular basis. The more we talked, the more I felt a longing for him. It grew so strong that I couldn't shake it. It began to consume my every waking moment. When I realized that, I started trying like hell to fight my feelings and convince myself to let him go and forget all about him.

I had my life situated the way I wanted it. I had my five-year plan and I wanted to stick to it come hell or high water. I didn't want to go off course and mess up everything I had worked so hard to build. It would be unacceptable to uproot myself from my own goals and dreams and throw them to the wayside, like a spoiled child who is done playing with their toys. I had come too far to give up now. I had come so very far.

As more time went by, and we became more serious with each other through hours of conversation Jason extended an informal invitation for me to come to California. Apparently, he couldn't shake me off either. It was madness. Pure insanity. We barely just met and had only spent a handful of days together. Why the hell would I go across the country to be with a man I'd hardly even known? It was complete and utter nonsense. Next thing I knew, I found myself packing up my entire life in Georgia. I quit my job, dropped out of college, backed out of my lease agreement on the rental property, loaded up the Jeep with my belongings and my dogs, then said goodbye to my friends. And just like that, in the snap of a finger, my time there came to a sudden dead end. I had done it all so quickly I didn't even have time to let it sink in. Mama had come down to help me in my hasty endeavor. It was February and I had been very ill with the flu all that week, so my mind was fogged up from that alone. It didn't fully hit me, what I had just done, till I was on the road following Mom to West Virginia. When it finally did sink in, it hit me like a ton of bricks. The whole trip to WV, I was completely dazed and confused. What about my plan? What was I doing? Why did I just up and leave? Where was I going? What would happen next? Am I making the biggest mistake of my life? Was I on the road to what God had planned for me? Or was I on a highway to hell and eternal damnation? Did the Devil make me do it? Question after question played over and over through my mind like a broken record. I was in a state of disbelief and panic. I finally broke down and cried, trying to see the Interstate through tears falling down like a monsoon of torrential rain. My heart was racing 90 miles a minute. But somehow, it all felt destined. Like it was going to happen even against my will; as though the entire universe was spinning so that all the planets and stars would align just right to make it happen; like it was forecasted into my future before I even existed, and I had been betrothed to this man since birth.

By the time we arrived in West Virginia, I had finally pulled my big girl panties up, wiped the tears from my eyes, took a deep breath, and made my peace with whatever unforeseeable chain of events were lined up ahead of me. It was too late to turn back now, and I couldn't even if I wanted to. I had permanently severed all ties to my life in Georgia. But Jason and I didn't even have a decent plan. We had no plan at all really. But it was time to make one. All I knew was that I had to find a way to make it three thousand miles across the continent to California. So whatever it took to make that happen, was what I had to do next.

Jason was a poor Marine, they don't pay soldiers much, poverty wage actually. He was living in the barracks on base. He didn't have money laying around to buy me a plane ticket. I was short on funds from paying rent and being a poor college student, so I couldn't afford airfare either. I considered driving my Jeep cross-country. But it already had a lot of miles on it and risked the chance of breaking down, so Peepaw advised against that. And I didn't want to bother my family for money, since they were just standing on the sidelines of what must have looked like a complete train wreck, shaking their heads about my sudden unpredictable change of plans. So I did the only logical thing I could do, I got a job for the meantime in West Virginia. I would buy time to regroup myself and save money to make my way out West.

I found a job working at a privately owned horse stable in Mt. Nebo, West Virginia. The barn was filled with world champion Saddlebred horses that were worth at least 30k each. I had never worked in such high caliber equestrian facility like this before. I was accustomed to country barns and Western saddles. This place was like a show horse mansion with English saddles. And it was my first time working with horses since my bad accident back in '97. I didn't even want to ride. I ended up being employed for the sole sake of brushing and braiding the manes and tails of those fancy upscale horses. That was my job. Granted, it was harder than it sounds. Their manes were long and thick, and their tales dragged the ground four feet behind them. With my bad back, it was tedious and strenuous work.

I stayed with Mama in the house of her in-laws. They were a prominent Italian family and their cooking lived up to their heritage. I would return after a long day at work, soak my sore back in a hot bath, and feast on their Italian cuisine. Wasn't so bad staying there, besides as I said before.. that family was my extended family and they all treated me well, except for my stepdad. He was still a damned tyrant. Jason and I were in the process of making our plans if you could call them that. Was more of a haphazard series of scattered ideas. One of which ended up being a drunken half-ass marriage proposal over the phone. To which I ignorantly accepted, like a stupid little puppy love school girl. Mind you we hadn't even seen each other since our winter whirlwind romance. But I took it seriously, regardless.

My stepdad had wrecked and totaled his Dodge Neon about this time.. and had no form of transportation. So he and my mother presented me with the proposition of letting him borrow my Jeep intermittently when I wasn't using it for work. I hesitantly agreed, based on the plea that they needed to be able to get my little brother to and from places. A few days later when I had a day off and was about to walk out the door to go visit Grandma Sparks, he asked me if he could take the Cherokee for a test drive. I told him of my plans and implied for him to be quick about it. About an hour later he came back. I asked for my keys to my vehicle, and he wouldn't give them to me. What the fuck? He seriously was holding my Jeep, that Peepaw bought me, as his hostage. Even his own mother came to my defense and gave him a good scolding when I blew the whistle on him. But he got away with it in the long run. I never drove my Jeep Cherokee again after that. Still makes me sick to think about how it was stolen right out from under me, by my worst enemy, like a thief in the night. I hated him. Why do the bad guys always seem to win? I should have put up more of a fight.

I could have gone to Peepaw and reported the case to him, knowing full well he would resolve the situation immediately. But I didn't want to burden him or involve him in what would possibly wind up being a big battle... with Mama caught right in the line of fire. And at that point, I just wanted to get the hell outta dodge. I was furious and madder than I'd ever been. I wanted to find some way to make this dictator Hitler wanna-be, parading around as my stepdad, disappear.. rid the world of his evil bullshit once and for all. He was just a giant bully, like the kid I stabbed with my pencil in the first grade. If I had been "Lady Outlaw Tiff" back then, I would have certainly killed him (or at least attempted to), over what he had done. He would have never gotten away with it. But instead of committing murder, as much as I felt viciously compelled to.. I sat my mother down that same night and made a proposition of my own. I told her this, "Get me a one-way ticket to

California and buy me a wedding dress. In exchange, your asshole husband can have my vehicle, on the condition that I can drive it when I come back to WV to visit." She agreed to my terms.

The next day, Mama drove me to the horse stable so I could quit my job and collect my wages. To top everything else off, I was sexually harassed by my perverted old man boss before I could make my exit. He didn't know my mom was in a car in the parking lot. I was humiliated. Disgusted. He had pinned me up against the barn and groped me while he whispered inappropriate things in my ear. I had been violated and was completely mortified. Mama was upset when I told her. When I informed Jason of it that night, he called and ripped the nasty son-of-a-bitch a new asshole. I should have pressed charges and exposed him for what he was. All arrows pointed to get out of West Virginia ASAP. Mama did as agreed and bought my plane ticket right away, but my trip was scheduled for a few weeks out still. So meanwhile she and I went shopping for a wedding dress. We went to a bridal boutique in Beckley, and I tried a few on. Then I saw one in a catalog that I fell in love with. We placed the order for it. So here I was with an unofficial engagement and a wedding gown on the way. It wouldn't arrive till weeks after my departure across the country.

March came in like a lion. And I found myself at the airport in Charleston, holding my one-way ticket to California. I had a trunk filled plumb full of whatever I could stuff inside, and a big suitcase that I'd had to sit on in order to get it zipped up. That's all I could take on my venture to the Wild West. I had to leave the stolen Jeep and my dogs behind, and I did have a good cry about that. But otherwise, I was relieved to finally be on my way in what had so far been a horrendous and exhausting journey. I was weary and tired. I slept for most of the eight-hour flight, aside from the long layover in Chicago. During my wait there, I tried to envision what my new life with Jason on the West Coast would look like. Would he regret inviting me there? Would I regret going? Or would everything work out for the best? Maybe we would end up living happily ever after in some storybook fairy tale romance. That's what I was hoping for. That's what every girl wishes and hopes for. It's what our dreams are made of.

As the jet plane started to prepare for landing, I began to feel a sense of excitement. I was going to a place I had never been before, or ever even thought I would have any reason to go to. I was looking forward to getting a view of the scenery and landscape of this far away destination. I felt like a pioneer about to stake my claim on a California gold rush. Open range and room for countless possibilities. Unchartered territory awaited me. I could breathe a breath of fresh air. And there he was when I came through the gate. My Marine. So handsome in his camouflage battledress military uniform, looking even more dashing than I remembered. But with the same striking green eyes and dazzling smile that I recalled so well. My whole new life stood directly before me. And suddenly I felt like the luckiest girl in the whole world. I fell into his arms like that was where I was meant to be.

And in that moment, my heart belonged to him alone. He was my new home now. And I could be anywhere on earth with him, and still, be home.

We held hands and kissed all the way from the luggage claim and throughout the San Diego International Airport. We were making out on the escalator, in the elevator, and in his car in the parking garage. Yep, the sparks were still very much alive and well. We like to never got out of there and on our way up the coast. And I sat as close to him as I could get, on the bench seat of his '73 Oldsmobile, for the entire trip. Holding hands and smiling, catching up and kissing, all along the way. I barely even noticed the scenery that I had been so excited to see before I landed. It was raining that day, the only time I ever saw it rain while I lived in California. Jason had moved out of the barracks on Camp Pendleton Marine Corps Base, to an off base neighborhood in the town of Oceanside.. in preparation for my arrival. He had explained to me before I came out there that we would be sharing a house with other Marine soldier roommates, which was fine with me. I didn't care where we lived as long as we were together. I just wanted to be with him.

We pulled into the drive on Nixon Circle. It was a typical California house of Spanish style architecture. And all the other houses in the suburban neighborhood were similar. We made it there before the other roommates had come in from work. So we had the place to ourselves momentarily and used that to our advantage if you catch my drift (wink, wink). Then he showed me around the house. It was a charming little place with three bedrooms, a garage and a fireplace.. along with a hot tub and a hammock on the back covered patio. The back yard was like its own little Garden of Eden. There was a privacy fence enclosing a green lawn with palm trees, lemon trees, orange trees and banana trees, along with native flowers of Southern California. It was small, but a tropical piece of paradise.

Our living quarters were to be the dining room of the house, since three other Marines lived there already, and all the bedrooms were spoken for. So that's where we set up camp. We inflated an air mattress which we covered in cheap bedding. I pushed my trunk up against the wall with my suitcase on top so I could access my clothes. He had his belongings stuffed into trash bags and his military sea bags with his uniforms and gear. It was very makeshift and unorganized by anyone's standards. But we would make do with what we had. It was our introduction to playing house.

Before that first day ended, I was already busy at work doing a thorough cleaning and tidying of the place. It had been a disaster with four men making messes and no women to clean up after them. It needed a woman's touch. And I was always very good and efficient at housework. I had done laundry and every form of cleaning since I was 8 years old. And I was born organized. Have always been major OCD. (You could draw a line down the bedrooms Haley and I shared as kids, and tell whose side was which). But I busted ass on the house till it sparkled and shined. The other Marines were stunned when they walked through the door. It was a pleasant surprise for them to see their house turned into a home. Obviously, I didn't touch their bedrooms. But still, they were pleased and accepted me into their pack based on my efforts to make the place livable. And I think Jason was impressed with the skills of his new female companion. He could see I would earn my keep at least on that level.

Cooking was another matter entirely. Mama had never really given me instructions in the kitchen. (Hamburger Helper has always been strictly forbidden in my own household) And although I had watched Grandma Sparks prepare meals countless times, she never measured anything or had written recipes. All I knew how to make thus far were fried eggs, grilled cheese sandwiches and ramen noodles. Lame and pathetic. I would have to learn the culinary arts and teach myself to be a chef as I went along. I was only 18, so there was still plenty of time for that.

Our daily lives and routines began right off the bat. Jason couldn't just stay with me in La-La land. He had to do his duties as a soldier of the United States military. Jason was five years older than me, 23 at the time. So I looked to him as the adult of the pair of us and followed his lead. Besides that, he was exceedingly smart and physically strong. I knew he would steer us right and always protect me. He was now my guardian. And I trusted him completely to make all decisions.

Jason had lost his base driving privileges over a speeding incident off base on his motorcycle. So when he was up at 5am, dressed in his uniform and ready for work; it was my duty to drive him there. We would commute in his big hooptie boat of an automobile, through the toll road in Oceanside and the gates of Camp Pendleton. The base itself is enormous. I was always worried I would get lost after I dropped him off since I've never had any sense of direction. I didn't know my way around California. And me behind the wheel of what felt like a cruise ship floating down the roadways making my way back home was a major feat and accomplishment in itself.

I enjoyed those drives though, taking in all the West Coast scenery. It was so drastically different than anything I had seen on the East Coast. There are different species of trees, other plant life and vegetation, the mountains are shaped differently and more barren... with sagebrush being prevalent. I even saw big lawns entirely cloaked with a pretty purple ground-cover of tiny flower blooms. California just has its own vibe too. If you have been there, you can imagine it in your mind. You can close your eyes and revisit it without even going there. I vote it as the best weather of any state I have lived in; altogether, it is unlike any other place I've ever been.

Days rolled on, and I had pretty much settled in as "Cali Tiff". I started looking for jobs in the area so I could contribute to our cause. I dropped him off at work every day, did my housework, picked him back up. We would stop by Ralph's Grocery on the way home and get something to make for dinner and a bottle of California vintage wine, (we tried a different bottle every time, till we had tried every local wine there was). I had progressed my cooking skills enough to add at least one more menu item to the short list of what I could make. Spaghetti, we ate it like every night of the week. We even had a designated spot on the kitchen wall that we would throw pasta against, to see if it would stick. I perfected my recipe for it and then forced us to eat it repeatedly. It would have to suffice until I could broaden my skills and move on to something more advanced; anything but more spaghetti. After dinner our nights were spent hanging out...playing card games with the other Marines, watching tv, soaking in the hot tub with our glasses of wine, or swinging in the hammock. And we would go to bed and make love, once the house was quiet and our roommates had retired to their quarters. Then I'd fall asleep, feeling safe and content in his arms. We would wake up several times in the night to a completely deflated air mattress. It had a steady leak. In which case Jason would get up and hand pump the air back into it every time, with me still half asleep on top of it. Was just part of our daily routine. One of our roommates was deployed to another base, so we finally got to move out of the dining room and into an actual bedroom. It was the smallest room of the house but we didn't care. We were just happy to have our privacy and a place to properly store our belongings. And especially happy to have a real bed where we could get a good night's sleep for a change. Once we moved into that room, Jason would give me my 5am wake-up calls by blasting Korn on the speakers and jumping up and down on our upgraded bed.

April came around, and we were in a good rhythm with our life together so far. I still hadn't found work yet, because every job opening I found required a college degree. And since I had just dropped out of college, I couldn't supply one. But I started looking for jobs on local farms and ranches, shoveling manure or something that didn't require a degree. I finally found one that I qualified for, which also included room and board on the ranch. Seemed like a perfect fit. We could both live there, save on rent, and I would have a job. For the time being, I was babysitting children of active-duty soldiers, for some extra money on the side.

Before I had a chance to apply for the ranch job, a turn of events took precedence. I was late for my period and thought I may be pregnant. Jason had taken me for a weekend outing to the cliffs of La Jolla to see the seals on the beach. That is where I told him that there was a possibility of pregnancy. A sense of urgency came over him, and he took me that same day to the mall in Carlsbad, California and let me browse the jewelry store to look at engagement rings. A few days later on April 11th, my 19th birthday Jason got down on one knee and proposed to me. He put a diamond engagement ring on my left hand and gave me a box that contained gold wedding bands for both of us, that he had also picked out and purchased. I was over the moon happy. I was going to marry my Knight in Shining Armor and be with him forever. We called our families and told them the news of our official engagement. My pre-ordered wedding gown had already arrived in WV. And we set a date for our hometown wedding. July 3, 1999.

Less than two weeks later, Jason got a call from home. His grandmother had been hospitalized, and they didn't think she would pull through. He asked for leave time from the military, which they respectfully granted. Jason then came to me with a new plan. He wanted to keep our original wedding date back home. But in mapping out our current necessary cross-country trip to West Virginia, it dawned on him that we could get married on our route through Las Vegas. That way we could go ahead and start collecting married and housing pay from the military.

He sprung all this on me the day before we were to leave on our trip. But I loved him and trusted his judgment, and agreed to this new idea. I was ready to commit to him. He took me that night to a department store to find a dress to wear. We were still poor and had to put everything we had into our upcoming travel expenses. So I chose a simple white lace dress and some modest but elegant pearly white shoes to match. I think they totaled up to under thirty dollars altogether. But while I was in the dressing room trying on what was to be my wedding dress, my time of the month showed up. Two weeks later than it was supposed to. I immediately told Jason as we were on our way out of the store. I figured he wouldn't want to rush and go through with a quick Vegas wedding, due to the finding that I was not pregnant. I assumed that had been the reason behind his abrupt change of plans in the first place. He was relieved at the fact that we didn't have a baby on the way. We weren't set up yet with suitable circumstances to bring a child into the world. But he insisted that we go ahead as planned. Getting the married pay from the military sooner than July would help us tremendously with our financial stability.

The next day, April 26, 1999. Jason had to work for half the day, and I had to babysit for one of his sergeants. When the children were picked up and Jason got home, we loaded up the Oldsmobile and set out for Las Vegas, Nevada. It was hot that day and the car was overheating before we even made it past the California line. So we had to crank the heater up to cool the engine down. We sat through bumper to bumper L.A. traffic, sweating our asses off. We had to keep a tight schedule on our way across the country as his grandmother's condition was getting increasingly worse. Once we hit the open road on Route 66 through the Mojave Desert, we finally cooled off. I painted my nails and put my makeup on to save time. I hopped over the seat into the back to change clothes into my wedding attire. We had agreed when this plan was first hatched, that we wouldn't tell a soul about it. We would just keep it as our secret, and carry on with our WV wedding plans. We swore on it. Both sides of our families were excited about our wedding and had already sent out the invitations, so we didn't want to ruin it for them.

I had never been to Vegas before. As it came into view like a mirage in the distance of the desert, it was magnificent to see standing there… with tumbleweeds, sand and cactuses on all sides. This huge lit up cityscape erected right in the middle of nowhere, against the background of the desert landscape. It was impressive to see. We arrived just as the sun was setting. Jason was wearing his Marine Corps Dress Blues, the most admirable uniform of all the military branches. It was the first time I had seen him wearing it. He was so fiercely handsome, such a distinguished gentleman. He looked like royalty. And I in my white lace dress, a blushing bride. We were young and in love. We were about to commit ourselves to each other; to bind our lives together forever. And we were both glowing radiant with the happiness of our occasion.

We rode down the main strip. He had been there many times before and wanted me to see all the monumental buildings with their neon lights. It was every bit as impressive as I imagined it to be. You're probably imagining that since we were in Vegas, we had an Elvis themed wedding, right? We did try a few places with that in mind, but we were too poor and couldn't afford any of them. It was a Monday, of all days, between 8 and 9 pm Western Standard Time. And with no luck at the Elvis gigs or Little White Chapels. We made our way downtown to the Clark County Courthouse. Who goes to Las Vegas, and gets married at the courthouse, on a Monday night? We did! And it was just as magical as any full-blown big scale wedding with pomp and circumstance could be. It was actually even better (having had both types I can testify). Everything about our ceremony was intimate. It wasn't a show to put on for spectators. It was just the Groom and the Bride. And the Holy sacrament of marriage.

We had a female judge who performed our ceremony. And her assistant took pictures with our film camera. We were both on the nervous and shy side in that courtroom. But we stood there before one another, holding both our left and right hands together. We said our vows, exchanged wedding rings, were announced as man and wife, and he kissed the bride. We were both smiling and crying at the same time. It was short and sweet and straight to the point. It was perfect. And it was official. I was his forever, and he was mine. Till death do us part. And for all eternity. In the moment that we sealed our marriage with a kiss, I knew with pure conviction that it had indeed been God's plan, that He had paved this path for me and led me directly where I was intended to be. I was very young at the time, yes. But I meant what I said when we exchanged vows and I pledged myself to him. I meant it with all my heart and soul. I was ready to be his wife. I gave him my hand, and he gave me his last name.

After we tied the knot, we took turns photographing each other in front of the Oldsmobile, in the parking lot of the courthouse. (Present day, Jason keeps the picture he took of me posted on the front of his refrigerator). We went to the strip of town to a place called the Holy Cow. We splurged and celebrated with a nice steak dinner and a glass of wine (that he had to sneak across the table to me since I wasn't drinking age). We were both grinning from ear to ear the entire time. And everyone was giving us well wishes when they would see his uniform and my white dress. We were elated and on Cloud 9. I was proud to be seen on his arm as his wife, and he was proud to have me there. We got a shot glass with the Holy Cow logo on it, to commemorate our first dinner as husband and wife. We still have that shot glass twenty years later. We didn't go to any of the casinos in Vegas. I was underage and couldn't enter them. We didn't stay at any of the grand resorts. We spent that night at the Howard Johnson Hotel, on the edge of town. With a 4am wakeup call to get up and on the road towards West Virginia.

Part 2

We barely stopped the rest of the way. We were trying to make it there in time for him to say his goodbyes to his grandmother. We drove three thousand miles in three days, (which included our stop in Las Vegas). We were full steam ahead with the hammer down on the Oldsmobile V-8 350 Rocket, making record time. Pedal to the metal. We did upwards of 120 mph in some stretches. We didn't stop to eat. We didn't stop to sleep. We were just wide open. That big green tank, (nicknamed The Bomb), was so loud and intimidating, that the other cars on the road would part like the Red Sea when we came upon them. We only stopped to gas up, and we took turns driving and sleeping. The entire back floorboard was littered with empty Marlboro boxes and caffeinated drink containers. That was our honeymoon.

We decided somewhere along our trip, that once we got there. I would stay and make the final arrangements for our big wedding coming up in July. And he would fly back to California leaving the Oldsmobile with me. And all throughout that road trip, Jason kept looking over at me and saying, "I love you Wifey." And I kept looking down at my shiny gold rings with sparkly diamonds. I was so proud to be his wife. I didn't want to be away from him. I was dreading that part. He was my everything. Just before we reached Lexington, Kentucky for a pit stop to pick up his sister, we got word that his grandmother passed away. We were too late. We didn't make it in time. So now we slowed our roll. We had agreed to tell one person each of our marriage. I would tell my sister Haley, and he would tell his sister Brandy. We were too excited to keep it completely to ourselves. So he told his sister, who seemed genuinely happy for us. And we proceeded to West Virginia.

Once there, we removed our wedding rings and I tucked them away for safe keeping, leaving only my engagement ring on my left hand. There was a somber tone, as we were now there for a funeral. It was a time of mourning. But even so, it was hard for me to keep our secret. I wanted to shout it from the rooftops for everyone to hear. But I played the part my husband asked me to play. And hid our news well. I had met his grandmother back in the winter. She was nice to me and seemed happy that he had a girl with him. After she was laid to rest, it was decided that we would inherit her furniture, to give us a start for our home after our July wedding. So we helped his parents pack up her household, and put everything in storage. The time came for Jason to fly out. I took him to the airport and cried my eyes out telling him goodbye. I had just married him and now I had to be separated from him for the next two months. And I couldn't even let on to anyone that we were already married. I was so sad that day. It was all I could do to let him go. I ended up staying in his parent's home with them for those two months, so his mother and I could take care of the last-minute details for the wedding together, along with my mother. I had fittings for my dress, chose flowers from the florist, booked the reception hall, hired the DJ, hired the caterers and all the other things involved with planning a big wedding. It kept me very busy and I hardly even had time to miss Jason. Plus I was cleaning house for a sweet little old lady, to make some cash. But our impending wedding day was all the buzz on both sides of our families. And a bridal shower was held in my honor during that time.

I drove the Oldsmobile everywhere I went. And since the idler had been set for California terrain, it was too slow for the mountains of West Virginia. And I would pop the hood to adjust it constantly, just couldn't get it in the right groove. Seemed like I was under the hood of The Bomb more than I was behind the wheel. But at least you can find what you're looking for in those older cars, and tell which part is which, before the computerized shit came along. I went to Braxton County to visit with Grandma Sparks at my Aunt Alta's farm, which was always one of my favorite places. (Daddy's Jeep had broken down near there when we were little, and he packed us girls, one under each arm all the way to Alta's). Well after we visited there that day, I offered to drive Grandma to her house on the Elk River. She got in and we headed down the long gravel driveway. Then the idler cut out again making the engine stop. When that would happen, all power steering and brakes would be inoperable. Grandma who was 78 at the time, and having never driven in her life, was always scared of cars. When she realized we were in a runaway automobile, she said, "Come on Tiffy, let's jump!" She aimed to bail out and wanted me to join her. Before I could say, "I have to get this thing stopped." She swung her heavy steel passenger-side door open, and made her grand exit. I saw her in the rear-view. She took a tactical roll on the ground, stood up, brushed herself off, and started marching up the gravel road back towards Alta's house. When I finally got the big boat of a hooptie halted, I left it where it sat and ran to check on Grandma. She wasn't even phased. She was half laughing at her own rebellious act of bolting out the car, and half scolding me for my failure to properly operate a vehicle. She refused to ever ride with me after that. Bless her heart. Grandma was the toughest, feistiest, sassiest lady I've ever known.

That few months flew by in the blink of an eye. On June 23, ten days before the big day, it was time for me to pick my husband up from the airport in Charleston. I couldn't wait to see my handsome fella. I got all cleaned up and dressed up, put on makeup and perfume. I wanted to look extra pretty for him. His plane landed and I could tell he was not feeling well as soon as I saw him. He had received a round of Anthrax vaccinations from the Marine Corps right before his flight out of San Diego. He made mention of it and was still wearing the bandage on his arm, issued by the military doctor. I took our rings out of hiding and we put them back on in their rightful places, just to wear until we got to our hometown.

We had dinner together then checked into a room for the evening at the Holiday Inn in Charleston, instead of making the hour plus long drive to Summerville. We wanted time alone to reunite since we had been apart. We consummated our reunion that night. And I remember thinking to myself after the fact, "I just got pregnant." Then wondered why on earth I would think such a thing. I never said it out loud. I just brushed it off and never thought on it again.

Our wedding day arrived, July 3, 1999. It was set for 7pm at Carnifex Ferry Battlefield State Park in Kessler's Cross Lanes, WV. My dad had worked there as a young man, making signs for the park. I chose that location because I wanted to incorporate my father into our wedding. And since Daddy couldn't be there to walk me down the aisle, Peepaw was the only one who had earned the right to give me away. He was the man who raised me. Meemaw worked hard making our wedding cake. She was a professional at it, having run her own cake business in her younger days and had made hundreds of wedding cakes. But this was the first one she made for one of her grandchildren, so it was special.

Mama helped me get ready at her house. My Aunt Vicki who was a hairdresser, fixed my hair really pretty. Haley was up from Miami to be my maid of honor, and I had told her of the secret. All the ladies had a bridal brunch that morning. My little brother Andrew and cousin Tyler were my ring bearers, they were both 3 years old and so adorable in their bow ties. Everyone had a part to play. And family members came in from all over the country.

The stage was set for the big day. I had been moody and rather short-tempered all that afternoon. I chalked it up to a case of PMS. I'm sure it just came across as a regular episode of Bridezilla. Mama even said to me at one point, "You're so grouchy, you need to go smoke a cigarette and chill out." And it was literally the hottest day on record for that year, but at least the rain held off since it was an outdoor wedding. I remember thinking how I just couldn't wait for it to all be over, I was tired of trying to hold in the fact that we were already married. It was a difficult charade to keep up.

Even though it was an evening wedding, it took me all day to get myself ready. Peepaw stuffed me and my big dress into his van and escorted me to Carnifex. I was very pleased with the wedding gown I had chosen, I felt like a Queen. It was a white silk and lace, off the shoulder, intricately beaded dress with a dramatic cathedral length train. And my veil was equally ornate. Jason donned his military Dress Blues, looking as stunning and regal as he had at our first wedding. I had chosen a red, white and blue theme to match his uniform, which also went along with the location of the Civil War battlefield where the ceremony took place. My bouquet of red carnations, white roses, blue delphiniums and baby's breath was so beautiful. When I got out of the van and saw how everything had come together, I was glad that we decided to go on with the big wedding. I observed all of our family there, and they looked so happy to be celebrating our day with us. This was for them.

Peepaw walked me down the aisle to the tune of "Canon In D". I couldn't take my eyes off of my Groom/ Husband. I don't think I even saw anyone else but him during the processional. Peepaw did the honors of giving me away. I had his blessing, so I felt I could be truly happy now. Jason and I were in truth having our vows renewed in the sight of God. But we were also joining ourselves in union, in the presence of our families, with them as witnesses to our sacrament. Pastor Phil, (who became our family preacher), performed the ceremony. Everything went perfectly. And Jason kissed the bride, again. It was officially official!

A great time was had by all at the reception, with family and friends, dancing and food. The cake Meemaw made was beyond lovely. (It had tipped over in the van while in route, but if she hadn't told me that, I would have never known). There were toasts given by our best man and maid of honor. I saved the father/daughter dance for my Peepaw. And Jason and I danced our first dance to "I Don't Want To Miss A Thing" by Aerosmith. It was our song. We cut the cake, drank champagne, threw the garter and a bouquet. Then we made our big exit through a sea of bubbles blown by our guests. It was a happy celebration.

We drove off in the red Ford Ranger that Jason had bought for us a few days earlier. It was all decked out with tin cans, condoms, and shaving cream. With Just Married on the rear windshield. We headed to the town of Gauley Bridge where we spent our wedding night at the Glen Ferris Inn, a historic bed & breakfast. He carried me across the threshold and helped me out of my big dress. We scarfed down the to-go plates that had been packed up for us. And sat there opening all the cards we had received from the reception gift table. The monetary gifts would fund our honeymoon. We were so tired after all the festivities. If I recollect correctly, I think we skipped the romance and just passed out.

The next few days were spent loading up a U-Haul with his grandmother's furniture, to take back across the country for our own settlement. When we finished that task and were ready to hit the road, we made our rounds to say farewell to our families, not knowing when we would see any of them again. I hugged Mama (who was three months pregnant with her second son) and told her goodbye. As I was walking away, I opened my mouth and started to say to her, "I'll call you when I find out I'm pregnant." But I instantly stopped myself before the words came out. And in my mind, I was wondering. Why would I say that? Where did that even come from? To my knowledge, I was not with child.

Happily Never After

It was July 5th when we set out to make way back towards California. We planned to take our time on this trip. It was to be our honeymoon. (Jason's dad said he wouldn't send us on a "real honeymoon" until we were married for five years, and stated that he didn't think we would make it that long). But with the gathered money that was given to us as wedding gifts, we made out like bandits and intended to use it for the sake of sightseeing on our way back West. Also, we were pulling the loaded down U-Haul trailer, so we were forced to take it somewhat slow. The used '93 Ford Ranger that we had just recently bought, broke down with a blown thermostat near Amarillo, Texas along I-40. When we were back up and running, Jason got us a lavish hotel room in Albuquerque, New Mexico for the night. We swam in the indoor heated pool, had a nice dinner and a romantic evening.

We travelled through the Painted Desert of Arizona. That was my favorite scenery of the entire trip. The Petrified Forest was also fascinating to see. Then we took a slight detour to visit the Meteor Crater Natural Landmark near Winslow. We spent several hours there exploring. Jason bought me a souvenir from the gift shop, a black horse figure attached to a piece of the meteorite rock. We didn't make it to the Grand Canyon (and I still to this day have yet to see that wonder of the world). We then passed back through Nevada. We drove by the Joshua Tree National Park in California. And 29 Palms, where Jason had done his MOS training. We stood along the San Andreas Fault in the Mojave Desert, where we also saw a series of dust tornados. Altogether I think we travelled for six days on that road trip. We were happy to be together and spend quality time as newlyweds... the first length of time that we had been able to set aside for just the two of us since our initial wedding.

Arriving back in Oceanside, we unloaded the contents of the U-Haul into the garage. We gradually brought his late grandmother's furniture into the house, but most of the boxes stayed packed until we would have a place of our own. While we had been away, another of our roommates had been shipped off to a different base. So now we had the master bedroom of the house all to ourselves, with its own ensuite bathroom and two closets. A huge upgrade.

It hadn't quite occurred to me until after both of our weddings the full extent of how messy of a man my new husband was, till I saw the state of the small bedroom we had occupied before. He had made a complete disaster of it while he was there for the two months I had been in WV. I'm talkin' about one of the biggest messes I have ever had to clean up. It was almost impressive really, the grand scale of his disorganizational skills. He had mastered it like a trade. It was that bad. I could tell then that this man clearly needed my help in that arena. I had managed to marry the messiest man in America, twice.

I got both of us and all of our belongings perfectly organized and settled into our new living quarters. I was "Wifey Tiff" now so it was my official role to be the homemaker and take care of Jason.

And I wanted to do a good job and make him proud of me. Right away, I dove into domestic life on a higher level than I had attempted when I was just his girlfriend and fiancé. I had done it well enough then. But as a wife now, I took my tasks way more seriously. I knew he would depend on me to keep everything straight for us, and to be his helpmate. I felt more of a sense of pride and accomplishment in doing my wifely duties.

Our honeymoon was over and Jason went back to work at Camp Pendleton. I was readjusting to life in California after my long absence. Aside from settling into our new bedroom, I also kicked into super extra, major Obsessive Compulsive Disorder, overdrive for two days straight. Cleaning, ironing, washing, scrubbing, dusting, vacuuming, mopping, rearranging. Then when I would finish everything I had done. I would go back behind myself and do it all again even though it wasn't necessary. During the few days since we had returned back home, I was so tired and weak, it was all I could do to make it through a full day without having to stop several times and rest. I just felt completely drained. And assumed I was just still recovering from the excitement of both weddings, the wear and tear of travelling six thousand miles over the course of two months, and the work I had done to get everything resituated in the house. I kept trying to brush it off and carry on as normal. But subconsciously, I knew that something was different about me. I was extra emotional too. I figured I was just in a state of exhaustion, surely that's all it was. But then I noticed that my breasts were hurting. Felt like there had been an elephant laying on my chest. And the pain of it kept getting progressively worse.

On July 14th, I was on the phone with Mama and just brought up in passing about my chest being sore. I have always told Mom everything. She raised us girls to know that we could openly discuss anything with her. And to this day she is the first person I talk to about all of my life happenings. She has never been judgmental or closed minded. My mother is one of my closest confidants. And one of my best friends. As soon as I had begun to make mention of my strange condition, I had no more than completed my sentence before she butted in and abruptly announced, "You're pregnant!" I said "What? No, surely not. I'm not pregnant." But as I was saying that out loud, my mind quickly raced back to the night in Charleston at the Holiday Inn, where I had thought it to myself silently. And then to the moment where I had almost said it out loud to Mom when I was leaving West Virginia.

Once all that came back to me, along with my recent more intense nesting instincts, added to me being so tired and emotional, I knew she was right. I had known it all along, without really knowing it. My intuition had told me plain and clear on at least those two occasions and had dropped hints all this time. Since the instance that it first happened. Since the moment of conception. I had tried to hush my intuitive voice, and not listen. But now it all made perfect sense. I was with child.

Mama told me to go immediately to get a pregnancy test. I hung up with her and rushed to the nearest pharmacy. I wanted to be sure before I told Jason this time, after the false alarm back in April. On my way to town, I realized that I had in fact entirely skipped my last monthly cycle. I guess I had just been so busy with everything that I never even noticed.

When I got back home, I went straight to the bathroom, and within seconds the test read positive. I was so overwhelmed in that moment. So many emotions came over me all at once. I was now "Mommy Tiff", the most vital and honorable role of my entire lifetime. Something I had wanted to be since I was a little girl. I had dreamed of the day when I would have a family of my own. And this was that day.

I wanted Jason to be the first one to know, (although my mom already knew unofficially). I called him at work to tell him I was coming to see him. I got in the truck and drove straight to his workshop on the base. It was around midday when I got there. I found him at his desk and told him the big news. He was smiling brighter than I'd ever seen before. He picked me up and twirled me around. His company Staff Sergeant congratulated us and gave him leave for the rest of the day.

We spent that afternoon and evening together just in absolute shock and excitement. I took another test just to double check. We called our families and told them the news. They were all happy for us. And I set up a doctor's appointment at the military clinic, to have the blood test done to verify.

We weren't just husband and wife now, we were a family. We were a mother and a father. We started talking about names. I had already decided that my first son would be named after his father, and my first girl would be named Grace. So we settled that. But he wanted to come up with some alternate boy names on his own. So I entertained his ideas. We talked about what kind of parents we would be, how we would raise our child, what our future would be like, who the baby would look like. My maternal instincts took over me immediately. Starting that day, I quit smoking as soon as I had taken the test. Stopped drinking caffeine and alcohol. Quit taking hot baths and using the jacuzzi hot tub. Stopped using harsh cleaning chemicals. I started eating healthy. I altered every lifestyle choice I could think of. It wasn't about me anymore. Everything was automatically about my unborn child and the health and safety of the life that had formed inside of me. The baby that was made out of the love between Jason and I. Nothing else mattered anymore. I would live or die for my child. I would protect this baby like a fierce mama bear. My life took on a whole new meaning, worth, and purpose. The most important role I would ever play was this. Life as I knew it would never be the same. And I couldn't be happier.

I went to my appointment, and of course, the tests there confirmed my condition. I was given a due date of March 23, 2000. My doctor put me on prenatal vitamins and set me up on the WIC program, which I immediately took advantage of at the base commissary. Choosing only what was best for me and my baby. I weighed 103 pounds at the time, with a very tiny frame, so I was also put on a high-fat diet right away to gain weight. I got every book on pregnancy and read them all. Every step I took and every decision I made revolved around the baby.

Jason found a second job. His fatherly instincts had also kicked in, and he was in a nesting phase of his own. He did everything he could to take care of us. He became like a male bird frantically gathering materials to build a nest for his unhatched young. His trade in the military was network engineering. So he carried that over to his new civilian job as a computer repair tech, at a business located on the coastal highway in downtown Oceanside. I started working there with him as his part-time assistant, to bring in even more money. We couldn't live with roommates forever. We had to find a place of our own before the baby's arrival. A safe and peaceful home to raise our family. When we weren't working, we would search for alternative residential options. California had a very high cost of living, even twenty years ago, so it was impossible to find something within our means; even with housing and married pay from the Marine Corps. Jason was promoted to Corporal early in my pregnancy, so that helped us out some. Every little bit helped.

As my pregnancy progressed, and I was starting to show, I began to get more severe cases of morning sickness, but they would hit me mostly in the evenings. I couldn't stomach red meat. I mostly craved other foods that contained iron, which was my body's way of telling me what nutrients I was deficient in.

Otherwise, I felt good, and healthy, besides the fact that my back pain was getting drastically worse. But I went to my appointments regularly and everything was right on track where it should be with the baby. I was putting on weight and doing everything the doctor instructed.

When we weren't working, we would take time out to enjoy our newly married status. He would take me to the drive-in theater on a regular basis (where we would watch the movies from a mattress in the bed of the truck), to the Pacific Ocean to walk along the beach and listen to the waves and to the mountains further North to go camping at a lakeside retreat. He took me on a special trip to Palm Springs once, where we rode the aerial tram up the Chino Canyon, and enjoyed the beautiful California weather and scenery. He had bought me a pair of overalls shortly before that, since I was too big for regular clothes but still not ready for maternity clothes. I wore my overalls that day, and he kept telling me how cute I looked in them. We were so in love and so happy.

Meanwhile at home, we had rotated roommates a few times. We let a married couple we had become friends with move in, another Marine from Jason's unit, and his wife. They started out being nice but turned out to be very rude and destructive. They were trying to completely take over the house. And had torn up several pieces of the furniture that we had from Jason's grandmother. The territorial side of me got to a point where I seriously couldn't deal with them anymore. And I needed a calm atmosphere for the sake of the baby. We had actively been looking at real estate. But we would find fallen down shacks on less than 1/4 acre lots for around 300 grand. We just couldn't afford anything in California's economy. And the base housing was completely filled up, with at least a year-long waiting list. So we ended up meeting a civilian guy who was seeking roommates for his house where he lived alone.

Jason packed up everything we owned and we left Oceanside behind... relocating to the town of Temecula, in the Wine Country region of the state. It made a longer commute for him to work, but his base driving privileges had been reinstated, and it was our only available option at the time. So that's where we went. The place in Temecula was in a private gated McMansion community. Every house in the neighborhood looked like identical clones of each other, with only about four feet of space in between them. It was a large two-story, three-bedroom, modern California style house. Since the owner was only using the master bedroom, we were able to claim the other two bedrooms. One for us, and one for the baby's nursery.

Although we were in the wine region, it was more of an arid desert-like climate. I remember the first time I went to the grocery store there, I saw tumbleweed blowing across the fields. It was way more upper class than the surfer beach town of Oceanside. There were huge estates and vineyards all over the landscape. Jason pointed out one mansion in particular that belonged to Burt Reynolds. Some of Hollywood's elite lived in and around Temecula. It had an Old Town area that was very charming and historical. There was a Knott's Berry Farm amusement park nearby that Jason took me to once.. to ride the Ferris wheel, eat funnel cake, and play carnival games. Altogether, I liked the feel of this location better than being on the coast. Temecula was more eccentric, refined and sophisticated. Jason took me shopping, and we bought a baby crib for the nursery, along with the bedding and a mobile to go with it. We took it home and he went straight to work assembling it. I washed the baby bedding and lovingly put it in place. The sheets, blanket and crib bumper were decorated with a theme of teddy bears. We assembled the matching mobile, with plush teddy bears and hung it above the crib. I was near the end of the first trimester of my pregnancy, and we were so excited we just couldn't wait. Plus, we wanted to make sure we were fully prepared, well in advance, for when the time came for the arrival of our baby.

One night, shortly after we had settled into our new town and new home… we were sound asleep, and I was abruptly awakened around 2 am in our bedroom on the second floor. I sat straight up in bed and felt like I had an extreme case of vertigo. I thought maybe I was sick. The room was moving. Then I realized the entire house was moving, swaying back and forth like a ship on a stormy sea. At first, I thought it was a dream or my imagination. But when the sway became more violent and I realized what it was, I woke Jason up and asked him, "Is this an earthquake?" He instantly jumped out of bed and escorted me quickly down the stairs, outside, and away from the house. All the other neighbors had already made way outdoors. Everyone was just standing there in their pajamas, in a panicked state of fear. You could feel the ground moving and the earth shifting, see the buildings rocking back and forth. It was terrifying, to say the least.

We waited till the threat of the aftershocks were over. Then went back inside to assess the damage. It looked as though the house had been picked up and rattled. Everything was crooked and sideways. But it could have been way worse. It had been a 7.1 magnitude earthquake, that had radiated from its epicenter near the Hector Mine quarry in the Mojave Desert. It had been a rolling quake instead of the shaking kind. That's what kept it from being a bigger disaster than it was, despite its high level on the Richter scale.

When I was around four months along, Mama was about seven months along in her pregnancy. So I would call her daily to compare notes on both of our current stages. Since she was carrying her fourth child, she had plenty of experience and could inform me on what to expect during each stage. At this point in my pregnancy, I was starting to feel the baby move. The little flutters that only the mother can detect. There's nothing like it in the world, feeling the active life inside your own body. It is a miracle. I would talk to the baby, sing songs, read books and play Mozart. I would pet my belly and have entire one-way conversations with the little one on board. I loved being pregnant. That first few months of carrying my first child was the absolute happiest time of my entire life. I couldn't wait for the day to come when I would meet my baby, hold it and kiss its precious little face.

The twenty-week, halfway mark, was quickly approaching.. when I would have my first ultrasound. So far we had heard the baby's heartbeat, which is the most reassuring sound a parent can hear. But soon we would get to see our child on film. And all I could think about was finding out if the baby was a boy or girl. I was getting so impatient for the big reveal of the gender. I wanted to give my little one a name, to make all preparations for the arrival and to stock up on everything in pink or blue whichever was the case.

Around this same timeframe, Jason received military orders to be transferred of duty stations to the United States Marine Corps base in Okinawa, Japan for one year. He had about one month till he would be shipped out. Since he wasn't an officer, I would not be permitted to relocate with him. Official orders from the military are not negotiable. It was devastating to think that not only would he be leaving me, but he would be away during the birth of our child.. and not even get to meet his son or daughter till they were over six months old. This was horrible news, and we were both very upset by it. But there was nothing we could do about it.. and I knew exactly what I had signed up for when I married a soldier. So we started making plans to accommodate this sudden change of events.

October 29, 1999 we had our scheduled ultrasound for the halfway point of my pregnancy. It was time to find out if we were having a boy or girl. We were on the edge of our seats with anticipation all day leading up to the appointment. We were so excited and couldn't wait. I especially looked forward to seeing our little bundle of joy on screen and having the pictures printed out to take home.

We arrived at the Camp Pendleton medical clinic and waited impatiently in the waiting room for them to call me back. I had my regular exam first. Everything checked out fine. Then we went into the ultrasound room. The technician came in and began. I was listening to my baby's heartbeat, and watching the screen.. mesmerized by the tiny little human I was carrying, trying to study every detail. I kept waiting for the tech to say something, or to announce the gender. We had informed them that we wanted to know. She just sat there scanning and taking a thousand measurements. She never said a word to us. She got up and quietly left the room.

Several minutes later, a nurse came back and called us in to our doctor's private office. We were confused by what was happening. Why had they not told us the gender? Why were we summoned to speak with the doctor privately? If I could go back to that few moments of just wondering, and stay there in an ignorant state of not knowing, I would have. Because what happened next changed the rest of my life, and shattered my soul, forever.

The doctor began to speak, and by the time she finished what she had to say my world was turned completely upside down. My heart would never be whole again. She told us that our baby had a genetic condition. That there was something wrong with the baby's heart. And that our child would not live to be born. Then the doctor revealed to us that our baby was a girl. I don't remember much after that. I recall falling into the floor, crying in a way I had never cried before. The cry of a mourning mother. It is a battle cry of pure agony, not one that comes from your voice or from your eyes; It comes from the innermost depths of your very soul. There is no sound more sorrowful on Earth, than the sound of a mother who has lost her child. I hadn't lost mine yet, but I felt as though she had been taken from me in that moment. I don't even recall leaving the clinic, or the long drive home. Next thing I knew, I was in our bed, and Jason was holding me while I cried for what was left of that day. What would be the worst day of my life thus far. My heart was destroyed. I would never be the same after that. I was forever changed.

On November 1st, I was sent to the Naval Medical Center in San Diego. I had been referred there to have an amniocentesis. I was now considered high risk. I was terrified, but I was hoping this test would prove my doctor's prognosis wrong. I was praying that there had been a terrible mistake and that everything would be okay after all; that my baby girl would be alright, that she would be born, survive and grow up to be healthy and strong. They sent us home with a set of ultrasound pictures of our daughter. I clung to them and held them, while I felt my baby kicking inside me, not knowing if I would ever hold her alive in my arms.

It took ten days for the amnio results to come back. On November 11th, we got the call. We were told that our baby had a chromosome disorder, called Trisomy 13. That she had a heart defect. And that she was indeed, a girl. They said she would not survive to birth, that if I managed to carry her to full-term, she would be stillborn. But that I most likely would lose her before then. My world completely stopped spinning that day. It all came crashing down.

I named my daughter, Grace Josephine.

I could feel her alive and active in my womb. How could this be? How could God be so cruel, to take a child away from their mother? Why us? We were young and healthy and strong. What had we done to deserve such a fate for our innocent unborn child? Then it suddenly hit me like a storm surge rising going back to the day she was conceived; the day Jason had been given the rounds of Anthrax. The day I subconsciously knew I was with child.

When I spoke of this to Jason, he instantly knew it to be true. He then told me of seven other military wives in our Unit, who had conceived around the same time as us. They had all miscarried. I was the only one who didn't. It had to have been the Anthrax. They tell female soldiers in the military not to conceive within two years of receiving the vaccinations. But they say nothing to the men, of the dangers it can cause to their unborn children. (I have since researched and discovered that the particular strain of Anthrax he had been inoculated with was recalled due to extreme adverse side effects).

When I inquired about this with my doctor, I was sent almost immediately back to San Diego Naval Medical Center. Jason and I were escorted to a private board room. Seated around the long table, were at least a dozen of the highest level military doctors and officers, from all branches. And in keeping with Marine Corps standard procedure, they tried to sweep what they viewed as a controversial issue, under the rug. When I mentioned Anthrax, they all (everyone at that table), proceeded to advise me to have an abortion. All the other mothers with my case had miscarried. My baby was the lone survivor. They didn't want her to be born, because they didn't want to be held liable for what they had ultimately caused. And they assumed since I was young and distraught, that they could convince me to abort my child. They presented it like it was the only option, and as though I had no choice. They all but physically forced me, in their attempts to persuade me, to let them kill my child. They were determined to sentence my daughter to death. Any mother who could knowingly do harm, or intentionally take the life of her own child, before or after birth.. is the worst kind of evil that walks this planet. It goes against nature and everything a mother should be and all of the maternal instincts that a woman should have within herself to love, protect, and keep her child safe. I addressed the military doctors and officers, in their uniforms, with their high ranks and Ph.D.'s. And I told them directly. "I am this child's mother. There is absolutely nothing and nobody that could ever convince me to murder my own child. I will live or die to protect her, and do everything in my power to save her life, and keep her alive."

I went home and stood in her nursery over her baby crib. I turned the mobile on. I watched the little teddy bears spin around in their circle, and listened to the song the mobile played, Brahms Lullaby. I cradled my baby, with my arms wrapped around my belly. I cried, and prayed, pleaded and begged and prayed and cried some more. Please God, please, don't take my baby away from me. Not my innocent baby girl. Not my Grace. She was in God's hands. Only the Lord could determine the fate of Grace.

Jason went to his commanding officers and relayed to them our tragic news. They had already been informed by my doctors. They instantly went up the chain of command and had his orders to Okinawa revoked. Then they issued him new orders and switched his duty station to Marine Corps Base Quantico, Virginia. On the grounds that it was close to our home state of West Virginia, and we were advised to seek family support for our crisis situation. Also, we were being referred to the number one military hospital in the country due to the high-risk level of my pregnancy, the National Naval Medical Center.

The Marine Corps signed off on the PCS (Permanent Change of Station) order. They obtained a military TMO (Traffic Management Office) service for us, which packed up and loaded all of our belongings into a cargo freight carrier to be delivered to the base housing they had prearranged for us at MCB Quantico. They granted Jason leave time to relocate. The direct commanding officers of his unit were very respectful to us both during this difficult time and had everything taken care of for us in the quickest possible state of emergency manner and turnaround time.

On November 21st, we left California behind, for good. Everything had happened so fast that I didn't have time to process any of it. I was mentally, emotionally and physically depleted. I was in a state of total shock and devastation. That entire final trip across the country was mostly just a blur. We took a different route that time, travelling along I-70 through the center of the country.

We hit a bad snow blizzard near Vail, Colorado. It was a complete white-out, so bad that they ended up shutting down the interstate and we were detoured off of an exit where we stayed the night. That is where I had a premonition about the time of 4:44. (I have since then seen this exact time on a clock every day, am and pm, on the dot.. for over twenty years now. I still don't know for certain what it means but I believe it will be the time of my death). After that, we were literally chased by an outbreak of tornados that spun across the Midwest. I was too upset and exhausted to care about the weather.

Jason was trying to make it to West Virginia in time for Thanksgiving Day. We pulled into Summersville late that night before. The holiday was an even bigger blur to me. I didn't even care about seeing family. There was nothing anyone could do to comfort me. And their failed attempts were just lost on me. All I cared about was Grace. And if the only time I would have with her was the time during my pregnancy, then every second she lived within me, as part of me, were the most crucial and sacred moments I had. I didn't want anyone to interrupt that time. I wanted to be left alone by everyone else. Except for Jason, the father of my child.

We left WV and drove towards our new duty station in Virginia. It was a sunny fall day. We entered the gates of MCB Quantico. Then Jason reported to his command post, where he was given his new orders, along with the keys and directions to our assigned base housing. We pulled up to the place with our new address on it. It was a brick two-story 1940s Sears Catalog mail-order house, divided into two separate townhouses. Ours was the one on the right. It would be the first place where we would reside without roommates. The first home we would share together alone, as a family.

Part 2

We walked through the house, room by room. And waited for the freight carrier to arrive and deliver everything we owned. They showed up, unloaded and put everything where I directed. Placing the furniture, and leaving the boxes in each designated room, for me to unpack gradually. My nesting instincts were still very strong, so even though I felt defeated, I steadily sorted through and organized everything. It didn't take me long to turn that house into a home.

My first appointment at the National Naval Medical Center in Bethesda, Maryland had already been scheduled before we arrived at Quantico. I went in and registered right away. Being acutely high risk, I was to be seen at least weekly for the duration of my pregnancy and have extensive tests and ultrasounds performed every time. I had also been scheduled to have heart tests and EKGs done on the baby. Our medical case was extremely rare, so I became their guinea pig being poked and prodded, evaluated and monitored hundreds of times over, for the sake of research.

At home, I decided to set the spare bedroom up as Grace's nursery. Jason didn't set her crib up though, he thought it best to leave it in the box. I felt compelled to try as hard as I could to be hopeful that we would bring our baby home, despite the fact that I had been informed repeatedly that she would not survive in-utero, or be born alive. As her mother, I could not accept the cruel determination that had been made. I had to move forward through the remainder of my pregnancy with faith, hope and love.

From family, there was no talk of baby showers, no gift registry, no discussion of anything about the future of Grace. We had been told that she had no future to speak of. Mama had given me some of her maternity clothes to wear. But no one had given me anything for the baby. I went shopping anyways. I bought newborn diapers, baby wipes, one pink infant girl outfit with a matching toboggan and the softest fleece baby blanket I could find. I took the items home and placed them in her nursery. I had decorated the room in lavender, white and spring green colors, with a theme of bunnies and chicks (since she was due to be born in the springtime). I had a full sized bed in her room with flowered bedding on it, to use for changing diapers and dressing her just in case God answered my prayers and let me bring her home. I spent a great deal of time in Gracie's room, just laying on that bed crying my eyes out and praying my heart out.

Between appointments, depression, anxiety, tears and sleepless nights. Most of my time was consumed by just waiting to feel the baby move. To make sure she was still okay. I would play music for her and sing to her. I would find her tiny feet through my belly and try to tickle them, causing her to kick me. I would do anything I could to keep her awake and moving. I needed to know she was still alive. Feeling her activity was the only thing that brought me peace of mind and joy. Every single time she would make even the slightest movement, they were all precious moments that meant everything to me. Absolutely everything.

I was at the stage where I was showing very well now, and Jason could feel her moving too. We would sit for hours, with both our hands on my belly, just watching and feeling her move around inside me. You can tell when you're pregnant how your child's nature will be if they will be hyper or calm. You can also tell what time of day or night you will give birth, based on their most active time frame. Grace was calm. And I knew she would be born in the morning.

Jason took such good care of me throughout my pregnancy. But he became much more attentive the further along I got. He would massage my sore back, rub cocoa butter on my big belly and bring me Chinese take-out or order pizza delivery, so I wouldn't have to fix dinner. I was still a lousy cook. He was a good husband, and I could already tell he was a good daddy too.

In the sixth month of my pregnancy, we went to our hometown of Summersville, WV for Christmas time. I didn't want to celebrate the holiday with anyone, except for Grace. I knew this may be my only Christmas I would ever have with her. So I withdrew from everyone else. I was, however, given some presents by my Godmother, Beth. A baby Bible, adorable little baby girl clothes, blankets and more. I cherished them. Someone had a big enough heart to shower Grace with gifts, even under the hopeless circumstances. It meant more to me than I could say to her, more than she probably ever knew.

While I was in for the holidays, Mama gave birth to her son. My youngest brother, Anthony, was born on Christmas Day. I had been there when she went into labor. And I went to the hospital after he arrived. I was truly happy for her. But it was very difficult for me to witness the process, knowing mine would not be the same. That mine was foretold to not have a happy ending.

In the seventh month of my pregnancy, Jason received a phone call one night, from one of his family members (whose name I won't mention). They began to talk of funeral arrangements for Grace. This person advised that she should be transported to West Virginia in the back of his company work van, then cremated to save money. I heard the conversation and became thoroughly outraged. Completely mortified that there was talk of my baby's death before she was even born. It made me so sick, that I literally threw up right where I stood. I couldn't even make it to the bathroom in time. Jason and I got in a big argument about the whole disturbing conversation.

The doctors spoke of her nonexistent chances of survival at every appointment, but this was the first time something of this topic came directly from family. And in such an insulting, uncompassionate, and unforgivable way. With no regard for my baby or me. Even dogs have been given more dignity and more honorable funerals than that. Why were they trying to infringe upon something that hadn't even happened yet? Why did they think they had any sort of rights to decide how my unborn child's death would be handled? They thought I would be too weak to make those decisions or to make the arrangements myself, if and when the time would come. That one conversation forced me to have to do something that no mother should ever be faced with.

I had Jason take me to Summersville, West Virginia. Where I spent a weekend making the arrangements that I knew for myself, I would not be able to make when the time came, if we should lose Grace. And I definitely didn't trust anyone else to handle these matters with integrity. I first went to the Baptist Church and spoke to the preacher that had performed the ceremony at our big wedding. I didn't want to have her services in a funeral home, I wanted them to be held in the house of God. Pastor Phil agreed to be the one to preside over the ceremony and gave me a detailed outline of the service prayers, songs and eulogy.

Next, I went to a funeral home, owned by one of Peepaw's closest friends, Waters Funeral Chapel. I was shown a selection of infant sized caskets. I chose a white one. The funeral director also arranged for a hearse to carry Grace from Virginia to West Virginia at the time of death. I went to the local florist, and selected the flowers for her service… pink roses, white carnations, and baby's breath. All these arrangements were being made one at a time, with mournful maternal tears streaming down my face throughout all of them, and my heart breaking even more than I could bear. And the entire time I was in the church, the funeral home and the florist I could feel Grace moving and kicking more than ever before as though she was trying to say to me, "No Mommy. I'm still here." There are no words that can even come close to describing the devastation of making funeral arrangements for your still living, unborn child. It is one of the worst forms of torture I have ever had to endure. But I was her mother, it had to be me. I was the only one who would bestow the love, care, honor, worth, respect, decency and dignity that my precious Grace deserved.

I proceeded to the cemetery, West Virginia Memorial Gardens, where I chose a headstone for Grace's final resting place. And was shown the gravesite where my baby would be laid to rest, in the white casket I had chosen, with the headstone I selected. Jason and I also picked out side by side graves, with Grace's being at the head of my burial plot. The Marine Corps paid the expenses for all of the arrangements. It hadn't been their direct fault. The orders for the Anthrax had been handed down from the Pentagon. But the Marine Corps did what they thought they could to help us now. It was the least they could do in a minimal attempt to reconcile what had happened to one of their soldiers. To compensate us in some small way, but with efforts that could never replace the life of our child that might be taken from us.

I should have been happy, preparing for my daughter's birth. Not preparing for her death. It wasn't natural. It wasn't right. I should have been picking out lovely things for my baby girl... dolls, dresses and ponies, everything little girls love. Not picking out caskets and headstones and burial sites. Why her? Why my baby Grace? Everything was all wrong. This is not what I dreamed of for my precious child. This was not how it was supposed to be.

This was never how motherhood was meant to be. Parents are not supposed to bury their children. It is supposed to be the other way around.

The somber trip back to Quantico was silent. I just kept thinking about how I wished I could stay pregnant with her forever. She was full of life inside of me. I felt that as long as I was carrying her in my body, she would be safe and protected from this evil world and from certain death. I faced my due date with dread and complete sadness. I couldn't even speak. I was in a state of desperation, completely beyond despair. I was crushed and irreparable. My soul was shattered into a million pieces, like a broken mirror, with sharp shrouds of glass in all shapes and sizes. No matter which piece of broken glass you look into, you will never see your full reflection again. There is no possible way to ever put it all back together, the way it was before it broke. That's how I felt. But words cannot express.

A few weeks later, on Valentine's Day, Jason took me out to a fancy dinner date and showered me with gifts. We got our picture taken together at the restaurant, with my belly the size of a basketball. I had gained forty pounds during my pregnancy. And I was wearing the same dress I had worn the day I got pregnant. We had a nice evening. It was the first time since we had initially been given our bad news, that I actually felt the slightest ray of happiness. Being there with my husband on a date, and with my Gracie onboard.

My final phase of nesting instincts kicked into full mode. I got a sudden burst of energy and went through the entire house from upstairs to downstairs and back again. From one room to another room. Over and over I cleaned and organized everything, with a sense of urgency. As my due date began to draw near, family members started to send packages, containing gifts for the baby. I guess they suddenly felt compelled to pitch in and help us prepare, just on the off chance that the doctors and prognosis had been wrong. I opened each one with mixed emotions. I was happy to have gifts for Grace but sad at the dooming forecast that she may never use any of them. They had sent diapers, blankets, bibs, little lace ruffled socks, mittens, dolls, stuffed animals, baby bath products, clothes, etc... an entire collection of pretty pink girly things. I lovingly placed all of them in her room. And continued praying for a miracle, to bring her home.

I had prepared two hospital bags, one for me and Jason.. and a diaper bag that I had filled with a few of Grace's prettiest baby outfits along with the soft blanket I had bought for her. We kept the bags packed and ready to go for a moment's notice when the time came for us to go to the hospital. On the Friday night of February 25th, Jason and I were laying on the couch watching the movie, *Nothing To Lose*. I didn't feel well that day, I had been very weak and tired. Suddenly, my contractions began. It wasn't time yet. She wasn't due for another month. But I had already been to the hospital once a few days before with signs of preterm labor. Now the contractions were beginning to get stronger and closer together. Jason gathered the hospital bags we had prepared. He loaded them up. Then came back and got me, took my picture on the doorstep and helped me into the Ranger. We left for the hospital in Bethesda, Maryland. It was time.

Falling From Grace

Grace: a gift from God, that He gives us through His mercy. Something that we don't deserve. He gives it to us because He loves us.

I was so afraid to go into labor. Not because of the pain associated with it. I would endure that pain infinitely to welcome any of my children into the world. It should be painful, to bring a sacred being onto this planet. That is what sets the female species apart from man. Women are the stronger of the two genders when it comes to pain. And we as women are given the invaluable role of carrying, birthing, and nurturing the human race. I think God made it hurt so we would understand the profound importance of the honor He bestowed upon us, to bring about the existence of life.

My Grace had made it this far, even though every medical theory and doctor didn't believe it was possible. She survived throughout my pregnancy and beat all the odds that were stacked against her. But I had been her lifeline all this time. I had been her safe temple. I was afraid because I feared that once she left the safety of her mother and the chord that connected us was cut, that it would be the equivalent of taking her off of life support.

I had been told by all authorities, that she would not be born alive. But here I was, in labor, hooked up to every possible monitor. And her heart was still beating strong. She was fighting with every ounce of her tiny being. She was a survivor. Grace was telling me again, "I'm still here." It was late at night when we made it to the National Naval Medical Center. The top hospital in the country, where they take the President of the United States, should he require emergency medical care. Because of the acute high-risk nature of Grace's condition, I was assigned to an entire team of doctors, nurses, physicians assistants and interns. I was given a private room. And I was under tight surveillance, due to the fact that I was never theoretically supposed to make it even this far along. So nobody knew what to expect because it wasn't a textbook case. They even had residency medical students come in to study me. Like I was some exhibit in a zoo.

The anesthesiologist came in to give me an epidural. Most of the pain I was experiencing was in my back. He tried three times to get it placed but was unsuccessful due to my scoliosis and other spinal issues from the bad riding accident I had been in years earlier. I remember the doctor asking me specifically if I liked to go fishing, (a distraction method so I wouldn't freak out about the failed attempts to get the catheter into my crooked spine), to which I snapped back "This is no time to talk about fishing!" He finally got it half situated in a somewhat general area of where it was supposed to go, but it never worked properly.

I didn't have much to eat that entire day since I wasn't feeling well. I had only consumed a half a pack of pop tarts on the way to the hospital. But suddenly I was very hungry. So I asked the nurses for food. They wouldn't grant my request. They won't let women in labor eat at all, for fear they will regurgitate the remnants if they are put under sedation. So then I pleaded with Jason to order me some pizza delivery, that's what I was really craving. One of the doctors overheard me and scolded me for trying to sneak food. I felt like I needed it to restore my energy. At this point, I would have settled for hospital food from the cafeteria. So I proceeded to beg everyone that entered my chambers, to feed me something—anything, to which I was catered with a cup of ice.

Jason called and notified both sides of our families about the inevitable state of labor I was in, to which some of them proceeded to make travel arrangements to come into Bethesda from their locations. I didn't really want anyone to come. Everything was so uncertain, especially the outcome once it was time for delivery. I was adamant that I wanted my privacy with my daughter, no matter which way it went. But regardless, people started making way towards us.

I labored all that night of February 25th. Then all throughout the next day, on the 26th. And I labored during the entire second night. But I continued to be prohibited from eating, not one bite of anything. I was literally starving by this time, and beginning to become delirious as a result. I recall on the second night, after 24 hours of labor, yanking out my IV's and stumbling around the room. Jason pushed the red button on the wall and I was escorted back to bed by the orderlies.

Sunday, February 27, 2000: In the early morning hours around 4am, I finally had a spell of rest come over me. After my body had been in hard labor for 36 hours straight. I opened my eyes at exactly 7 am, wide awake. My water had broken. I turned my head towards Jason who had fallen asleep sitting up in the chair next to me. I reached my hand out and touched his hand. I said, "Wake up Honey, it's time."

Jason jumped up like he'd been shot, pushed the red button again, and ran out into the hallways to recruit the team of physicians. They all poured into my room within a matter of seconds. Lights on, monitors checked, and time to push. I wasn't afraid anymore. In that moment, God covered me in a blanket of calmness and peace. I was ready to meet my Grace. To hold her in my arms. At 7:15 am, after eight months of pregnancy, thirty-six hours of labor and fifteen minutes of pushing, I delivered and welcomed my firstborn child into this world. Grace Josephine. They placed her on my chest, let her daddy cut the cord, and there she was, in my arms. My baby. Safe and sound.

She instantly began crying. The best sound I have ever heard in all of my life. It was the sweetest music my ears will ever hear, in all of my days, no matter how long I live. And happy tears of relief and pure indescribable gratitude poured from my eyes. She was alive. My precious Grace was alive. She was the most beautiful sight I have ever seen. I kissed her on her precious face and said, "Hello Little Girl, I'm your Mommy."

I stood as a witness to a miracle that day. God performed a miracle right in front of me, without disguising His almighty presence. He came to me in my hour of need. The Lord was in that room with us, and He let it be known that He was among us. He was there to see to it that I held my little baby in my arms, and heard her voice, and felt her breathing. He was there to make sure that I could look into the beautiful eyes of my child, and see my whole reflection put back together, and projected back at me, through her eyes. He was there to make sure this child had the strength to hold firm onto her mother's finger, with her tiny little warm hand. He gave a mother and daughter a bond that could never be broken—that would last forever. A moment that could never be taken away. He made sure that this innocent baby, and her loving mother, would both feel safe and loved with the faith He embraced us in together, like a veil of protection. He was there because He heard all of my prayers and cries for help. He heard my unending plea to protect my child and keep her safe. God was watching over Grace all along, from the moment of conception, and even before that. Every path and turn and trial in my life that God ever led me down to this point. He did it all to bring me right here. To this precious and sacred moment. He delivered her to me and breathed His life into her. Grace was a gift. A gift of His love, that I didn't deserve. The good Lord gave me His true and graceful mercy that day.

The look on every face in that room was of the same consent. We had all been witness to a divine miracle, and we all knew it. There were tears in everyone's eyes and smiles on every single face. Jason was in complete tears of joy too, he was a proud father. He stood by her side when the nurses took Grace to the warming table, to weigh her, clean her up and give her the APGAR test, which she got a high score on and passed with flying colors. She weighed 4 pounds and .098 ounces, and was 16 inches long. She had a full head of beautiful shiny golden hair that looked and felt like silk.

They took her tiny footprints in ink and stamped them onto paper. They suctioned her mouth, diapered her, dressed her, swaddled her in a blanket and gave her back to me. She was so very little that I was afraid to hold her. She was so delicate and fragile. I was as gentle as a lamb with her in my arms. She fell asleep safe and warm on my chest.

During the time that they were cleaning her up and sewing me up.. I didn't even realize what was happening. Once the staff knew that the baby was secure, they went into full on emergency mode with me. I was losing way more blood than was normal with delivery. They were trying every method they knew and couldn't get the bleeding to stop. At that point they had Jason hold Grace. And he had a look of horror on his face. I was fading away. His child was alive, but he was losing his wife. I could feel myself slipping off into a different dimension. It hit me so suddenly. I was falling into a deep slumber, drifting away. About that time, they finally got the bleeding to stop, and stabilized my vital signs.

They moved us from the delivery room into a recovery room. I made it very clear that under no conditions was my baby to be taken out of my room, under any circumstances. The nurse came in and taught us how to tube feed her with formula, until my milk came in and we would feed her that instead. Grace had a cleft lip and palate. We knew of this early on, from the numerous ultrasounds that had been done. She would not be able to nurse, or feed from a bottle. I was still very weak when we were given the instructions and shown how to do the tube feedings. So Jason stepped up, like a daddy bird, and took this under his wing. He made it his mission to be able to feed his child.

Once we were settled in the recovery room, Grace had been fed, then we took pictures of her, changed her diaper, bundled her back up and she fell asleep soundly. We stared at her as she slept like an angel, mesmerized by our sweet baby and content to be together as a family.

Soon Jason's parents came in to meet their first grandchild. They fell in love with Grace instantly. They took turns holding her, talking to her, and taking photographs as proud grandparents. They were so happy to be there spending time with their grandbaby. While the grandparents were there, the nurses came in and insisted that they needed to take Grace to the NICU for further testing. I again, strongly stated, that the baby was not to leave me or my room. I said that they needed to do the necessary tests where we were. They argued, claiming that they could not perform the tests there. And I argued back. Jason finally convinced me to let them take her to the NICU just long enough for the tests to be done. The nurses promised it wouldn't take long, and said they would bring her back right away. Shortly after, there was some commotion going on in the hallway outside my room. Jason was summoned to come out. I got up, still very weak, and quickly followed him out the door. They had Grace on the nursery cart, and said something was wrong. As soon as I saw her I could see that she was not breathing, and her color was changing drastically. I picked her up immediately and gave her several firm pats on the back. I was crying hysterically, and frantically rocking her at the same time, so frightened that I was about to lose my Grace, on the very day she was born. She started breathing again. I took her back to my bed and held her with her face close to mine, so I could hear her breathe and feel her breath on my skin. I yelled at the nurses for taking her away from me in the first place, and commanded them to never do so again. I told the family members to leave. I wanted to be left alone with Grace. Jason went to the waiting room for a while to explain what had happened to his parents. They were all very distraught too. I just cried, my tears running down my face and onto her head, soaking her beautiful gold hair. I rocked her back and forth, and held her tight. I kissed her face over and over and said to her, "Please stay with me Baby Girl, please don't leave your Mommy."

After that moment, I subconsciously knew that God didn't give her to me to keep. He gave her to me on borrowed time. So that I would be able to hold her, rock her to sleep, feed her, bathe her, dress her, sing lullabies to her, hear her voice, make her feel safe and tell her how much I loved her. To have memories with her, to hold onto. But I subdued this knowledge and carried on with hope. Hoping I would be allowed to keep her forever. Hoping that He would make that possible, and perform another miracle. Soon after everything had stabilized, we were alone for the first time, just the three of us. We just held each other and thanked God for giving Grace to us. We shared a quiet moment together, and rested for a brief time.

Mama, Anthony, Meemaw, Haley and Vicki had all made it in to Bethesda late the night before, and they were staying at the hospital's on-site lodging reserved for the family members of patients. They had arrived past visiting hours that night, so I hadn't seen them yet. They got up and ready that Sunday morning and came over to the hospital to check in and visit. They had no clue that I had already had the baby till they got there, and the nurse told them. It had all happened so fast that we hadn't even been able to inform them yet that she had arrived. The staff wouldn't let them come in the room to visit until everything had settled down.

Once all was calm, they finally came in. Mama said, "Dang Tiffy, you pushed that baby out fast." Then she praised me and told me I had done good. They all took turns hugging me, congratulating us, and holding Grace. I was happy to have them there. Proud to introduce them all to my beautiful newborn daughter. Meemaw especially seemed so happy to meet her first great grandchild. She rocked her in the rocking chair, and smiled the whole time.

When I presented Mama to my nurses as the "Grandma", they all seemed rather perplexed. Grace was her first grandchild. Mom was only 36 at the time, and she was holding her two month old son. After she saw the nurses trying to put two and two together, Mama told them, "This is Uncle Anthony." Then they understood.

Aunt Haley and Great Aunt Vicki were proud to meet Grace too. Haley bought her a plush white lamb from the giftshop. We had a nice visit.

That night, we changed Grace into one of the outfits I had packed for her. The one I had bought for her myself. And I wrapped her in the soft fleece blanket I had also picked out when I was pregnant. We took a million pictures. We were celebrating her birthday. Jason ordered pizza. I had been given a tray of hospital food earlier, but now I could eat real food. It was the best pizza I ever had. The nurses tried their best to persuade me to put Grace down for the night in the nursery cart. But I refused. I would not put her down even for one second, other than to change her diaper. I held her on my chest. And we all snuggled together in the one person hospital bed. Our first night together as a family. I didn't sleep that night, I stayed awake staring at my beautiful daughter.

The second day, they moved us into a private suite room, that had more of a home atmosphere and felt less like a hospital. It had a Queen sized bed instead of a hospital bed, and a nice bathroom. That particular room was reserved for special care patients that are expected to have an extra-long stay. Since Grace had made it through her first day and night, they saw fit to give us the more long term accommodations.

They had checked her vitals throughout the night before and all that day and every time, they came back perfectly normal. And her heart appeared to be perfectly healthy. Grace seemed to be just fine after that one episode. She was in fact, stronger than most premature babies. She arrived one month before her due date. Grace was a fighter. And she surprised the entire medical staff with her determination to survive. We were congratulated all throughout that day by every staff member on that floor.

Once we were settled into our new room, I showered for the first time in three days, and I traded my hospital gown in for my own comfortable clothes. Jason and I bathed Grace for the first time, and smiled as she made little cooing noises while he washed her hair. We put lotion on her, powdered her, diapered her and dressed her in another one of the pretty little outfits I had brought for her.

We were doing things with her, all these things that most parents take for granted, or even complain about. The crying, and the sleepless nights. They were blessings to us. Everything that we had been told would never happen, that we would never have the chance to do. These moments were priceless and irreplaceable. They were everything to us.

We all slept together in the big bed, with Gracie on my chest. We were up a few times in the night to feed her and change her diaper. And I kept one eye open to watch her and make sure she was safe throughout the night. I was so happy and content, to be there with my perfect angel, and her handsome daddy beside us.

My milk had come in, so I was pumping regularly to supply for her feedings. Grace was already gaining weight, and getting stronger by the day. She did have a slight case of jaundice. So they wheeled in the special light table on a nursery cart. They supplied little cloth glasses that we placed over her eyes for protection, and she had to lay under the lamp for periods of time.

Jason's parents had gone back home after the first day. My family stayed around for a few days. They spent as much time with us as they could. Meemaw couldn't wait for her turn to hold Grace, and looked so content and happy in her designated seat of the rocking chair. There were four generations of girls together. We had several photographs taken to commemorate the special occasion. They said their goodbyes. Then they all left to go home.

It was just the three of us now, with no family left to visit with at the hospital. I ended up being happy they had all come to be with us. And I was sad to see them go. But by this time we were getting into a regular routine with Grace. So I was only focused on taking care of her. And everything seemed to be as it should.

On the fourth night, we were told by the doctors that we would be released the next day. They could see no reason to detain us any longer. My prayer had been answered. I was going to get to take Grace home. We were so beyond happy and blessed to be given this good news. It meant the world to us to be able to leave the hospital, with our baby, and go home as a complete family. It was another gift from God.

It took all the next day for the hospital to get all of our medical records and release forms in order. We had somewhat of a debriefing meeting. There was a process, and a chain of command, being a military facility. All the staff came through and said goodbye to Gracie. They had all become her fans. They were so proud of her fighting spirit, and how far she had come. The hospital gave us an infant car seat to use for our drive. We didn't have one because we had been told we would never take her home. They also provided us with an infant weight scale, since she had arrived a month early. They gave me a big bag full of baby supplies to take home too, to help get us started.

As that evening set in.. Jason installed the car seat, packed the vehicle, and got us ready. We gave Grace another sponge bath, dressed her, and bundled her up. Then we waited. After nightfall, they finally came in and gave us the greenlight to go. We had walked into that hospital, scared and not knowing what the outcome would be. But we walked out of there, as the two proudest and happiest parents that ever were with our baby. Grace sat between us in the Ranger on the way home, all snug in her car seat. I kept a constant eye on her. She never fussed at all. It was like she knew we were going home. Jason was nervous to drive his child for the first time, so he drove extra slowly. We arrived back to MCB Quantico late that night, and pulled in to our parking spot. We walked through the front door with our precious baby. And we went straight upstairs to our bedroom, where Jason tucked his girls into bed, and came to snuggle with us. We were home. The Lord granted this request.

The next day, Jason assembled her baby crib and placed it at the end of our bed. I washed and put the teddy bear bedding back in place, and hung the matching mobile. We laid her down and turned the mobile on. We all listened as it played Brahms Lullaby.

And we watched Grace while she was looking at the little teddy bears spinning around in their circle above her. We took several pictures. We never thought we would see this sight. It was a beautiful sight to behold. It was one of the very most precious moments my eyes have ever seen.

I used the room I had set up as the nursery. I would bathe Grace, change her diaper, and dress her on the same bed I had laid on and soaked with tears so many times during my pregnancy. The same bed I had said so many prayers on, for God to let me bring her home. And here she was. The greatest answered prayer of all time. It was Gracie's room. And I had decorated it for her when she was in my belly. But now that she was home, she and I spent most of our time in her nursery. I would walk her around and show her all the decorations I had put in place. I would go to the window, draw the curtains back, and show her the sky and all the trees in our back yard. I would hum a lullaby or sing a song to her. I would gather all her toys and dolls up, and show them to her one by one. It was all sacred to me. Our mother-daughter time together.

Soon after we returned home, gifts for Grace started pouring in from all over. We received packages daily. And we opened each one with great joy. We received a lot of preemie sized clothes and diapers, since she was so tiny. They sent everything you can think of for our little girl. It was her baby shower. I would hold her while her daddy would open the presents. And he would hold each item up and show them to her. Jason's parents came to visit shortly after we brought Grace home. They came bearing a car full of gifts too, from friends and family. So we had another baby shower with them present. And they had brought us one of their cars, which they gave to us so we would have more of a practical vehicle than the truck to pack with a stroller, car seat, or playpen if we should decide to travel with Grace to West Virginia. It was a white four door Oldsmobile Ciera. We were happy to have more of a family car to travel in.

They stayed all one day, then spent the night and returned home the following day. They took turns again holding their baby granddaughter, and taking pictures with her, happy as could be to see each other in new roles as grandparents. It was obvious that they were proud of their son, and enjoyed watching him in his fatherly role with his firstborn child.

Jason was a good daddy. He would sing songs and dance with Grace. Put his sunglasses on her, and pose her toys around her for pictures. He was just so natural and great at being a father. She instantly had him wrapped around her little finger. I knew he would swim any ocean or climb any mountain for his daughter. I loved to sit back and watch them together. It was priceless. And having lost my own daddy, it meant even more to me. I was so happy that my little girl had hers.

Grace was a Daddy's Girl. I was always afraid to do her tube feedings, but he handled it like a pro. I provided the milk, and he's the one who always fed her. So they shared that bond. And there were times when she would cry and I couldn't calm her but as soon as Jason held her, she settled down right away. Specifically when we would bathe her, or take her clothes off to weigh her. Grace never liked to be naked. She would pitch a fit every time. But she was always content when she was fully dressed and bundled up.

The National Naval Medical Center scheduled reconstructive surgery for Grace, to repair her cleft lip and palate. Her appointment was a few weeks out still and they said she would require more than one surgery. It would allow for her to breast feed and bottle feed. I didn't want them to alter her appearance. She was completely perfect in my eyes. But I agreed to the procedure, because it would help her to be fed in a natural way. And I wanted that for her.

We had settled into a good rhythm and routine as new parents. It was so nice to be home with just our little family, away from the hospital and everyone. Jason was on paternity leave from the Marine Corps. We did everything like clockwork. I would get up in the nights to change her diapers every few hours, and we would both get up when it was time to feed the baby. I never slept. I didn't want to miss a second with Grace, even when she was sleeping. I just wanted to gaze upon her constantly. She was my miracle.

Grace had the sweetest soul. She had a calm nature, like I had predicted when I was pregnant with her. She always seemed to be as happy to have time with us as we were to have time with her. She would always look up at me with her beautiful deep blue eyes. I felt like she could see into my soul, and knew exactly how much I loved her. The most unconditional love I have ever known. She was my heartbeat. She was my every wish and dream. She was my whole entire world and universe. She was my Angel on Earth. And everything I had ever hoped and prayed for. She was the greatest blessing of my entire lifetime.

Everything had gone perfectly our first week at home. Grace was gaining weight and thriving. She seemed to be in complete good health. I believed that my prayers for God to allow me to keep her and watch her grow up, would be answered. I thought about and planned for her future. I became more and more hopeful with each passing day. And continued to pray my heart out.

After our first week home Jason had gone out on the base to get some supplies from the commissary. While he was away, Grace had another episode where she quit breathing. As soon as it happened, I did the same thing as before, patting her on the back firmly. It didn't work. I was panicking and sobbing. I was screaming, "No, no, no! Wake up Baby Girl, don't leave me! Please don't leave me!" I held my mouth up to hers, and blew air into her mouth to revive her. The moment I did that, she started breathing again. Thank God.

When Jason came home, I was still in a state of complete panic. Crying uncontrollably. I told him what had happened. He called the hospital, and they sent a nurse to our home. It wasn't safe for us to take her back to the hospital after we had been released. Because Grace had been premature and had a rare condition, she could possibly have a weak immune system. Plus she received tube feedings. So she had to be in a sterile environment. I had made our house as sterile as possible. The hospital would expose her to outside germs and viruses. So they sent someone to us.

The nurse they assigned to Grace, was a home Hospice nurse. I wasn't aware of what that meant until she came the first time that day, and explained it to us about the Hospice organization. I was devastated when I found out. All the hope I had stored up, drained from me like sand within an hourglass. I suddenly felt like my time with my sweet precious Grace was running out.

When the nurse examined Grace, everything checked out fine. Her heart rate was strong. Her breathing was normal. The nurse could find nothing out of the ordinary. The nurse was going to arrange for a breathing machine to be delivered within the month, in case we should need it for Grace if the same thing was to happen again.

Aside from the one breathing episode she had in the hospital, and the one she just had at home, she otherwise maintained a clean bill of health. And that gave me another glimmer of hope. But still I prayed even harder. Everything seemed fine after that. We were still keeping our regular routines. And Grace was growing bigger by the day. She was taking more feedings throughout the day and night. I was bottling my milk as fast as I could, to keep my supply up with her demand. My sleep deprivation was starting to catch up with me though. I would stick ice cubes on my eyes to wake myself up. Also, I would take dizzy spells and get very light-headed, from the massive loss of blood I had endured in delivery.

So I had to be very careful going up and down the stairs, and careful not to stand up too quickly.

It had been weeks since I had slept other than short cat naps I would take with one eye open and her face right next to mine, while she was sleeping. I had to always listen to her breathe, every second of every day and night. I was so scared another breathing episode would happen again. I never ever put her down other than when I was bathing her or changing her. She had only been laid in her crib twice altogether, when we would play the mobile for her and take photographs. And her daddy would hold her while I took a two minute shower, and when I was getting her milk bottled. One of us was always holding Grace.

Part 2

Grace had such an adorable collection of clothing, from all the gifts she received. I would change her clothes several times a day just to play dress-up with her. And take her picture each time. She had all sorts of baby caps, bonnets, dresses and outfits, cute little girly socks, pretty blankets and mittens (which we always kept on her little hands so she wouldn't scratch her face with her fingernails). I loved to dress her up, she always looked like a little baby doll. She always smelled so good. I washed all her clothes with Dreft baby detergent. And all the baby bath wash, shampoo and lotions we used on her were lavender scented. We would brush her beautiful golden hair all the time. She absolutely loved to have her hair washed or brushed. That was her most favorite thing. The second week, after we brought her home, we decided to take her on her first outing. It was starting to feel like Spring now in early March. And we had only taken her outside in the sunshine once before, which she seemed to enjoy. So on a warm sunny day, Jason had the idea for us to go on a picnic lunch at a local forest park. I dressed Grace extra warm and bundled her up in her thickest blanket. I packed her diaper bag with everything she would need.

We took the white Oldsmobile his parents had given us. I sat in the backseat, beside Grace in her car seat. And Jason drove us first to the Kentucky Fried Chicken drive-thru for our picnic food. Then we went on to the Prince William Forest Park. We had a lovely time. Jason and I took turns holding the baby and eating our picnic lunch. We walked around the park and took photographs of each other with our daughter.

We all enjoyed the fresh air and sunshine. Grace especially seemed content with the spring breeze blowing softly over her, hearing the sounds of the birds singing and feeling the warmth of the sun shining upon her precious little face. Everything was peaceful and happy. It was the time of year when new life is beginning to emerge and awaken. We were so proud to take our little girl on a nice outing. To let her experience the beauty of nature. It was a beautiful day, in every way. The following day, Jason went out and bought a video camera. He came home so excited about it, he got it so we could make home videos of Grace. He took it out of the box and charged the battery. He recorded some footage of me and Grace together. The next day was Saint Patrick's Day. We relaxed all that evening. We had a nice dinner, then we watched movies while we snuggled on the couch. All three of us, together as a family.

Being Grace's mother has been the most honorable role of my life. I had always wanted to be a Mommy as long as I could remember. It seemed as though I had been gifted with an extra dose of maternal instincts. Not just because of the difficult trials of my pregnancy, although that exponentially expanded my motherly love but also because I was just made that way. I loved my child so much that I felt like my heart would explode and burst out of my chest. It doesn't seem possible for one heart to contain such a vast and infinite amount of eternal love. I felt like it would spill out and overflow, filling up all the oceans, covering up every mountain top, then flooding the sky full and reaching every corner of Heaven above.. and still not be contained.

Every second, of every minute, of every hour, of every day and night that I had to spend with my Grace…all of those moments alone and combined, they were absolutely everything to me. They were then, are now, and always will be the happiest and most sacred, treasured, priceless, and precious moments of my entire lifetime. As long as I shall live.

What I am about to share next, are my innermost personal thoughts and feelings of the darkest hours of my existence. They are words I have never spoken to anyone, not even to Jason. It has been nearly twenty years.. and all this time, I have not been able to bring myself to speak of this. Until now.

March 18th, 2000: In the early morning hours of March 18th, before the sun had arisen, I got up with Grace. I took her to change her diaper in the nursery. I swaddled her back up, talked to her, smiled at her and kissed her beautiful face. I told her, "Mommy loves you Grace." I took her back to bed and laid her on my chest, where she always slept. We drifted off to sleep, together.

Once the sun had risen in the sky, before I even opened my eyes, I knew. The Lord was there in that room. For the second time in my life, God revealed His presence to me. This time, in the form of the Holy Spirit. I opened my eyes. And I felt Him take Grace from my arms, and lift her away from me. I felt her soul rising up above me. And with her soul, He also took mine.

I was awakened by God, coming back to claim her. I was awake the very moment that it happened. I was awake when she took her last breath. I was awake when her heart beat for the last time. The moment my sweet precious Grace left me. My baby was taken from me. My firstborn child. My heart and my soul went with her. I woke up that morning, but my little girl didn't. Please, please God no. Please don't take my baby girl away from me.

Jason awoke immediately, he knew what had happened. I begged him to do something, anything... to somehow undo what had been done. To please help her and bring her back to me. She was still warm. He took her tiny body from my arms and laid her down. He tried over and over to resuscitate her with CPR. He breathed into her mouth and pressed on her chest repeatedly. He tried his best to revive her, to get her to breathe again and to make her heart beat again. It was too late.

My Grace became an Angel in Heaven. God gave her to me, and He took her away.

The most deafening sound is the sound of silence.

My baby wasn't crying. She was sleeping for all eternity. Forever in the arms of the Lord. I would never look into her beautiful eyes again. I would never feel her soft breath on my skin again. I would never hear her sweet voice, ever again. Then I heard the cry of a mourning mother. The most sorrowful sound on Earth.

I would never watch my Grace grow up. I would never hear her speak her first words, or hear her laugh. I would never see her take her first steps, or walk. I would never get to watch her play. I would never see her pick flowers and chase butterflies, or pet animals, or watch her dance to music. I would never have her run up to me, wrap her arms around me, and give me a hug. I would never get to celebrate her birthdays with her, or holidays, or special occasions. I would never hear her call me Mommy, or hear her say I love you. Everything was taken away from me when God took Grace.

I laid holding her close to me for most of that day. Kissing her head, holding her little hands, running my hand over her beautiful golden hair. God had taken her soul, but I couldn't let anyone take her tiny body out of my arms. I could not say goodbye to my baby girl.

Jason called the funeral home, and they arranged for someone to come carry her to West Virginia. He told me they were on the way. I wanted to hold her and carry her myself. But he wouldn't let me. The Hospice nurse came, the ambulance came and the military police came. And no matter what any of them said, I refused to let her go.

Jason helped me into the nursery. He prepared a warm lavender bath for her. I bathed her tiny body and washed her hair. I dried her and dressed her in the pretty pink outfit I first bought her, the one I had put on her the day she was born. I brushed her beautiful silky golden hair for the last time… and cut a lock of it to keep for myself.

I bundled her in her softest fleece blanket, the one I had chosen for her. I held her in my arms, rocking her back and forth, kissing her precious face and telling her over and over how much I love her.

The hearse arrived to pick her up. Jason met the driver downstairs at the door. He came back carrying a woven baby Moses basket. I still refused to let go of Grace. I begged Jason not to take her away from me. I yelled and screamed at him. He held me and told me that I had to let her go. I laid her down in the basket. And he took her away. I would never hold my baby girl, ever again. I was completely broken and beyond devastation, far beyond all repair. There are no words that can describe the pain of losing a child. That is why I have never spoken of it. There are no words that can possibly do this most tragic of all losses, any justice. Or even come close. It is the worst possible pain and torment to endure. Far worse than the worst feeling of despair you can ever even imagine. It tore my heart into so many pieces, it could never be put back together. It shattered every ounce of my soul, forever. There is absolutely nothing, and no one, that can ever prepare you for losing a child. It is not natural. It is not right. It is not the way the circle of life is supposed to be.

I don't remember Jason driving me to West Virginia or anything that happened over the next few days. I woke up in a dark hotel room. Our preacher was praying over me. I didn't want to live or breathe, I wanted to fade away and find my baby in Heaven. My soul was already gone. I didn't understand how my broken heart was still beating. Why was I left here without Grace? I had to be with her.

The next thing I remember was going to the funeral home. I asked to see her. I couldn't even walk without Jason helping me. I was too weak and too far gone. He sat me down and they brought her to me, in the little white casket I had chosen. I held her hand and kissed her face. Then Jason escorted me out and took me away. And I didn't see her again until her funeral service.

On March 21st, Jason took me to the Baptist Church I had selected. It was where my mother and father were married. And where Pastor Phil preached his sermons. I remember seeing the black hearse parked outside, and thinking no, no this cannot be real. I was praying it had all just been a bad dream, a nightmare. I was so weak I couldn't see straight. I made my way to the front of the House of God, at the altar where Grace laid. Among the flowers, I had selected for her. I had her little white lamb, (that Aunt Haley had bought her on her birthday), in the little white casket with her. I kissed her face as many times as I could until I was pulled away from her and made to sit down.

I know the church was full of people, but I don't remember seeing their faces. I don't know who was there. I don't remember what was said, or what songs were played at my daughter's service. All I heard was my own cry of mourning. But I do recall the words that the preacher said. He said, "Grace is a gift from God. Something we don't deserve. He gives Grace because of His love."

The service came to an end. It was time for me to say my final goodbye to my baby, for the last time. I kissed her, my tears running over her beautiful face. I held her tiny hand. I told her how much I loved her. And I said goodbye to my Grace. I was dragged away from her and escorted down the aisle. I would never see her again. My time with my sweet innocent baby was over.

I don't remember leaving the church or riding to the cemetery. The next thing I remember is Jason helping me out of the car. I was dressed all in black. And he was wearing his Marine Corps Dress Blues. He had me hold onto his arm, while he carried our daughter, in the little white casket to the resting place we had chosen for her. All I recall from that part of the service is that it was a cold rainy day. And I remember Peepaw and Mama singing the most beautiful duet of "Amazing Grace". I remember laying a single pink rose on her casket. My sweet precious baby Grace was laid to rest. Never to be in my arms again.

The funeral arrangements I had made for her while I was pregnant, I had forgotten about them all, until I was there at her service. Once she had been born I had hidden all of that away, in some secret dark corner of my mind, and put it under tight lock and key. I never even once that about any of it while she was alive. But here it all was, right before me. Everything I had prepared for her had come together for the final farewell of Grace, in a mother's honor for her child. I collapsed when I was being escorted away from her burial. I have no memory of what happened next. I don't remember the rest of that day or anything about the day after that.

My next memory was on March 23rd, which had been the date Grace was due to be born. But by this time, she had already been born, had lived and passed away. Jason took me to her grave, so I could lay fresh flowers there. I saw her headstone for the first time that day, the one I had picked out for her. Seeing her name and the dates of her birth and death, all beside a gold engraved pacifier with a ribbon.. it brought me to my knees. I laid over the top of my daughter's final resting place and soaked the cold ground with my tears. The next thing I knew, I was back home in Quantico. Surrounded only by the deafening sound of silence. In our bed, where my Angel said goodbye.

As I write this with fresh tears streaming down my face. It has been nearly twenty years now since Grace came into my life, and left from this world. I remain a mother in mourning. All my memories of her are as fresh in my mind today as they were then. It does not get easier with time. If anything, it gets more difficult.. because there is that much more time I have missed out on what should have been. The only solace I have is that God allowed me to have my precious time with her, to have memories of her. And He took her peacefully. She passed away, safe and sound, in the arms of the one who loved her above all... her mother. We were heart to heart in her final moments. I held her on my chest when she came into this world, and I held her on my chest when she left this world. I was there for her first breath, and I was there for her last breath. The pain of losing a child I would endure that pain infinitely, just to hold my Grace for one more moment. I have missed my baby girl every second of every day, with every beat of my broken heart. My soul has never been fully restored, and never will be. Until I hold my Grace again, in Heaven.

Blue Mountain

In the following weeks after the funeral, baby gifts for Grace were still finding their way to our doorstep. I opened all of them. But to this day, they remain in their gift bags, with the tags still on them, packed inside of the boxes that they were originally shipped in. Condolence cards were arriving at the same time. We would open the gifts of congratulations, then open several sympathy cards. All in the same sitting. And that pattern repeated daily for a while. Eventually, when everyone had been informed of our loss, we only received the sympathy cards. They arrived in the mail for months.

I was completely inconsolable for the next six months. I didn't eat anything. I didn't talk to anyone. I didn't go anywhere. I was stuck in the *Valley of the Shadow of Death*. And I wanted to stay there. I wanted to sink further into the dark until it consumed whatever was left of me. I had nothing to lose. And nothing else to live for. I just laid in our bed and cried constantly. I couldn't function in even the most basic or minimal ways. There was no use or reason for me to even try.

Our marriage fell apart and disintegrated into thin air. In less than one year's time we had met, moved in together, gotten engaged, were married twice, relocated twice and travelled across the country three times. We went through the pregnancy of our first child, had Grace, and lost her. It was too much too fast. Our marriage received a fatal blow.

Jason and I dealt with our grief differently and separately. He had returned to work on base after his bereavement leave granted by the military was up. He couldn't be there constantly to console me. Any of his efforts to comfort me were in vain anyways. There was nothing he could do to save me. Jason was broken-hearted and devastated too, but he was trying to be the strong one, for both of us. He was trying to hide his feelings and move forward, and trying to lead me out of the dark. But I couldn't follow him. I was too far out of his reach. Too far gone.

Like the captain of a sinking ship, I resolved myself to hold tight and go down with it without even putting up a fight. I wanted the waves to drag me under, and the current to carry me away into some deep abyss where no one would ever find me. Jason instead resorted to bailing off of the same ship and tried to keep his head above water long enough to swim to the nearest shore. He wanted to recuperate and carry on with living. He wanted to build a new ship. In the aftermath of this storm, we couldn't find anything left to salvage from the wreckage of the devastation we had been through.

Jason eventually just handed me over to the solitude that he couldn't rescue me from. He tried to console me, he really did. But it was pointless. No one could save me. There was no reason for me to even try to pretend that I had anything left to give to anyone, anything left to offer. There was nothing left of me. I was empty and hollow. The steady stream of tears falling from my eyes was the only indication that I was even still human.

I spent my first Mother's Day alone. I was still a mother, but I didn't have my one and only child there with me. Jason went to West Virginia to spend the weekend with his mother. I spent the day in our silent house. With nothing but the sound of my despair. All the busy days and sleepless nights of hearing my baby crying, soothing her, feeding her, bathing her, diapering her, dressing her and rocking her; all of those most cherished moments I had as a mother, were suddenly gone. They left with her. Our home that had been so full of love and happiness with Grace, was now empty.

I cried so hard that Mother's Day, that I literally started to hallucinate. I blacked out and fell into the floor. When I came to, I laid there and watched my bedroom curtains blowing, from a window that was closed. I was seeing something that wasn't actually happening. There was no fan, no air blowing in that room, and the window was locked tight. But I watched the curtains blowing like there was a strong breeze, with no explanation. I was weak from not eating or sleeping. I didn't want to sleep. If I had only stayed awake on the morning that I lost Grace, maybe I could have saved her. It was all my fault. I should have never let myself fall to sleep. I should have stayed awake. If I could only go back to that moment.

I was severely dehydrated and my iron level was still dangerously low from the blood loss of delivery. But I was still producing milk, without my child to feed it to. Being a mother without her child is the single most confusing and contradictory state I have ever been in. I didn't have her there to nurture and take care of. I had all my maternal instincts, with no way to express them. I had all my love for her, without her there for me to give it to. All I could do was bottle everything up and store it away inside the empty chamber that used to be my heart. And I was constantly tormented by it.

I finally got to the point where I couldn't take the pain anymore. I didn't see any way to go on. My purpose in life had been served. There was nothing left for me to fight for. No one left for me to live for. Jason and I were still married, but we were strangers now. It was like we had never even known each other to begin with. Our identities as parents had to be suppressed against our will. We were no longer a family. I wanted it all to end, to be put out of my misery. It wasn't fair that I was still here and my daughter was gone.

I made several attempts to end my life. Each one failed by Jason coming along to rescue me. My suffering was so extremely overwhelming, that ending it all was the only way I saw to escape the torture I had been subjected to and the hell I had been walking through. I held guns to my head. I held knives to my heart. I was within seconds away from going through with it. But something always stopped me.

Aside from my husband deterring me, the only other thing that stood in my way, was the fear that if I took myself out of this world on my own accord I may be locked out of Heaven, and never be reunited with my Grace. That is what really stopped me.

Because that was all I had left to look forward to. I am still here today because I am waiting for God to take me home to my baby.

I became angry with God. I had always prayed to Him before, especially about Grace. But now I had no prayers left to say. I only had harsh thoughts and cruel words for God. I didn't understand why He took my baby away. I told Him that He was selfish to claim her as His own. She was mine. How could He take my innocent child from her mother, and inflict such a cruel pain upon me? But at the same time, God was the only one I had. He was the only one that was with me in the *Valley of the Shadow of Death.* He did not leave me or forsake me in my time of need. He held my hand every step of the way. He knew the pain of losing your only child. He was the only one who truly understood. He knew every ounce of my heart and soul, every pain that I felt. He counted every tear that fell from my eyes. And because of that, my personal relationship with God grew even stronger. I had been stripped down to nothing, completely bare and exposed. And He didn't shame me for it. He loved me even more because He saw me for who I really was. And He was all I had.

After six months of seclusion, I finally started communicating with people who were reaching out to me, but I kept those lines of communication on a minimum level. Letting people in just made everything even worse. No one knows what to say or how to say it. They are not always to blame. Mostly they were cases of pure ignorance. I heard everything from, "Oh well it was just a baby, you'll get over it," to "Well you're young, you can have more children," and "I know how you feel, I've had a miscarriage."

And much more. I truly started hating people during this time. And I hated that the world outside my door was still spinning after my entire world had come crashing down. Nobody knows how I feel or what I have been through. No one has ever walked in anyone else's shoes. And I wouldn't wish even my worst enemy to walk a mile in mine.

My child was not someone that could be replaced.

She was mine. I never got over it. And I never ever will. There is no such thing as getting over the loss of your child. And time does not heal. My baby girl could never be replaced, even if I had a thousand more babies. Grace was mine. I loved her from the moment she was conceived. The age of a child is irrelevant to a mother. My child is my child no matter how old they are… a baby, or a hundred years old, or any age in between. A mother's love knows no age, no boundaries and no end. It is always unwavering and eternal. It is powerful and constant. It is the most undying love that has ever existed. It transcends above all other forms of love.

Jason forced me to go to a psychiatrist. That just made me hate people even more. Losing a child is not a form of depression that you can fix with prescriptions. It doesn't fit into any category of clinical illnesses. There is no medical diagnosis for it. You can't mask it or pretend that there is a magic cure for it. They put me on two types of depression medicine, and both of them made me more suicidal. You cannot numb the pain of losing your child. It is impossible. There is no grief counseling, ten-step program, therapy or pills that can fix the most tragic of all losses. No doctor can heal that. Nothing on Earth can mend that.

Let me just say to anyone out there who needs to hear this.. don't presume to try and relate to someone who has gone through the devastation of losing a child, unless you have lost one of your own. There is no possible way to ever understand the magnitude of that kind of pain unless you have personally experienced it yourself. People who say, "Oh I can't even imagine," well that is true. Even if you think you can imagine losing a child, the reality of it is nothing even close in comparison to your very worst imaginations or nightmares. Losing one of your children is a hell that is worse than a million other hells combined.

And even parents who have lost children, never compare their pain with any other parent who has lost theirs. It is not the same. Every loss is like a snowflake. There are no two the same. There is a unique and personal bond that is individual between every parent and every child. No comparisons can be made. Every case is special, and every case is different.

The way to show compassion is to hold that person's hand, give them a hug, tell them you are thinking of them and keep them in your prayers. Don't just blurt out the first nonsense that comes to your mind. That usually ends up being an unintentional insult, and the equivalent to pouring salt on an open wound. There is nothing that you can say or do to make anything better. All you can do is offer a small token of kindness or comfort. True compassion, is the result of having suffered yourself and reaching your hand out to help someone else when you recognize that they are also suffering even though you are still drowning in your own sorrow. Unfortunately, it is an art that I eventually mastered myself, from years and years of experience and heartache. It takes a broken soul, to know another broken soul.

After enough people showed me their lack of compassion, I withdrew from everyone again. And stayed hidden away at home. I didn't want to go anywhere or see anyone. I couldn't stand to see other babies, or especially to hear them cry. I would turn my head to keep from seeing pregnant women, or mothers pushing babies in strollers. Or parents yelling at their children in public. All of it made me sick. Because my child was not with me. Why did they get to keep theirs?

By the end of that summer, Jason insisted that I get a job. He thought it would help me function if I could start taking small steps towards some form of moving forward if I had some sense of purpose to get out of bed. He didn't want me to waste away in my sorrow. But that's all I could do at this point. I didn't know how I would ever be able to even put one foot in front of the other, or where to even begin. I was completely off balance and disoriented. I was scattered like dust in the wind.

That September, I got a job at the Marine Corps Base Quantico Riding Stables. Being around horses had always been a source of therapeutic remedy for me in the past. But what I was going through now far surpassed anything I had ever been through.

Everything I had suffered before, all of them combined, they were nothing compared to the grief of losing a child. All the other deaths I had dealt with, were way beyond overshadowed by this. But I made a frail attempt to pick myself up off the ground and get back in the saddle so to speak. I chose a black Tennessee Walker horse named Buddy. He became my work partner and my friend. It was my first time riding since my bad horse accident. But I held no value on my own life at this point, so I wasn't afraid of having another accident. I had no fear at all regarding my safety. I was a trail guide on the base, leading Marine Corps soldiers on what felt like a Calvary Regiment ride through the woods. I was also hired to run heavy equipment for the Corps since I had prior experience of working with machinery on my resume. I operated tractors and a hydraulic dump truck on the military base. I worked that job for a few months. Jason and I had been on the brink of divorce all that summer. I was still completely inconsolable, and he had been skipping town every chance he got, leaving me alone to my own defenses. He started exhibiting signs of a bad temper. I packed a suitcase and tried to leave him one night, but he stopped me. After that, he started trying to rekindle our relationship.

And on October 22nd, for the second time in my life, my intuition told me, "You just got pregnant." This time I listened instead of trying to hush that voice. As soon as I was late for my monthly cycle, I went straight to the base PX and got a pregnancy test. It was positive. That day, I hung up my riding reigns and quit my job. And I told Jason that we were expecting our second child.

I was terrified of being pregnant again. I was so afraid that another one of my children would be taken from me, or that the distress of losing Grace would cause me to miscarry. During my first pregnancy, I started off at 103 pounds and gained 40 pounds on top of that by the time Grace was born. But after losing Grace, I had almost completely quit eating altogether. So I only weighed 96 pounds at the beginning of my second pregnancy. I was not in good condition physically to support carrying a child. Besides the fact that I was also thoroughly emotionally exhausted and distraught, and mentally unstable. But my maternal instincts were all very much intact, still bottled up from all the suppression of them, and waiting to be released. And I proceeded to do as I had done the day I found out I was pregnant with Grace. This time again, I immediately put down the cigarettes I had been smoking for the past few months. I started eating again. I quit drinking caffeine. I quit my riding job and said goodbye to Buddy. I wanted to do everything I could to make sure that I was taking the best possible care of this baby, just as I had done with my Grace. I also knew as instantly as my intuition had told me I was pregnant again, that this baby was a boy. I hadn't sensed the gender in the beginning of my pregnancy with Grace. But this time I knew. I can't explain how or why; I just knew. I was carrying my first son. God knew I needed another child to hold, and He blessed me with my one and only little boy.

I wanted to be overjoyed with the blessing of my second child. But I was so cautiously optimistic and hesitant to be happy. Fate had already left me with empty arms once. I was so very afraid that God would see fit to take this child as an Angel in Heaven too. It had only been eight months since He had taken Grace. And I was still reeling with grief.

I immediately began my prenatal appointments. I was given a due date of July 22, 2001. Having been classified as high risk during my first pregnancy, I was automatically considered as high-risk for this one. So I would have more frequent visits to the OB doctors. And I was so scared, every single time I went, that they would give me bad news for the second time.

Meanwhile, Jason's five-year active duty contract with the United States Marine Corps was almost up. He was trying to make decisions on whether or not to reenlist or to take an honorable discharge and seek civilian employment. The Marine Corps presented good terms for reenlistment. Jason would receive a large sign-on bonus, he would move up in rank becoming a Sergeant, and he would have a choice of any active duty station. Also, I would be permitted to relocate with him. We discussed it at length several times and even talked about choosing Hawaii as his duty station. Just to start over somewhere new, somewhere we had never even been before. A beautiful place to welcome our new son when he came along.

Jason was invited to attend a career fair where he was being recruited for civilian jobs in Washington D.C. He went and came back, with a job offer from a very large and reputable government contracting agency, to work for the Department of Defense at the

Pentagon. He didn't have a college degree, but he was exceedingly skilled and well respected at his job in the military. So he was highly sought after in his field of expertise. And this offer was a high paying job. Through several hours of ongoing discussion, we weighed out both of his current options against one another. Reenlisting in the Marine Corps and remaining as an active duty soldier stationed in Hawaii.. versus working as a civilian contractor for the Department of Defense at the Pentagon, making more money.

My fear of him ending up in a wartime combat situation if he was to reenlist, caused me to persuade him to choose the job at the Pentagon. Although we had grown apart and our marriage had been on shaky and unstable ground, I didn't want to lose him should our nation end up going to war during his time of service. And even though he was the head of our household, he had a difficult time making big decisions, so he would turn to me for advice. And that was the advice I gave him. Ultimately, that turned out to be the decision he made. Plus, he felt it was the best plan of action based on our current circumstances of expecting another child.

He applied for the job and was hired to start upon completion of his military EAS (End of Active Service). He received an honorable discharge from the Marine Corps and was released in January, a month early due to accrued leave time he had on the books. We were given a deadline to move out of our base housing.

So we started searching for real estate. He started his new job at the Pentagon on January 2, 2001.

I was having an extremely difficult time dealing with the fact that I would soon be forced to leave my home. That house wasn't just any home. It was mine and Jason's first real home. It was the home where I had spent half of my pregnancy with Grace. It was where I brought Grace home from the hospital. It was the only home that she ever lived in. It was the home where she passed away. The only home that would ever contain all of my memories of the time I spent with Grace. I couldn't bear the thought of leaving. I didn't know how I would ever be able to walk out that door and never return. I would have stayed there for the rest of my life if I could have.

But I had no choice. So we looked for a new home. We didn't want to be in the D.C. metro area. It was too crowded with people, and the real estate was way too expensive, even with the new high paying salary he would receive with his new job. So we looked further West, to a town Jason's dad had worked in and recommended to us. His dad thought we would like it there. We drove to the Shenandoah Valley, to the town of Front Royal. We fell in love with the area immediately. It brought us back to our mountain roots and heritage. Of everywhere I have ever lived, I always loved the Appalachian Mountains the most. They were in my blood. Those mountains always called to me, like I belonged to them. We ended up finding a place for sale on the top of a huge mountain ridge. It was called Blue Mountain. It would be our new home. The place we would bring our son home to.

Also, that January I was scheduled to have my twenty-week appointment for an ultrasound. I had already received several ultrasounds before this one since I was high-risk. And they had all turned out fine. But this was the one I was extra nervous about because I kept reliving the same twenty-week mark I had with Grace, where I received the devastating news of her condition. I was so scared I would hear the same for this child. But thankfully, all was well. And we were told immediately and happily, "It's a boy!"

I had known all along I was carrying my son, but now that it had been officially declared, I named my boy after his father. Jason Edward, Jr. ("J.J."). And at that point, although I was still very scared that something would go wrong, I breathed a sigh of relief. And I began to let myself feel the joy and hope of expecting our second child. He was another blessing from God. My son was a rainbow in the promise that God would never put us through the same devastation again.

We stayed in our home at Quantico long enough to honor Grace's first birthday. I have always celebrated all of her birthdays, in any meaningful way that I possibly can as her mother. The actual day of her birth was the greatest cause of celebration I have ever had. And although she was taken from me, and the chance to celebrate any of her other birthdays with her was also taken away from me; I have always honored her birthday in devotion and remembrance of my sweet baby girl. And her birthday has always been one of the most difficult days of every year for me to get through. We were also there during the first anniversary of her death. A day in which I always relive all the events of what remains as the worst day of my life. It is the absolute very most difficult day of every year for me to endure. But again, I do what I can on that day, as a mother, to honor Grace's memory and commemorate her life.

At the end of March, we closed on our new house in Front Royal, Virginia. It was a big deal to us because we had never been homeowners. This was the first home that we bought together. When we went to the house after the closing. We were walking around the yard, Jason picked me up and swung me around in a big bear hug. He was so proud that he could provide his wife and son with a nice place of our own to call home. We had come a long way from our deflated air mattress days in the dining room of the Marine bunkhouse in California, where we started off.

That April, we packed up our lives and our belongings in Quantico. I literally waited until the very night of our big move before I started packing all of Gracie's belongings. They were all just as they had been when she was still there. I hadn't been able to force myself to put any of it away. Her bedroom still smelled of lavender, like her. Leaving our home there behind, was one of the hardest things I have ever done in my life. I had memorized everything about that house. The way the sun shined through each window, at any given time of day. The smell of each separate room. The sound of each part of the floor and stairs. Everything. It took all the strength I could conjure to shut that door behind me and walk away knowing I would never be able to return.

We made our way to Blue Mountain in the middle of the night where I would spend the next five years in isolation, solitude, mourning and restoration. Our new house was near the top crest of the mountain, on Scarlet Tanager Lane. It was a three-bedroom ranch style, cedar-sided house, with a full walk-out basement underneath. It sat on close to two acres of land, nestled down over a hillside, and surrounded by tall Poplar trees. Not far from our house was a small lake and a playground. Blue Mountain had a special beauty of its own. It was a magical place. It was quiet there. All you could hear was the sound of the wind blowing through the Poplars. It was peaceful and secluded. And I was glad to be far away from any kind of civilization.

When we moved in, the first order of business was to paint the walls. And since we owned the house, we could do anything we wanted. I picked a different color for every room. I chose the smallest of the three bedrooms as the new nursery for my son. I had Jason paint it two shades of blue, baby blue and midnight blue. He reassembled the crib in J.J.'s room. And I selected a Noah's Ark theme since my son was my rainbow promise from God. When I assembled the bedding and mobile, with all the little Ark animals on them, I stood over that crib again, listening to the lullaby play and praying for my son. I prayed to bring him home safe and sound.

Jason seemed to like his new job at the Pentagon. He worked the night shift and had an hour and a half commute from Front Royal to Arlington. So he slept during the day while I was slowly turning the house into a home. At night while he was gone, I would lay on the couch in the quiet, and feel every movement the baby made. Jason had given me a kitten when we still lived in Quantico. It was a striped grey male cat, I named him Roscoe. He would perch himself on my belly at night and take beatings from the baby. Roscoe seemed as if he didn't mind it, cause he always just stayed right there purring like a motor, no matter how many times he got kicked by the little feet in my big belly.

This one was hyper, and I could tell he would be born at night time. He was constantly moving, which I was happy about because it set my mind at ease. I could tell he was strong. It felt like he was always doing karate or gymnastics in my belly. My ribs were literally bruised from him repeatedly kicking me like a little mule. It seemed like he was claustrophobic in there, and was trying to make a prison break of his own, into the world.

I went into labor with J.J. when I was six months pregnant. Jason rushed me to the hospital, which was an hour away in Manassas, Virginia. We arrived at Prince William Medical Center, and I was given six shots of Terbutaline to stop my labor. I was put on strict permanent bed rest and a prescription of Terbutaline for the duration of my pregnancy. I had gained a significant amount of weight so far but I had been way too underweight when I first became pregnant. My body was just too tiny and frail to support a full-term pregnancy. So J.J. almost got his prison break that time but not quite. I followed my orders of strict bedrest. I took my medicine and drank plenty of water. I stayed lying down, getting up only to use the bathroom or refill my water cup. I let all my housework slide. I did everything I was told to do in order to carry my son to full term. I craved only red meat and Fruit Loops with this pregnancy. That's all I wanted. And watermelon. I would sit and eat an entire watermelon at a time.

I went into labor again at seven months pregnant, in J.J.'s second attempt at a prison break. This time I had Jason stop by the McDonalds connected to a gas station in the town of Marshall, on the way. I didn't want to be starved again like I had been in my 36 hours of labor with Grace. I got a double cheeseburger, large fries, a chocolate milkshake, a Cherry Coke, and a candy bar. And I ate it all while we rushed to the hospital. I was so far progressed in the labor stages, that the doctors said if he had been a girl, they would have let the baby arrive then. But since boys have weaker lungs, they gave me more steroids and stopped my labor, again.

That June, after the second round of labor, Meemaw and Peepaw came to visit us at our home. They brought gifts for J.J., and Meemaw had sewn him a handmade baby blanket. We had a mini baby shower with them. Then a few weeks later, all of our parents came to visit. I was supposed to have had a baby shower back home in West Virginia, but my bedrest prohibited me from being able to travel long distances or go anywhere for that matter. So they came and brought gifts for the baby. Everything blue. It was obvious that I wouldn't make it to the baby's due date of July 22nd. So we all took bets on when we thought J.J. would actually make his prison break escape. My mom guessed it would be July 2nd, her birthday. I said he would arrive on July 3rd, mine and Jason's WV wedding anniversary. And Jason's mom thought he would come along on the Fourth of July.

Tuesday, July 3, 2001, on our second wedding anniversary, I went into full-blown labor again with J.J., for the third time. Jason rushed me down Blue Mountain and headed towards Manassas on I-66. I made him stop again at the same Marshall McDonalds, where I got the same order of food as the last time I was in labor. And ate it all. (In total I had gained 36 pounds during this pregnancy). I knew this time that J.J. was actually going to be set free from the confines of my belly. The labor pains were much more severe than my other two go-rounds with him. There was no stopping him now.

Part 2

We arrived at the Prince William Medical Center, and I was admitted to my delivery room. Jason had made the calls to our families while we had been in route, so our parents were on their way from West Virginia. My water broke shortly after I arrived at the hospital, and again the epidural was a no go. They couldn't place it properly and it did permanent nerve damage to my spine. After four short hours of labor, J.J. made his final prison break. J.J. was a strong and healthy 7 pounds, 1 ounce baby boy. He was 19 inches long. And arrived at 8:52 pm. He looked a lot like his sister Grace, but much bigger and with less hair. Jason and I cried tears of joy at the welcoming of our handsome son. God had truly blessed us again, with our second child. They put him on my chest, and my heart was automatically full again. Full of never-ending love and devotion for my precious son. I said to him, "Hello Little Man, I'm your Mommy." I held him in my arms and vowed to always protect him. To be his safe haven, for as long as I lived. And he became my whole world.

The nurses took him to the warming table to clean him up, diaper, and dress him. Jason stood close by to the baby and talked to him the whole time. He was proud to have a son. And we were happy and relieved that our son was healthy. We had been so afraid that we would lose another child. But God kept true to His promise. J.J. was the best anniversary gift of all time. He was the renewal of our wedding vows. He was a treasured gift from God.

J.J. and I had incompatible blood types, and because of that, the nurses said they had to take him to the nursery for a while to run some tests. I automatically protested against them taking him out of my room, but then agreed, to make sure he was okay. The tests came back fine. They moved me to my recovery room. And still, they kept him in the nursery. They fed him formula, against my wishes. I intended to breastfeed him. So I finally got up, yanked my IVs out, and marched to the nursery. I threw a giant mama bear fit and yelled at everyone there demanding that they give me my baby immediately. To which they quickly handed him over. And knew to never take him out of my sight again.

Jason's parents made it in that night after J.J. was born. And my mother arrived the following day. The grandparents took turns holding him and taking pictures. He was completely adored by all of them. They had all suffered from the loss of their first grandchild. They were extra appreciative to be able to spend time with their second grandbaby.

It took me half of the first night to get the baby to nurse since they had given him a bottle, it threw him off on how to feed from his mother. And it was my first time trying to nurse a baby. But we both finally got the hang of it, and I became his personal milk cow. I spent all that night just looking at him and kissing his little face. Telling him all about how much I loved him. Telling him how proud I was to be his mother.

We spent July 4th in the hospital, sharing a room with a Latina mother and her baby. There was a curtain between my bed and hers. The room only had one TV, and we each had our own remote control. That night, I would put the channel on to watch the National Fireworks from nearby D.C., and she would then change it to a foreign channel which was broadcasting a Spanish Soap Opera. We went back and forth like that for half an hour or longer, flipping between the two channels. Till I finally gave in and let her have her way. I found it comical after about the twentieth time, and so I just had a good laugh about it.

We were released to go home on the afternoon of July 5th. Jason drove the three of us carefully in the Ranger, with J.J. in the middle. Jason's parents followed behind. And Mama stopped by Toys R Us on her way, to buy more gifts for her grandson. They all wanted to be there with us to help us settle in. I was so happy to be taking my baby boy to his home on Blue Mountain. Where I would raise him and watch him grow.

They had all brought even more gifts, from family and friends back home. There were so many it was overwhelming. Everyone was trying to be extra considerate, knowing what we had been through with Grace. Our son was also a miracle baby. After losing Grace, no one knew if we would ever be given another chance to raise a child. With J.J., we were given a promise of tomorrow. And he became the most showered baby ever. We opened all the gifts as soon as we were settled in. Then our parents said goodbye, and left us to our privacy, with our new son in our new home.

We did everything we could do with J.J. right away, we didn't want to waste any precious time. Just within the first week, we took him on stroller rides to the lake and park near our house. We took him to Chuck E. Cheese when he was five days old, and to the Pentagon that night, so he could see his daddy's office. We wanted to show him everything. The sun, the moon, the stars and the whole wide world. I read a dozen books to him every day. Played every baby video for him that we had. Sang every song I knew. Talked to him constantly, and kissed him so many times a day he would start to get fussy about it after the hundredth time.

I never put him down. Ever. If I showered, I held him in the shower. If I did anything, I was holding him. And I learned how to do everything with one hand, cleaning, cooking and laundry. I did it all while I held him. He slept on my chest, like Grace. But I never slept at night. I refused to sleep, except for cat naps I would take during the day when J.J. was awake and his daddy was taking care of him. Jason's sleep schedule was backwards since he worked night shift. But he would come home from work and spend time with his son, and didn't sleep much either.

When J.J. was about one month old, we took him on his first road trip to West Virginia. Our families were hosting a baby shower for us there since we couldn't make it when I was pregnant. Everyone wanted to hold J.J. Grandma Sparks came in and said, "Whoever has that baby, give him to me. I'm the great grandma!" He had at least a hundred more presents there. Everything you could think of. His nursery at home was already filled full from the gifts he had previously received. Now it would be overflowing.

We took our son to church that Sunday. To the church where I last saw Grace, at her service. It was beyond difficult for me to walk back through those doors. I knew it would bring me back to relive the day of her funeral, and seeing her there at the altar. But I wanted Pastor Phil to bless my newborn son. The preacher was glowing with happiness when I handed the baby to him. He knew what this meant to me. He held J.J. up at the altar, in front of the congregation (like baby Simba on *The Lion King*). He prayed over my son and blessed him. I cried tears of grief and tears of joy, at the same time.

We went back home, loaded down with baby presents like Santa's sleigh. We all settled back into our routines on Blue Mountain. J.J. was growing fast. The first two months with him flew by. And other than a slight case of jaundice which was too low to even require treatment, he was perfectly healthy. Our home was filled with love and happiness again. I thanked God constantly for blessing me with another child.

On the morning of September 11, 2001. I received a call from my sister Haley. I didn't have cable tv at the time, so I knew absolutely nothing of what was happening in New York City, Pennsylvania, or the Pentagon where Jason worked. And when she called me, everyone was still very uncertain of exactly what was happening. She told me there had been a massive explosion at the Pentagon. And I told her that Jason was still there working. Around the time she called, was when he was supposed to be getting off work for the day and leaving to come home.

Jason had a cellphone, but it wasn't working. The entire D.C. area traffic was gridlocked, and all cellular service had gone down. I tried repeatedly to call him, with no answer. I made several other calls to family members, trying to find out what had happened. I sat there holding my two-month-old son, crying. I thought, based on what I had been told, that I had lost my husband. I was trying to prepare myself for the harsh reality that I may be a widow and a single mother. He should have been home by now. My mind was racing with thoughts of wondering how I would raise my son without his father.

About three hours later, he finally made it home. I was so relieved to see him, so happy to know that my husband and the father of my children was alive and unharmed. But he was badly and visibly shaken. He explained to me that he had been in the parking lot of the Pentagon, getting ready to leave for the day. He saw the airplane come in, and he watched as it crashed into the Pentagon. He witnessed the massive explosion of the Boeing 757 American Airlines Flight #77, along with all 64 passengers and the jet fuel onboard, colliding into the Pentagon killing an additional 125 military and civilian employees in the building. He watched as the defenses of the United States of America's most vital military fortress, were breached and destroyed, the headquarters which housed our nation's Department of Defense, and his own personal workplace. He tried to stay and help however he could. It was his second nature instinct and drilled combat training, to act in a time of crisis. He felt a crucial sense of responsibility to immediately assist the emergency services personnel with rescue and recovery. As a Marine Corps Veteran, he had been properly prepared and was thoroughly qualified to offer support aid in such an extreme situation. But the authorities began an immediate evacuation of everyone they could remove from the premises. So his hands were tied and he was forced to leave.

Jason relayed to me that he believed it had been a terrorist attack, even though that hadn't been officially determined or confirmed yet. He had me hastily pack some overnight bags for all of us. He packed guns and survival supplies for preparation in case the attacks continued or escalated, then rushed us out the door. He proceeded to take us to our hometown. He wanted to get his family away from D.C. and the East Coast, and into the safety zone of the mountains in West Virginia. I remember as we travelled, thinking what a beautiful blue sky day it was, how it could have just been a nice day. But also thinking about how it was ruined and what a tragic day it had turned out to be. I was thankful that my husband survived, but shocked and saddened by all the lives that had been lost.

No more than we had made the five-hour drive, and gotten out of the vehicle, Jason received a call from the Department of Defense. They gave him orders to return to the Pentagon. He wanted me and J.J. to stay in WV, but I insisted on us returning with him, so our son and I could be home for him during such a stressful event. We drove all the way back and he dropped me and J.J. off on Blue Mountain. Jason returned to work that evening, with the Pentagon still on fire and billowing with smoke. With the explosion of the terrorist attack still smoldering. He worked steadily all that night, and for days and nights in a row after that. And nonstop for several months. He was responsible for getting the Pentagon network back up and running.

We were now in a war on terrorism, and the Department of Defense had to be able to function. He was working directly under the Secretary of Defense, Donald Rumsfeld. And providing support for the war efforts. Jason later received many accolades and awards for his personal service to the Pentagon and the nation during that critical time. [I am writing this chapter on September 11th, 2019. Jason was a guest speaker at the local high school, with J.J. also present (although he graduated last May). Jason prepared and delivered a speech to the students. He spoke to them about the tragic events of 9/11, and his role at the Pentagon during one of the most catastrophic events on U.S. soil eighteen years ago today.]

As his wife, I felt guilty and partially responsible for the trauma he was subjected to on 9/11. Here I had persuaded him to take the Pentagon job, for fear of him going to war if he stayed in the Marine Corps. And he could have been killed on that day, in the Pentagon. It was a very uneasy scary time, for everyone in the country. But Jason had to work right through it. And had no time to deal with the PTSD factor he had experienced.

After 9/11, Jason started to age rapidly. He was plagued with survivor's guilt. He was literally not sleeping at all. And he was commuting three hours a day to work in the very place that had been a strategic target of terrorism. It caught up with him, and he was basically operating on survival mode. It was all starting to take a major toll on him. And I noticed his temperament started to change drastically around the same timeframe. There was nothing I could do to ease the amount of stress he was under.

I spent every second with my son, watching him grow and change. Experiencing all the "firsts" with him. When he got his first teeth and started eating solid food. When he first started talking, saying "Dada" and "Mama", when he started crawling, when he first started walking, all of those moments and every moment in between were priceless treasures to me. Celebrating holidays with him, taking him on outings, watching him play and learn, I didn't miss a second of it, and I never let him out of my sight. I didn't put him down for the entire first year of his life. He started walking a little later than he should have because I was always holding him. (Actually, he started climbing before he started walking). But I was always right behind him when he was on the move. I just wanted to keep him from all harm and dangers. I was a super hovercraft mom.

Most of our time together was mother-son time. It was mainly just me and J.J. since Jason was always at work. I took him to the playground, we played toys, we watched cartoons, colored pictures, sang songs, laughed and danced together; every day was full of life and happiness. J.J. was a happy child, full of energy and mischief. Just like little boys should be. He could do no wrong in my eyes. Everything my son has ever done, I have always smiled at him and said, "You're the best boy in the whole world." And I mean every word of it every time.

J.J.'s first birthday was an extra big celebration. I spent months planning every detail of an elaborate party for him. All the decorations, the cake, his outfit, the presents, the location, everything, it was all such an enormous deal to me and I wanted him to have a party fit for a King. I wanted him to know how special he was. We had it at the same place where our big wedding was held, Carnifex Ferry Battlefield. It was also our third anniversary. Family and friends poured in to celebrate both occasions with us. J.J. was showered with many gifts, again. Watching him blow out his candle, eat his birthday cake and open presents, it all meant so much to me. I have always treated my son like a little Prince. Anything and everything he ever wanted, I got it for him. I could never say no to him, and still can't to this day. I wanted him to know he would always be taken care of. So I spoiled him every chance I got. He was so bright and radiated like the rays of the sun. He was the absolute light of my life. Having him made my broken heart beat again. He will never know how he came to my rescue and saved me. He brought me back from the darkness I had been in from losing Grace. He gave my life meaning and worth again. To hear him call me Mommy, to have him hug my neck, to listen to him laugh, or watch him run and play. A thousand little moments, each one as special to me as the next. My little boy, my only son, he made me the proudest mother in the world.

That July 22nd, a few weeks after J.J.s first birthday, for the third time, I knew I was pregnant. But this time it was confirmed through a dream before I was even late enough for my cycle to take a pregnancy test. I had a dream that I was giving birth at home, to a baby girl. So instantly, I knew this one was another girl. My second daughter. I named her right away, she would be my Faith. I took the test before I had even missed my monthly time. It took a little while for it to show up, but it was positive. I went straight to the doctor, to confirm. Faith was given a due date of April 14, 2003. I was put on bed rest very early on this time, as high risk again and because I had both of my other children prematurely. I started off this time at 103 pounds again. I was going to try to gain more weight with this one, in hopes that might help me carry longer.

I craved ice cream and strawberry milk with my third baby. Once I could feel her moving, I could tell that Faith was a calm one. So calm that it scared me, so I would shake my belly frequently and wait for her to kick me, just to make sure she was okay. And she only moved at night. I knew she was a night owl, and I predicted she would be born in the middle of the night. My sister Haley helped me to decide on Faith's middle name, Abigail.

I went into preterm labor with her for the first time when I was thirty weeks pregnant. There had been a massive blizzard the day before that. It was labeled as the "Presidents Day Snowstorm". We had five feet of snow piled up against the house and covering the vehicles. And the power was out for days. Jason had to recruit a snow removal crew to get us dug out so he could take me to the hospital. I was scared I would give birth at home, like in the dream I had about Faith at the beginning of my pregnancy. We finally made it to the hospital. The labor was stopped.

I was assigned a preterm labor specialist nurse. It was a program, where the nurse called a few times a day to check in on me. I had to give reports on how much water I was drinking, and if I'd had any contractions. At my next doctor's appointment, I was told that because of my preterm labor history, if I wanted to have any more children after Faith, I would be required to have a cerclage procedure done, and deliver only by cesarean section. I decided then that Faith would be my last one. All three of my pregnancies had been so stressful and scary. I never got to just enjoy being pregnant. I always had such a deeply instilled fear for the safety and health of my babies. And after starting labor so early with Faith, I was afraid that I would have one so premature that they would be kept in the hospital for months, or wouldn't survive being born prematurely. So I informed my doctor that I was choosing to have my tubes tied after Faith was born.

The strict bed rest I was on made it challenging to try to keep up with J.J. He was full steam ahead and nonstop at his age, he had a steady supply of endless energy. But he was very well behaved during the rest of my pregnancy. He seemed to sense the seriousness and importance of what was going on. He would stick close to me when I was lying down, which was pretty much constantly. He would snuggle with me and watch cartoons, or let me read a hundred books to him. I would only get up to feed him or tend to his needs, or to refill my water and grab something for me to eat. He was interested in why my belly kept getting bigger. I would put his little hand over Faith, so he could feel her kick him. But he didn't quite understand the concept of what was in there. I managed to gain fifty pounds with this pregnancy. And I made it to thirty-seven weeks before I went into full-blown labor again. I couldn't wait to meet my second daughter. I loved being a mom to my little boy. We played trucks, played ball and went fishing. All the things boys like to do. But I was also looking forward to having a little girl again; to playing dress up, and dolls and having tea parties together. I wanted to do all the things with Faith that I never got to do with Grace.

On Tuesday, March 25, 2003, it was time. Jason packed me and J.J. and our hospital bags up into our new Ford Explorer that he had recently bought for our growing family. We set off for the Fair Oaks Hospital in Fairfax, Virginia. It was just on the outskirts of D.C., further away than the town where J.J. was born, and further from home. We got there in the afternoon. Jason called both of our mothers while we were on the way. I had invited both of them to be present during Faith's birth since she was to be my last baby.

I had Jason stop again, at my pit stop in Marshall for my McDonalds supply of labor energy junk food. He knew the drill by now. It was a beautiful Spring day. I was smiling the whole way to the hospital. I couldn't wait to meet my Faith. And I was still smiling through contractions by the time I checked into the hospital. The doctor said that I looked "too happy to be in labor", and tried to send me home. I said, "No, you can't send me home; I'll give birth at home, she's going to be born today". (Thinking back to the dream I had of giving birth to Faith at home. I was certain if they sent me home, that it would come true).

When the doctor checked me, he confirmed that I was, in fact, quite ready for the birthing phase. I told him I was just happy because I couldn't wait to meet my daughter. I have always had a high pain tolerance. I never did scream, or carry on, or even make a sound any of the times I had been in labor or delivery. I just did what I had to do quietly, and looked forward to meeting all of my beautiful children. So as soon as the doctor realized that my labor was imminent, I was admitted to my hospital room.

I told the nurses that I didn't want an epidural. The one I got with Grace didn't work, and the one I got with J.J. did more harm than good. But they insisted that I had to have one since I was scheduled to have my tubes tied after delivery. They had a hard time placing the epidural again because of my bad back. And of course, it didn't work.

Our mothers made it in time. I watched American Idol on TV from my hospital bed that night. Then waited for after midnight, when I had predicted Faith would arrive. J.J. snuggled with me until it was time for delivery. One of the nurses who attended me had been our nurse at Prince William Hospital when J.J. was born. She recognized me, then said to J.J., "Hey, I remember you."

When it was time for Faith to arrive, J.J. went to the waiting room with his grandpa, while our two moms and Jason stayed with me.

I was in delivery for a few hours this time. I kept telling the doctor and nurses that the baby's shoulders were stuck. They finally saw for themselves that I was correct when her head came out but the rest of her wouldn't follow. They called in several more doctors and nurses. Then turned on every bright light they had, and a swarm of physicians came rushing at me and did some intricate maneuver to get her dislodged. It was a stressful moment, but thankfully it worked.

Wednesday, March 26, 2003, at 1:51 am, I welcomed Faith Abigail into the world. She was my biggest baby, at 7 pounds 11 ounces, and 21 inches long. When they put her on my chest I said, "Hi Baby Girl, I'm your Mama." She looked just like my other two babies. All my babies looked very similar when they were first born. (I keep a frame on display in my home, with all three of their newborn pictures side by side. And it's hard to tell them apart). But I could tell right away that Faith looked the most like me of my three babies. And she was perfectly healthy. God truly blessed us, for the third time.

The grandmothers were happy to be present for Faith's arrival. They were both so proud to be there, and witness the miracle of her birth. And as soon as the baby and I were all cleaned up, I had J.J. come in to meet his little sister. She was bundled up and asleep when he saw her for the first time. He was not even two years old yet, so he didn't really understand that she was a baby human.

I think he thought she was a toy baby doll. But he was happy to see her all the same. I had taken him to Build A Bear Workshop a few weeks before; he made a custom bear for himself dressed in blue, and a matching bear with a pink outfit for his new baby sissy. He proudly presented to Faith the teddy bear he had made for her. Seeing the two of my children together, being able to hold them both made my heart so happy and content.

They took me back to the operating room for my surgery a few hours after Faith arrived, while I still had my useless epidural. I told them it wasn't working properly. They began anyways, and I could feel every cut they were making. So I started yelling at the doctors, and then they put me under general anesthesia. I was sad to have my tubes tied. I had always wanted at least seven children. But the risk was very high with all three of my babies, and my body and mind just couldn't go through the stress or emotional turmoil of having any more. That was one of the most difficult decisions I have ever made.

Mama stayed up with me all throughout my second night in the hospital. Faith was a night owl like I knew she was during my pregnancy. She would take little cat naps while me and my mom were talking quietly. Then she would wake up to nurse. Instead of crying like a baby, Faith would make a sudden loud squall that sounded like a cat meowing. It startled me the first few times she made that sound. I started calling her "Kitty Cat" right then. And that has been nickname ever since.

We were released the next day to go home. And since I had been on such strict bedrest through my entire pregnancy, I hadn't been able to completely set up her nursery. Jason had bought and assembled a new crib in her room, but I hadn't decorated yet. So as soon as we got home, I worked on getting everything settled for Faith. Her room was painted lavender, and I used a butterfly theme with flowers, in pink and purple. I had crocheted a baby blanket for her while I was pregnant, and it matched her room perfectly.

So far, J.J. had only seen his baby sister sleeping. And the first evening we were home, he was studying her little face while she was asleep, bundled up in her blanket. When she woke up and let out one of her cat cries, it startled him, and he was confused for a moment. When he realized that she wasn't a baby doll, he was even more intrigued. Then he seemed to understand that she was a little friend for him, and he was a proud big brother.

Faith was instantly a Mama's Girl and always has been. From the time she was a newborn, she didn't want anyone to hold her except for me. She would throw a giant fit if I would hand her to someone else, even her daddy. He never really got to hold her until she was three months old, while we were on vacation at the Outer Banks, for J.J.'s second birthday. Faith had a very calm nature, other than her loud cat cries. My night owl kitty had her days and nights confused and all backwards. Faith would sleep all day, and stay up all night. And J.J. would sleep all night, and stay up all day. (So I was literally awake 24 hours a day for the first nine months of her life, till I finally got her pattern reversed). And I loved every second of it. I was so happy to be actively engaged in my most valuable role as a mother. I was filled with pride and joy to be able to tend to and take care of J.J. and Faith. I counted all of my blessings, all the time. J.J. had become my new heart and Faith became my new soul.

Faith was my little princess. I was so happy to have another baby girl of my own, to take care of and raise. I was looking forward to doing all the girly things with her, that I didn't get to do with her sister. It was happy and sad for me at the same time. Faith was not a replacement for Grace. But she was Grace's sister. I love all three of my children equally. Although there are attributes that are special to me about each one of them individually. And my relationship with each one has its own unique connection. But I know that Faith was the Lord's special gift to me. She restored my faith in God, and she restored the biggest part of my soul that was taken when I lost my Grace.

I couldn't wait to have tea parties, play dress up, play dollies, put ribbons and bows in her hair and have girl time. I painted Faith's nails for the first time when she was five days old. Aunt Haley bought her a bracelet with her initials on it, so she was already wearing jewelry as soon as I brought her home. Some babies, you can't really tell by their faces if they are a boy or a girl. Faith looked like a girl right away, even if she wasn't wearing pink. She had rosy cheeks and lips, and she was just breathtakingly beautiful.

Shortly after Faith was born, Meemaw and Peepaw drove their camper to Front Royal, and we went to the campground to visit with them. They were proud great grandparents, and always lit up when they would see J.J. and spend time with him. They were happy to finally meet miss Faith. She stole their hearts right away.

Faith was also showered with many gifts. Presents poured in from all over. We had her official baby shower on the weekend of her first Easter, that April. And at Easter Sunday service in our hometown church, Faith was held up and blessed by Pastor Phil. He was proud and happy to do the honors of announcing my youngest child. He had been with us and supported us throughout our marriage, and with all three of our children.

Part 3

At home, I did everything on my own. Jason was working around the clock. And I was stingy with the babies anyways, so I was happy to have them all to myself. I was happy to have a home full of life and energy and round the clock motherly duties. It was a huge blessing for me to have my hands full taking care of two little ones. They were only 22 months apart, so most of the time I had J.J. on my hip, and Faith in my other arm. They clung to me, and I never wanted to put them down. We were all inseparable. The sleepless nights, diaper changes, potty-training, crying and toddler fits, I cherished every minute of all of that. And they never slept in their rooms. I kept them both in bed with me so I could keep a constant eye on them.

I could tell early on that Faith was stubborn and independent like me, and messy like her father. As she got to be old enough to sit up, I would set her in her crib while I cleaned her bedroom. She would tangle every baby doll's hair, and throw every blanket and toy out onto the floor. And when she started eating baby food, she never let me feed her from the spoon. She would throw a giant Kitty fit until I let her do it on her own. (To this day, sixteen years later, I have never fed the child from my hand). I thought to myself back then, I have finally found someone more stubborn than me, which I didn't think was even possible.

When Jason was off on the weekends, we would take the children sight-seeing and exploring around the Shenandoah Valley.

There was so much to do in that area; wineries, petting zoos, cave tours, hot air balloon festivals, parades, holiday festivities, etc. We had settled into our lives there in Front Royal. J.J. especially loved going to all the different places and seeing all the people. He was always a social little man and an explorer. The town of Winchester was where we usually went for shopping and activities. We took the kids to the Apple Blossom Mall there, to ride the carousel and go to the movie theater. We took them for Sunday drives along the Shenandoah River, into downtown Front Royal to the ice cream shop. Sometimes we would take them to Washington D.C., to tour the monuments and museums. And we watched the National Fireworks from the steps of the Pentagon on the Fourth of July one year.

One time when the kids were little, an F-5 tornado touched down in the valley town of Winchester, which was more than twenty miles away from us. It was so powerful that it sounded like a freight train was on top of our house, and rattled every window. Also, an earthquake once hit near Richmond, and it shook our house violently. Every time it came a bad storm, I would take the children down to the basement. We were in a windy ridge near the top of Blue Mountain. There were power outages frequently there. We experienced lots of lightning storms in the summers, snow and ice storms in the winter and windy springs and falls. But that mountain was majestic and beautiful in all weather. I loved to see the changing of all the seasons there.

On Blue Mountain, almost every day, I would pull the children in a little red wagon, down the gravel roads that led to the playground and the lake. We would spend hours there, just enjoying the outdoors and the beautiful scenery. I would swing them on the swing set, we would draw with sidewalk chalk, blow bottles of bubbles, have picnics, they would ride their bikes, run and play. At home, we would play with every toy they owned. And I always read to my children and sang songs to them. When Faith was nine months old and just starting to stand up, she found my grocery list on the coffee table. She picked up the pen and started drawing. And she has drawn ever since then. She inherited her artistic talent from my father. And I could tell early on that J.J. was left-handed, like him.

I did all the girly things with Faith that I had planned to. We had tea parties literally every day. I brushed and braided her hair, and put fancy bows and ribbons in it. We played hours of dress-up and dollies. I put makeup and jewelry on her. She picked me flowers and drew pictures for me. I watched her chase butterflies, and pet animals. We baked cookies together. All the mother-daughter things I ever wanted to do. And she was J.J.'s little baby doll. He would pick her up and swing her around. He hugged her and tried to cheer her up when she cried. He shared his toys with her. He was the best big brother, so proud to help his Mommy with his baby sister.

Jason did all the manly things with J.J., teaching him how to throw and catch a ball, how to fish, how to use his toy tools and how to ride a bike. He was always so proud to have a son to pass his knowledge and skills down to. He wanted to teach our boy everything he knew. I always liked to do boy things too though, so any time I got to play trucks or action figures, and find frogs or lizards to stick in his pockets, I was right there with my little man. I finally learned how to cook, in my kitchen there on Blue Mountain. As the children grew bigger and began eating more, I wanted to be the kind of mom that baked treats for them, and I wanted to fix nice suppers like my Meemaw and Grandma Sparks always did. So I began experimenting with cooking. At first, I ruined or burnt everything I made. And I tried to make Grandma's biscuits, which she never had a recipe for. But I had eaten loads of her raw biscuit dough when I was a kid, so I knew what it was supposed to taste like. I threw out fifty pans of my bad biscuits, opened the kitchen door and tossed them into the back yard. Then finally, on the 51st pan, I got them right. I have made them ever since and never messed up another batch.

One year at Christmas time I decided to bake a pie for each of our neighbors. I had a recipe for chocolate pecan pie. I had made this recipe several times before, and it always turned out really good. It was one of Jason's favorites. This occasion, I was making four at a time. I was on the phone with Mama while I was busy at work on them. I assembled them all and put them in the preheated oven, feeling all proud of myself, like I was Martha Stewart. When I hung up with my mom, I realized I had been distracted and accidentally left out one key ingredient, the eggs. Dammit, I thought, it's not too late. So I yanked them all out of the oven and stirred the eggs into each one, causing the heated chocolate chips to melt into the swirl of yellow egg yolks. I put them back in the oven and set the timer. When they came out, they looked just like cow manure patties in pie plates. Like someone had literally baked cow shit. And they were hard as a rock. I had Jason taste test a bite of one, and he made a funny face. But he told a giant falsehood and said, "Mmm, this is good honey." Even our dog Rocky could tell that they weren't fit to eat. Rocky was smart. He ran away from the pies. Dogs don't tell lies when it comes to food.

Jason insisted on distributing them anyways. He loaded all the indecent pies into the kids' little red wagon and proceeded uphill on our driveway through the snow. I was watching from the window thinking, "Oh no! I didn't even cover those pies or wrap them up with anything, and it's snowing on them." About that time, I saw (in slow motion) Jason hit a rough spot in the road, and the wagon tipped over. All the cow patty pies slid out into the deep snow. They were welded to their tin pans with the half beaten petrified egg yolks, so they were still intact, but he was inspecting them for damage. I ran out onto the porch and yelled, commanding him to cease and desist this faulty mission at once. He ignored me, picked the shit pies up, brushed the snow off the tops and put them back in the little red wagon.

He proceeded to parade them around the neighborhood and pass them out to our poor neighbors, whose houses were all far apart. It was below freezing that day, so the already rock hard pies were probably also frozen by the time Jason delivered them. Oh to have seen the looks on their faces when they received our neighborly holiday gift of inedible manure pies. That's the most horrible kind gesture I ever did in my life. Shameful. Those people probably still refer to me as "The Frozen Cow Shit Pie Lady".

It was one of our annual traditions, to go to a local Christmas tree farm to pick out and cut down our own tree. On Faith's first Christmas we selected the prettiest tree. On our way home that night, we were singing along to Jingle Bells when our tree suddenly fell off the top of the Explorer. We watched as a semi-truck ran over it. There was nothing left but one little twig by the time Jason tried to recover it. We went back to the tree farm and got another one.

And another year, we went to the same tree farm and got the biggest Christmas tree we ever had. It was about eight-feet-tall. When we got it home, Jason was in the front yard trimming it. I thought it was taking him too long, so I started watching from the window. First I saw a few branches. Then I looked outside awhile later, and the whole entire front yard was covered in pine boughs. I ran outside to see what he had done. Jason had gotten carried away with his chainsaw. He scalped it. All that was left of that big beautiful tree, was a two-foot tall pitiful Charlie Brown bush. I had to prop it up on a coffee table just to be able to fit presents under the thing. It looked ridiculous.

I always treasured holidays with my children. I did everything I could to go above and beyond so every one of them would be special for my babies. I loved all of it; hunting eggs with them for Easter, having them bring me breakfast in bed on Mother's Day, helping them make cards for their daddy on Father's Day, watching fireworks with them on the Fourth of July, dressing them up in costumes and taking them trick or treating for Halloween, having a big feast with them for Thanksgiving, opening presents together on Christmas. I had traditions for each holiday, that I added to every year. I loved being the Tooth Fairy, the Easter Bunny and Santa Claus. It made me feel special to add magic to my children's lives. And their birthday parties were always huge extravaganzas with themes, that I put a lot of time and Jason put a lot of money into. Every year I was given to celebrate their birthdays, I did all I could to make sure they knew how special they were, and how happy I was to have them and to celebrate their lives with them. I always strived to make everything magical for the children. Seeing the smiles on their precious little faces was everything to me. Watching them experience all the first times and new things, seeing it all through their eyes, was priceless to me.

We took family vacations to the beaches of the Outer Banks in North Carolina. We took regular trips to West Virginia to visit family. We took the children to zoos, carnivals, fairs, festivals and amusement parks. We had camping trips, fishing trips, hiking trips and took the children swimming. On our fifth wedding anniversary, as Jason's dad had promised, he sent us on our official honeymoon. We planned a Disney Cruise to the Bahamas.

But I couldn't leave my babies behind. I had never been away from them, even for one minute. So instead of sending just the two of us, Jason's dad sent all four of us on the cruise. We drove to Florida and stopped by Tallahassee to see Aunt Haley. She took us to a phosphate lake where we swam and the kids ate melted Hershey bars. Then we went to Aunt Vicki's, where the kids played with their cousins Tyler and Hayden. We took the kids to Disney World for the first time. Faith was scared of Mickey Mouse, and she was too little to have much fun, but J.J. had a blast riding the rides and seeing the characters. Then we boarded the ship at Cape Canaveral and set sail on a 4 day trip to a Disney island called Castaway Cay, and to Nassau Bahamas. We had a really nice time. It was our best family vacation.

It wasn't just the big moments though. It was all the little moments that I mostly lived for, the hugs and kisses, bath time and story time, standing back watching them play and have fun and interact with each other as siblings. Seeing them smile and listening to them laugh. Hearing them call me "Mommy", and saying, "I love you." Watching them grow, change, learn and develop into their own personalities. A million little moments that made up the very best parts of my life. They were my reason for living and breathing. They were my happiness in the present, my hope for the future, and my greatest loves forever and always.

And I documented everything. I always had film and video cameras on them, following them around and capturing every moment I could. I have a million pictures and countless hours of home movies featuring J.J. and Faith. I measured their heights and weights regularly. I took ink stampings of their little hands and feet every year on their birthdays. I wanted to record and remember every single detail of watching them grow up.

We lived on Blue Mountain for five years. I mostly stayed isolated there other than our family outings, getting groceries and taking the kids to their pediatrician appointments. I was pretty much a hermit. I just wanted time with my two children, and time to begin moving forward from my grief of losing our first child. I kept my distance from everyone else mostly.

I remained in a state of mourning during those five years, but I tried to never let the kids see me sad or crying. I kept a happy mask in front of them. Throughout that time, I made my peace with God. I knew that I would never recover from losing Grace. But I came to terms with the fact that I would have to find a way to learn how to pick up my heavy burdens and pain and carry that heartache with me for the rest of my life. I knew that I had to find the strength within myself to keep moving forward, for the sake of my other children. I had to be strong for them. I was happy and blessed with J.J. and Faith. Everything I did, revolved around them. I thanked God several times, every single day, for giving me the blessings of all three of my precious children.

We turned our little piece of Blue Mountain into a home. We planned to stay there and raise our children in the home we made as husband and wife, and as parents. Jason landscaped, built a toolshed, made sidewalks, a patio, and a dog house. We planted a flower garden of roses in the backyard, in honor of Grace. We had a swing set for the kids, a sandbox, a kiddie pool, bikes and toys to play outside. We had a four-wheeler to ride around on Blue Mountain. We had a gazebo with a picnic table where Jason would cook out, or I would host parties for the kids. We had pretty redbud trees in the front yard. We had everything that looked like a picture-perfect family home life.

Jason always provided very well for his family. He busted his ass to give us everything we needed and wanted. I was never materialistic, I always made do with what I had. But I wanted the best of everything for the kids. He took care of us financially and even worked a second job for a while to make ends meet. He always wanted me to be a career woman. So I chose photography as a profession. My daddy had been a professional photographer. I thought I might be good at it since he was. So I studied and took a course on Film Photography and Photojournalism for three years, from home while I was raising my babies. I graduated from the New York Institute of Photography, becoming certified as a Professional Photographer. My plan was that when the children became school age, I would start a business from home and help contribute financially to our household.

I worked hard doing everything I thought a wife and mother should do. I was a homemaker, a housewife and a stay at home mom. I cooked three meals a day and prepared snacks and desserts. I cleaned the house immaculately and kept the laundry done. I always took the best possible care of our children. I kept them fed, clean and safe. I taught them their letters and numbers, how to read and about geography maps along with other various subjects. I taught them about the Lord and the Bible. I taught them songs and nursery rhymes. I taught them morals and values.

We had a nice house and yard. We had our smart handsome son J.J., who looked just like Jason and our sweet beautiful daughter Faith, who looked just like me. We had pets, Rocky the dog and Roscoe the cat. We had nice vehicles, the Ranger and the Explorer. We were financially stable. We had built a respectable and worthy life there together. For all intents and purposes, we appeared to have a classic American love story. Jason and I weren't always doing well during that time though. From the outside looking in, no one would ever know. But on the inside, it wasn't at all a fairy tale. We had countless good moments and happy memories. We still loved each other, although our love was buried underneath the many layers of all our pain. But we had a lot of bad moments with one another there too. I won't go into details about any of the bad times, out of respect for him as the father of my children. But the hardcore Marine combat training he had been through, the night shift along with his long commute and long hours of work at the Pentagon, being the provider for all of us, his suppressed grief from losing Grace, trying to be strong for me, plus the PTSD he experienced on 9/11 all combined to wreak havoc within him and subsequently spilled over into our marriage. Not to mention everything I had been through—emotionally, mentally and physically; that combination resulted in major negative effects on me. I was not perfect. To be honest, I was defective in many ways. I was too clingy to him as my husband and required too much affection from him. I had severe abandonment issues. I have never been the easiest person to live with. I was immensely overprotective of the children, to a fault sometimes. I hovered over them day and night and micromanaged their every move. I majorly freaked out about every little thing that I thought could potentially be harmful or dangerous for them. I instilled fear into them over things they shouldn't have been afraid of because I was so scared to lose one of them. I was germophobic and OCD regarding the house order and cleanliness because I didn't want the children to get sick. I was infuriatingly stubborn and downright bossy. Plus I have always had a bad temper too. I truly wanted to be a submissive wife, but I just wasn't wired that way. I was harder on Jason than he deserved, about everything in general.

We were barely holding it together, for the sake of our children. He was a good father to them. But he wasn't always a good husband to me during that period of our lives together. And I was so focused on being a mother, that I neglected him as a wife. It wasn't his fault, and it wasn't my fault. Nobody was to blame. It was just the hand of cards we had been dealt. We were handed so many so fast, that we couldn't hold all those cards together, no matter how hard we tried. We were on a long runaway train headed down a track that was too short to keep us moving forward. We either had to stop in our tracks or back up in reverse. And neither of those was a valid option. Divorce was never an option for me. I married my husband, intending to honor our vows and stay married for life. For better or for worse.

Jason's stressful work schedule and lack of sleep was getting to him, and he was weary of his long commute. He was aware of the repercussions all of that was imposing upon our marriage. And I was always afraid to travel, it completely stressed me out putting the children on the dangerous road for our five hour trip to West Virginia to visit family. It seemed like we spent more holidays there rather than at our own home. Family would come to visit us too, especially Mama since she had finally divorced "Captain Ass-hat the Jeep Thief". But I was tired of all the back and forth between Virginia and West Virginia. I didn't feel completely settled. Also, we were starting to outgrow our starter home. The kids were getting bigger and I wanted them to have more room to run and play. So it was time to either finish our basement as extra living space or find a house with more square footage. We were at a crossroads.

After five years of calling Blue Mountain our home, I talked to Jason and suggested that we relocate to West Virginia. We would have family support there. And since J.J. was getting close to school age, if we were ever going to move, I wanted to do it beforehand, so we wouldn't rip him from one school to another. And I thought perhaps a major life change would help our failing marriage, and reconnect us with each other. He was in agreement. The decision was made.

I started looking at jobs for him, and real estate. I found a position that fit his skills, as a government contractor at an FBI center in Clarksburg, WV with the same company he had been working for at the Pentagon, Lockheed Martin. His resume was already so impressive that he could work anywhere he wanted to. He applied and got the job. I found a house with acreage online, a newly built, bigger, two-story house on the outskirts of the rural community of Birch River, WV. The very second I saw the picture of it, I knew it was meant to be our next home.

We went as soon as possible to view the house in person. It was twice as big as our current home. The children loved it as soon as we walked through the door. While we were touring it with the realtor, Faith disappeared. I searched in every room until I found her. She was in the master bathroom, had removed every stitch of her clothing, and was sitting in the big jacuzzi tub ready to take a bath. She had made herself at home. J.J. picked out the bedroom he wanted as his own and was having fun running all throughout the house. Jason was scoping out the big yard and the surrounding woodlands. I sat on the front porch swing looking out over the land and the West Virginia mountains. I said to myself, "This is where I am going to live until I die. This is our forever home."

Farm Sweet Farm

We immediately put an offer on the property in Birch River. It was accepted. We listed our home for sale on the real estate market, which was booming at the time, especially since the D.C. metro area was expanding towards Warren County, where we lived. Ironically, the couple selling us their WV house was relocating to the town we were moving from, Front Royal. We signed a rental agreement on the new house while we were waiting for our house in Front Royal to sell.

I started packing up our lives on Blue Mountain. Jason had to start straight away to work at his new job in West Virginia. So he stayed with his parents there during the week and came home on the weekends to start hauling truck and trailer loads from VA to WV. We were living separately for a few months while I packed and took care of the babies, and he was working one state away.

That April my sister Haley married her long time sweetheart that she had been with since college, Javier. They were living in Lexington, Kentucky. My kids stayed with Jason at his parents' house, while I travelled with Meemaw and Peepaw to the wedding. It was my first trip ever away from J.J. and Faith and I cried most of the way there. All the rest of our family made the drive to Lexington to take part in celebrating Haley's big day. I helped her get dressed then took some bridal portraits of her. I was her matron of honor and Peepaw walked her down the aisle. It was a beautiful and elegant ceremony and reception. I was proud to be there to share my sister's special occasion, but I was very happy to return to my babies and to go home.

Back on Blue Mountain, once I finished packing everything in boxes, Peepaw, Jason and his dad came with the biggest U-Haul they make for our big final load of belongings. It amazes me every time I've ever moved, how much stuff you can accumulate over time. I have always been a packrat of everything that holds any sentimental value to me. I swore then that I would never move again. We all worked together that Friday and Saturday to get everything loaded up. It was strenuous, exhausting, and stressful.

With everyone else outside and ready to go, I did one more walk-through of the house alone. I was sad to leave our home there. It was the place I brought J.J. and Faith home to, where I had raised them so far and watched them grow. Faith was barely three years old, and J.J. was almost five at the time. That home had been a symbol of a new life for me, a new beginning. Tears ran down my face and onto the floor as I did a final tour around every room, recalling all the memories that had been made in each one.. all the happiness, love and laughter, the holidays, special occasions, and regular every-day moments of our lives that had been contained within those walls. If it is possible to haunt a place while you're still alive, I know my ghost still resides at the house in Quantico, and the house on Blue Mountain, two of my true homes where I have left a part of myself behind after I closed the door behind me for the last time. My spirit still cries at Quantico, and still roams the halls on Blue Mountain.

J.J. was sad to leave Virginia. I was also sad to say farewell to Blue Mountain and all its majesty. The Shenandoah Valley area is one of the most beautiful places I have ever lived. I cried all the way from our driveway, down the mountain, to the Interstate. I questioned if moving was the right decision. It was too late to turn back now. We were travelling in a caravan, with Jason and J.J. in the big U-Haul up front, followed by me and Faith in the Explorer, Peepaw in his van, and Jason's dad. I had the entire five-hour drive to collect myself and begin looking forward to our next venture.

On May 31, 2006, we officially moved into our new house in Birch River. Peepaw, Meemaw, Mama, and Haley all came to help us unpack and settle in. It was the best moving party I've ever seen. We danced around the living room to Johnny Cash and Loretta Lynn. Peepaw liked our home on Blue Mountain but he seemed especially happy about our new place. He was happy to have us all closer, only twenty minutes from where he lived in Summersville. He seemed so proud for me to have such a nice property but it also seemed like he felt some sort of personal connection to this place.

Our new house was up a quarter-mile long gravel tree-lined drive on top of a big hill. It sat on three acres, surrounded by a 112-acre farm that it had once been a part of. It was very secluded and peaceful, set way back off the main road. The majority of the land laid level in a big meadow in front of the house with the back yard sloping upward towards the tree line. The house was a two-story Cape Cod style structure with a green shingle roof, hemlock siding, and a stone foundation. It was newly built and over two-thousand square feet. The crown jewel of the house was the enormous covered front porch. It was definitely the most impressive porch I've ever seen with a beautiful view of the big meadow and mountains as the backdrop in the distance.

The layout of the land automatically reminded me of Grandpa Sparks' farm in Canvas. There were several very similar attributes. When I had been to the property for the first time to view the place, I pictured what the land could be. It was a blank slate. We could write whatever we wanted to on it. I wanted to write a very specific story on this land, a story about a farm. I wanted to transform this place into the closest thing I could get to my best nostalgic childhood memories spent on my grandparent's farm. I wanted to give my own children a homestead filled with the same kind of memories. Having my own farm had been a lifelong dream of mine and this was where I was going to see that dream come true. I knew it the first time I ever sat on that front porch swing. The inside of the house was twice as big as our house in Front Royal. It had a kitchen with a big island, open to the dining room and living room. A small back porch was through sliding glass doors off the dining room, and the big front porch was entered from the living room door. A long hallway led from the kitchen to the master bedroom, which had a ridiculously large master bathroom. Along the same hallway was the laundry room and an office. The staircase went from the living room to the children's two L-shaped bedrooms and a bathroom between them upstairs.

In our former home, I could see or hear the children wherever they were, just based on the size of the house. There was a lot more room in this new house for the kids to run and hide from me. There was too much square footage to make it logistically possible for me to hover over them constantly as I had religiously done before. They had their first taste of freedom. Faith was always so quiet that she was the harder of the two to locate. J.J. usually gave his location away. While I was unpacking boxes and getting the house organized, the two of them joined forces for the first time to do some trouble-making together. They were at the ages where they wanted to see what they could get away with. Faith called J.J. "Bubby", and he called her "Faif" since he couldn't pronounce her name. (The nicknames they gave each other as toddlers, I still use for both of them present day). But yes, Bubby and Faif made good teamwork of their mission for misconduct.

I was getting my bedroom settled when I heard several loud crashes on the side landing of the entry door off the dining room. I ran down the hall and opened the door. Through the glass storm door, I saw a collection of toys piled up, and a dollhouse midair on its way to crashing down. They were both launching the toys out of Faith's bedroom window, and laughing maniacally about the outcome below. They were testing the gravity of our new two-story house and were thoroughly entertained by the mischief they were making. I ran upstairs, shut and locked the window. I scolded them for the danger of them possibly falling out of the window themselves. By that night I installed alarms on every window in both their bedrooms and child proofed every door and electrical outlet in the house.

That same week, I was getting the office organized while the kids were playing in the living room and watching cartoons. They got really quiet. Quiet toddlers equals up-to-no-good. When I went to investigate, J.J. and Faith had gotten a hold of red Sharpie markers, and they colored the entire side of the oak staircase, almost every square inch. It took me a bottle of rubbing alcohol, a pack of Magic Erasers and hours of scrubbing to undo that particular mess.

Also, both the kids had taken a spell that caused them to flush Mickey Mouse shaped cheese down the toilet. That phase started at Blue Mountain, but they were still continuing it at our new house. I don't know exactly what brought that cheese flushing era about, but they sure liked to watch those mouse ears swirl around the potty when they pulled the handle. Faith must have wanted to experiment further with the flushing because she somehow managed to flush an entire package of Q-tips down the toilet in the master bathroom. I had to unbolt the toilet from the floor, lay it on its side, and pull every single Q-tip out by hand.

It took me about two weeks to completely settle in, by which time the little ones had worn themselves out with their preschool crime spree around our new house. And over the course of that few weeks, I had established new rules and routines for the kids. I couldn't get mad at them for anything. Every ornery thing they had done, I would scold them in a pretend serious tone of voice, then turn my head so they couldn't see me and laugh to myself at their creative mischievous endeavors. I tried to see everything through their eyes. I was understanding and sympathetic to their toddler-sized exploration. I was always just so happy to have my children.. and glad that they were healthy and able to push their boundaries and make mischief and that they had each other as accomplices. Plus I recognized early on that they both inherited extra doses of my stubbornness and rebellious ways. I could never get upset with them no matter what they did. I never did much fussing at them at all, unless they were doing something dangerous or harmful. All I truly cared about was that they were safe, healthy and happy.

Once I could relax after settling in and focus all of my attention on the kids, the fun began. We played games of hide and seek all over the house. They rode their tricycles and bicycles down the hallway and on the big front porch. We ran and played in the meadow and explored the creek that ran along our driveway. We rode the four-wheeler all over the surrounding farmland. There was so much open free range at our new location that it was like being on our own frontier, on top of the world. It felt like home right away.

In mid-June, we took our first family trip out West. We flew this time, from Pittsburgh to Seattle. We were going to Washington state to visit with Jason's sister who lived in Seattle at the time. Jason's parents also went on the trip with us. It was mine and Jason's first time flying together, and the children's first time flying at all. Faith threw a big fit before take-off and almost got us kicked off the flight. She settled down as soon as we were in the air. Then the aircraft was hit with violent turbulence for a long duration of the flight and Jason got really nervous. He still had a fear of airplanes and PTSD from what he had witnessed on 09/11. It was an extremely stressful ordeal travelling to get there.

Once we landed, everything was fine. We spent several days in Washington. We explored Seattle, making our way to the top of the Space Needle and touring Pike Place Market. We visited the German Alpine village of Leavenworth, where the kids had the biggest ice cream cones I've ever seen, and the adults taste-tested German beer. We hiked over two thousand feet elevation up a mountain to see a glacial lake near Mount Index, called Lake Serene. It had flakes of gold floating on the surface and it was the coldest water I've ever felt. We also saw Bridal Veil Falls on that hike. Then we spectated as a Naked Bicycle Parade rolled through downtown Seattle. That was a bit of a culture shock. Overall, I was rather impressed by the state of Washington, and the grand scale of everything in the Northwest. The mountains, trees, wildlife and plant life.. all of it is massive, way bigger than anything on the East Coast. We had a nice trip, but I was happy to get back to our new place in West Virginia.

Near the end of June, our house in Front Royal sold and we were able to close on our new home. It officially became our piece of the world. So we started making more permanent alterations and planning ahead for our future there. Jason went to work on mowing and manicuring the three acres. There was a small patch of woods in the backyard and he began clearing that out and made a place to hang a hammock. He would lie in his hammock up there in the woods. It was like his secret man hideaway.

Our neighbor from across the street came to welcome us. Her name was Susie and she brought housewarming gifts of canned goods from her garden along with toys for the children. The house had been built by her nephew, and he was the one who sold it to us. She explained that the ground it sat on was once the hayfield of her family farm, the bigger 112-acre farm that surrounded our three acres. It had all been in her family for four generations. And another family by the last name of Fox had been the settlers of the land before her family came to live there.

Susie asked me if I had found the cemetery in our back yard. I had seen one in the upper field of her land, so I referenced it. She told me it wasn't that one, that there was one in the small patch of woods directly behind our house. I thought she was kidding but after she left, I walked up to the place where Jason had hung the hammock.. and sure enough, I started counting graves. There were at least twelve. They were only marked with a flat flagstone at the head, and smaller stones at the foot of each one. The hammock Jason had been lounging in was hanging directly over top of one of the graves. I had him take the hammock down immediately. In his previous tidying of that patch of woods, he had also mistakenly removed some of the flagstones, not knowing that they were grave markers. We replaced them all back as best we could. I told him that we had disturbed this cemetery and feared we would be haunted for doing so. That night we were awakened by strange noises. We both got up and loaded shotguns, thinking at first that it may be trespassers. We sat on the couch side by side with our weapons at the ready, just listening and waiting to act on our suspicions. We startled at every noise we heard. Then it dawned on me, this isn't a case of burglary. I told Jason, this must be the repercussions of disturbing the cemetery in the back yard. I thought we were being haunted. We sat there on the edge of our seats for the rest of that night, concerned with every single sound. It wasn't until later that we realized it was just the sounds of the newly-built house settling. We weren't being burglarized or haunted at all. We had stayed up all that night for no good reason.

The oversized front porch became our actual living room. It was so grand that it designated itself as the heart of the house. Most of our time and activities took place on that porch. It was the granddaddy of all porches. I could have lived just on that porch. I kept it swept and tidy and pretty. I hung wind chimes for their musical sound and placed potted star jasmine trees to scent the air. I really wanted a double rocking chair to put on the opposite side of the porch swing. Peepaw knew I wanted one, so he bought a white double rocker for me. He came to visit and surprised me with it, then assembled it for me on the porch. It was one of my favorite gifts I ever received. Peep and I sat there rocking, looking out over the mountains, and talking about the place. He loved my new property so much that he brought his best friend Earl over to see it one day. I realized early on that this house wasn't just a home for me, Jason, and our kids. This house was a home for all of our family and friends. A meeting place of common ground.

I felt peaceful and at ease to be back home in the hills and hollers of West Virginia. It was the first time I had lived there since I was five years old. I was now twenty-six. I was mostly happy because it was the first time I had lived near family since I left for college when I was eighteen. Now that I had come down from my Blue Mountain hideaway of isolation where I had no relatives around, I was ready to let them all back into my life on a more regular basis. I wanted the children to get to know their extended family better and to spend quality time with them. I wanted my kids to make memories with all their relations.

When we first moved back we had Meemaw, Peepaw, Mama and my brothers, plus Jason's parents and his grandpa just south of us in Nicholas County. Then we had Grandma Sparks, some of my aunts and uncles, and a bunch of my cousins north of us in neighboring Braxton County. So we were right in the middle of all those relatives and I had my sister Haley only four hours away in Lexington, Kentucky.

It was very important to me as a woman, wife, and mother to feel completely settled. I had been shuffled around and relocated so many times throughout my life, that I was just done with moving. I was never going to move again. I swore an oath on it. Of the six states, I had lived in, West Virginia was my truest home. When I first sat on my porch there and told myself I would live there till I died, I meant it. It was a promise to myself, for me and my children. I didn't want them to be rearranged all over the place like I had been. I wanted to plant firm roots in solid ground.. for them to have something to hold onto, to maintain a sense of home, in a state where their ancestral history was firmly established.

For the first time in my life, I felt like I had a clear picture of what the rest of my life would look like. I had the man I married. I had my only son and my youngest daughter. I had the home of my dreams that I could turn into the farm of my dreams. I had a respectable education in photography that I planned to use for a new career path. I was surrounded by my family. Everything had fallen into place as much as possible, aside from all the hardships and tragedies I had been through. I intended to raise J.J. and Faith, and grow old with Jason in our home.. and stay there until I was taken to Heaven to be with my Grace. This was the peace I had made with my life at this point and I felt like I could allow myself to be settled with where I was, even with all the pain that I still carried with me. I owed it to myself and my children, to carry on and move forward. My picture would never be complete with my first child missing. But it was at least a picture I could look at and feel some sense of pride and contentment with how far I had come in life. I found new strength within me, and determination to smile and make the most of every day.

There were three things I wanted to be ever since I was a little girl.. a mother, a farmer, and a wife.. in that order. So far I had been two out of the three. But the other one was within reach now. My intuition had told me when we first arrived at our new home, that we would have more land there someday. I had such a strong feeling about it that I felt compelled to tell Jason. He had seen my intuition proven right every time before, so he believed me. I told him that I didn't know how or why, but we would have a big farm. However, in the meantime, I planned to start drawing my farm picture on the three acres that currently belonged to us. I wanted to have animals of every kind, fruit trees, vegetable gardens, fences, barns and tractors. I envisioned everything and the way it would all be situated. We would have to work on all of this gradually over time. I knew it wouldn't happen overnight, but it gave me something to plan for and look forward to.

That July, we had J.J.'s fifth birthday party. His big present from us was a Jack Russell terrier puppy that I had Jason smuggle in the night before and hide where the kids wouldn't find it. We stuck the pup down in a gift bag and presented her to him on the morning of his birthday. When she jumped out of the bag, he was so surprised and excited to have his own doggy. We named her Cabela.

The kids were so happy. J.J. and Faith both loved her immediately. That afternoon we threw a big birthday party with a Pixar Cars theme. (That was J.J.'s favorite at the time, and I had decorated his new bedroom in the same theme.) The family came over and we cooked out. There were presents and balloons, cake and food all over the place. It was our first big celebration in our new home. When we took Cabela to the vet to be spayed, J.J. saw kittens there for sale. He wanted a black and white tuxedo kitten from the litter. Of course, I couldn't say no. I can never say no to a cute fur baby. Our Roscoe cat had gone feral as a great hunter on Blue Mountain, and we left him where he seemed happy, so we didn't have a cat in our new house. We took the tuxedo kitten home and named him Puss 'N' Boots. He fit right into all our chaos. Faith would dress him in her dolly clothes and force him to play in her dollhouse. He became her best friend. And Cabella was J.J.'s best buddy.

I was contemplating whether or not to homeschool J.J. for kindergarten or to send him to public school. I had never been away from him for long periods of time, and I wasn't ready to send him out into the big world. He was extremely intelligent for his age. He knew all the letters and numbers, he could read and write, he knew all fifty states and their capitals, and much more. I felt like he was too smart to wait another year before starting kindergarten but he hadn't acquired many social skills yet. We had lived secluded on Blue Mountain for all his formative years and he only had one friend there since we didn't live in a traditional neighborhood. Now we didn't live in a neighborhood at all. We were in the middle of nowhere. Considering all that, I decided to homeschool him and also to become proactive in getting the children involved in social activities so they could make some friends and become more socialized. I had sheltered them all their lives so far. It was time that they were given opportunities to broaden their horizons. I knew I couldn't trap them in a cage forever, as much as I wanted to. It would be unfair for me to hold them back from interacting with others.

That fall, I set up the home office as a schoolroom. I ordered accredited curriculum. I bought supplies and books, crafts and games. I filled the entire room with educational materials. I started taking the children to Sunday School and service every Sunday at our hometown church. It was always hard for me to walk through those doors but I went for the sake of the children. Jason and J.J. signed up for a karate class. I signed J.J. up for a soccer team and cub scouts. I signed Faith up for ballet classes. I got a library card and began taking the children for weekly visits to check out books and to participate in events held for kids at the library.

I started daily structured lessons and routines with J.J. for kindergarten and Faith for preschool. We began in the morning and spent hours working on lessons and crafts. We had a recess and lunch break, then a few more hours of lessons and games in the afternoon. In the evenings I drove them to their activities. Suddenly they went from toddler ages of cartoons and toys to busy little people with schedules of sports and disciplined activities. I made charts and hung them on the wall in the schoolroom, so the kids could be rewarded with stickers for all their good deeds and for doing small chores. I had only ever been away from the kids once when Jason took me out on a date for our anniversary while his parents babysat, and I cried the whole time. Plus the trip I took to Kentucky. I was having a hard time with being away from them while they were busy at practices. Most of the time I would stay and watch them, but sometimes I had to leave to go drop off or pick up the other one from their activity. J.J. was fine with that, but Faith would throw a giant fit if I had to leave her at ballet class to go get her brother. She was still a mama's girl. I carried her on my hip till she was four years old. She was my mini-me. I would also alternate spending one-on-one time with each of the kids while the other was at practice. They always liked that. I would take one or the other of them to the playground, to get a Happy Meal or to the library. Sometimes when J.J. was busy, I would take Faith to visit with Meemaw and Peepaw and when Faith was busy, I would take J.J. to visit them. Peepaw always called Faith his "Little Princess" and he would twirl around for her like a ballerina. He would help J.J. recite the Boy Scout Pledge.

Peepaw had hung his pilot wings up for good and taken an early retirement from his flying career. He and Meemaw had moved again from Florida, this time to stay. Peepaw was diagnosed with leukemia during the summer of the year 2000. It was discovered while he was having a routine physical for his job as a flight instructor but was in remission now. Shortly after he had initially received the diagnosis, he sat us all down one day and told us the bad news. He never spoke of it again other than to tell us that the cancer was in remission. He didn't want his illness to alter our view of him. He was still very active in golfing and fishing and he remained actively involved with the church he and Meemaw had been founders of when they were younger, New Life Assembly. He played his guitar and sang every Sunday. His church remained one of the biggest reasons why he was always drawn back to West Virginia. I was happy to have them so close by. I felt safe knowing they were down the road and a phone call away. I wanted to spend all the time with them that I could.

Grandma Sparks was living in an apartment when we first moved back to West Virginia. I would take the children and go at least once a week to visit her. We would sit and talk, I would take her to the grocery store, and I would tidy her house. It always made her so happy to see the kids. Her mind was starting to slip with Alzheimer's though. She had struggled with dementia for many years already. When she lived on the river she still kept a garden, ran a tiller, canned, weed-eated, mowed, cleaned gutters and worked nonstop. (I once saw her trim the grass along her entire driveway with a pair of scissors.) Now that she had moved into a smaller unfamiliar space, her mind was getting drastically worse but she would still sit and tell me stories, the ones she had always told. She would show me every picture she had and talk about Daddy. She had a small vegetable garden in what was supposed to be the flower bed in front of her apartment and she always fixed us something to eat. She would never let a guest enter her door and leave hungry. I never argued against her cooking. Grandma was still the best cook in the whole world.

We all became very busy with our new lives in Birch River. There was always something to do, people to see, and places to go. I had no friends or activities of my own. Everything I did revolved around J.J. and Faith with their busy schedules. I was basically a soccer mom type during this time. Jason seemed much better off with his new job, although he still had a long commute. He was on day shift and getting a normal night's sleep for the most part. (I still had the kids sleep with us so I could make sure they were okay.) I could tell a difference in Jason's temperament though. We were getting along better than we had in years. Everything we did involved and included the children.

I became an even better cook in my big modern kitchen. I would wear an apron and sometimes high heels when I was cooking up a storm. I was like a Stepford Wife. The family would come often and I would prepare big spreads of hors d'oeuvres and entrées. People began to take notice of my finally-acquired chef skills. It made me proud to be able to host and entertain my family members in my home. Meemaw especially complimented me and remarked on my hostess hospitality. We had family gatherings every chance we got. I loved having a house full of life and loved ones. Everyone seemed to feel at home there. I worked hard to keep the house and porches clean and make it a welcoming place where everyone felt relaxed and comfortable.

Jason worked hard on the outside. He kept the big lawn mowed. He made horseshoe pits and a baseball field in the front yard and kept the grill ready for cookouts. He cut a circle in the tall grass around the upper field on the neighbors' farm and she gave us permission to use it. I would take the kids and Cabela on daily walks up there in the big field, where Faith would pick me flowers and chase butterflies and J.J. would find caterpillars and catch lightning bugs. We all got plenty of fresh air and exercise.

Part 2

We spent a lot of time visiting our family at their homes too. We would go to Mama's, where she and Peepaw would play their guitars and sing together, my all-time favorite family gathering pastime. My kids would play toys and games with my little brothers. Uncle Andrew was especially loving and protective of J.J. and Faith, from the time they were babies. We would go to my Aunt Alta and Uncle Bud's farm where I had spent much of my childhood time in the summers. We would sit on the porch and watch the kids play while the elders told stories of the old days. (That porch was the place where I had my first chew of tobacco when I was 16 years old. Aunt Alta handed me a pouch of Red Man and said, "Try this Tiffy.") Alta always fixed a big feast for visitors. She was the next best cook to Grandma in my family. Also, we would take the kids hiking on the trails in the woods, through the caves and creeks, at Jason's parents' property. We had cookouts and family dinners there too. And we would meet Jason's grandfather in Craigsville to have lunch out with him at his favorite restaurant, then follow him to his house for coffee and dessert. We were always having get-togethers with family. It was a big part of why I made the choice to move us back to West Virginia. I wanted my children to really get to know all their family members, and they did.

I especially treasured my time when it was just me and the kids at home. A big part of me missed how it was on Blue

Mountain when it was just them and me. Now I had to share them with everyone else and all the activities they were involved in. But when we were home, playing with their toys and our pets, watching cartoons, baking cookies, having bath time and story time, then snuggling at the end of each day; those were always my favorite moments with J.J. and Faith.

Their personalities were developing even more as they got older and bigger. They were both very smart and creative. Faith was the quiet and independent one of the two. J.J. was very active and demanded more attention. I always knew exactly where he was and what he was doing. A lot of times I would be preoccupied with entertaining J.J., while Faith was happy to entertain herself and didn't want me to bother her or interfere. Faith was also a thrill seeker and that became more evident with a few stunts she pulled.

We were all out in the yard one day while Jason and I were putting a new swing set together for the kids. Faith suddenly just disappeared. I had already given her many talks, about how when mommy calls for her she needs to answer because she had scared me before with being so quiet and trying to play hide-and-seek when she wasn't supposed to. When I couldn't find her this time, I went into a full on panic attack. I ran all throughout the yard and in every room of the house. I was crying and screaming her name, searching everywhere for her. I was two seconds away from dialing 911 when she finally showed up. She had gone over the steepest side of the property, following the cat. Faith emerged with Puss-N-Boots under one arm, with her hair and clothes full of sticks and leaves. She had been on her own adventure. When I rushed to her and grabbed her up, I scolded her and yelled at her to never wander off like that again.

Also, Faith had taken a notion to ride a rocking horse from the top of the stairs to the bottom. Plus she proceeded to make way down the stairs, (on two separate occasions), wearing roller skates. Her second attempt at skating downstairs resulted in several cartwheels and somersaults before she reached the bottom. We didn't have a banister on the open side of the staircase and I was always worried sick that the kids would fall over the edge. She wasn't hurt in any of her daredevil tricks but I freaked out so dramatically each time that it would scare her and make her cry. She finally learned that these dangerous things were a big no-no, although I never spanked her. Faith has never once had a whipping her entire life. I never wanted to whip either one of my kids. I only wanted to keep them safe. My reaction of fear was enough to teach her not to do scary things anymore. In yet another incident, Faith was at the top of the hill in the back yard, sitting in the little red wagon. J.J. had caught a hop toad and it pleased him to throw it on his sister's head, in hopes of making her squall. Well, his plan worked. She threw such a gigantic fit that the wagon was propelled into forward motion, rolling fast all the way down the hill, across the gravel driveway and headed towards the cliffside. I yelled at Jason to intercept the runaway wagon, with a screaming Faith on board and bound for certain danger. He managed to jump in front of the wagon, stopping it just in time before it flew over the cliff.

Faith was furious and raring to punish J.J. for his foul play. She aimed to open up a can of whoop-ass on Bubby. (Did I mention she has my temper?) Somehow, the hop toad managed to hang on for the entirety of the wild ride.

We had our first winter in our Birch River home. We found a local tree farm and continued our tradition of picking out our Christmas tree, cutting it down and taking it home. We had a nice Christmas that year. Jason was making more money at his job, and we bought the children everything they asked for and more. We played in the snow all winter, building snowmen, sledding and snow skiing. We had a fireplace with a stone chimney and log mantle built onto the living room, including a big cast-iron wood-burning stove and a large stone hearth to sit on. It kept us warm all season. I missed my front porch-sitting weather, but we were cozy and comfortable by the fireplace in our pajamas, with hot chocolate and blankets, watching through the windows as the snow fell outside. I was always thankful for the changing of the seasons since I had returned to the mountains. Florida doesn't have four seasons, and that took much of the majesty of nature away during my childhood (even though we lived in the "lightning capital of the world" when I was a kid and I liked to see those spectacular storms roll in). I was happy that my children were being raised in the mountains. They have always lived in places where they could experience the beauty of all weather and all seasons, the flowers in the spring, the green grass of summer, the colorful leaves of fall and white snow in the winter. I loved to pick flowers with them, catch fireflies with them, rake up leaves for them to jump into, throw snowballs and build snowmen with them; any seasonal fun that can be had, we did it all.

Our pets were the children's number one source of entertainment during the cold months. We spent countless hours with Cabela and Puss-N-Boots. We taught Cabela tricks. She would jump through hula hoops and stand on her hind legs twirling around in circles. She was high-strung like J.J. so they were perfect companions for each other. He had a pair of garden boots that Cabela took a liking to. She was always trying to steal them, whether he was wearing them or not. One time she chased him up the satellite dish pole and stole one of his boots off his foot. Then while he clung to the pole, she pulled his pants clear off with her teeth, trying to get him to climb down and play with her. She snuggled with him at night, in a big pile with all of us and Puss 'N' Boots. There is nothing sweeter than a little boy with his pup.

That next spring, Cabela ran down the driveway and was killed on the main road. My mom and brothers were leaving and saw the whole horrific scene unfold. A car didn't hit her; she ran headfirst into the car and died instantly. She was running so fast she never even saw it coming. J.J. was at karate practice when it happened. I dreaded having to tell him when he got home. When the kids were babies, I came very close to deciding against allowing them to ever have pets because I never wanted them to feel the heartache of losing one. I ended up, instead, coming to the conclusion that the joy pets bring us is worth the pain of losing them in the long run.

I knew I was going to have to tell my son something that would break his heart that day which was the last thing on earth I ever wanted to do. When he got home, I sat him down in his bedroom and told him about his doggy in the most gentle and age-appropriate way I could. He was devastated. Faith was too. Seeing my children crying and heartbroken broke my heart in a way I had never known before. I would have done anything to take that hurt away from them and claim it for myself, to spare them from sadness of the loss of their loved one. We buried Cabela under the dogwood tree in the meadow, and Jason made a cross for her with her name on it. That was my children's first experience with death. They knew all about their sister Grace and how she was an angel in Heaven. They had been to her grave frequently with us to take flowers, but they were too young to comprehend the finality of death.

The only thing I knew to do to cheer them up was to get them another dog. I researched different breeds, trying to find one that was good with kids and not as prone to roam. I decided on the Dachshund breed. I searched the internet and found a female mini-weenie dog named Faith. She was located in Missouri. I paid the fee for the puppy, along with airfare for her to be delivered on a flight. Jason and I kept it a secret from the kids. We wanted it to be a surprise.

The puppy was scheduled to arrive on St. Patrick's Day. Jason made arrangements to pick her up from the airport in Charleston, where she would land from St. Louis. I decided to name her Clover (since two Faiths would be confusing). I bought a green teddy bear with a four-leafed clover for the pup. I made St. Patrick's Day cookies for the kids. Jason called ahead to tell me when he would arrive. I sat the children down on the floor, making them close their eyes when I heard Jason coming up the gravel driveway.

He brought the tiny five-week-old puppy in and placed her on the floor in front of the kids. Then I told them to open their eyes. They saw Clover and their little faces lit up with big smiles and bright eyes. They loved her as soon as they met her and I knew I had made the right decision. (We had no idea that day what a long-standing legacy that dog would leave.) Clover wasn't a replacement for Cabela, but she gave J.J. and Faith something else to love. She brought joy to them in their time of sadness just as they had done for me in my sadness. That same spring, we took the kids and Clover to hike a section of the Appalachian Trail on Mount Rogers in Virginia. Jason's dad was doing the entire trail and he had told us of the wild ponies in the Grayson Highlands State Park, so I wanted to go see them. Jason and I had backpacks full of camping gear, with Clover on a leash and the kids hiking along like troopers. We found the wild ponies, and they ran around me in a circle formation, getting closer and closer to me. It was magical. I took several pictures of them with my new professional camera. I still keep one of those pictures framed above my kitchen stove. One of the photographs I took of the alpha stallion of the herd, was published in a book the called *Appalachian Trail Guide for Southwest Virginia*, Fourth Edition. That night we set up camp at the top of Mount Rogers. We built a fire, roasted hotdogs and marshmallows, then settled into our tent and experienced the worst thunderstorm I've ever encountered.

That summer I got my business license, business cards, plus all the equipment I thought I would need and started my photography business. J.J. was set to attend public school in the fall. So the room that had been our homeschool room was transformed into my office. I named my business Sparks Photography, in honor of my father, Mark Sparks. Daddy studied photography at Yellowbird Photography School in White Sulphur Springs, WV when he and Mama were first married and Haley was a baby. They lived in a cabin on the school's property. That is where I was conceived, at that cabin in Greenbrier County. He was as naturally gifted at photography as he was with his artwork. I was always told I had an eye for it too.

I started getting business clients immediately. I was focusing my work mostly on wedding photojournalism. My first real job was the wedding of Jason's co-worker. The bride and groom came to our house for a consultation, and I became instant friends with the bride, Kerri. I shot their wedding that summer and picked up several other jobs too. I became swamped with hours of editing and designing custom-made, top-of-the-line Italian leather and silk coffee-table books, working with a highly reputable company based in the Province of Pordenone, Italy. Word of mouth kept bringing more and more customers. Before I knew it, my business turned into a successful full-time job.

At the end of that summer, we traded the Ford Explorer SUV in on a Chevy Avalanche 4wd truck. We planned a trip to Maine to pick Jason's dad up from his completion of the Appalachian Trail. I mapped our trip out so that we could take the children to see the Statue of Liberty on the way but I wanted to visit it from the Jersey side in order to avoid Manhattan traffic altogether. We packed up and set out to travel north. I had never been to New York City before but I could see the smog looming over it when we were about thirty miles out and I could smell it. I could tell from a distance that it was a dirty city. We made it to the New Jersey side of the Hudson River where we boarded a ferry that took us to the Statue of Liberty. Some things you see on TV or in pictures and it doesn't do them justice. Some sights are way more impressive in person. The Statue of Liberty is not one of those sights. It looks way more grand and majestic on film than it does in person. I was not impressed by it at all but I was happy that the kids got to see it. We climbed up to the torch, herded like tourist cattle. I could feel ten layers of filth on my skin from the nastiness of the Manhattan skyline. I was just ready to get the hell out of there and find a place to wash off. I took a wrong turn headed towards Connecticut where we had reserved a camping spot for the night on a river. My entire plan of that part of the trip to avoid New York City, well that was an epic fail. I ended up driving our new Avalanche through every ghetto hood, the Holland Tunnel, the Bronx, Harlem, Queens and Brooklyn. We saw them all up close and personal. And the traffic was so bad, I just knew I was going to get our expensive new truck scratched and banged up. I swore I would never go near New York City again. No thanks. Places like that remind me of why I'm a country girl. I like to visit some cities but that was not one of them. I've been there, I've seen it. Once in a lifetime thing.

We made it to Connecticut way behind schedule on account of the ghetto detour. We set up camp and I jumped in the river to rinse off but I still felt dirty. The next morning I found the shower house, and it was the best shower I ever took. We made our way up to Maine. We camped in a harbor there, on a bay as still and smooth as glass. You couldn't tell where the grey water met the grey sky that day. We took the kids kayaking on the harbor. It was a location known for whales and I was just waiting for one to tip our boat over. The harbor was eerily calm.

We travelled north along the coastal highway, stopping at lighthouses and any place that looked interesting. I photographed all the New England architecture that caught my eye. We dined at a fancy restaurant on Maine lobster. J.J. freaked out when the waitress brought it to the table, with its eyeballs intact. It was one of the best meals I ever ate but he was scared to death of it. He always had a fear of crawfish and this made it worse. That lobster, in his mind, was a monster crawfish. I joked and told him I was going to put the lobster in his sleeping bag that night.

We arrived at Mount Katahdin, the end of the Appalachian Trail, to pick Jason's dad up from his thru-hike. His dad had written a blog during his journey on the trail and we had read along and followed his adventures. We met up with him at the bottom of the mountain. He was waiting for Jason to hike with him to the top to complete the last leg of his long journey. He was happy to see the kids and to know we would be taking him home after his months away. Jason and his dad hiked to the top and I took the children as far as we could go on the trail. We fed chipmunks and I looked for moose. I was bound and determined to see a moose in Maine. We camped that night at the base of the mountain and headed back home the next day. I never saw a one damn moose in Maine. But I got a lot of great pictures on that trip, some of which still hang on the walls of my home.

Back in WV, it was time for J.J. to start public school for the first grade. I knew he would be fine but I was worried about how I would handle it. I knew I was going to have a severe case of separation anxiety. We signed them both up for t-ball that fall, where they made some new friends. Faith was back in ballet class and J.J. was still in Cub Scouts. I reluctantly took my little man to his first day of school. I walked him to his classroom with his backpack and lunchbox, helped him find his desk, hugged him tightly, told him to have a good day and told him I loved him at least a dozen times, then I sat in the parking lot and cried for over an hour. When I made it back home, I took Faith for a four-wheeler ride. She looked up at me and said, "You can dwive

Mama?" She could tell I was sad and she picked me a bouquet of flowers. We planted apple trees that day with Jason. It was the beginning phase of turning our land into a farm. We also planted cherry trees and started a small grape vineyard.

I was back working steady with my photography business shooting weddings, sports, pets, senior pictures, etc. I had so much work coming in that my housework was piled up and neglected. My OCD tendencies were forced to be put on the back burner. And this was the beginning of the kids' Lego phase, so I was always stepping on the little jagged-edged blocks, and figures with their swords sticking up… they were all out to get me. I was having a hard time juggling everything that we all had going on but I tried my best every day.

I spent a lot of one-on-one time with Faith while J.J. was at school. Her bedroom was decorated all Disney Princess. We had daily tea parties, played hours of Barbie dolls, baby dolls and dress-up. She would come down the stairs a hundred times a day and every time she would be wearing a different wardrobe of princess dresses, jewelry, high heels and crowns. She was my little princess. We would play with Clover and Puss 'N' Boots, forcing them to dress up too. Faith was still constantly drawing. If she ran out of paper she would make art on a paper towel, an envelope, herself and eventually the walls of the house. She would draw and paint on any and every surface she could find. It was her obsession and her talent. I was always finding new murals on the walls. I left them there on display because they were all precious to me. Faith was still a night owl too. Sometimes she would get up in the middle of the night to play Legos or video games. She has always maintained a case of her original night owl tendencies.

Toward the end of that year, I decided to have Clover bred to a male mini-weenie dog. Clover was a registered piebald Dachshund. Her parents' names were Ardy Fardy and Rosie Tulip. I found a red long-haired male named Mr. Skittles. The vet had suggested it would be a bad idea to breed Clover because she had a case of the buck teeth and her puppies could inherit that trait. I didn't heed the vet's advice. I took Clover for a conjugal visit to Mr. Skittles and she came home with baby puppies onboard. We pampered her with cheese and vanilla ice cream during her entire pregnancy.

On the night of January 13, 2008, Clover gave birth to two puppies—first a blonde female pup and second was a brown male pup. She delivered them in our living room beside the warm fireplace with me attending as midwife. Because of Clover's buck teeth, I had to remove the sacks from the pups. She tried but wasn't able to. The children had been in the bathtub when the puppies were born, but they came out in time to see them within seconds of their arrival. They were the size of mice, so tiny and cute. The kids were very happy and excited to have little baby newborn animals. We named the girl Latte and the boy Mocha, based on their colors.

We watched the puppies grow and change. We saw every phase of them crawling, opening their eyes, learning to walk and wag their tails; we heard their first whines, barks and growls.

Clover could never pick them up with her mouth but she would roll them around with her snout. She was a good little mama. Jason said we couldn't keep both the puppies but the kids and I were so attached to them, we couldn't possibly part from them.

Peepaw had a little dog named Rascal. He was Peep's best friend and travelling buddy and he had Rascal for a very long time. That little dog was like a child to my grandfather. He had passed away shortly before Clover's puppies were born. Peepaw was broken-hearted. I went to his house soon afterward to offer my condolences. He walked me up to the wood-line on the hillside in his back yard and showed me the place where he had buried Rascal. Peepaw hung his head and cried. I just stood there and held his hand. Seeing my big strong hero with tears falling from his gentle eyes, was one of the saddest things I have ever seen in all my life.

I wanted to cheer him up. So when the new pups were weaned from Clover, I took them to Peepaw's house and placed them both on his lap. I told him to choose one for himself, or that he could even have both of them if he wanted. He held the puppies and studied them. I could tell he was thinking it over. He favored the brown male of the two but, after considering taking Mocha, Peepaw decided against it. He was still too upset about Rascal and didn't want to subject himself to getting attached to another companion. I told him I would keep both the pups in case he changed his mind.

The kids and I ended up somehow converting their names from Mocha and Latte to MoMo and LaLa. We have always had a tendency of giving our animals multiple names but the new versions of their names stuck and that's what they came to be permanently known by. Puss 'N' Boots had become the puppies' uncle. He snuggled with them and bathed them, and Clover didn't mind. Uncle Puss was their babysitter. We had a weenie dog family; Clover, MoMo and LaLa. We watched them run and play together. We snuggled with them and played with them constantly. They brought us all so much joy.

I worked all that winter organizing a local art festival. I booked live music, catering and as many local artists and craftsmen as I could gather. I called it Appalachian Artisan Festival, and I intended for it to be an annual event. That spring, I hosted the event in Summersville at the historic Brown Oaks mansion. The local newspapers and radio stations promoted the event. I had local artists, painters, pottery makers, jewelers and photographers. I had my own display for Sparks Photography. Some of us set up on the lawn with tents, and others set up in the grand house. The catering company brought fancy hors d'oeuvres and beverages. Three local bluegrass bands played on the covered porch. All my family came out to support me. The city and county were also very supportive of my endeavor. It turned out to be a very successful event. Peepaw sat beside me and told me that I was starting my own legacy, that it was basically my turn to carry the torch and pass it on. He was genuinely proud of me that day for what I had accomplished.

In May, we lost three of our beloved pets. Puss-N-Boots was hit by a car on the main road. I went to the county animal shelter immediately and adopted a female Calico kitten. She was the only Calico one of her litter, all the rest were solid black. I took her home and we named her Ellie May. Then a pack of wild dogs came to the farm and killed Clover and Latte while they were playing in the meadow. They almost got MoMo too but Jason managed to save him and run the pack of dogs away. It was a tragic time for us all. We buried our pets underneath the dogwood tree, beside Cabela, and I saw the saddest thing I've ever seen an animal do. MoMo buried his own mother. We dug the hole but we watched as he piled dirt over Clover. He would get down in her grave and spread the dirt with his nose and pat the dirt down on her with his paws, then get back out and rake more dirt into the hole with his paws. He did this until he had completely covered her grave. MoMo was the only one we had left of our little weenie dog family. He became the king of the farm.

J.J. finished first grade at Birch River Elementary. He seemed to like public school. However, he did get called to the principal's office a few times. Once they called me down to the school and had me join a meeting with the principal. J.J. was in trouble that time for "fixing a computer" because he was not supposed to be on the computer in the first place. I was like really? Pat the boy on the back and tell him, "good job", instead of calling me down here for an innocent misdemeanor. They also made a common practice of taking his recess away if he was too hyper. That's the stupidest thing schools can do to punish children, especially active little boys. They weren't meant to sit in a desk all day like statues. They are not programmed like robots. Little boys are meant to run and play and get all their orneriness out of their systems. Regardless, J.J. made it through his first year of public school, and I was very proud of him.

That summer I began expanding on my lifelong dream of having my own farm. I was "Photographer Tiff", but I really wanted to be "Farmer Tiff". Farms need lots of animals, so I started with baby ducks, baby bunnies and baby chicks. I wanted to raise all of my animals and tame them myself. MoMo especially loved the baby animals; he became a mother hen to every one of them. Jason and his dad built a chicken coop and put up fencing beside it for a vegetable garden. We planted seeds and watched them grow. It was a start but we still had a long ways to go.

Fall came, and it was time for Faith to start kindergarten. I never adjusted to J.J. being away at school for first grade; now he would be in second grade and Faith would be at school too. I was dreading the thought of both my little ones setting out into the big world away from me and the safety net of home. I didn't ever want to be apart from them. On their first day of school, I packed their lunches, laid out their clothes, prepared their backpacks and took their first-day-of-school picture. I drove them to Birch River Elementary and walked each of them into their classrooms. I kissed them, hugged them and told them to have a good day so many times that their teachers finally had to shoo me away. I sat in the parking lot, in my truck and cried for hours. When parents say, "kids grow up too fast," that is the honest to God's truth. You blink your eyes, and time slips through your hands. The older they get, the faster time flies by. Every step they take is another step closer to the day they will be full grown and fly from your nest. I just wanted time to slow down and stand still so I could always keep them with me. I always told them and still do, "Just stay with me and be Mommy's little babies forever."

The kids were involved in after-school activities—ballet, Cub Scouts, T-ball, etc. Their schedules were busier than ever. Faith's teachers called me in for a meeting at school. They were concerned about her because she wasn't speaking at all in the classroom. They asked me if she was capable of talking. Faith was always very shy around people that she didn't know and I think she was having a hard time being away from me. We had always been inseparable. I assured them she would eventually warm up to them and there was no need to worry. Faith did finally become more comfortable at school and started to make friends. Her teachers were relieved to find out that she could, in fact, speak.

Also that fall, after 9 years I finally tracked down my little sister Marci for the first time since she was eleven years old and I had seen her at Daytona Beach. Now she was twenty-one years old and had a son of her own close to two years old, named Anthony. Haley was twenty-nine at the time and had still never even met

Marci. We made plans for all of us to meet at Haley's apartment in Lexington, KY on October 14th. With me in West Virginia, and Marci living in Ohio, Haley's location was the halfway point. It was a monumental moment for all three of us sisters to be together for the first time. I travelled towards Lexington but I got lost in a town called Versailles along the way. I was running early so I spent some time wandering around a cemetery there as I tried to emotionally prepare myself for our meeting. I finally arrived at Haley's. We waited impatiently, so excited and nervous to see our now grown-up baby sister and to meet our little nephew.

Part 3

Marci and Anthony arrived and there were hugs and tears, smiles and laughter, all at the same time. It was an extremely emotional reunion for all of us, to say the least. Marci had been raised as an only child by her widowed mother. She didn't get to grow up with her sisters or have anyone the way Haley and I had always had each other. She had a difficult upbringing too but she had to walk her journey alone. She never got to meet our father, since he passed before she was born. Marci was our father's best legacy. She was a beautiful final tribute that he left behind, the last mark he made on this world. Haley and I had been deprived of our little sister all her life. Although we weren't raised with Marci and had been separated from her for 21 years, there was no denying that we were all sisters. She looked like us and she had the same personality traits as us. It was as if we had all just seen each other yesterday, like no time had ever passed by at all. Marci wasn't a stranger. She was one of us; part of our daddy and part of me and Haley. We were cut from the same cloth, made with the same fabric. Our deeply rooted genetic and hereditary connection bonded us all together instantly.

We talked and talked, catching up on all the years we had been involuntarily separated. We spent hours looking through old pictures and telling each other stories about our childhoods and family history. We laughed and cried and reminisced about all that had transpired and what could have been. We wondered what Daddy would think of all his girls together. If he had lived, our estrangement never would have happened. He would have seen to it that we sisters had been together all along. He would have united us but, even though our father had been gone for almost twenty-two years, he still united us. We were all three his greatest works of art, his masterpieces. And that drew us all together with such a strong magnetic pull that no universal force could have kept us apart forever. We were bound to one another through our father. All the time that had passed before suddenly became irrelevant. The three of us sisters were together now; that's what mattered most.

Marci was born in Somerset, KY like me and she had been mostly raised there. She told us about two of Dad's best friends that still lived in Somerset, Blaine and Mark Purcell. They were Cherokee brothers and they had known our father very well for many years. They were also pallbearers at Dad's funeral. We had already planned to visit our father's grave together in Somerset that same day. We all agreed that we should try to meet up with Blaine and Mark. Marci still kept in touch with them and had their phone numbers, so she called and arranged for us to get together with them.

We drove to Somerset, the three of us and Anthony. We stopped along the way to buy silk flowers in fall colors. We found our father's grave and replaced the old flowers with the new bouquet we had carefully arranged. It was the first time I had been to Somerset, or to his grave, since the day of his funeral. We surrounded his graveside, all of us holding hands. It was a somber and sentimental moment for us girls. It brought back feelings and memories that I had buried a long time ago. All of that rose to the surface when I stood there with both of my sisters but it felt right for the three of us to be there together, honoring the memory of our beloved father.

That evening, we went to Blaine's house, where we met with him and his brother Mark, as well as their families. There was an instant connection with them. They immediately felt like our own family. They told us stories and showed us pictures of them with Dad. They had all been members of a weight lifting club together, called, Touch of Class. I had seen a photograph of my dad with them years earlier in Grandma's collection but I didn't realize back then that they were two of his best friends. They remembered Haley and me from Dad's funeral when we were just little girls. It meant as much to them as it did to all of us, to have this common bond and connection. It seemed as though Daddy had orchestrated the whole reunion like he intended to bring us all together for a purpose. We were all destined to meet up at this crossroads. It was preordained.

We drove back to Lexington after dark, talking the whole way there. We stayed up late in the night having more girl talk and sister time. The following day we had breakfast together, made plans for our next gathering, and then we all went our separate ways. (I got lost in Versailles again on my way out of town.) During the four-hour drive back home, I was recounting all the memories we made during our long-awaited reunion, smiling with contentment in the knowledge that Marci had come into our lives to stay this time. I vowed to never lose track of her again.

That November we had Thanksgiving at Mama's place. Haley and Javier came from Kentucky and Mama's new boyfriend Jack was there. Javier prepared a Cuban style dinner for everyone. We feasted, visited, and then gathered around Peepaw while he played his guitar and sang to us, every tune we requested. Peepaw looked like a cross between Johnny Cash and Elvis and he could sing just like both of them too. They were his favorites. Peepaw was the most talented man I've ever known. He was my favorite. It was one of our best Thanksgivings on record. We all had much to be thankful for, especially our fellowship with family that day.

For Haley's 30th birthday on January 21, 2009, I had planned for Marci to meet me in Lexington to surprise Haley at her birthday party downtown. I got lost in Versailles again on my way there but I made it to Haley's apartment in time and went to the party with her. Marci showed up right on cue; Haley was very surprised and so excited. We celebrated and stayed up late again visiting. This time it was all just very light-hearted and fun. We had breakfast at a restaurant the next morning and said our goodbyes till our next sister-time.

In late winter, Grandma moved to downtown Gassaway and was living in a building on Main Street with my Aunt JoAnn. Aunt Jo and her husband, Tom had also opened a restaurant downtown called the Red Rooster Cafe. I was going to visit frequently with Grandma at their new place. Her mind had deteriorated even further with Alzheimer's. Every time I would take J.J. and Faith to see her, she would ask several times, "Now whose kids are these?" It was sad to see her suffer from memory loss. (Alzheimer's is one of the most difficult illnesses to witness, with the effects it has on its victim. Their memories are imprisoned within their mind.) She still told me the same stories she always had, although she began to change the endings with twist plots I had never heard before. She would show me all her pictures, drink her coffee then doze off, still holding her coffee cup, with her cat curled up on her lap.

Aunt Jo offered me space in her building to open a photography studio. I accepted and set up my lighting equipment and backdrops, plus an exhibit of my framed photography. I worked there while the kids were at school, happy to be running my business among a family where I could spend time with my aunt and uncle. Other family members would also drop in and see us during the time that I worked in Gassaway. I would walk down the road and visit with Grandma every day too, till it was time for me to go pick the kids up from school.

For Easter Sunday that year, Meemaw and Peepaw came to my house to have dinner. It was still cold outside, so we had a nice fire going. Peepaw had been having gallbladder problems. He sat on the hearth in front of the fireplace and said the heat helped to relieve his pain. Not long after that, Peepaw and Meemaw went to his Army reunion at Fort Benning Georgia, and then to Florida to check on a new property they had recently bought in Lakeland. He wasn't feeling well, so they came back home earlier than they had initially planned. He went in for surgery to have his gallbladder removed. I met him and Meemaw at their house as they were getting home from the hospital. Peepaw was having a hard time walking from the driveway to the door, so I held his arm and helped him inside to his recliner. I had never seen him so weak. Mama and my brothers came over, and Peepaw was speaking to Andrew and Anthony like he was telling them goodbye.

On May 2nd, I returned to Lexington to meet up with my sisters and attend the 135th Kentucky Derby. Guess what? I got lost in Versailles. Again. This time Haley and Javier got really mad at me because they were finally frustrated with the fact that I managed to get lost and end up there every single time, and we were running on a tight schedule to get to the Derby. I met up with them and Marci at their place. We all rode together to Louisville and we made it in time. I had never been to Churchill Downs before. I was super excited to see the Kentucky Derby for the first time in person, having watched it on tv for years. We were there during the Swine Flu epidemic and we had tickets for the infield. It was cold and rainy, crowded and chaotic. Everywhere you turned, people were wearing surgical masks. It was like a scene from a horror movie. We drank Mint Juleps, placed our bets and had a grand time. My favorite part was going into the paddock to get a good look at the Thoroughbreds and jockeys up close. I took a ton of pictures. We all stood as close as we could get to LeAnn Rimes while she performed the National Anthem. Then we spectated the fastest two minutes in sports. The longshot, Mine That Bird, won.

There was later a movie made about him, called "50 to 1". It was a once in a lifetime experience, and I was happy to share it with my sisters.

Back at home, my favorite cousin named Sissy, (who had always been an avid rider and a gifted horsewoman) offered to give me one of her horses, a paint, Missouri Fox Trotter filly. The foal had been born on my cousin Shane's land in Greenbank, West Virginia (Pocahontas County) on September 7, 2008. She was only 8 months old. She was exactly the kind of horse I had always wished for. After riding hundreds of horses in my life so far, I never had one of my own. It was another lifelong dream of mine and Sissy was making that dream come true. I was over-the-moon happy and grateful for the gift Sissy was giving me. I felt like the luckiest girl in the world.

In the same timeframe, my intuition about having more land also came true. Our neighbor Susie who owned the farmland surrounding our property offered to deed us a big portion of her land in exchange that we turn it back into a working farm like it had been when her grandmother was living and running the place. Susie added a condition that I help her find a horse for herself, plus I would have to be the caretaker of the land and the horses. She was past retirement age, with no family of her own. Susie had also always wanted a horse but she would have to rely on me to do the work and upkeep. It was agreed. It was the best deal I had ever been presented with. It all seemed too good to be true.

Peepaw hadn't recovered from his surgery and he was admitted to the hospital in Summersville. I went to see him straight away. He had gone downhill very quickly. Some of his closest friends were there visiting when I arrived. He got up to use the bathroom.. and I saw him standing at the mirror, looking at his reflection like he didn't recognize the man he saw. His hair was disheveled so I got his brush from his travel bag (the same hairbrush he had used as long as I could remember) and I brushed his hair for him. Peepaw had always practiced immaculate hygiene and always presented himself well-groomed. I thought maybe he was upset with his reflection because his hair had been a mess. When I fixed it for him, he looked back in the mirror and seemed almost child-like. He had an ornery grin and a sparkle in his eyes. He appeared as I would have imagined him to be when he was a mischievous little boy.

Peepaw returned to his hospital bed. His friends left and I sat by his side to visit with him. I told him about the Kentucky Derby. He seemed pleased that my sisters and I got to share that experience. I also told him that my cousin Sissy was going to give me a horse from her herd to have as my own. He was very happy about that. He knew it had been one of my biggest dreams to have my own horse. He said to me, "Peepaw will buy you a saddle for your horsey." I then told him about the deal with the land and how it would allow me to have the farm I had always hoped for. His eyes lit up with genuine pride, knowing that all these wishes of mine were finally coming true. He was the man who raised me and knew how much all this meant to me. He had the look of a proud father.

Peepaw was released from the hospital, and Meemaw took him home. I had been praying constantly for him and his health. I had faith that he would be healed. He had always been so strong. I believed that he would recover and go back to doing his normal Peepaw things.. fishing, golfing, watching NASCAR, playing his guitar and singing, going to church and travelling, reading his Bible and praying, spending time with his family and being our leader—everything he loved, and everything that made him the most legendary man I've ever known. He was such a monumental presence, I just always felt like he would be around forever. He was still young, only 67. Even having known that he had leukemia and that he had battled it for nearly ten years; I always saw him as invincible. He was my hero.

Mama called me and said that Peepaw had been taken to the hospital in Beckley. I could hear the urgency and fear in her voice. She told me I needed to come as quickly as possible. I got in my truck and drove straight there, as fast as I could. When I made it to his room, I wasn't at all prepared for what I would encounter. Peepaw was lying helpless in a hospital bed. He wasn't able to walk and he could no longer speak. He had gone from a big strong man to being completely incapacitated within a matter of days. All the years he had won his battle over leukemia, it all caught up with him at once. Aunt Vicki and Haley made it there as fast as they could from Florida. We all gathered around Peepaw. He had all "his girls" there by his side. That is exactly how he would have wanted it to be.

That look of disappointment in his gentle eyes, the look none of us ever wanted to see, it was there. But he was disappointed with himself this time because he had so much to say to all of us, especially to Meemaw, and he couldn't say a word. He had the look of worry in his eyes and the look of fear. He couldn't talk, but I knew what he was trying to say, just by looking into his eyes. He was worried about leaving us. He was worried about who would take care of his wife. He was afraid of not being able to say goodbye and not being able to tell us all how much he loved us. That look of disappointment was out of concern for his family, the ones he had given his whole life and his entire heart to. He knew how his departure from this world would irrevocably devastate us all to the core of our foundation. He was our foundation.

We all stayed at his bedside day and night for the next few days. Doctors and nurses came in and out. We were trying to get answers, asking how his health could have deteriorated so drastically. They were running as many tests as they could, but we were only given inconclusive explanations. It was becoming more apparent that our time with Peepaw was rapidly running out and there was nothing anyone could do to slow that time down or to stop what was happening. He had relayed his wishes to Meemaw when they were younger, that he never wanted to be hooked up to machines or have his life prolonged in any unnatural way. There was no choice but to respect his wishes.

I just held my Peepaw's hand, I talked to him and I played Elvis and Johnny Cash music for him. Haley and I got a chocolate milkshake from Dairy Queen for him and fed him. He loved Dairy Queen and had taken us there all our lives. (He even took his little doggies there for treats.) When we were little, he always fed us ice cream. Now we were feeding him. I went home from the hospital one night that week, and I read all of the letters Peepaw ever wrote to me. He had written to me every time distance separated us when I was at boarding school and college and in California. I kept all his letters. After I read them, I sat down and wrote a letter to Peepaw. I poured my heart into it and stained the paper with the tears that fell while I was writing it.

I went to the hospital the next morning. I asked that my family let me have some time alone with Peepaw. I sang to him, *Will The Circle Be Unbroken*. I sat beside him, holding his hand, and I read aloud to him the letter that I had written. When I finished reading it, I stood up and kissed him on his forehead. I was crying uncontrollably. I told him that it was okay, that he could let go and let the Lord take him to Heaven, where he had earned his place among the angels. I told him that we would all take care of Meemaw for him. Then I said to him, "I love you Peepaw." He looked into my eyes, squeezed my hand and with all of the strength he could find, he spoke to me. Peepaw said, "I love you too, babe."

I stayed all that night at his bedside. The next day, Peepaw was moved to the Hospice House. I followed the ambulance there and I stayed as he was settled into his room. I hadn't slept for days.

Meemaw suggested I should go home and get some rest. I hugged my Peepaw and kissed his cheek. I told him that I loved him. And I headed home. On my way, I stopped and bought a burning bush in honor of Peepaw. I planted it as soon as I got home. To this day, it still serves as a daily reminder, of the last time I saw the greatest man I have ever known.

On Sunday morning, May 17, 2009, Peepaw was called home by the Lord. He earned his eternal Pilot Wings. He soared in the Heavens and sang with the angels. If there was any lasting legacy he would have wanted to leave behind, I believe it to be his unconditional love of his family and his faithful love for the Lord. Both of those legacies continue to live on. His memorial service was held in the church that he helped to found and build, New Life Assembly. He had a dream, before the last time he and Meemaw moved to West Virginia. He saw it as a sign for them to return. He dreamed about daffodils growing out of the snow. We laid him to rest during the season when the white snow melts away and the sun raises the yellow daffodils up from the ground.. in his beloved mountains of West Virginia.

I was given my horse on May 25th. I named her Pocahontas Painted Mayflower. She is the best gift I have ever been given in all my life. I could never thank Sissy enough for her. I kept her at Aunt Alta's farm for a while, till I could get proper fencing and a nice place for her at home. I would go every chance I had to see her and spend as much time with her as I could so we would get to know each other and form a bond. We were also given the land from the deal we had made with our neighbor Susie. My intuition had been right again. I stood in the upper field that had just been deeded to us, and I felt Peepaw smiling down on me. He wasn't here on earth, but he saw my dreams come true from Heaven. He gave me his blessing to be happy. His presence was still with me. Peepaw became my guardian angel.

Jason and I celebrated our 10th wedding anniversary that year. He bought me a six-string Johnson acoustic guitar as an anniversary gift. Peepaw and Mama had taught me the basics of how to play when I was a kid. I still remembered the three chords of G, A, D and one strumming pattern that I had learned from them but I didn't have the natural musical talent that the rest of my family had been gifted with. I was happy to have an instrument of my own though and intended to progress enough in playing it just for the sake of making a racket on my front porch. I didn't even know how to tune it at first. That guitar was one of the nicest anniversary presents Jason ever gave me.

That summer was all about our farm expansion. We were all busy painting the picture we envisioned for the land. We went to the post office and picked up special deliveries for J.J. after he had selected and mail-ordered some endangered species of baby chicks and ducks for himself. He was in charge of all our feathered friends. Faith was a natural Snow White and tamed all of our furry friends.. they followed her everywhere she went. Our cat, Ellie May, had a litter of three kittens. MoMo was the reigning king of all the animals. The children helped me gather eggs from the chicken coop. They helped us bring in vegetables from the garden. I was proud to have our own homegrown food. I canned everything we harvested that season. We all had important roles to play on our big farm. I continued to count all of my blessings.

At the end of that summer, J.J. and Faith teamed up for another epic "Bubby and Faif" mission. I had worked hard cleaning the house all day. It was a big house and I would break my bad back to make it sparkle and shine. I had just mopped the floors and washed my bedding. Lastly, I put all the clean sheets, pillowcases and bedspread back together for the grand finale of my cleaning spree. I went outside to tend to the animals. When I came back in, I found a trail that led from the dining room door, down the hallway, all the way to my bedroom; a trail of chicken feathers and chicken shit on my freshly mopped floors. I'm sure the look on my face was priceless. When I followed where the trail led I found, on my clean reassembled bed a chicken. "Bubby" and "Faif" took off running and laughing maniacally. I wrestled the Golden Comet hen to catch her. Chicken feathers were flying everywhere. It looked like I had ripped open a feather bed and was having a pillow fight. I finally caught her, dodged my way around the land mines through the hallway, and set the confounded hen free outside. I was madder than an old wet hen. I hollered to the kids, who were already hiding from me, and told them they better hide where I won't find them. It was an angry mama bear game of hide-and-seek. I hid in the laundry room where I busted out laughing at what my little trouble makers had done. I secretly thought it was clever and hilarious, but I couldn't let them off the hook. Aunt Alta had given me a fly swatter that had a miniature flip-flop attached to the end of it. I grabbed that flip-flop fly swatter and started chasing the little rebels. They revealed their locations but they were faster than me. Faith got away. I barely caught up with J.J., then he and I went round in circles while I paddled his behind with the flip-flop fly swatter. He was laughing the whole time and I was trying my best not to laugh. He got set loose from the mean ole mama bear. I yelled at both the kids in my most authoritative voice and said, "Don't you ever put a chicken on my bed again!" Then I hid myself again and had another big laugh. That particular fly swatter went missing after the fact. I have never seen it since. The "chicken on the bed incident", remains as the most capital crime my children have ever committed.

The first three years at our new home had been the best years of mine and Jason's entire marriage. We were doing really well during that time. The move to West Virginia had been the right decision, I believed. I think we had even fallen back in love with each other. But it seemed as though, overnight, our marriage was headed downhill again. He became overwhelmed with everything we had going on. His bad temper started to erupt again. I had tried to convince myself many times that, as he got older, he would settle down and become more calm. That was not the case. It seemed like, no matter what I did, I could never do anything right by him. I was never good enough. And I was having an extremely difficult time dealing with my Peepaw's passing. It hit me very hard. He was the single most influential person in all my life. He was the only person I turned to for advice and wisdom. I couldn't cope without him. As busy as we all were and as happy as I was to finally have a farm to run, I was also struggling on many different levels.

While the kids were at school, I occupied myself with my housework, farm work and photography work. I tried to distract my mind from everything that was weighing me down. I cleaned every square inch of our home, did all the laundry, fed the animals, gathered eggs, shoveled stalls, groomed the horses and worked for hours in my home office editing thousands of pictures. Aunt JoAnn and Grandma had relocated to Georgia and so I shut my studio down but my business continued to be successful. I was backed up with jobs I still had left to complete and there were new clients and more work pouring in faster than I could keep up.

I became the unofficial staff photographer for an exotic animal farm in Canvas, WV, called, Good Evening Ranch. I would take trips there some days while the kids were at school, photographing the animals. I especially liked to visit with the lion, named Leo, and pet his big paws through the fence. I also photographed rodeos and other events there on different occasions for the ranch. I made the brochures for them and supplied their pictures for advertisements on their website. I was hired to photograph a St. Jude's benefit concert there that June. A West Virginia native was the opening act for the Kentucky Headhunters, Sammy Kershaw and Aaron Tippin. I met all of the bands and hung out backstage with Aaron Tippin after the concert. The guy who had been the opening act for the concert, also a Nashville recording artist, contacted me and hired me to do a shoot of him for his next album cover.

Around that same timeframe, my cousin Sissy invited me to go to a local outdoor concert with her and some other ladies in the nearby town of Flatwoods. I knew of the band that was playing there that day. My friend Kerri had given me a CD of theirs, that I listened to often. They had a song about chickens on that album, and the kids and I danced to the chicken song regularly. (That same song was also later used by my cousin Tyler, as the track on a chicken documentary he made at the farm.) So I went to the concert, to see them in person. After the show, the band members invited me backstage, and we exchanged introductions. The lead singer and the lead guitarist were brothers. They were very well known in West Virginia as natives of the state and were also Nashville recording artists. I was already a fan of theirs, but I liked them, even more, when I met them in person. They seemed to be my kind of people, down to earth, country mountain folks. I didn't think much of it the first time I met them though. I thought it was just a meeting in passing and assumed I would never see them again.

I was starting to get burnt out on my photography business. By this time I had worked with one too many bridezillas. They killed my inspiration and I got to where I hated editing pictures. Money flowed in during the spring through fall months but in the winter season, it slowed way down. I wanted to just wrap up the jobs I had left to finish and throw in the towel on my business. Anything that starts out as a passion and turns into a headache makes you forget why you ever enjoyed it in the first place. I ended up getting a part-time job at Tractor Supply for the sake of having employee discounts on livestock grain and farm necessities. It was the only retail work I have ever done. There is zero job satisfaction in selling shit from China, sticking it in a plastic bag and telling people to have a nice day. I didn't work that job for very long. I continued my photography.

That fall, J.J. started third grade and Faith was in first grade. I would go have lunch with the kids, then walk around the track with Faith and her friends at their recess. I was a homeroom mother and brought treats to school for both the kids' classes. I got to know a lot of the staff and students at Birch River Elementary. Both the kids had friends that they would invite over on a regular basis. I would host them for sleepovers, tea parties, games, and holiday festivities. The children's' friends enjoyed coming to the farm and seeing all the animals. It was like our own personal petting zoo.

Grownups liked to come to the farm too. We would take guests out to shoot guns in the lower field for target practice, take poles and fish in the pond at the horse field, go on four-wheeler rides all over the property, and whatever else we could do to entertain them. We would have cookouts and bonfires. I would half-ass try to play my guitar on the front porch. The farm became a refuge for everyone who wanted to come be part of it. It seemed as though anyone who came once wanted to keep coming back. The farm always drew certain people in and made them want to stick around awhile. Those people became our honorary guests.

Part 4

In the winter season that year, the kids had a lot of snow days and I was happy to have them home with me more. We played in the snow with all the animals and they played video games and Legos. We drank hot chocolate and baked cookies. We did all the regular snow day things there were to do. Jason had taken them snow skiing every winter since we moved back to West Virginia. It was a tradition Jason and his dad started together with the kids. I had attempted to snow ski the first year they went. I hated it. I took my skis off and slid all the way down the mountain on my ass cussing the whole time. I swore I would never go again but I went a few more times after that because I wanted to learn so I could go with the kids. I started to get better at it. I took a private ski lesson once and then I actually began to enjoy skiing. During Christmas break, I invited Haley and her husband Javier to come with us. We had a discount ski day with the Cub Scouts at Winterplace Resort. They drove in from Lexington. We went to Jason's parents' house where we fitted them with ski bibs and gloves in the attic. Javier ended up with a pair of snow bibs that Jason's dad had from the 1970s. They looked just like they came straight outta Rainbow Brite's wardrobe. Bright red, yellow, and blue. Hideous. To make it worse, Javier put them on backward and inside out by accident. We all rolled, laughing at him.

We drove to the ski resort, got out of the vehicle and suited up for our day of adventure. Javier put his Rainbow Brite coveralls on backwards, again. We about fell in the parking lot laughing at him.

He finally got them on right and we made way to the bunny slope. They were having a short lesson for beginners there. I just stood by and watched since I was a half-decent skier by now. Jason, his dad and the kids took off for the black diamonds. They were all skilled skiers. In the mini ski course Haley and Javier participated in, Javier showed Haley up, he looked like he knew what he was doing. It was both of their first time ever attempting to snow ski. It was time to leave the bunny slope. Me, Haley, and Javier set out together. Haley was doing a good job. Even she was impressed with how well she was staying upright. I didn't fall down at all; I actually felt comfortable on skis. Javier, who had done so well in the lesson, was busting ass all over the place and he could be seen from twelve miles away in his Rainbow Brites. Plus did I mention Javier is of full-blooded Cuban descent? Cubans don't mix well with snow. He hailed from a tropical culture. Javi wiped out every possible which way a person can on the snow. He did splits, he did face plants, he fell off the ski lift, he lost his ski poles over a snowbank and went sliding after them. Haley and I laughed so hard we almost peed our snow bibs. It was seriously one of the funniest scenes I have ever had the pleasure of witnessing. We were thoroughly entertained by Rainbow Brite Javi.

In January of 2010, I was finally able to bring my Pocahontas horse home to the farm and Susie bought herself a palomino Quarter Horse mare named Valentine. Jason and his dad had rebuilt all the fences along the big field across the road. We cleared the overgrown pasture, tore down old buildings, and fixed up the two big barns that we left standing. I had completely cleaned out and prepared the smaller of the two barns to house Pocahontas and Valentine. There was a nice size spring-fed pond at the top of the pasture, stocked with bass and brim. There was plenty of acreage to sustain the two mares. It was a good and proper place for our horses. We had completely transformed the land from decades of neglect back to its former glory days.

I spent all that spring working with Pocahontas, to raise and train her. I did ground work with her for a long time. Then I trained her using only natural horsemanship techniques. I lunged her in circles. First I rode her bareback with no reigns. I would just hold on to her mane and use body language to steer her. Then when she was ready, I started riding her with a saddle and a bridle. I groomed her every day, spent hours with her, and led the children around in pony rides on her. She was everything I had ever wanted in a horse and more. My little filly imprinted on me. She would follow me every step I took, and halt when I stopped. Pocahontas became my best friend and my partner.

By that summer, my vision of having my own farm had become a full-blown picture. The place was filled with horses, chickens, ducks, bunnies, cats, and MoMo. The land was full of life. The garden was overflowing and the fruit trees were thriving. We bought a John Deere tractor. Aunt Vicki's son, Tyler, came up from Florida to spend some time with Meemaw. She brought Tyler to the farm to spend a few days with us and he loved it. He filmed a documentary about the chickens and the kids. He drove the tractor. He became big buddies with MoMo. Tyler seemed to feel right at home on the farm. He fit right into country life in the mountains.

That June, I took a flight to Miami, Florida. Haley and Javier had relocated there from Lexington, Kentucky, and they bought me a ticket to so I could come to spend a few days with Haley. She was pregnant with her first child and we needed some sister-time. While the airplane prepared for landing, my phone started blowing up. Someone had turned the horses loose from the barnyard and they were running up and down the two-lane highway that runs through the farm. I was thinking that I would have to get off the plane and immediately book the next flight back home, to catch the horses. But I got ahold of Jason and he left from work (over an hour away) to go home and wrangle them. So Haley picked me up and I relied on Jason to save the day. By the time he got there, he located Pocahontas and Valentine on the other side of the mountain near a coal mine, on someone else's farm, consorting with a jackass donkey. Jason got them safely back home to their pasture.

Javier, Haley and I spent part of a day on the ocean at South Beach. We went to a port-side outdoor restaurant for lunch. They took me to Little Havana where we dined on Cuban pastelitos and plantains. We watched the old men play chess games while they smoked their Cuban cigars.. that was my favorite part of the city. They showed me all around Miami that day. The next morning we drove to Key West and spent a day there, touring some of the places that are prime for sight-seeing. We went to the

Southernmost Point, the Boars Head Saloon, the historic cemeteries, and the Birthplace of the Pan American World Airways. Then we swam in the warm turquoise water. It was my first time to the Keys. I thought Islamorada was the prettiest one. We spent some much-needed sister-time together. I was happy to make more memories with Haley and so excited for her and Javi to be expecting their first baby.

In July of that year, Mama got married to her sweetheart, Jack. She had moved from Summersville (two hours away) to Parkersburg, WV. That's where their wedding was. I was the photographer, J.J. was the ring bearer, Faith was the flower girl, and my brothers were groomsmen. Plus I gained two stepbrothers Mathew and Nicholas. Mama seemed happier than she had ever been. She finally found someone that completed her. She seemed at peace after a long life of her own struggles. All I cared about with this stepdad was that he treated my mother well.

In August Susie bought an Amish-built two-stall horse stable for Pocahontas and Valentine. It was a big operation the day they delivered it. We had prepared the site for it ahead of time and they brought it in on a big semi-truck with a flatbed trailer. They used a Mule machine to maneuver it into place. It was my ideal concept of the perfect horse stable, complete with a copper horse weathervane, iron horseshoe hardware for the Dutch stall doors, and a nice tack room. We poured concrete under the overhang. We installed fancy lighting in the stalls, put a ceiling fan, a mini-fridge, and a saddle rack in the tack room, then filled it with horse supplies. It was the perfect home for our horses.. as nice a barn as I have ever seen.

Later that month we invested in a herd of three goats to help clear the brush from the horse pasture. We named the goats Pepé Le Pew, Bessie, and Priscilla. The kids and I spent almost that entire summer at the horse field. We fished, picked up rocks, dug up antique metal from the old dirt road, threw hay up to the barn loft, groomed and rode the horses, cleaned the stalls, anything we could find to do in the barnyard. We worked hard and we played hard. We even hung the hammock up to relax in, where we were constantly harassed by the goats and horses. We would be covered in dirt, sweat, and hay by the time we crossed to the other side of the road to go up the driveway back home in the late evenings.

We had adopted a barn cat who had been a stray at nearby Trinity Baptist Church. She was a calico cat. We named her Trinity. In October, she gave birth to five kittens in the loft of one of our barns. I found the newborn kittens in between the square bales of hay. I gathered them all up, put them in a basket, and made a home for them and Trinity in the tack room of the stable. We couldn't keep all five of them. We still had Ellie May and two of her kittens who were full-grown, Dandelion and Pixar. Jason's mom had one of Ellie's kittens too. Plus we had a Himalayan kitten that J.J. got as a get-well gift from Susie after he had been in the hospital with a kidney infection back in June. (That kitty had about ten different names.) We ended up keeping the only calico kitten from Trinity's litter, and we named her Hermione.

For Jason's birthday on November 4th, I bought him a puppy. She was a copper-nosed lemon beagle, only six weeks old. The kids and I drove to the Frametown Fire Department to pick her up. We took her home and surprised Jason with her when he got off of work. He loved her. We named her Copper. She was the prettiest puppy I've ever seen. And MoMo was very happy to have a companion of his own.

That Christmas, Jason and I planned to get the kids a miniature horse. I had seen the advertisement for the mini-mare on the classified board at Tractor Supply. We didn't have a livestock trailer so we borrowed one. It was a thirty footer. We hitched it to the Chevy Avalanche and drove far away in the middle of a blizzard to pick her up. When we got there and loaded this tiny little horse onto the livestock trailer, (that was big enough to fit fifty head of cattle), it was laughable. She was so small, I could have held her on my lap in the cab of the truck.

We got the mini horse home and hid her away in the horse stable. She was to be a surprise. On Christmas morning, after we opened presents under the tree, we took J.J. and Faith down the driveway and across the road to the horse stable. I opened the stall door and their present came trotting out into the snow. I had tied Christmas ribbons onto her mane and tail. The children loved her and chased her all around the horse field. The big mares, Pocahontas and Valentine, treated the mini mare like she was their baby. We named the miniature horse Ginger.

On March 15, 2011.. my sister Haley gave birth to her first child, a son, they named Javier Jr. They waited until his arrival to find out the gender of their baby. I was proud to have another nephew. Haley and Javier had moved from Miami to Lakeland. For Spring Break in April, my family had scheduled separate vacations. Jason and J.J. were flying to Washington state to see Jason's sister; Faith and I were flying to Florida to see my sister and to meet my nephew, Little Javi. We also had plans to celebrate Faith's 8th birthday and my 31st birthday at Disney World with Aunt Vicki and her daughter, Hayden, and to visit with Meemaw who had also relocated back to Florida.

Before our separate trips, I was shopping for some travel treats for the kids. J.J. helped me pick out some candy from the store for Faith. He got her the fanciest lollipop there was (from the Easter candy aisle), it even had pretty ribbons on it. We took off on our separate destinations, with the boys heading West, and the girls going South. Once mine and Faith's airplane got up in altitude, I gave her the fancy lollipop from her brother. She took the wrapper off and put it in her mouth. She made a funny face, and said, "This tastes funny, Mommy." To which I casually replied, "I'm sure it's fine, try it again honey." Then she took a bite out of the lollipop. Faith made an even funnier face. I licked it myself and was appalled by the taste. I looked back over at Faith; she had foam coming out of her mouth. I grabbed the wrapper and read it, worrying she was having an allergic reaction to it. The package read, in fine print, "soap". J.J. had selected a soapy lollipop for his sister. We laughed about it for the rest of the flight to Florida.

When we arrived at Lakeland, we went straight to see Haley and the baby. Faith and I were both so excited to meet Little Javi. He was absolutely adorable. We took turns holding him. Haley was a good mother. I was proud of my big sister. She had dealt with gestational diabetes during her pregnancy but she was a trooper and made it through, with a beautiful baby boy. Little Javi was born with only one good kidney and ended up having to undergo major surgery to have the other one removed. We spent as much time as we could with my sister and new nephew. We visited with Meemaw too. She had settled into her new place in Florida, the last property she and Peepaw had bought together.

On my birthday, we spent the day at Disney World with Aunt Vicki and Hayden, who was six months younger than Faith. Aunt Vicki raised her kids in Florida but we had gotten our girls together whenever we could throughout their lives. Since they were close in age, they always had similar interests. They would play toys and have tea parties when they were little. Although Hayden was younger than Faith, she was always the taller of the two. Faith would pick on Hayden when they were toddlers and take baby dolls away from her. I would say, "Faith, don't pick on Hayden. She's bigger than you." They were at the ages now where they got along well and the girls were happy to see each other.

The trip to Disney was my gift to Faith for her birthday, which is sixteen days before mine. Vicki and I made appointments for our daughters to have princess makeovers done at the Boutique in the Castle that day. Faith and Hayden were treated like royalty and looked so beautiful. We all had a fun day riding rides, having meet-and-greets with the characters, then watching the parade and fireworks that night. We did everything there was to do at the Magic Kingdom. It was a fun girls' day out. I was happy to have time together with my Aunt Vicki. She was only ten years older than me and was always more like a sister than an aunt.

Faith and I flew back into Huntington, WV. We had a rough landing. The runway at that airport is way too short and it's always scary to touch down there but this landing was so rough that the airplane hit the runway with such an impact that it bounced way back up off the ground, then landed sideways and came to a turbulent screeching halt. All the passengers screamed, including me. Faith was the only one on board who thought it was fun. She even said, "Whee!" She is still a thrill seeker. Jason and J.J. enjoyed their man trip to the Northwest, where they had explored and adventured around Seattle, and along the Pacific Coast. We all met back up at home in West Virginia. We exchanged stories about our trips and showed pictures from our separate travels. We were happy to be back on the farm with each other and all our animals.

We spent that summer working together on the land. It was pretty well complete with being established as a full running self-sufficient farm but work on a farm is never done. Jason and his dad fenced in the big meadow in front of our house, so we would have a separate field to rotate the horses too. I liked being able to have the horses where I could keep a better eye on them after the prankster had set them loose back in the springtime. We threw a lot of hay that season, filled the barn loft full. We grew a big garden and I did a lot of canning. I loved the constant busy activity of farm life. It was exactly what I had always dreamed of. I never took any of it for granted. I thanked God for all the blessings He had given me.

It was important to me to teach my children the way of life on a farm. I wanted them to learn how to grow and harvest their own food, how to raise and tend to animals, how to live a simple country lifestyle. I felt like all of that was a lost art for most kids of J.J. and Faith's generation. What was even more important to me, was to have something to pass down to my children. Most modern-day families live in suburban neighborhoods. Those places aren't passed down through generations. They are sold off as assets after the owner works all their life to pay the mortgage, then they die, and the bank decides what becomes of the property. I intended to leave an entire estate to my children when the day came for me and Jason to leave this world. I wanted J.J. and Faith to always have a familiar place to come home to once they were grown and for them to gain something they could, in turn, pass down to their children, and their grandchildren, and on down the line of succession. I was planning ahead for the future and for all my descendants. My dream of a farm was as much for them as it was for myself. I wanted to pour my blood, sweat, and tears into the soil and streams, the meadows and woodlands, the hills and valleys. I knew every acre like the back of my hand. I wanted every part of this land to contain a piece of my soul, like a time capsule of love, for my children and future generations of my family, like wish flower seeds floating through the air, and replanting firmly in the ground, for the sake of posterity. I named the farm Almost Heaven Homestead. I planned to leave it behind, as my lasting legacy.

Fight or Flight

Horses are wired with the "Fight or Flight" response. When they are threatened by predators or opposition, or if they experience fear, they will do one of two things; they will either stand their ground and fight or run away and take flight. This happens when they feel that their dominance is rivaled, or their lives are at risk. Depending on the horse, sometimes these responses are activated by something insignificant because it is a matter of unfamiliar territory. Sometimes it takes a great deal to compel them into this mode. Wild horses are more prone to be in tune with these instincts. It is more common for them to rear up and flee running. They are untamed. Domestic horses have been bred and trained to be coerced into disregarding their initial gut instincts. They force themselves to move on and dismiss the impulses in which their natural intuition would otherwise cause them to react accordingly. Fight or flight responses are survival modes. They are acts of resistance. Rebellion against confines and potential threats. These innate senses are designed to assist their host in avoiding danger, ensuring safety and prolonging life span. They are natural behaviors and self-defense mechanisms. When a horse is triggered into fight or flight, they will break all boundaries; either to settle a score or to set themselves free. The key to surviving is knowing how and when to switch from one response to the other—deciding at a moment's notice, or with no warning at all. It comes down to judging when to stay, and when to go. It could be a matter of freedom or entrapment. It could be a matter of life or death.

I moved our horses back across the road that fall, where they had more room to run. In August, J.J. started fifth grade, and Faith was in third grade. I would saddle Pocahontas up almost every day before school let out, and wait for the kids to come home on the school bus. Copper and MoMo would greet the children daily; they always knew when to expect them and would be sitting at the end of the driveway, waiting for the big yellow bus. J.J. would run to the house to play video games, with the dogs following up the hill behind him. Faith would come straight to the barnyard, and take a ride on Pocahontas. For some reason, Pocahontas was always extra gentle around Faith and acted motherly towards her. Faith was born an animal whisperer. She could tame even the wildest of animals. We added more furry and feathered friends to the farm that season. In all.. we had horses, goats, pigs, bunnies, ducks, chickens, dogs and cats. Animals were everywhere. MoMo (mini Dachshund) climbed a stepladder and managed to get Copper (Beagle) pregnant. I could tell she had a big litter because she looked like she swallowed a basketball. As Copper got closer to her due date, she kept trying to hide in the creek bed. Faith and I took turns carrying her back to the house. She was heavy and it took all our strength to pick her up and tote her up the driveway. We were afraid she would give birth in the creek. In September, her litter of puppies arrived. I managed to trap her in the house that day. She had nine pups sired by MoMo, and I assisted with the delivery of the entire litter. The children were there to see them born. And MoMo stood on the sidelines as his offspring entered the world, one by one.

The puppies became our obsession. The mix between beagle and weenie dog made for the most adorable combination. They were all different colors and sizes. Copper was a good mama. MoMo, (who had always loved every baby animal he ever met), didn't like his own babies. He was jealous of the attention we gave them. We named every one of the nine puppies and handled them constantly. We watched them grow and play. Jason would only allow us to keep one, a tricolored male we named Scout. And I decided to give one to my cousin Tyler, who had never had a dog of his own.

When the puppies were weaned from Copper at the end of October, I went to the Tractor Supply and bought vaccinations for all of them. I had always done my own animal vaccines, I was properly trained on how to administer shots when I worked at the veterinarian clinic in high school, and in hands-on livestock health administration during college. I had given eight of the puppies a Canine Spectra 5-way shot and was on pup number 9. It wriggled when I went to inject the needle subcutaneously under the hide of its neck. I missed the puppy and plunged the full needle into my hand on accident. (I didn't think twice about it when it happened, because I knew that canine Parvo couldn't be transmitted to humans.) I then successfully injected the puppy and went on about my day.

That accident almost cost me my life. It was one of the worst mistakes I have ever made. Within 24 hours, I was deathly ill. I had chills and a high fever. I broke out into hives all over my body. After one week, I started having neurological issues with my hands and feet going numb, extreme fatigue then a severe case of arthritis set in. All my fingernails became bruised and turned black as coal, looked like I had banged every one of them with a hammer. And I started having kidney problems. I went to the doctor, trying to figure out what was wrong with me. The original prognosis was lupus, since every symptom I had coincided with that. They ran every test they could, and a Lyme's disease test came back as a false positive, so they put me on high doses of antibiotics and pain pills. It never crossed my mind to tell the doctors about the accidental injection.

I called Grandma Sparks on November 13th, her 90th birthday. We talked for a long time, and her memory seemed to have come back to her. She recalled things and people I hadn't heard her mention in years. I told her Happy Birthday, and said, "I love you, Grandma." I had no idea at the time, that was the last conversation I would ever have with my grandmother. On November 17th, she peacefully passed away. She lived a long life. She was a hard worker. Everything she ever did was for her family. Her funeral service was a beautiful tribute of remembrance. I was devastated to lose her. She had been one of the most important figures in my lifetime. She was one of the key elders who had a major role in my upbringing. She was my female hero, and I had always tried to conduct myself in the same image that she portrayed. Grandma was the epitome of a strong, resilient mountain woman. She was the last great storyteller of my relations. But she had been patiently awaiting her turn to go to Heaven ever since 1986, the year that she lost her husband and her son. I knew she was at peace, reunited with them, and because of that, I was able to find some peace in the wake of her absence. However, I was still very sick when Grandma passed. Everything was such a foggy blur to me. I kept having to remind myself that she was gone. I would even pick up the phone to call her, and then I would remember that she wasn't there. She was the matriarch of my father's side of the family, and nothing would ever be the same without her. She was the end of an era.

With the effects of my illness, I was continuing to get drastically worse. I was going to scheduled doctor's appointments at least three times a week, and they ran a full spectrum of tests every time. All of them were coming back inconclusive. The Lyme test came back negative after they had treated me for months with high powered antibiotics. My blood work was all over the place and my doctors didn't know what to do with me. I saw every physician in that clinic till they unanimously shook their heads at the lost cause. Then they started sending me to specialists.. neurologists, rheumatologists, internal health and infectious disease doctors. The Rheumatoid Arthritis test came back positive, and the doctor said it was already present in my system, but triggered by an autoimmune response. I was also diagnosed with fibromyalgia but my overall condition was still a mystery. Every symptom I had was getting severely worse by the day. Then my hair started falling out in handfuls. I ended up losing almost all of my hair. My blood pressure was dangerously low. I had a fever day and night, (which went on to last 24-7 for five consecutive years). Every lymph node in my body was swollen. My kidney problems became chronic (and still are). The arthritis and neurological issues progressed throughout my anatomy, to such a state, that I became bedridden, not being able to walk or bathe myself or dress myself. My body was attacking itself from the inside out. I was only 31 at the time, but I felt like I was 131 years old. After months with no confirmed cause of illness, it finally occurred to me to mention the accidental injection of the 5-way vaccination. Bloodwork came back and revealed three of the five live viruses that were present in the strain I had stuck myself with. That one isolated incident plagued me with an autoimmune disease that nearly killed me, literally. I was fighting for my life. I was on my deathbed and making post mortem arrangements for my own demise. I still suffer from that permanent illness daily, even eight years later. It has tried its best to destroy me. It remains an ongoing battle that I fight incessantly, and try to hide.

Jason couldn't take care of work, the kids, the house, the farm, me and all my doctor's appointments. It was too much. And I was too sick to take care of anyone or anything. Word had gotten out of the dire state we were all in. So my Uncle Stanley and his wife Janet, drove all the way across the country from Oregon to come and help us. Stanley immediately took to doing all the farm work and tending to the animals. Janet did all the housework and cooking. And they both pitched in to take care of J.J. and Faith. They also got me to my appointments and took care of me. They were selfless and invaluable, they were Angels on Earth. I have never in my life had someone come so far out of their way to my rescue like they did. Stanley and Janet stayed with us for almost two months throughout that winter, till I finally became stabilized enough to start walking on my own again with a cane. It was the most valuable time I ever got to spend with my dad's only brother. I felt safe while he was there. The kids and I were sad to see Stanley and Janet go. They had become such a vital part of our everyday lives. They were the definition of family. We never could have survived that trial if they hadn't been there with their love and support.

On top of everything else Jason and I had managed to survive.. my state of poor health ended up being the straw that broke the camel's back. We had done so well when we first relocated to West Virginia, considering the extreme rollercoaster ride we had been on together up to that point. However, we were on a steady decline since 2009. And after the emotional turmoil of losing two of my grandparents, having a near-death experience myself, and inadvertently dropping the ball on everything I had always taken care of; I was incapacitated. I was the glue that held us all together, but I was coming undone. And our marriage suffered further fatality. It derailed and there was no foreseeable way to get it back on track.

After twelve years of keeping all of our homes in perfect order, our house was now a total disaster. I was still too weak to keep up with cooking, cleaning, and laundry. The children suffered because I wasn't capable of doing all the things I had done with them before I got sick. They knew I wasn't well, and they were very concerned about me. I knew I was letting them down, and I felt like a failure as a mother for the first time in their lives. That killed me more than anything. I never wanted them to see me like that. I only wanted to be a perfect mother and make them feel safe and happy. The most important thing to me was to make sure J.J and Faith were always taken the best possible care of, by their own mother. And I simply couldn't do everything I had always done for them. It made me even sicker to realize that I wasn't readily available to take care of them as they were accustomed to. I was also failing as a wife. Jason had extra weight on his shoulders because he had to pick up my slack of tending to all the animals, meal preparation, and the housework that was neglected. Plus, he was having to step up as a parent.. and do things for the children that I had always done. I just physically wasn't able to keep up with any of my duties. Everything I had worked so hard for, was falling into decay and disrepair. And I was forced to helplessly lay there and watch it happen.

You know how when you are completely exhausted, but as long as you keep moving, you continue to catch a second wind?

Then if you slow down or stop, your exhaustion sneaks up on you, catches you off guard, and knocks you down. And you have an even harder time getting back up and carrying on. It's easier to just stay in constant motion than it is to rest and restart. Well, that's what happened to me during this time. I had been going and going constantly and nonstop. One foot in front of the other. One day at a time. For ten years straight. Ever since we first moved to Blue Mountain. But once I was knocked down and forced to stop, on account of my illness.. it all came rushing at me, it all caught up with me, it all hit me at once. Everything I had been through in my life. Every heartache and pain. Every loss I had suffered. Anything I had worked so hard to cover up and hide with a smile and consistent perseverance. All the walls I had built around myself in a fortress of strength and steady determination—they all came crumbling down around me in debris; crashing in on top of me and burying me alive.

My relentless physical ailment, along with the emotional turmoil and mental strain that was triggered because of my forced stop of forward motion; turned me into the worst version of myself to date. I hated how all that had changed me. Right at a time when everything in my life had finally come together to form a more complete, almost full circle of existence. It was devastating to stand back and watch everything unravel at the seams. To see myself become someone I didn't recognize anymore. I knew my prior happiness on the farm was too good to be true. This was the damnation I received for allowing myself to be happy in the first place. Every time life had knocked me down before I had stood back up, brushed myself off, and tried my best to carry on. So after having a long pity party for myself, wallowing in my physical pain, I couldn't take it anymore. I had to make a stand to find a way to harness my disease and steer it into submission. I attempted to regain some of my momentum and strength. At least enough to try and pull myself out from under the rubble of everything that had me trapped. I had to start with the small stones and work my way up to the big boulders. I finally climbed out enough to see the light of day. And that was no small task. I had to fight for it, I had to fight hard to continue living. If not for myself, for my children, who were my only reason for being, and my inspiration to march onward like a wounded warrior in combat.

In the spring of 2012, I slowly stood up on my feet and made an effort to try and pull everything back together. To rebuild all that had fallen to the wayside during the many months of my sickness. My photography business had gone under while I was ill. But I tried to get the house and farm back in order. That March, we bought Faith her very own dairy cow, a Holstein calf from Amish country, that she named Merrybelle. She had asked for a cow for years.. and we surprised her on her birthday. Merrybelle became Faith's best friend and her giant baby. We had also rescued a miniature horse that past December, a stallion named Napoleon. And Ginger was pregnant with his baby. For my birthday in April, Susie bought me a Great Pyrenees dog. I named him Gandalf. He was the most regal and noble dog I have ever had, majestic in every way. And he assisted me in my recovery efforts. Every day, I would walk him along the fence-line, so he would learn the parameters and get acquainted with the livestock that he was to guard. Gandalf became my physical therapy service dog and Merrybelle's personal guardian.

Things were starting to get back on track after all. I was hopeful that I would overcome the obstacle of having to deal with an autoimmune illness. I intended to grab life back by the horns, with a vengeance. I was angry about the bad health that had befallen me. And I used that anger as fuel to thrust myself forward.

Although Jason had always been a hard worker and a good provider, he hadn't always treated me with honor and dignity. I got to the point where I wasn't in my marriage for the sake of love, but for the sake of my kids having both their parents present. I stayed for a long time believing that's what was best for them. And up to this point, I had enough love for Jason to keep us both afloat. He was still my home. He was everything familiar to me. He was my only husband and the father of all my children. I had no intention of ever divorcing him. I had never even considered divorce. It wasn't even in my vocabulary. We were supposed to stay together, in sickness and in health.

On May 4th of that year, I worked for several hours cleaning up our tractor shed, where we kept all the farm equipment. (While Stanley was staying with us, he had cleaned out a two-hundred-year-old cellar. He and Jason found hundreds of Mason jars, and had stacked them all in boxes on the front porch.) That day I had a fever of 103, a kidney infection, and lingering neurological issues. I carried every one of those boxes from the front porch, loaded them into the bed of the truck, and unloaded them into the tractor shed I had tidied. The whole time I was working, I was thinking of how proud Jason would be of me for what I had done. It was a huge accomplishment for me in my still very weak state of sickness. That night after the kids had been fed and bathed, I sat on the four-wheeler in the equipment building and waited for Jason to come home from work. I was hoping he would be happy with the results of my days-worth of work.

It didn't go at all as I had imagined. I listened as he came up the long driveway. I could always tell by the sound of his tires on the gravel road, what kind of day he had. It sounded like he was in a bad mood. And as soon as he got out of his vehicle, there was obvious confirmation that he indeed had a bad day, and was stressed out from work. Of all the good I had done, he found the one thing I did wrong. I had thrown one of his shoes away because I couldn't find the other one from the pair. I placed it on top of the trash can so he could claim it if he wanted to. He immediately flew into a fit of rage about that one minor offense. During that time, I was still in such excruciating pain from my illness, that I couldn't stand to be touched in any way. I hurt so bad I even flinched at the thought of being hugged. I had built an imaginary force field around myself to protect my body from further pain.

I am not going to elaborate on what happened next, other than this, Mama had bought me a beautiful turquoise beaded bracelet for my birthday. She gave it to me a few weeks late, and I had just received it two days prior. I wore it proudly for the first time on my wrist the day before and showed it to Jason when he took me out to lunch after my rheumatology appointment. I had also been wearing it all that day of the 4th, and admiring it every time I stopped to take a break from working. Fast forward to later that night, I found myself deflated, with the wind knocked out of my sails. I raised myself up on my hands and knees, then crawled around the front porch. I was frantically trying to find and gather up all of the beads that had fallen when the bracelet was broken. They were scattered everywhere. I never did find them all. The children heard me screaming and sobbing, and came out to see what was wrong. Jason had gone to his recliner, turned on the tv, and popped open a cold beer. Cool and collected, like nothing ever happened.

The flight response took effect as soon as I saw J.J. and Faith. I abandoned my mission of searching for the missing parts of my bracelet. I escorted the kids quietly around the house and buckled them up in the truck. My keys were still in the ignition from where I had hauled the loads of jars that afternoon. I made a quick getaway, with no money, and no clue where I was going. I drove twenty miles, then pulled off the road in the next town, and called my sister Haley. I asked her what I should do. I didn't have enough gas to even get very far. She paid for a hotel room for us to stay the night in, till I could figure out which move to make next. It was past the kids' bedtime, on a school night. They didn't even have shoes on their feet when I had snuck us all out. I carried them into the hotel; one on each hip since they were both barefoot. They were crying and upset because I was visibly shaken, clearly confused, and still very sick. There was pure concern on their innocent little faces. That is when it hit me like a slap in the face.. this is not best for my children. I had been wrong to stay in an unhealthy marriage all this time.

The next morning, I kept the kids out of school. I went directly to the courthouse and got divorce papers. I headed towards the farm, where I had planned to pack us all some bags, and flee the state. I was trying to rush and tackle all of this while Jason was away at work. But when we arrived home, instead of packing and leaving, I took a deep breath and tried to collect myself in order to do some rational thinking. I settled down enough to untangle the thoughts running through my mind. I really wanted to wage war. At the same time, what I mostly needed, was peace. I was torn. I came to the conclusion that if I was going to pursue a divorce, I should take the high road, and do it in the most peaceful way possible. The last thing I wanted to do was to uproot the kids from everything familiar in their lives. I didn't want to pull the rug out from under them. They weren't old enough to understand divorce and the separation of home and parents. But a switch was flipped in me that day, a switch that I could never flip back. The man that was supposed to protect me, had done the opposite. I was in a fight or flight mode. I could stand my ground and fight for what I believed in. Or I could pack up and fly away, and never look back.

Just take off running. My initial gut instinct had been the flight response, but after contemplating that decision, I forced my instinct into the fight response.

When Jason got home that evening, I presented him with the divorce papers. He thought I was just bluffing. He didn't believe that I would actually follow through with it. Part of me desperately wished he was right about that. But I already knew there was no way to possibly reconcile our relationship after that switch was flipped in me. It was over. Our marriage that had endured every test and trial we had ever been through, had finally reached its bitter end. It was irretrievable. There was nothing that could be done to reverse the final blow. It wasn't just one thing that did our marriage in though. It was the fatal blow in the beginning. It was every element combined. It was years of trying to hold it together. It was a consolidation of all that had been out of our control, and all that was within our power to sway. It was every aspect we encountered between the beginning and the end. It started off as a fairy tale love story, then led to a broken road paved with detours every mile along the way, and turned out to have a tragic ending. It was sad. It was heartbreaking to see the end.

I mourned the loss of our marriage like a death. All the hopes and dreams I always had for me and Jason, the family we made, and the life we built together; I felt like it was all tarnished now. I was forced to let go of the death grip I had kept on our marriage for the past thirteen years. But I didn't want to. It went against all my religious morals and family values. It was against everything that I believed to be right and holy. My marriage was sacred to me. My husband had been my constant companion since I was eighteen years old. I had been with him my entire adult life. I couldn't even begin to imagine a life without him. He had been my true North and my home. I was so lost, even though I hadn't left him yet. We were still under the same roof, living like roommates. (We hadn't even slept in the same bed for a few years before the final straw broke.) But I was already lost at the prospect of losing him. I was spinning with no sense of direction. And I had no idea which way to stumble towards. I was resentful of him because he had driven me to this crossroads. He left me with no choice but to dissolve our marriage. I hated him for it. He took all of our history and what could have been of our future and ruined it with his temper. He gave me an ultimatum, and I was forced to choose. Every other time, I had chosen him. This time was different. I chose peace.

And meanwhile, still sick with my autoimmune disease and a stomach injury, I lost sixty pounds over the course of four months. (During the time I had been healthy and happy on the farm, I had gone from my typical 103 pounds, up to 158 pounds. It was the heaviest I had ever been. You know how they say.. when you're happy, you get fat? Yeah, that's what happened to me.) But now I couldn't keep anything down. I was projectile vomiting everything I tried to consume. And it happened wherever I stood. I never had enough warning to even make it to the bathroom. I would have to pull over several times just to get the kids up or down the driveway, to and from the school bus. I kept having to stop and open the truck door to throw up every time we made the quarter-mile trip. I was conducting an involuntary pukefest marathon. It was taking a whole other toll on me physically. It made me even weaker than I already was.

I had quit going to any of my doctor's appointments. My frustration with clinic visits and repeat tests had caused me to completely cease seeking medical help from physicians. All they accomplished was prescribing me with hydrocodone, highly addictive narcotic pills, and more powerful antibiotics. I didn't want to be all drugged up. I only took the pain meds at night so I could rest. I never took the Neurontin and I quit taking the antibiotics. I was trying to rehabilitate my health using naturopathic remedies. I did go to the doctor to see if anything could be done about my stomach issues. They told me I possibly had stomach cancer, did an endoscopy procedure, and gave me a prescription of Ondansetron, which I did take. I had dropped down to 98 lbs. And still couldn't hold any food or liquids down. I was withering away to nothing but a skeleton.

The close-knit circle of women on my mother's side of the family convened to do an intervention of sorts when they realized the extent of how my health issues and emotional well-being had deteriorated. Meemaw and Haley drove up from Florida. Mama took me to meet with them at their hotel. And I rode back to Florida with them. They wanted to remove me from the stressful situation I was in, so I could focus directly on my recovery. They were trying to rescue me from declining into a more critical condition. It became somewhat of an emergency situation. I agreed to let my family help me get back on my feet again. I was too weak to even argue against them taking me.

I explained to J.J. and Faith why I had to go on a trip out of town. I hugged them and told them how much I loved them. I cried and said goodbye to my babies. I felt like I was failing them even more by leaving. They were sympathetic and understanding because they wanted me to get better. They had seen firsthand how I was suffering from sickness. I arranged for them to spend time with Jason's parents while I was gone. Jason's mother was the only person I trusted to babysit my children. Almost all of my local family had moved away or passed away. And so we set off on our way to Florida. I took the male puppy I had kept to give to my cousin Tyler. I held him on my lap for the entire 14-hour long ride. I cried the whole way there.. having to leave my children, our home, and the farm animals.. was more than I could take on top of everything else. I knew it was temporary and for my own good. But I wanted to revolt on the mission and return home. About halfway there, I finally submitted to the plan. As soon as we arrived, I gave the puppy over to his new owner. Tyler named him Buck and was happy to have a doggy of his own. Then my recovery began.

I stayed with Haley in her new home for a few weeks. And my health improved immensely. That was when I first realized that the autoimmune illness was greatly exacerbated, and also triggered, by stress.. which in turn caused massive flare-ups of my symptoms.

When I was removed from the stressful environment I had been in due to the pending divorce, all my symptoms receded a great deal. I almost felt normal again physically, and my constant vomiting almost completely stopped. Haley took care of me. Meemaw and Aunt Vicki spent as much time with me as they could, trying to help me heal. Their plan of intervention was successful.

Part 2

Towards the end of my stay, Aunt Vicki took me to the ocean for a day. Then she took me to a tattoo parlor. I got new ink around my wrist, like a bracelet. It was the last line of a Johnny Cash quote, that says, "Life and love go on, let the music play". I had it written in Elvish script (from the Lord of the Rings), so only I would know what it said. And I had the tattoo artist add a small turquoise heart at the end of the quote (which signified my broken turquoise bracelet). The tattoo was a note to myself, a reminder to always move forward and never give up. It was my permanent bracelet that no one could ever break.

Back in West Virginia, feeling much better physically, and relieved to be home with my children; I caught a second wind. I was determined to remain emotionally calm and to learn how to manage my physical ailments, but I went into my own mentally dark period, similar to the one I had seen my mother go through when I was a young girl. But mine was different. I spent most of my darkness outdoors in the sunshine. I wanted to air out the dirty laundry, instead of containing it behind closed doors. I wanted to shed light on it. I wanted more space to sort through it. I wanted to hang it out to dry. I was enveloped in deep thought, prayer, and meditation.. sifting through every finite detail again and again in my mind. Trying to talk myself out of what I was about to do. Then replaying the reasons why I couldn't allow myself to change my mind. I kept circling around to the same answer.. divorce was the only available option.

Next, I was trying to figure out the best and most peaceful course of action., the least intrusive way to go through with divorce. I wanted it to be as fair a process as possible for J.J., Faith, Jason, and myself. There is no easy way to go through a divorce. But I intended to go about it in a way that would not completely disassemble the entire foundation we had built our lives upon. I knew everything would have to shift.. but I wanted to calibrate for the dust to settle in a way that would cause the most minimal amount of distress. I carefully calculated all possible avenues and variable outcomes.. until I had exhausted every option.

The only outcome I could live with, make peace with, and finally decided on (against the advice of everyone)... was for all of us to stay on the farm. That way none of us were losing our homeland. And more importantly, the children wouldn't lose either of their parents. They would have both of us available day and night. Nothing would have to be sold off or split up and divided as assets. The animals would all stay and be taken care of. The familiar world we had created for J.J. and Faith would remain intact. That was of the utmost importance to me. We didn't work so hard to see the farm come together, just to destroy it. It had been one of my lifelong dreams that I saw to fruition. Undoing that would be unacceptable. And it was still my fervent wish to leave the farm behind to J.J. and Faith. To leave a trace of history.

I couldn't rip my children's lives apart just because I could no longer live with their father. That would be a cruel injustice. Jason had been a good dad for the most part. Although he had been way too rough on our son, and my protective mama bear instincts over my boy, is what provoked most of the fights between Jason and I. We had conflicting parenting styles. He was the hard-ass, with a tough-love method. I was the gentle, nurturing and affectionate parent. He thought his hardcore rough ways would make a man out of our boy. I would interject myself between them, hiding our son behind my apron strings. I was J.J.'s safe place, as I vowed to him I would be when he was born. I was his soft place to fall. Without hesitation, I would readily kill or die for my children. But regardless, I didn't want Jason to be a part-time dad. He didn't deserve to only see his kids on just the weekends. I didn't want to remove him from their daily lives. I had grown up without my daddy, and I didn't want that for my kids.

My plan was to share 50/50 co-parent custody. We would raise them together, but separately, in two different houses. There would be no drop-offs and pick-ups, no third-party intervention. No fighting over holidays and birthdays. The children would choose which parent they wanted to be with, and which house they preferred to be in at any given time. We would put this ball in their court, let them openly choose how they wanted to divide their time among us, without being pressured. We would share the driveway between our two homes. They could come and go, up or down the hill, as they pleased. And we would all cohabitate peacefully, on the land which was our united home. This was my vision. This is what I set out to create.

The last thing I wanted to do, was to put J.J. and Faith in the line of fire of a nasty divorce and custody battle. They were innocent and didn't deserve to be caught in a tug of war battle. So every step I had to take to rearrange things.. had to be done with that at the forefront of the entire operation. Wanting peace for my children is what led the way for my divorce plan. That was my ultimate end goal in what I was setting out to do. The only aspects that would incur direct change were that Jason and I would not be married anymore, and we would no longer live together. But we could finish what we started, and raise our children together until they were ready to fly from the nest. And we would maintain the farm for them, in case they ever wanted to return to stake their own claim on the land.

Staying together on the farm was my big bright idea. It was a long-shot gamble, with everything at stake. It was a game of Russian Roulette that could backfire. I could end up on the wrong end of a losing streak bet. The wagering is unknown until the end of a game. It was a risky endeavor of reformation. This plan didn't make sense to anyone else that I presented it to. But it made logical sense to me. It had to make sense to me. I needed a detailed roadmap and a compass. A sense of direction and a predetermined route was crucial to me. This was it. A carefully thought out design that would become my highway to freedom and lead to the destination of peace. Where there's a will, there's a way. My stubborn ass was going to see this carefully devised plan through to the end and make it work, no matter what anyone else thought or said about it. I was bound and determined. And it was a transition that I could accept. It could go badly, but I honestly believed it to be the best decision at the time. After conveying this bright idea to Jason, he was agreeance with it. Reluctantly at first, but he agreed. It was settled. So that became my official map to Independence.

Now we would have to find a way to execute this unorthodox divorce blueprint. It wasn't a traditional path to the separation of man and wife, by any means. This was not how Americans were taught and conditioned to handle divorce in our culture. We were going to do something almost unheard of, and by all modern standards, considered downright insane. There was no handbook on the topic of "Co-op Divorce for Dummies". We had to write the manual ourselves. Jason and I would have to learn how to navigate these troubled waters carefully, without disturbing or disrupting the essence of a secure home-life for our children in the process. We would have to figure out how to coexist on the same land in separate dwellings. In the long run, it took two years total for our divorce plan to reach completion and become finalized, and we stayed under the same roof for most of that duration period.

My extended family was understandably concerned with and completely confused by my final decision; it was lost in translation to them. So I turned to my dad's friend Mark Purcell, the Cherokee man from Somerset, Kentucky. I had kept in touch with him and his brother Blaine, and they had become father figures for me since the loss of my Peepaw. Mark was also a photographer, so we had that in common. Plus he was an acclaimed author and a renowned psychotherapist. He was the one who saw me through, in hours and hours of therapy and advice. He took on an immensely complicated case when he took me under his wing. And he wasn't even getting paid for it. He became my counselor and my mentor, out of respect for my late father, who had been his friend. He felt responsible for me because we shared a bond through Daddy. And we had developed our own friendship that drew us together more like family. I could never thank him enough for helping to lead me towards the light at the end of the dark tunnel of divorce.

I initiated the first phase for executing the logistics of my plan. That June, Jason and I commissioned a Dutch crew to build an Amish one-room cabin on top of the old cellar that Uncle Stanley had cleaned out. It was located down the quarter-mile-long gravel driveway, closer to the main road.. and within viewing distance of the barnyard and horse pasture across the highway. It had two creeks running close by, one in the front and the other on the side of the cellar.. the streams converged at the driveway. Jason and his dad prepared the frame on top of the cellar, where the Amish cabin would be positioned. The day it arrived on a semi-truck, Jason and I sat on the hillside and watched as two young Dutch men went to work on assembling the precut lumber. They worked nonstop for seven hours, putting their signature Amish craftsmanship into every board and nail. The Dutch men never took a break or even paused for a drink of water. They didn't speak English, so Jason and I became fascinated by listening to their foreign discussions. It was impressive to see them in action. We watched till their masterpiece was complete.

The one-room cabin was to be the beginning of my new residence. I was still too sick to stay on top of the upkeep in our big house on the hill.. so we agreed that Jason would remain in our marital home, and the children would keep their bedrooms there. We made a subsequent plan to add onto the one-room cabin, to create a new smaller scaled, more manageable home for me and the kids down the hill. I drew the plans out for the expanded addition on a piece of sheet music, which later became the officially unofficial blueprint for my house. Jason would fund the construction of my new house, in lieu of child support and alimony. That was the deal we shook on. During the summer season, I spent a few nights camping in the one-room cabin so I could begin to get an idea of what it would be like to live in a different location. We also held J.J.'s 11th birthday party in the cabin. The kids saw it as a playhouse. They were happy to have a new place to explore on the farm. It was evolving into an entire village.

My brother Andrew came to visit me at the farm one day. I had taken him into the lower field to shoot guns. Firing weapons had become a therapeutic source of stress relief for me. I frequently loaded the four-wheeler down with ammunition, rifles, and pistols.. then blasted holes in targets. Andrew was a good marksman, and I wasn't too bad myself. We shared the shooting range side by side on a regular basis. It was a hobby we enjoyed together. He was a regular honorary guest on the farm, he loved the land. My baby brother was a big grown man now, and protective of me as his older sister. While we were wading through the field in the tall grass, Andrew said, "Be careful Sis, watch for snakes." I said, "Don't worry Brother, I have never seen a poisonous snake on this land, only black snakes." I was soon proven otherwise.

The very next day, I went down the hill to clean the cabin. A black preacher and his family from Maryland, (who were friends with our neighbor Susie), asked to stay over in the one-room cabin. They were due to arrive for their visit in a few days' time. I wanted to make the place welcoming for them. I took a break in the midst of sprucing up. I was sitting on a chair near the back door, hidden from the traffic on the highway. It was hot that day, and I had taken my jeans off while I was cleaning. I sat there in a tank top, my underwear, and my cowboy boots. I heard something rustling in the grass behind me, and turned around to look. I saw it coming. A five-foot-long rattlesnake. It slithered across the top of my boot, from its head to its rattler. I sat there petrified, sure that I was going to be found dead by snake bite, in my underwear and boots. The snake made way past me, and I jumped into the cabin. Then I jabbed a stick at it, as the snake coiled up and tried to strike out at me. I quickly slammed the door shut, and stayed held up inside the cabin till nightfall when Jason came and rescued me. The preacher and his family took up lodgings there that weekend and he performed a holy blessing of the cabin. That made me feel better about my future living quarters. It was a place of transition for me. I felt reassured that it would be cloaked in peace and blessed by God.

During that entire summer, Jason was trying his best to make amends with me. He finally realized that I hadn't been bluffing about the divorce. And he saw that I was getting a handle on keeping my illness at bay. He began trying to court me again like he had done when we were young and in love. Ironically, I think he also became more physically attracted to me since my massive weight loss. He seemed as though I had put some sort of witchcraft love spell on him like I slipped a magic potion into his drink or something. It had been a long time since he looked at me that way. And I still found him extremely attractive. I always thought he was so incredibly handsome. It was hard for me to not give into him, his mesmerizing green eyes, and all his charms. I remembered how and why I had fallen so deeply in love with him in the first place. That was never lost on me. The fire and sparks we first felt were still there, buried deep underneath all the layers of life we had experienced along the way of our eventful and traumatic journey. He was very convincing and had my full attention when he gazed at me like a lovesick fool.

He finally recognized and openly admitted the error of his ways, and wanted to do better by me. He apologized and begged for my forgiveness. I forgave him and we made peace. I knew how hard he had worked all along; he slaved to provide for his family, at his job and on the farm. I would never deny that he is one of the hardest working men I have ever seen in all my life. The stress he took on, and the tragedy he had been through himself, is what led to him treating me unkindly. I knew that. He didn't even have to explain.. I had known that all along. It was one of the reasons I stayed as long as I did. I knew him well enough to know that he never had bad intentions; he never purposefully meant to do harm. He didn't know how to express emotions, other than to release them through anger. He was doing the best he could with what he had. Deep down, he really was a good man with a good heart. He had just been tainted by misfortune. It really wasn't his own doing.

I honestly considered going back to him, several times. I wanted to believe that Jason had changed and was ready to settle himself down for good... that he was capable of finding happiness in the life we had worked so hard to build together. He showed great signs of improvement already. He displayed more emotions than I had never seen from him before, in all our years together. He really was trying to put his best foot forward. I came so very close to grabbing him in my arms and holding him tight. I wanted to console and assure the man I had loved for so long, the one I believed to be my soulmate, the husband I had been to hell and back with so many times, the father of my children. I wanted to tell him everything would be okay, that we would live happily ever after, growing old together and dying in each other's arms.

The biggest part of me wanted nothing more than to reconcile our marriage. I wanted to fix what had been damaged between us. I had always tried to show consideration towards him. But it was too late. I just knew with all conviction in the smallest part of myself, my broken heart.. that I could never withstand another battle if he was to ever get angry with me again. I just couldn't. That was the cold hard truth, and I had to live with it. As much as I wanted to stand by my man, I had to stand by my final decision instead. For my own sanity, and most importantly, for the best interest of our kids. I was so afraid that if I changed my mind and decided to stay with him, that his temper would flare again someday, sooner or later.. and I would be back to square one in the whole process. I couldn't let myself backtrack. I knew I was too damaged to ever find the strength to retrace my steps again.

For the children so far, life was going on mostly uninterrupted and as normal as could be expected, during the time that we began proceeding with our divorce arrangements. J.J. had graduated from grade school and was going on to middle school. Faith was busier than ever, tending to Merrybelle and helping to take care of all the animals. We still had much to be proud of and thankful for, regardless of the decision to divorce. Everything was basically the same as before this latest tidal wave of catastrophe struck, and definitely better on the other side of those fairly recent hard times, we had fallen on. Jason and I were getting along more peacefully than we had in years. We didn't discuss the pending divorce in front of the kids. Our farm lives didn't slow down much at all. I was getting increasingly more stable health-wise. Although I wasn't as active or nowhere near as thorough, in my work around the house and on the land. I was always a perfectionist before I got struck with the sickness, and now I had to settle for whatever I could manage. But I was making small steps in progress, slowly regaining some of my lost will power and strength.

There was always something to do on the farm, and we were all constantly entertained by our big collection of animals. MoMo, Copper, and Scout played and patrolled as a pack on the farm. Gandalf and Merrybelle had taken center stage and were in the spotlight more than the others. They had a unique relationship that demanded most of our attention. We had moved them both to the big fenced meadow in front of the house. Gandalf did his rounds and managed to re-enforce the entire fence line with items he collected. He would thieve anything for this mission. Every time I would see him, he was packing something in his mouth, to add to his ever-growing collection. He stole trash, he stole horse supplies, he stole the kids' toys, he stole patio furniture cushions off the front porch. Whatever he could find was his for the taking. His philosophy was finders, keepers.

I decided to walk the entire fence line one day—just out of curiosity of what Gandalf had been working so hard on. It was rather amazing what he had done. I couldn't help but be proud of my big white polar bear dog. He had every square inch of that fence arranged with his stolen objects, in an organized manner. He was brilliant. He had dug potatoes out of the garden down the hill. He carried them up the hill, and placed them at measured distances apart, along the fence line. I saw a pair of Jason's underwear. I came across an unopened package of Mary Kate & Ashley perfume. I found one of the kids' missing iPods. I discovered trash that had been sorted by material, like a recycling center. He had put glass bottles in one place, aluminum cans in another, and plastics somewhere else. Gandalf was a pure genius. He had lined the entire fence, to protect his cow, Merrybelle. It looked like he was practicing an intricate art form of warding off evil spirits. I had chosen the right name for him. He was like a real-life wizard.

Gandalf ended up getting into a brawl with a juvenile black bear that came too close to his fence and Merrybelle. He would have died protecting his cow. The bear nearly ripped his tail clear off. Luckily I rushed him to the vet in time for them to sew it back on. Gandalf made a full recovery from his injuries. I made him come off of his duties and into the house while he was healing. He was terrified of the ceiling fan. Even though I would turn it off while he was inside, he would never walk directly underneath it. In many ways, as big and brave as he was, that dog was a giant scaredy-cat. He allowed little lowrider MoMo to bully him away from food. He never let any humans near him, other than me and the children. I made him watch the Santa Buddies movie repeatedly, in all seasons, and he always seemed to enjoy it. Also, he was adamant about holding hands when he was with us. Gandalf was the first dog I encountered that insisted on holding hands. I have never seen another dog like him. He was one of a kind, and very special. I always felt indebted to him, because he had helped me to walk again, in my physical therapy on the farm.

I finally learned how to play my guitar and sing at the same time. So I would sit on a bucket out in the front meadow and perform for the animals. They would all gather around me in a semi-circle, and listen intently to the racket I made. The first song I learned on the guitar was an old Merle Haggard tune, "The Way I Am". I bet I played and sang that one a hundred times. Animals don't care.. they make for the best nonjudgmental audience. I had sung to animals all my life, but now that I could half-ass accompany myself on the guitar, I felt like I had accomplished something that somewhat resembled music. My vocal cords were permanently weakened by my illness, to the point that my speaking voice became so quiet that, to this day, people have a hard time hearing me talk. My voice was also dialed down a few notches to a lower octave range, with a more raspy sound. I sang soprano before, but now I was altered to alto range. Arthritis in my stiff hands made it hard for me to play the guitar. But I gave it hell anyways. I just wanted to do anything that didn't involve lying in my sickbed. I was tired of being sick. I wanted to feel alive.

In the fall of that year, I did something I regret to this day, and will always be remorseful for. I had gone all through my twenties without smoking or drinking or using foul language. I had been a good and decent person for the most part. Now I was pursuing all three of these bad habits. I was using them as coping mechanisms for the disease I was dealing with, and the divorce still in progress. I was invited out by a girlfriend, one night at the end of August, to the local Tractor Bar. The guy that I met at the St. Jude's benefit concert years earlier was set to play. He and I had become somewhat of friends since I had photographed his album cover. It started out as a professional relationship and grew into an innocent friendship. I never even looked at another man inappropriately the whole time I had been married. I had no intentions of ever cheating. I wasn't the cheating kind. I have always been an extremely loyal person to those I love.

I got dressed and ready to go. Jason knew I was going. It would be my first time ever at a bar without him. He was not happy about it and called me some bad names on my way out the door. We were still separated even though we still resided in the same house. But that was no excuse for what I did next. I went, I got drunk, I danced with the guy I had been friends with, and then I let him kiss me in the parking lot at the end of the night. He knew I was having marital troubles, I had disclosed that to him in confidence as a friend. It was mostly innocent on his part. But I was plain guilty. Although I was headed for a planned divorce, I should have waited until it was final before seeking comfort from another man. It was out of line and out of character for myself to do such a thing. I was mortified that I kissed another man. I went back home, did the ultimate walk of shame, and kept it from Jason. It was my dirty little secret that I had to cover up and hide.

What's worse than that, is the fact that I allowed for this affair to continue and escalate. It became very serious by the end of that year. I told myself that because I was lonely, I needed affection from a man. I told myself that I deserved someone who would treat me like a prize to be won. This is how I made it okay in my mind. This is how I swept my guilty conscience under the rug during that time. I convinced myself, since I was on my way out the door of our marriage, that there was no harm done in beginning a new relationship. I was wrong. I should have just waited for the right time. I should have fixed myself before I got involved with someone new. Then it would have maybe been alright. But the longer I got away with it, without getting caught, the more it brought my born rebellion to the brink of danger. Then I continued the affair because it made me feel alive and wanted. It was a rush of adrenaline. I felt young again. It was my release of the flight response that had been initiated within me.

I knew for a fact if Jason ever caught me he would certainly kill me. That was the danger in it. I told myself that I was finally giving him something to actually warrant his wrath and I was okay with that. I almost wanted to be punished for what I had done. I knew it was a cardinal offense, even in our current circumstances. I subconsciously wanted to engage in something that was a valid reason and could justify being hurt by my spouse in the past. On the other hand, I also believed that I had fallen in love with this new guy. He was a guitar man and that drew me in and captivated me. I became naively fixated on him and the prospect of having a future together. It was all just smoke in mirrors. It was all a charade. But I didn't know that then. Although that path did somehow lead me to where I was supposed to go. However, that isolated incident is something I would change the timing of if I could. But life doesn't work that way, we don't get do-overs or what-ifs. Life is full of nasty tricks and dirty deeds. And the Devil was taking a shotgun ride in the front seat of my condemnation during that wild ride—with all my demons in the backseat, cheering me on.

Jason eventually did find out. But it didn't go as I had expected, not at all. He found text messages on my phone one morning while I was sleeping. He went on to work, without saying a word. But he left clues as to the fact that he was now aware of my moral indiscretions. So when I woke up and found these hints, I called him, expecting to hear the judgment for my crime. He calmly said we would discuss it when he got home. That was one of the longest waits I ever had. I didn't know what to expect. I was preparing myself for the verdict to be read, and the sentence to be carried out. I was ready to pay the Devil his dues. I was prepared to lay my head on the chopping block and to accept the consequences of my bad behavior. He hadn't killed me or even yelled at me upon his discovery. It scared me even more that I didn't get the reaction I originally anticipated. I just assumed he would lash out immediately.. which would have made me feel less guilty.

We hadn't officially filed for divorce yet. I was stalling till we had our plan in order, so the court wouldn't make our determinations for us. Jason had been holding off in hopes that we would get back together. When he got home that evening, he wasn't mad at all. I was in complete shock and disbelief. His pride was hurt. He felt betrayed and blindsided. He felt like there was no way for him to win me back after I had crossed that line. I hung my head in shame and listened to everything he had to say. He knew with no uncertainty, that I had officially cut my ties to him on a romantic level. It was the event that made him realize that our divorce decree was already sealed. He knew I would have never strayed off otherwise, it wasn't in my nature to be unfaithful. And so he took the divorce papers, and filed them himself, citing irreconcilable differences.

Jason continued to try and make up with me even after finding out what I did, and after filing our divorce with the court system. I opened up in complete honesty with him once the truth of my infidelity was revealed, and I told him how the affair came about. There was no sense in trying to sugar coat it at this interval. I had been caught red-handed. I had to fess up. Later, it became a competition for him to try to win me back. The affair had been on again off again and had taken a dramatic turn of its own when I found out that the guy I had been seeing, had a woman at home. So I wasn't invested in that relationship anymore. I had been burnt by my desire to be with someone else.

But I still couldn't go back to my failed marriage. Aside from my initial reasons for divorce, I felt uneasy about what I had done and how it made Jason feel. I recognized myself as a horrible person that deserved no one at all. I had consorted with a man that wasn't my husband. On the other hand, I got a glimpse of the fact that there are men out there who are calm and gentle. That gave me false hope. But I resolved to lead a life with no man at all—to be alone and lonely for the rest of my days. I never wanted to search for love, ever again. I had my fill of the pretend notion of love between a man and a woman. As far as I was concerned there was no such thing. It was all merely make-believe, lies, and nonsense. I grew numb and void of all emotions.

Part 3

After all, this was said and done, I became broken again. I didn't know how I could continue to look my children in the eyes and teach them right from wrong when I had done something so blatantly wrong myself. They weren't aware of what had transpired, but I knew. That's what brought me to my knees in atonement. I was convinced that I didn't deserve any of my blessings. I had become a low life piece of shit, not worthy of anyone or anything. I was shattered again, divided into more pieces, scattered all over the ground yet another time. I would never be able to put myself back together in a way that I could be proud of or feel any sense of self-worth or honor. I had been broken one too many times to ever even qualify for being repaired.

All my life, most every bad thing that had ever happened to me, had been out of my hands. I was an innocent victim in most every case (other than my first grade fit and my teenage trouble). And I had managed to overcome all of my past hardships, with the eternal exception of losing Grace. I have never been whole since then. But this kick in the gut was something I inflicted upon myself. That made it different and it was something I would never be able to brush off and walk away from. It became a permanent scar. And the stress that came along with my newfound predicament, caused my body to attack itself again, with a massive flare-up of my unrelenting autoimmune disorder.

I ended up in the hospital with a severe kidney stone attack. Then I was cursed with a much worse case of rheumatoid arthritis, another episode of pukefest, even more of my hair falling out, and a more intense round of intolerable pain. There was no position I could sit, stand, or lie down in to feel any relief. There was no way to alleviate the constant affliction. I took it just like I had taken that whipping in the first grade, knowing full well that I deserved it for the wrong I had done. I tucked tail and picked my own switch for a flogging. I was being punished by Karma. And I accepted my fate with unadulterated responsibility. I owned my disease and it owned me. I was set back in the mode of fight response again. But I had no fight left in me.

Rising From the Ashes

When I rose up again, I was like a Phoenix. My former self had been incinerated in the flames of every mortal Hell on Earth I ever walked through. When I came out on the other side of Purgatory, I disintegrated into ashes. My new self-emerged from the fire and was regenerated. I was rising from my own ashes, in renewal and rebirth. I felt like I could flap my broken wings and learn to fly again. Then I pieced myself back together in a mismatched Frankenstein style assembly line of creation. I was missing parts and stitched together in a random assortment of spare pieces. At first, I was repulsed by my new reflection. I was a monstrosity of sorts. I was like the Tin Man, tack welded at the seams, and rough around the edges, with a mechanical heart. I would have to get reacquainted with myself. But I knew I would grow into my new skin eventually, and become comfortable in it. I just had to break it in till it fit like a glove—wear it down like the tread on new tires, condition it like leather on a new saddle.

I was still sick, but I came to terms with the reality that it was just part of the territory. I would drag my disease with me like a life sentence of a ball and chain, I would force it to follow my lead.. and hope that someday I would finally find the key to unlock it and set myself free from this heavy burden. But for now, it was mine to carry. And I refused to let it slow me down or deter me anymore. I learned to read the warning signs of my flare-ups. They would start with the lymph nodes on my collarbone getting extremely swollen and sore, along with my hands feeling weaker and my vocal cords becoming more strained. I knew when these three things set in, that a bigger wave of worse symptoms, with my kidneys and arthritis, was soon to follow. If I could settle myself down or rest in time before the big wave hit, sometimes it would be subdued and take less of a toll on me. So that's what I tried to control. I couldn't let myself get worked up or overly stimulated. I had to remain calm and listen to my body when it demanded downtime. If I failed to manage it and get it under control, I knew to brace myself for impact, and hang on for dear life.

I gained a new fervor for life since I had survived what I thought was the end for me. I had a new appreciation for living in the moment like there was no tomorrow. I felt like I had been given a second chance at a new beginning. I wanted to devote myself and my time, only to people and causes that I deemed as worthy. I was part leather for the tough side of me, and part lace for the sensitive side that I kept. I maintained my gratitude to God for the good in my life. I reserved the soft side of myself solely for my children. And stored some of that away for the rest of my family, and my animals. I aimed to be passionate about anything I aspired to accomplish. I wanted to feel the wind beneath my wings. I needed to roam freely like a Mustang in open range, unbridled. I had been a domesticated horse, but I was breaking loose of my constraints. I was turning into a wild horse. I was becoming untamed. And I would never let anyone or anything try to break me, ever again.

I had been under the dictatorship of a man for over a decade. I was theoretically drafted into Jason's personal platoon as his own recruit, trained like an infantry grunt soldier. I was under his command, and he was my Marine Corps Drill Sergeant. I graduated from his boot camp. I earned my rank. I wore my battle scars. He turned me into a fierce and brave warrior. At this point, I wasn't going to take instructions from anyone else.. I didn't care who tried to bark orders at me. It could be the Pope of Rome, The President of the United States, anyone with authority, I didn't care. I feared no man. I dared anyone to even think about trying to rule over me, (Except for the Queen of England. God save the Queen. She could boss me around.), but I was fed up with the rest. I made up my mind that I was done being told what to do or how to be. And I wasn't going to wait for a knight to ride in on a white horse and rescue me. I was going to rescue myself from now on. I added the first amendment to my newly founded constitution, A Zero-Bullshit Tolerance Policy. I was sticking to my guns. I was finished with taking any shit from people, or from life. Period. Nothing and nobody was ever going to push me around or try to overpower me again. I would not allow it. I was done being reprimanded. I had enough of being bullied. I would start taking names and kicking ass of anyone who proceeded to step foot over my threshold or threaten me in any way.

When I was younger, I would wear my tough girl mask to cover up my pain and hide my sorrow. But this time, when I came back up swinging, it wasn't a mask anymore. It was actually part of me, a permanent fixture. I wasn't just pretending to be a badass now. I was the real deal. I had transformed into a legitimate hardcore five foot three force to be reckoned with. I was ready to take on the world, like a wrecking ball crashing in. I said to the universe, "You want to knock me down again? Come at me bitch. Here I am." I looked the Devil in the eye and laughed at him. I said, "Fuck you Satan, and the horse you rode in on. You're not going to imprison me in Hell again. I've been there and done that. I escaped to tell the tale." Then I drug all of my ugly demons out of the closet and dared them to defy me. I put them in the naughty corner and made them cower down before me like I was their queen and they were my subjects. I gave them a loud and clear proclamation.. to stay in the closet, until further notice, when I would send for them to come out of the shadows and do my bidding.

In this new Renaissance Period of my life, I came out of the gate at full gallop. I was ready to let the rubber meet the road, to keep truckin' ahead to the next chapter of my unwritten story. The year of 2013 brought about another blank slate that I was prepared to tell a new story on. I wasn't exactly sure what I wanted this new chapter to entail.. but I knew that change was on the horizon. Historically, I have never done well with change, even if it's for the better. I like for things to stay the same—to feel a sense of settlement. But if there is one thing that never changes about life, it is that life is always changing. I learned this lesson the hard way countless times throughout my years on this Earth. But this time, I knew that change was necessary. I felt like I may even be capable of embracing the wind as it switched directions, like I was a weathervane, and could spin freely and turn to face whichever way the soft warm breeze or the cold hard wind was blowing. I felt as though I could remain in constant centrifugal motion, steady under any and all elements of nature.

Meanwhile, the farm story was still unfolding mostly uninterrupted, but with a few previews, commercial breaks and brief intermissions. It resembled a Lifetime Movie Network miniseries. The most dramatic parts were based on the still-pending divorce. There were tearjerkers, requiring a box of tissues. But there were also plenty of heart-warming moments, laugh out loud comedy, action/adventure, horror scenes, plot twists and cliff hangers. There were main characters, cameo roles, and stunt doubles. There were heroes and villains. It contained a variety of scripted and non-scripted parts. The storylines flowed together in a way to keep the audience captivated and on the edge of their seats, wondering what would happen next. How would it end? I happened to be the producer, director, and one of the lead stars on the credit roll in this epic tale of heroism and defeat, tragedy and triumph. I was on the silver screen at my own premiere party. I provided plenty of entertainment for spectators, to grab a bag of popcorn and an ice cola. Then sit back in their theater seats and watch an unrated explicit version movie reel of film, as it was unraveled through the projector. (Depending on how close you were to the action, it might look more like a train wreck).

That spring, we welcomed new life on the farm. Ginger gave birth to her baby foal in March, a filly that we named, Mini Cooper. It was mine and the children's first time ever seeing a newborn horse. And since Cooper was of miniature equine breeding, she was extra tiny. After her mother cleaned her off and she was able to get to her feet, I picked her up and held her in my arms. She was the one and only horse I have ever held. Faith and J.J. watched in amusement as Cooper ran around in circles. She bucked, kicked, and reared up while she whinnied and neighed in her micro mini voice. It was magical. That event brought about a sense of renewal on the farm. In May, our two female goats (Bessie and Priscilla) both gave birth to two sets of kids. They were sired by our male goat, Pepé Le Pew. We were intrigued by all the cute and funny behaviors of the baby goats. All the new animals around the land brought us pure joy.

Sadly, Priscilla rejected one of her two babies, so I took that one up the hill and raised it inside on a bottle. Having a goat in the house was so much fun for me and the children. Who needs TV and video games when you have livestock in your living room? We had hours of free entertainment. I named that adopted male goat, Presley, but we accidentally called him Goat one too many times, so that is what he answered to and it subsequently became his official name. He was raised with the dogs in the house, so Goat behaved just like one of them. Canines were his tribe. He would go to the door to be let out if he had to use the bathroom. When he was weaned off the bottle, he preferred dog food. MoMo trained him and herded him around the house. Every animal on the farm accepted MoMo as the dominant alpha, and he was the smallest of them all.

Goat followed me around like him and I was the real-life version nursery rhyme of *Mary Had A Little Lamb*. He cried and carried on if I got two feet away from him. He became my little sidekick. He sat on my lap. He slept at my feet. He took rides inside the cooler on the front of the four-wheeler. Every time I would go to leave the farm, he would uninvitedly load up in the cab of the truck and perch himself on top of the dashboard. He designated that spot so he could see out through the windshield. When I drove to town and pulled into a parking lot, people would see him propped up there and do a double-take. Like "What the heck am I seeing?" I just nodded at them and announced, "Yep, that is a goat on my dash." He was a conversation starter everywhere we went. And he was also a mischief-maker. He would try to raid food off our plates. He tried to eat my burning bush. He climbed on top of the tractor. I was constantly having to scold him and say, "No Goat, behave yourself."

Jason didn't exactly approve of pet livestock in the house. He took Goat away from us and sold him off. Faith and I whined and cried, bawled and carried on about it the day that he left the farm, and for days on end afterwards. We were so sad. I guess Jason felt bad after seeing how torn up we were about it. Several days later, he left and came back. Faith and I were in the living room, still depressed from losing our friend. Jason came around the front porch and held a surprise up to the window for us to see. It was Goat! Jason brought him back to us. We were the happiest two girls in the world that day. And he was just as happy to be reunited with us. Weeks after Goat's return, the children and I were getting ready to go to a parade in Summersville. We planned to take Goat with us, and hook a leash to his dog collar to walk him around. We thought he would enjoy the festivities in town. I called for him when it was time to load up in the Avalanche. He didn't come. We ended up skipping the parade, to search for him because he always came when I called and was the first to jump in the truck. I looked high and low for the rest of that day and didn't find him. For days and weeks and months after that, I would call for him and hope that he would come back home. I never saw him again. I never knew what became of Goat. I still miss that little fella. After a while, I tried to adopt his brother. I named him Sue ("A Boy Named Sue"). That one did not make for a good pet.

The farm was expanding and abounding with life. Our orchard trees were mature, our garden was overflowing, the animals were content with their home and their human family. It all looked like a pretty picturesque setting. No one would have guessed that it was all an optical illusion. Very few people knew that we were in the process of dividing our marriage and our home. Everything just seemed normal and happy. We covered our hidden agenda very well and just went on about our business. I'm sure the close circle of our extended families must have assumed that we were never actually going to follow through with the divorce. It didn't appear that way. It most likely came across as though we had buried the hatchet and would continue to stay together. It was long and drawn out. But behind the scenes, most everything was being rearranged in some way or another. We were just trying to shield the kids from it, and maintain a sense of privacy in what was happening behind closed doors.

Our children were growing and changing more and more each day. They were doing well in school and sports. They were developing more into their own unique characters. J.J. was smart, funny, and creative. He was one of a kind and marched to the beat of his own drum. That's what I love most about him. There is no one else in the world like my son. To this day, that is my favorite aspect about my boy. There will never be another one like him. He is the most special person I have ever known. Faith was sweet, caring, and innocent. She was always a good girl, with a heart of gold. She would do anything to make someone smile or feel special. She would go out of her way to pick flowers for me, draw me pictures, and give me hugs. She is still my princess and my baby, always will be. Faith is the kindest and most beautiful person I have ever known. Both the kids have always had impeccable manners and high morals. They knew right from wrong. They would never intentionally hurt anyone or anything. They have good hearts and sharp minds. They were upstanding little citizens. I was beyond proud of how my kids were turning out. Jason and I must have done something right; we raised them the best that we could. We had J.J. and Faith to be grateful for.

In July of that year, we took our last vacation together as a family, to Florida. Haley and Javier planned an extended trip to Spain, where Javi Senior intended to check a big item off of his bucket list and take part in the Running Of The Bulls in Pamplona. They asked us to stay with Little Javi in their home while they were away. So Jason, the kids and I, packed up and drove down to Lakeland. We got there right at J.J.'s 12th birthday, so Haley graciously hosted a pool party for him at her house before she left for Europe. Once we wished my sister and brother-in-law bon voyage, we spent our time there with Javi Jr. We tried to make everything fun for him, so he wouldn't get upset with missing his parents. We took him to the beach, to the movies, and to Lego Land. I was happy to have quality time with my nephew, and my kids were so attentive to their little cousin. We all had great times and made good memories. However, It was bittersweet between Jason and I, knowing that after all our many travels, this would be our last trip together as man and wife. We would sit out by the pool at night and contemplate our current status. We held peaceful pow wow discussions.

Back home in West Virginia, it was time for us to begin the next phases of our full-scale invasion on the farm. We broke ground for the addition onto the cabin. It was time to get my new home plans underway. In August, on the morning of the day that the crews were due to arrive, Jason and I sat on the hillside to survey the site. He asked me one last time, "Are you sure this is what you want?" I briefly paused and reflected, then replied "Yes."

There was no need for either of us to say more than that. We had laid all of our cards out on the table, and this was the luck of the draw. So we continued to look out over the land together, while the workers began busting away the deep layers of sandstone with jackhammers, and moving the broken rock with excavators. The landscape was changing, right before our eyes. We sat there watching silently, side by side—close together but a million miles apart.

Construction began on my house. Jason hired a local crew of contractors to do the job. He gave them my kindergarten style drawing of plans. That's all they had to go on. I oversaw all the beginning stages of the building process. I had a front-row seat, and I was fascinated with observing every single step; the foundation being laid, the walls being raised, the roof trusses going up. Architecture has always been a subject I am extremely interested in. But this meant more to me than that. My future hopes and dreams for peace and happiness would be cultivated within these walls and under this roof. It would be "the house that built me." I did walk throughs daily and made last-minute changes as I saw fit. I could tell the builders were getting frustrated with my indecisiveness. But I would bring them beer and Subway sandwiches for their lunch break every afternoon, so they let me get away with changing my mind. There was one crew member that I felt an instant kinship with from the first time I saw him. He was a long-bearded, rough-looking character. The epitome of a West Virginia hillbilly. His name was Hippy. I didn't know it then, but he would soon become one of my very best friends of all times. We were destined to meet.

Now that my house structure was well underway; the next logical step for me was to get a job to support myself. Jason had always been the primary financial provider. But now I would have to pull my own weight. I hadn't worked full time since before my illness first struck. I had to carefully select something that wouldn't be physically demanding, as my body couldn't take hard labor now. It was still very fragile, and I had to be delicate with what I subjected my health too. And it couldn't be anything overly stressful, because I had to remain calm to keep from having a flare-up. So that summer season, I started an endeavor that I saw as a way to start providing for my children and myself. This is where "Untamed Tiff" stepped up to the plate. I decided to dabble in the black market of moonshine. I didn't know the art of the trade yet or how to make it, but I got my feet wet by stepping out as a bootlegger. Remember, since the reinvention of myself, I had no respect for any type of authority—including the law.

I originally procured an interest in the moonshine tradition when I was a young child. My fascination was sparked by my Grandma Sparks telling me a story. She told me about her mother dressing up as the Revenue Man, and shooting her father's still all to hell. She said moonshine ran off that mountain for a month. Then her dad tried to hide another still under the dining table, tucked away beneath the cover of the tablecloth. But he added too much yeast one time and caused the mash to overflow and spill out onto the floor, which got him into even more trouble with his wife. I was always curious about why my Great Grandmother got so mad at my Great Grandpa for what he was doing. I didn't understand what the big deal was. I felt sorry for the old man every time I heard that story. That is how I first became aware of the taboo subject of shine and enamored by it at the same time. Besides the fact, it was just a way of life in my native Appalachians. It was part of my culture and heritage.

I was making decent wages with my fees for bootlegging untaxed liquor. I picked up several regular customers and accumulated discreet outposts in different locations. I made for the perfect culprit in the transportation of illegal moonshine because I looked like a sweet innocent lady. The law was never onto me because I didn't seem suspicious at all. But I needed to secure a big purchase of a vehicle for myself, and moonshine money wasn't going to make me rich overnight. So I got a second, less incriminating full-time job, as a banker of all things. Which is funny, because I have always sucked at mathematics. But I could at least count, so surely it wouldn't be that hard. And the bank hours would be conducive to the school schedule of my kids.. that way I could still be home for them.

I didn't fit in well with the other bank ladies. It was my first time ever working with women in general. I had worked mostly male-dominated jobs all my life up to this point. I realized early on that groups of females are like a hen house of gossip and operators of rumor mills. And grown women can be just as immature as middle school girls, if not worse. But I ended up getting along with most of them after a while. They didn't approve of my inappropriate behavior in the bank though. I would shoot rubber bands at our male boss. I would catch spiders and insects outside, and put them in the tubes to send to customers I didn't like. I would wait on cops at the drive-through window and announce on the microphone that I needed a police escort to Mexico, cause I was fixin' to rob the vault. I would boss the officers, telling them not to come back unless they brought donuts to send me through the tubes. The other bank ladies would say "Shut up! You can't say that to policemen." I had no filter. But I looked professional in my business attire. And some of my customers loved me.

I bought myself a car in September. I needed something fuel-efficient for travels. I ended up getting a blue 2014 Chevy Spark. It was the first and only brand new vehicle I have ever had. The best thing about it was the butt warming feature. I felt like a real grown-up purchasing a car of my own. I didn't want to take any of the shared vehicles from our marital assets. I loved the Avalanche, it had been my primary ride for years.. but I couldn't afford the average of 8 MPG that it got. I wanted a reliable mode of transportation to get me to and from my bank job, and for my bootlegging career. The only problem is that the Spark only had a whopping 84 horsepower engine; it was like the equivalent motor of a go-cart. It was not an ideal hot rod to outrun the law if they ever caught onto me for hauling liquor. But I insisted on the car because it matched my last name. It was the main reasoning behind my selection of that particular model. I felt like it was custom made for me. The "Blue Spark" was going to be my ticket to freedom.

Which leads me to the second round of my dark period. This time it wasn't about airing out the dirty laundry—that ship had already sailed. I was on a new mission, to hit the highway and rack up miles. I was going to squall tires and burn rubber. I wanted to roll the windows down, turn the radio up loud, rev the RPMs and stomp the gas pedal to the floor. I needed to feel the wind in my hair and sing along to "Free Bird" on the stereo. I didn't really even care where I went, I just wanted to hit the green lights and go. It was part of spreading my new wings. Jason and I were in the practice now of dividing our time with the children. It was sort of a trial run to see how we would all adjust when I moved down the hill once my house was finished. So I had the kids while he was at work, and he had time with them on his days off. When they were with their dad, that's when I would take off and feel the freedom of the road. It was another form of stress relief for me.

I planned a road trip out of state for early November. There was a newly opened Johnny Cash Museum in Nashville, TN, and I wanted to visit it. I made a few previous trips to the general area while I was seeing the guitar guy recording artist from the affair.. but I didn't make it downtown on any of those occasions. I had never been in a metro area alone before, and Music City was new to me, so I didn't know my way around. I was still of the old school mindset of using maps instead of the modern-day GPS systems. So

I mapped out my trip into the city ahead of time then followed the road signs. It was a seven-hour drive from Birch River. I booked a hotel room on the outskirts of town. When I arrived in Nashville, I found a parking garage just before dark. I walked the rest of the way to 3rd Avenue South. I went right past Broadway and didn't even stop to take notice of the nightlife there, or the musicians on every street corner. The museum was my whole reason for going, the only sight I wanted to see.

I bought my ticket at the door, and slowly made way throughout the museum, stopping to admire every exhibit. The entire time, I was wishing my Peepaw could be there with me. He was the main reason I wanted to visit this place to begin with. He would have loved the tribute to Johnny Cash. It was an impressive collection of The Man In Black's personal items and memorabilia from his long-standing music career. Along with those of his second wife, June Carter. It was all remarkably done and well worth the trip. I met one of the curators on duty, his name was Chuck. I explained why I was there, and told him the story of how Johnny's brother Tommy taught my grandfather how to play guitar, and how much that gift of music meant to me and my relatives. He seemed interested in that connection between the Cash family and my family, then invited me to come back to the museum for Johnny's birthday celebration which would be the next February. Chuck and I added each other on social media and exchanged contact info. We became friends.

Back at home, and back to work; I kept busy with everything that I had going on. The progress on my new house was coming along nicely. It was under roof before winter, and the interior construction was underway. It was starting to look like a real dwelling. Hippy was a master craftsman by trade, and he had taken over as foreman on the job. He put his carpentry skills to fine form on every square inch of the place. I bossed him around about everything though. He wanted to knock the back wall of the original cabin down, and I demanded that it stay. We went back and forth about it several times for months.

Finally one day, after ordering a spiral staircase for the house, I walked in and said, "Okay Hippy, take that wall down." He was like, "Damn girl, what took ya so long to say that." We became the best of friends, even though I continued to be bossy to him. Like I stated before, it takes a broken soul to recognize another broken soul. That was the basis of our friendship. We were kindred spirits. Hippy became part of my tribe.

During that winter, I went out with two of my girl cousins from Braxton County, to a concert in Flatwoods. It was the same band that had invited me backstage in the same town years earlier. The whole time I was there, one of the brothers kept staring at me, the lead guitar player. We have already established that I had a thing for guitar men. Something about them caught my attention more than other guys. I think it was subconscious gravitation, due to the fact that my Peepaw was a guitar man, and he was the best example of a good man that I have ever seen. Maybe I thought that translated over to other guitar players. Anyways, I couldn't help but notice the way this one kept his eyes on me in the crowded room, like he was singling me out. I didn't speak to the band members this time, I was trying to keep my distance from falling for anyone else. I didn't need a man, and I didn't want one either. My divorce still wasn't final. And aside from that, I didn't want the hassle of being tied to anyone romantically. After I left, I went to the truck stop to put gas in the truck. The band was there fueling up their van, and the guitar player stared me down again. He looked at me like he belonged with me. It struck me. It haunted me. But I drove home and tried to put him out of my mind. It was the last thing I needed. I didn't want to be compelled by a man. I was in the process of trying to climb down from the tower I had been trapped in for nearly fifteen years.

After about a month, I still couldn't shake the way the guitar man made me feel. I felt like our paths were meant to cross for a reason. So I found him on Facebook in the beginning of that January and sent him a request. He accepted and immediately began a conversation with me on private messenger. It was just talk about the weather, our home state of West Virginia and about Nashville, where his band recorded for their albums. I told him I would be in Nashville for Johnny Cash's birthday party the following month, he said he would be there that same weekend. He was a country boy, so I told him a little about the farm. He was familiar with the Birch River area. Overall, he seemed like a genuinely nice guy. He invited me out to another one of their local shows, said he would put me on the guest list, and I accepted his invitation. One week later, I went to that concert, in his hometown an hour north of me. The weather was calling for snow, so I booked a hotel room within walking distance of the bar where the show was held. I saw his brother first, and he recognized me right away. We sat and talked, then I asked him where the other brother was. He took me to him just before they got on stage.

Part 2

The one I was there to see, put me in a side stage area and blocked it in with all their instrument cases. He was being protective of me, he didn't want anyone to bother me. That immediately made me feel something for him. All throughout their show, we kept making eye contact. He was looking at me the same way he had the last time I saw him. I was mesmerized by his guitar playing. He plays an electric acoustic and is one of the absolute best players I have ever heard. He is one of the best in the world actually, has a sound all of his own that you could pick out over a thousand other players. He was born to play the guitar. This man had a different look then other men I would have considered as my type. He had long hair, a goatee, jeans and cowboy boots; in general, he appeared as a rock-star/biker. I loved that about him. He looked like a badass but seemed calm and gentle. At the end of the concert, we sat in a corner booth and talked. I was shy, and I could tell he was too. He escorted me to the parking lot of the hotel where I was staying. He was a gentleman, continuing his protectiveness towards me. The snow was falling down all around us, looked like a winter wonderland. Standing there with him in the pouring snow, I felt safe and warm. I leaned in and kissed him before I even realized what I was doing. It just happened, as if it was meant to be, like it was natural. It felt like we were the only man and woman on Earth at that moment. Both of us blushing, we said goodnight in the parking lot and went our separate ways. We talked day and night after that. Although he seemed a little standoffish, I was too. If this was right, I wanted it to happen gradually.. slow and steady. I didn't want to force things. If it was meant to be, it would work itself out over time and play out the way it should.

This new relationship was not a secret to Jason. I told him about it right away. Our divorce still wasn't final, but we had the court date set and it was just around the corner. We had an unwritten agreement that it had dragged out long enough, to the point that it was okay to start seeing other people. Our relationship had evolved into more of a friend/roommate level. I think at this point, we were both just ready to get the show on the road and be done with the two-year ordeal of our divorce proceedings. But I was told by the guitar man that our relationship had to be kept a secret, because of the band's fame. I will not reveal his identity or the name of his band even now, out of my respect for him to this day. But back then, he all but had me sign a confidentiality agreement. I was dating a celebrity. He said it would cause me trouble if word got out about us. He was in the spotlight constantly, so I respected his wishes and did my best to maintain the privacy of our courtship. I didn't want to cause any problems with his career. He had worked all his life to get where he was. He was the one in charge of all the band's business and getting them to and from the hundreds of locations on their tour schedule. He was the boss. I was okay with keeping everything on the down-low. That's the way it had to be. I was on his rodeo circuit now. The other band members knew of course, and they all accepted me as the bosses girl. I played the part like a professional.

In mid-January, I unofficially moved into my new unfinished house. I had the keys to it, and I felt like it was time to start turning it into a home. Plus that winter was a bad one, my Chevy Spark couldn't make it up the steep driveway in the snow. And the gravel road stayed covered in a sheet of ice all that season. I had to be able to get out so I could make it to work. I didn't pack up my belongings from the house on the hill, the place that had been my home for almost a decade. I was waiting till spring and the driveway to thaw. I just gathered some clothes and basic necessities. The living room (which was the original one-room Amish cabin) wasn't finished yet. It still required insulation, electricity hook up, and drywall. There was no running water yet, no plumbing. (I lived there for six months total without water). I used a five-gallon bucket as my toilet and cleaned it out in the dirty creek. I had to gather water from the clean creek, and boil it on the cast iron wood burning stove for bathing. I didn't have central heat and air, so I had to keep the fire going. I had no cooking stove and only a mini refrigerator that I brought over from the tack room of the horse stable. I cooked beans from a can on a Coleman camp stove on the front porch. I was living primitively, to say the least, I may as well have been back in the 1800s. I didn't have the children come down to live in the new house until it was a proper place for them. I could live without modern-day amenities, but I wasn't going to ask them to live that way. They deserved only the best. I would walk up to the big house after work, to take care of the children there. And leave to go back to my house when Jason got home at night. Then on the weekends, he took care of the kids. That was a rough time for all of us.

Every weekend, I would travel to whichever town my guitar man was in, and watch him perform on stage. I went to the local Tractor Bar one night, where I hung out with him between sets. It was the first time we saw each other since our first kiss. He smiled the whole time we were together. He still seemed shy though. At the end of the night, he drove me back to Birch River in my car and had the band follow behind us in the van. He wanted to make sure I got home safely. The next time I saw him was in Ashland, Kentucky at the Paramount Arts Theater. The band was opening for Tracy Lawrence. I was escorted in the back door to the green room. The guitar man and I hid from the other band members and had some time alone. I was wearing a sparkly gold dress. He ended up with glitter all over him. Then I sat backstage with him after they finished their performance. Tracy Lawrence walked up behind us, he caught us holding hands and kissing. He said jokingly, "Knock it off lovebirds," and laughed. I said goodbye to the guitar man later that night and went to my hotel room, while he hit the road for the next stop on their busy tour schedule.

At the end of February, I headed back towards Music City. I stopped along the way to visit with my Cherokee friends Mark and Blaine in Somerset, Kentucky. We went out to have drinks and catch up. I stayed the night at Mark's house. We discussed the divorce status and I told him about my newfound relationship. Guitar man called me that night to make sure I arrived safely. I returned to Nashville to the Johnny Cash Museum for his birthday celebration. My new friend Chuck the curator, relayed my story about Tommy and Peepaw to the founder of the museum. And I was sent a personal invitation to the event. I felt so special and grateful for the opportunity. Chuck invited me to stay in the guest room of his house, to help me save money on lodgings. I arrived at his home in time to get cleaned up from travelling, and ready for the big party. He had his own personal collection in a showcase room, like a Johnny Cash mini-museum in his house. He showed all of it to me and told me the stories behind each item. Once I was ready, we rode downtown together and I was escorted through the back door of the museum. I had VIP access. I felt like a rock star, and of course, I was dressed in all black, like the legend himself.

I was led to a private elevator in the big building that housed the museum. I was taken to the top floor, to the presidential suite quarters. Chuck introduced me to the husband and wife owners of the museum, it was my first time meeting them in person. Their names were Bill and Shannon Miller, and they looked like glamorous Hollywood royalty. But they were just as nice and down to earth as could be. I liked them instantly and told them how much I loved their museum. Chuck asked me to tell them about how my grandfather came to know Tommy Cash. I told them, and they also seemed interested in the history. I was then escorted to the elegant dressing room for celebrities, where I was introduced to

Tommy, his lovely wife Marcy, and their cute little doggy. They were all very nice and gracious to me. I was nervous and star-struck, so I didn't say much at first. We left them to finish getting themselves ready and headed downstairs to the main room where the event would take place. We were there before the public ticket holders arrived. The room was filled with members of both the Cash and Carter families, as well as surviving members of Johnny's band, along with family of the late band members.

When I looked around that upscale room, my first reaction was, "Whoa, I don't have any business being here." I was a nobody farm girl from a one-horse town in the middle of nowhere West by God Virginia. And I was in the company of country music's elite legendary icons, Nashville Royalty. I was floored. Everything was so surreal. I felt like a fish out of water for a moment. I tried to compose myself in the manner I always stood by, treat the CEO like you would treat the janitor. I just conducted myself in a classy yet understated way and spoke to them as I would speak to anyone. As Chuck introduced me to all of them, one by one they all treated me like I was a guest of honor. They were all welcoming and kind. The Cash and Carter families are hands down the nicest group of people I have ever had the pleasure of meeting. I had one on one conversations with most of them. I met Johnny's sister Joanne Cash plus her husband. I met two of his daughters Tara and Kathy, June's daughter Carlene Carter, the drummer W.S. Fluke Holland, and original guitar player Luther Perkins' widow and daughter, Margie and Kathy, to name a few. I also met one of Johnny's best friends and tour managers, named Chance Martin, who hosts his own radio show on Sirius XM Outlaw Country.

Then I had another chance to speak with Mr. Tommy Cash. This time I told him why I was honored to meet him. I wanted to shake his hand and thank him for blessing my family with the gift of music. I asked him if he remembered the soldier in Germany, that he gave guitar lessons to in the attack of a castle. I saw the recollection in his eyes, and they lit up with a spark of memory. He asked me my grandfather's name. I said, "Gary Venable." He immediately replied, "Yes, I remember Gary." Then he went on to tell me personal stories of the time he had spent with my Peepaw. It was all I could do not to break down in tears of joy. It meant the absolute world to me. I was there not only to honor Johnny Cash but also in honor of my legendary Peepaw. I was an ambassador for my family. Tommy Cash tied us all together. He was one of my heroes before I ever even met him. But having the chance to look him in the eye and tell him that, was one of the best moments of my entire lifetime. It was golden.

I went on to have a private sit down five-star meal with several courses on fine linens and china, with the Cash and Carter families. I felt like I belonged there after meeting all these wonderful people. They treated me like family. The night was filled with tribute music and personal testimonies, slide shows and storytelling. When I was eating a piece of Johnny Cash's birthday cake, I felt like I officially arrived in Nashville. That was pretty epic in itself. I met and hung out with Tommy's son Mark, and we hit it off first thing. It seemed as though I had known these amazing people all my life. That's how warm and receptive they all were towards me. We had our pictures made together. It was something out of a Cinderella story for me, to be there in the presence of such outstanding company. Out of my farm attire, and dressed like a lady in black, at a red carpet event. I blended in with them and matched the occasion. It was a night I will never ever forget, as long as I live. I can never thank everyone enough, the ones who made that possible. I felt like Peepaw played a major role in orchestrating the experience for me. I hoped he was sitting with Johnny Cash, looking down from Heaven with each other, and smiling upon their families gathered together.

The following day, I spent time with my friend Chuck. We talked and talked about all the events of the celebration. He told me every story he knew about Johnny. We went back to the Museum for a Sunday service which featured the film *Gospel Road*, along with music performed by Joanne Cash. Then I packed up that afternoon and got on the road to head back to WV. I ran headfirst into a blizzard. There were severe winter weather warnings. Kentucky had already been hit with a bad case of it; a major ice storm, one of the worst on record. Some of the roadways were closed, so I stopped in Franklin, Kentucky just across the state line from Tennessee. I decided to stay at a hotel that night and wait for travel conditions to improve, then leave the next morning from there.

My guitar man was in Nashville with the band, but I hadn't heard from him most of the weekend. We were both busy doing our own thing. He called me shortly after I checked into my room and asked me to meet up with him that evening at a designated place. I got dressed up and headed back an hour South to Nashville, where I was to meet the band in a section of town near Music Row. I arrived at Winners and Losers bar and I found my fella. He wasn't performing that night, so we were able to just hang out together. We had drinks and talked, partied late into the night. He couldn't keep his hands off me, and I didn't mind. I was wearing a red dress because he liked me in that color. I ended up leaving my car in the parking lot under his instructions and rode with the band in their van to the hotel where they were staying. I spent the night with him there. He kept telling me I was the woman of his dreams, and saying over and over, "I want to marry you." I had sworn to myself I would never marry again once my divorce was final. But I had quickly and completely fallen in love with this man, and I said I would marry him someday. I felt like he was "The One". For some reason, he stated more than once that he wanted the wedding to be on December 14th. I don't know the significance of that specific date for him, but I agreed to it anyways. If he would have me in that way, I would have been his for the keeping, without hesitation.

I woke him up early that next Monday morning. I told him I had to hurry back home to take care of something important. He called me a cab, which took me back to my car, and I immediately hit the highway. My divorce court was scheduled for that very day. The weather was bad, and I had already stayed a day longer than planned. I was running way behind because of the storm. The travel conditions were some of the worst I've ever seen. There were huge sheets of ice flying from the tops of passing semi-trucks, gas pumps were coated in ice, roads were still being shut down. The band caught up with me on I-65 and followed behind me for a while. My guy was driving, and again, he was trying to make sure I was safe. I got separated from them when they pulled off an exit for gas. I knew I wasn't going to make it in time for the hearing. Two years of waiting, and I was late. I called Jason to let him know, and he said we may be able to do it over the phone through a conference call. Somewhere along the Bluegrass Parkway in Kentucky, I pulled off on the shoulder of the road and dialed in at the pre-arranged time. I was seriously present at divorce court on a cellphone, in my car on the side of the highway, one state away. The proceedings couldn't be completed, because there were documents that the judge required specifically from me. So the hearing was rescheduled for March 10th.

I made it back home and went back to work the next day. I hadn't really heard much from the guitar man since we left Nashville. When I did finally hear from him, he was acting strangely. I couldn't figure out why, but I knew there had to be a reason behind his change of behavior towards me. He ended up telling me that he didn't mean any of the things he said to me at the hotel. He blamed it all on the liquor he had been drinking that night. I was confused, but I wasn't going to force our relationship to work out. If it did fine, if not oh well. I told him I was okay with just keeping things casual. I wanted to be with this man, but I had no intentions of chasing him in a cat and mouse game. I felt like I deserved better than that. So I just backed off from him for the time being.

March had come in like a lion. Next thing I knew, it was the 10th, D-Day. Jason and I rode together to the Summersville Courthouse. We held hands on the way in the building, and on the elevator ride up to the courtroom where our almost 15-year-long marriage would be dissolved. I was crying as flashbacks played through my mind, of everything we had been through together, all the ups and downs, highs and lows, good times and bad times. It was a miracle we had even made it this far. It was impossible not to feel a surge of emotions, every feeling imaginable. It was a somber day. Jason had an attorney, and I represented myself. The presiding judge was struck by the unusual circumstances of our divorce arrangements, but he praised us for trying to keep everything civil for the sake of our children. The judge granted me my house and also tried to stamp down his seal and grant me a large monthly sum of child support. I stood up and told him that the house was in lieu of alimony and child support. I was adamant about the agreement Jason and I had made. I wanted to be fair to him. The judge then gave me the option of one year to change my mind, and handed me an official document that I could turn back in should I choose to claim child support. He stamped his gavel down, and it was done. We were married in a courtroom and divorced in a courtroom. Jason took me out to lunch afterwards, and we talked the whole time. Recollecting different aspects of our life together. It was the right way to end what we intended to be a peaceful divorce. Then we rode back to the farm together, to our shared homeland. He was freaking out about the child support document, so I gave it to him as a peace treaty so he would know that I would hold to our deal. We got the kids off the bus and told them of our divorce being final. They seemed happy about it. They knew their parents were better off apart than together.

My new house was just the right size, about a thousand square feet, less than half the size of the house on the hill. I would miss that home, even more than all the other places which were homes to me. That house is where I lived longer than any other place in my lifetime. I had memories of family gatherings and special occasions, and so many memories of my children were there. Leaving it was one of the hardest things I've ever done. But it wasn't the first time I had to start over from scratch, and if there is one thing I'm good at, it's turning a house into a home. This new place was to be a sanctuary of peace and love. I would not allow for it to be corrupted by evil of any kind. The building itself was shaped like a T (for Tiff) from an aerial view. It was two stories, with the cabin over top of the cellar, so from the street view, it looks to be three stories tall. The cabin was the living room, then the bigger two-floor addition was connected to the back of that. Hippy joined them seamlessly. You would never know that they were separate structures merged together. Hippy added his signature craftsmanship to every detail of his handy work, (and hid his autograph somewhere that I have yet to discover). Downstairs was the kitchen/dining room, a bathroom, and my room. The spiral stairs led up to J.J. and Faith's new rooms. All three of our bedrooms were the same size. There was an open space between the kids' rooms upstairs that led out onto a big bridge to the back hillside. There was a balcony off the living room, and a front porch off of the kitchen door. The living room had a cathedral ceiling and a small loft. This house had character. It was designed by me and had my name written all over it. I intended that my children and I would be the first and only ones to ever live in it. I swore that no man would ever reside under this roof.

When the driveway finally thawed out, I drove up the hill to start packing my belongings and whatever the kids wanted to bring down the hill. I knew it would be a massive undertaking to sort mine and Jason's possessions. He had brought some boxes down to me, what he didn't want, and was okay with me claiming. Most of what we had were jointly owned items. When I got to his house, as soon as I walked through the door, I noticed that a lot of things were missing. I asked the children where they were. And they told me that their dad had been sorting through everything, burning stuff and throwing it away. The kids said that he had also sold a lot of their things to a thrift store, or burned them. My blood started boiling immediately.

He hadn't even allowed for me to pack my own personal belongings. It was the things of deep sentimental value to me that I was concerned about. I felt myself going into a complete fit of rage, with smoke coming out of my ears and flames shooting from my eyes. He crossed my threshold in a most intrusive way. If he had been standing there I would have killed him right then and there. I felt like someone had burned my home and memories to the ground, purposefully as an act of pure hatred and evil arson. I went down the hill and tried to cool my temper. I didn't want my kids to see me that mad. It was the angriest I have ever been in my life. I was even afraid of what I may do next. I was like a bomb ready to go off with a big bang. I couldn't settle down. I flew back up the hill, went back into his house, and gathered as much of Jason's stuff as I could carry. I took several armloads of it. I piled it up in the driveway and looked for a can of gas. They were all empty. I went back in and grabbed a brand new bottle of Kraken Rum. I poured the entire contents of alcohol all over the pile I made. Then I struck a match, lit a cigarette, threw the match down and watched his shit burn while I stood there and smoked. Next, I was going to blow his truck up and set his house on fire. I stopped myself when I saw the fear in my children's eyes. They had never seen me that irate.

When Jason got home that night, WWIII was underway and waiting for him on the front lines. It took all I had to not put an end to him that day. But we engaged in a nasty drawn-out battle that went on for hours, (and would go on for years without a full cease-fire). It was the beginning attack from a small scale hand to hand combat version of a Hatfield-McCoy inspired feud in Birch River. He had never seen me fired up to that extent. It was scary. I was even afraid of my own self. I was a raving psycho lunatic, having a temporary moment of insanity—a meltdown. I invited my demons out of the closet for a showdown. I was the definition of batshit crazy that dark day. Jason should have listened. He should have been fair to me in return. I warned him beforehand. I told him I would never take any more bullshit or bad treatment. It was a knife in my back after I had tried to be so fair to him. I could have taken everything he owned if I had told the truth in the court of law. I took nothing from him. And this was my repayment. Fuck being nice. It doesn't pay to be nice nowadays. Everyone is out to get someone else and drag them down. I was madder than hell and about two seconds away from breaking bad in the biggest way possible. I would have been in prison for life if I had followed through with my temper. Instead, I made him tell me which thrift store he had taken the kids' belongings to. And then I made him get the fuck out of my sight before I murdered him right there on the spot in scornful vengeance. I wanted to leave him in a pile of ashes.

It took me that entire night to get a grip on myself. After the anger started to subside, the sadness began to set in. My entire plan of peace was up in smoke before I even had a chance to blink an eye. All the planning, contemplating, rearranging, figuring out how to make this impossible situation work; it was off to a catastrophic start right out the gate, and everything seemed doomed to damnation. My big bright idea was actually a big bad mistake. I hated him more than ever. The next day, I drove straight to the part of the county where the thrift shop was located. It was in the same town as the cemetery where Grace was laid to rest, so I stopped there first. And wondered what we would do with the gravesites Jason and I had already procured side by side. That was one aspect we had mutually agreed to keep the judge out of. We would decide upon how to handle that later down the road. But it was close to Gracie's 14-year anniversary of passing, so I wanted to honor her memory.

I went on to the thrift store and gasped as I walked around. Let me explain that because of the trauma of losing Grace, some of my memories of my other children were contained within items of theirs. Like time capsules. It was crucial for me to have something tangible to physically see or hold onto in order to bring back those particular memories. That's the dire state of how my mind was permanently scarred from losing my first child. As I saw some of those memories displayed around the store, with price tags on them, it killed me. Those things were priceless to me, and they were for sale for someone else to buy. I broke down crying. The owner of the store approached me and asked what was wrong. I told her as best I could through the tears racing down my face. She felt compassion and told me to please take everything I could back home with me.

I saw Grace's crib, with her bedding and mobile, along with the other children's nursery bedding sets and mobiles. I found J.J.s first Bible, and the baby blanket Meemaw made him. I found Faith's first Easter dress, the one she was wearing when Pastor Phil blessed her in church. I found a hand-sewn doll my great grandmother made for my mother, that was passed down to Faith. I found both the teddy bears J.J. had made for him and his baby sister before Faith was born. I found his first piggy bank. All the children's favorite books that I read to them countless times and several of their favorite toys. I saw Faith's first ballet recital dress and ballet slippers and so much more. I could go on and on with the memories of mine that were scattered around that store. Many of them had already been sold. I was devastated. I gathered as much as I could fit in my small car, which wasn't everything. I had to leave most of it behind, including Grace's crib that she once laid in while she watched the teddy bears dance above her. I cried the whole long way home. I would never forgive Jason for that. I never will. He should have known better.

Of course with all that stress, came another flare-up of my disease. I was down for the count again. There was nothing I could do to stop it. I didn't even want to. I just wanted it to drag me under. I felt defeated for another time. And if all that wasn't bad enough. Jason sold Faith's beloved Merrybelle, along with the cow's baby bull calf, to buy himself a new leather couch. I didn't find out till I saw them loaded up and hauled away from the farm. He was singlehandedly destroying everything, one piece at a time.

I guess he was trying to get back at me for wanting a divorce in the first place. He was trying to teach me a lesson. I was done dealing with him. We could never maintain a decent friendship after all that was said and done. I was proven right in my decision to leave him.

Back to the guitar man, we were still talking, but it wasn't the same. There was awkwardness since he was an Indian giver of words. But I needed to get my mind off everything else, so as soon as I was well enough to meet up with him again, I drove clear to the other side of the state, hours away. He had put me on the guest list and asked me to be there. I can't say exactly why, but he is the only man I have ever minded and been submissive to when it involved following instructions. I think it is because he had an authoritative presence, but was also very gentle in relaying directions. Anyways, I made the long trip to see him. Before I arrived at the venue, he sent me some cryptic messages.. basically telling me that my cousin was there, and for me to not say anything to her about our relationship. I thought it was odd, but in his line of business and constant publicity, I was used to his weird sets of instructions. There were different rules I had to follow in every location when I went to be with him, and I followed them all. I never questioned him about any of it.

I arrived and continued with guitar man's specific protocol that was in effect. I wasn't to go in the back door to the green room like I normally would to see him. I was supposed to go through the front door like a ticket-holding concert-goer. But I could feel tension in the air as soon as I walked in. My cousin turned around and had a puzzled look on her face when she saw me. She was one of the same cousins that I had gone to their show with the night guitar man stared me down. I just assumed she was a fan of the band. She was like 15 years younger than me, and much prettier. I was close to her older sisters, but never really knew her very well.

Part 3

She was fake nice to me that night and asked me what I was doing there. She seemed suspicious. But I minded the protocol and didn't answer accurately. She thought I was there to see the other brother in the band, the lead singer. And I assumed the same of her. Most girls were after that one instead of the lead guitar player that I was supposed to be with. I reluctantly danced beside my cousin in the front row and was fake nice right back to her, even though I can't stand that type of catty shit, but two can play that game. Mister guitar man had a look of horror on his face the entire night. He looked like he had seen a ghost and wanted to jump off stage then take off running. He tried his best not to glance in my direction. I wanted to walk out and leave. I was in no mood for playing games. I did exit shortly after I got there, but I returned to figure out what was going on.

Backstage after the show, it became evident to me that my cousin was there to see my guitar man. They were taking selfies together and she was acting like she knew him on an intimate level. It made me sick. I hung around long enough for her to leave, so I could tell him goodbye. He seemed ashamed of himself. I left and made the long drive home.. mad at myself for wasting my time and the fuel it took to go there for nothing but a bunch of insults. He called me later and tried to explain. Now, this is going to sound like some twisted West Virginia backwoods hood rat horseshit; come to find out, guitar man had dated this little cousin of mine, supposedly before him and I hooked up. I was like a deer in the headlights. Talk about a damn unforeseen plot twist of hillbilly love triangle, WV Edition. I had been taken for a complete fool. He apologized for my inconvenience in coming so far to see him. He swore they were a thing of the past. I was speechless. He asked me not to be mad at him.

I brushed guitar man off for a while after that disgusting turn of events. I couldn't deal with more drama along with everything else I was struggling with. I went on about my bootlegging business, my regular job, and trying to settle into my new house, (with most of my belongings ripped from me). I still had a war to fight on the home front. I needed to focus on getting my place in a livable condition for my kids. Hippy finally finished up the living room construction. I started laying into Jason about getting some running water in the house, along with a proper stove and refrigerator. Those were all on his end of the bargain. He was drawing it out on purpose, to hold our children over my head. He was still trying to control me, even after our divorce was final. And I was still trying not to kill him. It was a hostile timeframe on the farm. I also found out that he got our neighbor Susie persuaded to his side of the battle by making himself sound like a victim. They went in collaboration with each other to have my name removed from the rest of the property that had been deeded to both of us, and I had intended to pass down to my children. I never in a million years would have agreed to that. That was the beginning of a major falling out with Susie and a continued battle with Jason. It was another big knife in my back.

That May, on Mother's Day, I finally got running water. You just don't know how much people take for granted having indoor plumbing. You don't truly miss it until you have to do without it. I did without it for nearly half a year. My pissing in a bucket days were officially over. That was enough to make me want to celebrate. Jason also provided the stove and refrigerator that I had been doing without all that time. I could finally turn my house into a suitable home for my babies. That was the best Mother's Day gift I could have been given. I was thankful, and I made a temporary truce with Jason since he followed through with my requests. I went to work on transforming the place straight away and had Jason bring me down some of the kids' furniture from up the hill. He could afford to buy new, I couldn't. And it was the least he could do for stealing and selling my memories.

That same day, I also tried to make peace with guitar man, even though I was still hesitant about him and upset with the recent findings of my cousin's infatuation with the man I loved at the time. He responded and told me I could come to his concert that night if I wanted to. I couldn't make up my mind. Later I messaged him back, trying to get my protocol of place and time. He replied saying that something bad had happened, that the show was cancelled. His youngest brother had tragically passed away, on Mother's Day. My heart automatically went out to his mother. I had met her in passing only once, but I knew she was going through the worst thing that anyone could possibly experience. I cared about that whole family. I had become close to both of guitar man's brothers. The first time I met the youngest one, he said that I was perfect for his big brother. Then he and I became good friends and talked on a regular basis. I was very sad to learn of his passing. He was the same age as me. He was still young, and he was taken too soon. I wanted to comfort guitar man, but I backed off and respected the privacy of him and his family.

Shortly after, the band was scheduled to play at Myrtle Beach. I thought they would cancel, but they let the show go on; that's what their brother would have wanted them to do. I was supposed to be in another part of South Carolina visiting with family that same weekend, but I altered my plans to go out of the way to see the guitar man. I just wanted to give him a hug and be there for him, to show my support. I didn't see him before the concert, but during a set break, I walked on stage and went to him. I sat on his lap and hugged him, without saying a word. I left my car at the venue and rode with the band to their condo. All those guys had become my second family. I loved every one of them, the band members, the roadies, the sound and lighting engineers, and a cousin of the brothers that travelled with them. I had grown attached to the whole gang.

We all downed too much moonshine that night, except for guitar man who was driving the van. The rest of us were in the backseat singing acapella, every Randy Travis song we could think of. (That's who they were opening for the first time I met them.) It was hard for them to get up on stage after losing one of their brothers. Me and their cousin tried to cheer them up. Guitar man hit the brakes one time, and the cousin took off flying from the very back of the van all the way to the front. He probably slammed on the brakes to get us to shut up our singing. He was in no mood for our drunken behavior, although he had been a good sport for most of the ride. We made it to their condo on the beach, where guitar man cooked something for me to eat. Taking care of others was just part of how he rolled. He hugged me and said goodnight, then went to his own private room, where he requested to be left alone.

The cousin wanted to see the sunrise, it was his biggest wish. He had never seen the sun come up over the ocean. He even started drunk crying about how much it meant to him. I promised I would stay up to watch it with him. It was nearly time for it anyways. We pulled an all-nighter. I walked miles along the beach in the sand, wearing five-inch high heel boots. That's what moonshine does to ya. Some stupid shit comes from too much corn whiskey. We were still drunk come the dawn. But it was a beautiful sunrise. The next day, I said goodbye to them at a tattoo parlor, where they were getting ink in honor of their fallen brother. I was escorted back to my car and went on to Aiken, South Carolina to visit with three of my aunts and one of my cousins who was also my best friend, Sarah. We celebrated her birthday together and explored the Aiken Historical Museum and Thoroughbred Racing Hall of Fame. Then I headed back home to West Virginia.

Later that month, I went to another show at a riverside campground in the northeastern part of the state. I ended up following the band to a big bluegrass festival in Cumberland, Maryland. We stayed up most the night, socializing with some of the top stars of the genre. Guitar man and I ended up in someone's camper, listening to Eric Church music, and talking. I had decided to let the whole scandal with my cousin die down. If it was over between them like he said it was, I wanted it to be water under the bridge. I felt like he needed me to be there for him at this tragic time of his life. We stayed up all night. Shortly after sunrise, we gathered around a campfire, and I sang church hymns while he played his guitar. It was a peaceful morning. Afterwards, he was tired and getting kind of grouchy with me, so he went to sleep it off in his van. I left him and went on my way. I cried on my drive away from him. I was sad that I had fallen in love with this man because I knew deep down that we weren't going to stay together. It wasn't meant to be.

When all else fails, get a baby animal. I arranged to pick up a new puppy for me and the kids that afternoon, so I drove straight to Fayette County to get him. He was free to a good home, and I intended to give him one. The pup was a cross between Golden Retriever and Plott Hound. He was mostly black with some brindled gold fur. I named him after the Apache leader, "Chief Delshay." I took him to the farm, and he became our newest family member. He is the second dog I have had that insists on holding hands. It is his favorite thing. He is always the first one to greet me when I come home. Also, he leads what he sees as parades every time anyone goes up or down the driveway. He is one of the best dogs I've ever had. And speaking of Apache, that is one of my Native tribe lineages, which is why I named him Chief Delshay. I have always said, if I wake up on the Apache side of my bed, all hell is gonna break loose. Grandma Sparks use to say her Grandpa Roberts was where that heritage came from. She said he was a mean spirited man. I also have Cherokee and Potawatomi ancestral roots. I believe that my sixth sense of intuition comes directly from the Native American part of my bloodline. But I was happy for Delshay to be the chief.

In June of that year, I was invited back to Nashville by personal invitation, to the Grand Ole Opry. My friend Chuck had backstage passes for us thanks to the generous owners of the Johnny Cash Museum. It was a huge deal for me having been a lifelong fan of country music. Now I was getting an opportunity to witness the pinnacle of the industry firsthand. My main reason for wanting to go was to meet one of West Virginia's biggest icons, Little Jimmy Dickens.

I was running late to get to Nashville. I didn't have time to get ready at Chuck's place, and I didn't have enough money to get a hotel room. So I did the only thing I could think to do, I pulled into a truck stop. I had made a common practice of camping at truck stops during my travels. I would pull my little compact car in amidst the big rigs, and sleep to the sound of their diesel engines running. Then wake up and grab some coffee, and keep rolling. There was a Love's Travel Stop that I used frequently in Horse Cave, Kentucky. That's where I made my pit stop that day. I asked to use one of the trucker showers, which the manager obliged. I went in there looking like a trucker...wearing jeans, cowboy boots and a ballcap. I came out looking like a rhinestone cowgirl, all sparkled up in a dress and makeup. All the truckers that saw me emerge looked at me like, "What the hell?" And it was so steamy in the shower room, that my curling iron just made a big rats nest of my hair. Every time I see pictures from that night I think, "Oh dear, there's my damn truck stop hairdo."

But I met up with Chuck and we made it to the Opry House on time. We were VIP. We walked in through the artist entrance, where I met the lovely and talented Jaida Dryer, and iconic Jim Ed Brown. Then we went backstage to the celebrity dressing rooms. Chuck knew who I was there to see, and he was trying his best to make that happen, but Little Jimmy wasn't at his dressing room yet. I met Keith Anderson and all the other artists that were performing that night. Then I was finally introduced to the one and only Mr. Little Jimmy Dickens. He was so cute, I just wanted to pick him up and whirl him around. I shook his hand and told him where I was from. His eyes lit up when I said, "West Virginia." He gave me a big hug and asked me which part I lived in. I told him Birch River, and he knew exactly where it was on the map. We talked about our home state for a while, had our pictures made, gave each other several big hugs, and I kissed him on the cheek. It was a dream come true to meet the legendary Little Jimmy. During the Grand Ole Opry show, we were seated on the stage, directly behind the house band. It was epic. You can feel the energy in the air and sense the presence of every great legend who has ever stood in that circle of hallowed ground. It was a once in a lifetime experience. I felt so fortunate to be able to have that opportunity, to witness history in the making.

Chuck and I left from the Opry and headed to the Nashville Palace, where our night just continued to get even better. We hung out with Johnny Cash's drummer, W.S. Fluke Holland. He was so kind and generous to me. I had my picture taken with him, and he gave me an autographed drumstick, (which I display in my own Cash collection). He played a stage set on his drums, and I danced along to his legendary beat with my friend Randall, who also worked at the Cash Museum. Then I met the beautiful Catherine Bach. I was star struck when I hugged her. I couldn't even keep my cool. I was like a little girl meeting a real-life princess. "The Dukes of Hazzard" was and remains as what I consider to be the all-time absolute best program ever on television, and "Daisy Duke" was one of my biggest female idols when I was growing up. Meeting her made me feel like I was in the cool kids club. She was so sweet and kept telling me that I looked beautiful. I just couldn't believe that my role model was giving me compliments. She made me feel like I was someone special. It was a huge honor for me to meet such an amazing lady. Altogether, that was hands down one of the best nights of my life.

One of the star-studded characters I met at Cash's birthday party, (the one whom was one of Johnny's best friends and stage manager among other significant roles), Chance Martin. He added me on Facebook after we were introduced at the party, and we kept in contact through private messenger since the night we were first introduced. He suggested several times that he and I should record a duet together. I kept thinking, this guy is crazy, he doesn't even know if I can sing and he's a professional. His voice sounds exactly like Johnny Cash, and he was nicknamed by Johnny himself, as "The Voice In Black". Well, he knew I was in town that weekend, and he wanted to meet up with me, so I agreed to it. That Sunday was Father's Day, and he sent me the address of where to find him. I put it on a GPS and followed the directions. It felt like "Sunday Morning Coming Down" after the festivities of the night before. I ended up on Music Row, another place I had no business being. The address I was given was a big mansion with a for sale sign in front of it. I thought it was a mix-up. So I pulled into the next driveway down. I saw a runner coming towards me on the sidewalk. I stopped her in her tracks and asked if she knew where I could find this address. She confirmed it was the mansion for sale next door. I asked her to stick around a minute. I said to her, "I'm meeting a man there, and I don't really know him. He could be an axe murderer for all I know. Could you make sure I'm good to go before you leave?" She politely agreed and hid in the bushes. I pulled into the circular driveway of the mansion. Chance got out of his maroon car, and instantly, I knew we would be comrades. I hugged him and I gave the runner a thumbs up, to which she popped out of the bushes and continued on her morning jog.

We sat in Chance's car, properly named the Alamobile, which suited him since his on-air name for the Sirius XM Outlaw Country show he hosts is "Alamo Jones." But to me, he is Chance, because it was by pure chance and destiny that our paths crossed. He played several songs on the radio and he brought up again about us doing a duet together. I was too nervous to sing in front of him, so I played a recording from my phone of me singing and half-ass playing my guitar. (I still don't know how to play the damn thing). He didn't say anything, he just listened. I should have been intimidated by him because he is one of the few original living legends left in Music City, or as he refers to it, "Twang Town". His resume and career are insanely impressive. I probably would have pissed my pants if I had known back then what a big deal he really was. But I didn't know all this at the time. He just became my instant buddy, and I could tell we would become partners in crime. He told me personal accounts of Johnny Cash's life and career. From everything Chance has told me over the time I've known him, I feel like I know Johnny on a personal level, even though I never met The Man In Black. But still, I was honored to be chilling with one of his best friends, who would quickly turn out to be one of my own best friends. It's funny as hell now looking back.. the fact that I had told the runner he could be an axe murderer. Chance is one of my very most favorite people in the whole world. He is an exceptional and fascinating man. He is one of the most interesting characters I have ever known.

Chance turned off the engine of the Alamobile and took me into the mansion. It was the former home and recording studio of the late great Cowboy Jack Clement. It was known as The Cowboy Arms Hotel & Recording Spa. As soon as we walked through the door, I knew I was in another place that a nobody farmgirl like me has no right to be. There were gold records lining the walls, grand pianos, rare guitars, and a vast array of significant artifacts with historical importance. It was one of the most elite recording studios in all of country music. Countless artists have probably spent their entire careers trying to get their foot in the door of this place. And I just walked right through, with no claim to fame whatsoever. It was Cowboy Jack Clement's personal home, and he hosted recording sessions there with all the greats, Johnny Cash, Waylon Jennings, Kris Kristofferson, to name a few. And Chance had known all of these legends personally. Cowboy Jack was an award-winning Country Music Hall Of Famer, a singer, songwriter, a comedian and producer of music and films. He and Chance were partners and cohosted the Sirius XM show together in that mansion for years. So what on earth was I doing there? I held one of Johnny Cash's famous Martin guitars. Chance took me into the recording booth. Being a history nerd and a classic country music fan, I was like a kid in a candy store. All of it fascinated me. It was yet another surreal experience for me in Nashville. I left there that day, with a bond and a relationship that remains invaluable to me. Chance is a rare and precious friend. I love him dearly.

I gained a deep respect and love for Music City and its residents. It became my honorary home away from home. And I had made more lasting friendships there than I ever had in West Virginia, or anywhere else I ever lived for that matter. Throughout that entire year in general, music seemed to be the recurring theme for me. It was everywhere—my friends, my guitar man, my VIP trips to Nashville. Almost all arrows seemed to point towards the music industry. I didn't take it as a sign that I was supposed to be a part of it myself. I knew I didn't have the talent or the charisma to ever be a performer. But I was happy to be an onlooker, a fan and a cheerleader on the sidelines for the artists I knew, and anyone in the profession. I acquired an understanding of what it takes to work within the music industry. I saw it behind the scenes, up close and personal, every aspect it entails. These people bust their asses to follow their dreams. They have scraped and scrounged, nickeled and dimed and climbed their way from the bottom to the top. Even true legends didn't have overnight success stories, although they had the pure talent and presence to back them up. They all had harrowing tales of defeat too along the way. They fought for what they achieved and how they got it. They did whatever they needed to do in order to survive. These people never gave up no matter what stood in their way or who told them they weren't good enough. That's where I related to them. And that's where we understood each other. Music is the universal language.

Near the end of that month, I gave the guitar man one last chance. I went to see him in Charleston, WV. He tried to blow me off at first, so I just let him. Obviously, this wasn't working out. I sat in on a televised game show hosting that the lead singer of the band was a contestant of. It was a West Virginia celebrity edition of Hollywood Squares in our state's capital. We ended up in a legit real deal Jazz bar downtown, The Boulevard Tavern, listening to some of the best musicians in the business. I quickly made friends with the owner, a few bar tenders, and some regulars of the bar. Several of the stars that were on set of the tv show trickled into the Jazz club. There was the leading lady from "Three's Company" Joyce Dewitt, and Landau Eugene Murphy Jr. from "America's Got Talent", along with iconic artist and songwriter Billy Edd Wheeler, plus a few others. They were all West Virginia natives. I ended up getting drunk with guitar man's cousin again. And somehow, I wound up singing a duet of John Legend's current hit at the time, "All of Me", with Landau Eugene Murphy Jr., who is a phenomenal singer, and a blast to hang out with. Then we all gathered around a circle in a break out of gospel music, accompanied by a washboard player. It was awesome. It was one of those things, you just had to be there to appreciate the moment.

Later that night, I went and found guitar man in his hotel room. He was half asleep, although he never really slept much at all. We spent some time together. He dozed off. I couldn't find my hair tie, so I undid his ponytail to borrow one of his because he always wore two. I then sneaked and braided his long hair like an Indian Chief. He woke up after that and basically yelled at me to get out of his room. I started crying. It was the only time I ever cried in front of him. I walked out of his room knowing it really was over between us. He had never spoken to me like that before or tried to be intentionally hurtful. And I wasn't going to tolerate being done that way, by anyone—even him, although I really did love him. I don't know when he noticed that I braided his hair, but I'm sure he wasn't happy about it. I saw him briefly before I left the next morning, and gave him a hug as a farewell from me. I'm sure he could tell by the look in my eyes that I had enough of his games and rules. I was tired of playing along.

So a few days later, I received a call from my cousin, the one that was after guitar man. She tried to fill me in on the fact that she had still been seeing him, while he and I were together. She said he also asked her to marry him. That taught me everything I needed to know. I felt like the biggest idiot on the planet. I went the hell off on him, I was going to let him have it. He tried to settle me down, probably just out of fear that I would run my mouth about us. The whole time he wanted to keep everything between us hush, hush.. had nothing to do with his fame or reputation. It had everything to do with his habit of seeing multiple women at a time and trying to keep them from finding out about each other. I wanted no further involvement in romantic relationships with musicians. They are the definition of a rambling man. Regardless, out of my true feelings for him, I gave him my word that I wouldn't invoke a riot. Although my cousin and I did team up to attend one of his concerts together, just to make him nervous. Besides all that, I had asked him several times to take me fishing. I was sick of the spotlight and gigs with screaming fans and groupies. I was tired of following him all over the place, spinning my wheels and getting nowhere. I had racked up over 50k miles on my car in one year just from chasing him around. What I only ever wanted from him, was some quiet time for just the two of us, to get away from all that and really get to know each other. He even promised me a fishing trip that he ended up backing out on. That was my real basis for wanting rid of him. The cousin scandal was just my scapegoat. Guitar man never took me fishing. It was one simple request and he never granted it. He was one of those people that came into my life but wasn't meant to stay.

I woke up on the Apache side of my bed every day for a while after that. One of the stories Grandma Sparks always told, I interpreted as bravery on her part. When my daddy was a little boy, he asked to go play with his friend Kenny Bryant. Grandma said he could, but Grandpa said he couldn't. Well, he set out to see his friend anyways. Grandpa got hold of him and started whipping him with the belt. When Grandma saw this, she grabbed an old sour wet mop out of the bucket on the back porch. Then 4'11" feisty granny whipped 6'3" stern gramps with the dirty mop until his britches were falling down and he was pleading for her to stop. He turned loose of my dad and said, "There you go, he'll turn out to be a criminal." Grandma replied, "Then he'll be my criminal." She took dad and they went fishing, leaving Grandpa with no supper for the evening, which was a huge punishment for him since he didn't know how to prepare meals for himself. She also cut his leather belt up into tiny pieces with gardening shears. I love both those grandparents, and I was Grandpa's girl. But I admire my grandmother as the hero of this tale. That story has always stuck with me for some reason.

On two separate occasions, I beckoned my demons again, and literally tried to kill my ex-husband. Round one, he was in my house and tried to charge at me. That was his first strike. I was sweeping the floor when he came at me like a buffalo stampede. I went at him like he was a piñata at a party. I took that broom and whooped the devil out of him with it till it broke in two. I grabbed one half and he grabbed the other. It was a full-on duel of the exes, like the "War of the Roses". But I fluffed my feathers and got the better of him with my end. I kept flogging like a hateful old rooster, till he ran for the door. I didn't let up, I wasn't going to. I aimed to take him out like a varmint with that broom. J.J. was on the spiral stairs during the entire episode. He looked at me and said, "Mom, I think that's the biggest fit you've ever thrown." And I said to him, "Son, I think you're right."

His second strike also happened to be in my home, a place where I rebuked all evil. It wasn't welcome in the sanctuary I was trying to make for me and my kids. That time he yelled at me and pointed his finger at me. I would rather be punched than to have someone's finger in my face, and he had done it one too many times. I don't fight fair. I take hold of the first object I can find and go to town with it. That time, I grabbed the closest thing to me, which was a draft sized horseshoe and I beat the living shit out of him with that big iron shoe. I went at him like a farrier on steroids. I struck him all the way from one end of the house to the other, and clear out the front door. He was squalling that he thought his arm was broke, but I kept on; I was trying to do far worse damage than that. I tried to put an end to him. That didn't quite happen. But I did put an end to him ever trying to threaten me again.

I gave him a dose of his own medicine. My otherwise peaceful home was not going to be compromised by him or anyone else. He has never once even attempted to come at me since the Horseshoe Incident. He proceeds with caution when he comes anywhere near me. I taught him a lesson. I laid down my own law. I keep crosses on my walls to ward off evil. And I also keep a variety of items including guns, knives, iron skillets, antique farm tools, saws, deer antlers and pitchforks all throughout my house. I pose them as decorations on the walls and tables, but they are strategically placed weapons in disguise just waiting for someone to disturb the peace, so I can take matters into my own hands.

Introducing Lady Outlaw

I was living life like a modern day classic Western movie, and ironically, that's the only thing I watched at the time. I had no satellite or cable television (I haven't had either for over a decade) but I do have a flat-screen TV, a DVR player, and a big collection of Western movies. I had my favorites that I would watch repeatedly. I appreciated the old ones, with John Wayne and Clint Eastwood. And I enjoyed some of the newer ones too. My favorite cowboy flick is "Wyatt Earp", starring Kevin Costner as the lawman Deputy Sheriff Earp, and Doc Holliday is played by Dennis Quaid (who was my Peepaw's good golfing buddy). I especially love the featured overture song on that one. And I repeatedly replayed "Bury My Heart At Wounded Knee", which is my favorite Indian film about my absolute most favorite of historical figures, Chief Sitting Bull. I could fit the bill for any of these films.. with my cowboy boots and leather chaps, or my turquoise jewelry and fur moccasins. I sang sad cowboy songs, while I strummed my six-string beside a campfire. I survived a buffalo stampede, and I had a tough girl whoop ya with a horseshoe attitude. I liked this theme. My house decor looked like an old-time general store from the Wild West. And I was running my own portable saloon with the bootlegging business that I operated. Okay so maybe I've seen one too many Westerns. But I can play the part and this was all real-life shit.

I have always felt like a cross between an Indian and a Cowboy, (or a Cowgirl rather). But I was a mix of both worlds. I knew how to navigate open prairie, and also how to work with fences or corrals. I could go bareback with no reigns, or with a saddle and a bridle. I have a deep respect for the tribal way of life of American Indians, the true settlers of this great land. But I also sympathize with the rough lifestyle of Cowboys and how they came to be an icon of this country. Some days I feel like scalping my enemies and doing a ceremonial dance with a battle cry. Then again, sometimes I want to draw a six-shooter on them or hang them with a rope in the town square. I could see myself wearing a cowgirl hat and spurs with war paint and feathers, all at the same time. And being bred between both Natives and European settlers, I guess is how I can identify with my Indian blood and my inner white girl, in unison. I am a living contradiction of two separate clans, who were sworn enemies and stood on opposing sides of a never-ending war over this nation. I am most endeared to the forgotten and honorable plight of the Native Americans. In my opinion, they are the wisest of all cultures and were treated with the most injustice and dishonor of any human race on home soil. But either way, I could ride horses and sling pistols with the best of them, Cowboys or Indians.

Jason is the one who taught me how to shoot guns. I was trained by an expert Marine sharpshooter. I wasn't good with a bow at that time though and I almost accidentally shot him with his own compound bow after our divorce, when he tried to teach me that skill in our lower field shooting range. I would have assuredly been guilty until proven innocent and gone straight to prison for manslaughter if that arrow had flown one inch closer to him. He had the look of pure fear in his eyes when it went soaring past his head and he felt the tailwinds off of it. But I was a good shot with a rifle thanks to him and even better at firing a pistol. I am right handed, so I always handled weapons that way. I asked Jason one day, why I was better at shooting pistols rather than rifles. It is usually the other way around for marksmen. He had me do a test to figure out which of my eyes was the dominant one. It was my left eye. Once I figured that out and started holding weapons with my left hand I became an even more accurate shooter. It made a notable difference. My favorite gun to fire is a Ruger Super Redhawk44 magnum revolver with a 7-inch barrel. Jason and I have joint custody of one such gun. He purchased it after we lost Grace, with money left over from the military paid expenses. He named the Redhawk "Grace", in honor of her. He also bought a hand tooled black leather gun belt to go with the pistol. It was our home protection weapon when we were married. I used to practice loading and unloading it in my sleep. I am most accurate with it of any firearm I've ever shot. I never miss my target with that gun. It is my #1 weapon of choice. You feel the power in your hands when you pull the trigger. You have to hold a firm grip onto it with both hands, to keep it from kicking back and knocking your head off. It is a legit hand cannon, not to be taken lightly. You must handle it with the utmost care and regard for the damage it is capable of ensuing. It goes off with an intense big bang.. that resonates throughout your entire body and bounces deafening echoes off of the surrounding landscape. It penetrates deep fear into anything within hearing distance.

Back to the story of current happenings on the farm. After all the dust settled from the latest chain of random events and the Horseshoe Incident, Jason and I were starting to ease up on our great war with each other. We concurred to an armistice for the sake of the children. Meanwhile, our joint herd of seven goats were waging their own organized attack of rebellion, with Pepé Le Pew as their Commanding General. He once fell off of the tractor and broke his leg. We took him to the vet and had it mended, then kept him in the house for a while. He didn't learn his lesson. He would climb up anything. We had three re-enforcements of fence along the goats' parameters, woven wire, barbed wire and electric wire. The barnyard was like Fort Knox. And they could break out of it anyways. They went on a tactical mission, to ransack the neighborhood. Our postal zip code and mailing address is Birch River. But the physical address of the farm is a rural section of the county. We live in an unincorporated town, known as Bays. Well, these goats had become the unofficial Bays highway patrol. They were in the road constantly causing traffic jams, horn honking and near accidents with vehicles. They were violating our neighbor Susie. They would lounge on her patio furniture. They ate the wreath off her front door and destroyed her heat pump by climbing on it. The community was issuing valid complaints left and right. We had to do something about it before the villagers of Bays came at us with torches and pitchforks. We could be cited with a public violation of goat misconduct, or sued for property damage.

Jason found another farmer to lease the herd of goats to. He was located a few towns over in the same county, in an area known as Wilson Ridge. This farm bordered along a church property. He had other livestock and a kangaroo of all things. (This is a true story by the way). Our goats were relocated to this place, and Jason started getting phone calls right away, of havoc they were wreaking at their temporary home. The farmer was begging us to take them back. But we weren't adequately prepared to contain them yet. Then Jason gets more calls, about how the goats were going to the church on Sundays. They were standing on the hoods of parked cars. They were jumping up on members of the congregation, getting their good Sunday clothes dirty. Then the farmer calls and he was mad, really upset. The herd of seven goats crashed a funeral. They barged in on the burial part of the service with Pepé Le Pew as the ringleader. They proceeded to make a beeline straight for the casket and ate every one of the flower arrangements that were there. After that, we never heard from the farmer again. And we have yet to find out what became of our goat herd.

Other than that three-ring circus, everything else had taken on a new normal in our alternate reality of divorce and co-existing life on our homeland. Jason and I were back to being civil with one another. We did our own separate things with the kids, but sometimes we would also do things together with them. The farm was a community effort, that's how it worked best. I settled myself and the children into our new home. I was finally at peace and felt content in this place. I was able to set the tone for the three of us and create a safe harbor. I provided an atmosphere that was serene and pleasant. That's what I really wanted. It was the main reason for the decision I made to be on my own without someone else who could come along and ruin a perfectly fine day. If I had known the essence of how being able to have power over your own mood is so beneficial, I would have left much sooner than I did.

I always loved to watch horses run, and at my new home, I could see my herd all the time from the balcony, which is the heart of this house. I still rode Pocahontas, but not as often. Mostly I just wanted to see her be free, grazing or galloping, with her mane and tail blowing in the wind. I also loved the streams running close to the house. I would open my bedroom window at night so I could hear the rushing sound they make, along with the crickets and the Whippoorwills. The smaller house made for more simplified living. It just felt cozier and less foreboding than the big house on the hill. By today's standards, my house would be considered as a tiny home. But it is filled with so much detail and character, that it has the feel of a hobbit house or something of that nature. I was very happy with how it all turned out. It didn't take me long to make it a proper setting for J.J. and Faith. It was our own and we felt safe and comfortable in our little castle.

I decorated the house with colors that were calming and added my personal flair to every single space. I have always prided myself in being a good interior decorator, I have an eye for placement and Feng Shui. Creating an aesthetic ambiance is one of my best attributes as a woman. I feel like my home reflects my personality, and projects everything I hold dear to me. It's like wearing my heart on my sleeve. You can tell a lot about a person just by taking a tour of their house. Mine is almost always in order, even when I'm not expecting company. I function best when I can keep things tidy and organized. That helps me to declutter my mind. I love the fact that my house is a small scale structure, so much more manageable for me and my condition. And I'm not gonna lie, it was really nice to not have to clean up after a messy man for a change. Everything stayed clean and orderly when it was just the children and me.

It took me a few years before I could start eating regularly again after my stomach was so damaged. For a long time, I couldn't even look at food. But now I was starting to slowly regain my appetite and was putting weight back on. I felt inspired to get back into cooking, in my new tiny kitchen. And with that, visitors started to come around.. because I became known as a good cook. Also, the new location of my residence was an easier target to allow for folks to just drop in, since it was right off the main road. That never happened up the hill, it was way more isolated. Hippy was the number one culprit of doing drive-by's to the house he built for me. He was also there for me when I needed someone to vent to, or a shoulder to cry on. In the short time we had known each other, he knew me very well. I told him pretty much everything. He is going to hate me when he reads this.. but you know how gay guys make for good girlfriends? Well, Hippy is like that, even though he's not gay. But he's just a good friend for a girl to have. He would bring me flowers and snack cakes, and tell me I looked pretty. He let me rant and rave about my troubles and sorrows. And we devised evil plans together. That's what best friends do.

I guess as dues collection for volunteering to put up with me, (being the undeniable pain in the ass that I am), Hippy did a bad Hippy thing. I had window boxes for flowers on both sides of the cabin section of the house. I planted petunias in them. I would water and weed them every day. But I have never been very good at tending to plants, and sometimes don't know the difference between weeds and flowers. I'm lucky if I can keep a cactus alive. But Jason came down the hill one day and noticed something in one of the flower boxes. Something that wasn't supposed to be there. He started interrogating me. I'm sure I looked as clueless as I actually was about it. He discovered two baby pot plants in my flower box. I was like, what? I didn't even really know what a marijuana plant looked like in real life. I had only ever seen it on t-shirts and stuff. I could have easily plucked them mistaking them for wild weeds or poison ivy. It took us no more than a minute to solve the mystery. Dammit, Hippy. Jason called him immediately and told him to come remove his contraband from the premises. He came, and the plants disappeared from the flower box.

Overall, everything was going alright for a change. I finally got my own last name back legally. I really didn't want to change it when I got married in the first place. But I did take Jason's last name and kept it for fifteen years out of regard to him as my husband. Since my father Mark Sparks passed and had no sons to carry on his name, I felt entitled to hold the family name for him. Now that I was Tiffany Sparks again, I had a renewed sense of self as though I had been freed from prison and could reclaim my own identity. I was honoring my father in the most direct way I possibly could, in the name I was given by him, the name he passed down to me. It was more than a last name. It was in memory of my daddy. That's what Sparks meant to me. And I promised myself that I would never again change my last name. It would be written on my tombstone as it was written on my birth certificate. After tracing my ancestral genealogy, I discovered that the Sparks side of my people originated in Great Britain. The last name of Sparks was derived from the Old English original surname of Sparrowhawk. I can trace the origins of the shortened version back to the year 1550 in London, England to a direct ancestor which was my 13x great grandfather titled as, Sir Ludgate 'King's Knight' Sparrowhawk Sparks. He was the first one in my lineage to add Sparks to the Sparrowhawk name. There are records that the surname was also used as a descriptive title as early as 1327, in a document known as the "Suffolk Rolls" in which it is used as a reference to someone exhibiting fierce or rebellious character. In that capacity, it was referred to as Sparhawk the Outlaw.

My life was beginning to feel regular and provide some much-needed normalcy for the entire farm village. I felt like I reached the end of a jolting and windy roller coaster ride, and now I could disembark from it, and stabilize my balance. And just do something ordinary. Like metaphorically sit on a park bench and eat a funnel cake while I people-watch. Anything that didn't require me to exert my precious energy or take drastic measures of any sort. I could portray a Classic Western leading lady on any given day. But I also wanted to sit back and relax and just be boring for a change. I wanted to be surrounded by my children and animals and just do normal mom everyday uneventful things. I wanted to take bubble baths and light candles, shovel manure and throw hay, bake cookies and play board games with the kids. That's what I had in mind. That is not what happened next. Right at the point where I was just getting comfortable with thinking I had my life settled down and in a normal routine, guess again. Something was about to shake it up and change it all. I was about to embark on the most thrilling upside-down roller coaster ride in the entire amusement park, and I didn't even know it yet. I had no intention of thrill-seeking, in any way.

In the one-horse town of Birch River, there was buzz about a TV show. It was a reality show about the ginseng industry, on the History Channel. One season of it had already aired, but I never saw it because I didn't have TV. But I heard about it from the locals. And the star of the show was the ginseng buyer, Tony Coffman. His business is called Coffman's Metals, and it is less than five miles from the farm. He deals in metal, ginseng, and fur trading. I had taken scrap metal into his recycling center several times over the years, but I had never personally met him. We were friends on Facebook though.

In July of 2014, he made a post about the producers scouting for the first female character of the show. I didn't really know much about the program's content, but I thought based on the title "Appalachian Outlaws", that it sounded like a role I could fit into. I never expected to hear anything back from him but I half-joking sent Tony a private message, saying "I can be the Lady Outlaw." It was the first time I ever mentioned that title. But based on my lifestyle and my personality, it just came to mind and seemed to fit who I was. I just blurted it out. I had no idea when I said it, that it would become my very identity.

Tony quickly replied back to me and asked for my phone number. He said he wanted to give my name and number to producers. The very same day, I got a call from Hollywood. I seriously thought it was a prank. I thought I was being punked at first. It was the executive producer and creator of the show. He asked me some questions and requested a headshot from me. We talked for a while and he seemed like a really cool guy. He was a native of West Virginia, from the Bluefield area. The next thing I knew, the production company was arranging for a date to meet with me. They wanted me to sign a talent hold contract and shoot a sizzle reel of me on the farm. I told the creator that I honestly didn't know much about ginseng, other than having harvested it with my grandmother as a kid. I told him I knew way more about moonshine, and I should be on that show instead of this one. He said that it was alright, then assured me I didn't need to be an expert on the plant species. Well, I immediately started studying everything I could about ginseng and the industry. I became thoroughly educated on the topic. Then Hippy and I scoured every square inch on the farm searching for the elusive red berries and green prongs with five-leaf stems. He was already an avid hunter of the root. We found nothing, not one single sign of it anywhere. The farm had been logged several times in the past, and that had wiped it clean of ginseng.

It was never anywhere on my radar to ever be on television. Hell, I didn't even watch tv. I was never in any school plays. I was shy and reserved for the most part. I wasn't outgoing or seeking any sort of fame or notoriety. This Hollywood show business was a foreign concept for me altogether. I was like shit, I never should have raised my hand and spoke up. What have I signed myself up for? What have I got myself into this time? I knew the music industry side of exposure. And I knew what fame was all about. I saw it firsthand from my famous friends in Nashville.. the screaming fans, taking pictures, and signing autographs. But I knew nothing about acting, or the tv industry, or reality shows. I wasn't cut out for being in the spotlight. I wasn't sure if I could handle publicity on any level. I was a nobody farmgirl with nothing special to offer in the entertainment business. I didn't possess the kind of larger than life charisma that would translate through a television. But my thinking was.. if the History Channel comes knocking on your door, you better answer. That doesn't just happen to anyone. It's like winning the lottery. Besides, it was my favorite network back when I did have TV. Opportunities like that don't simply fall from the sky and land in your lap for no good reason. I decided to see where this led. If nothing else, it would be a new adventure and an extra source of income. What could possibly go wrong?

Within a week of my initial call from the creator, a crew was scheduled to film with me. They gave me a briefing of what they wanted me to do on the farm. So I borrowed Jason's Avalanche, (because a Spark doesn't look Appalachian). I got the horses groomed, got the tractor ready to roll, and had the Redhawk ready to fire. On July 14th, I met the crew at Coffman's Metals, where I signed my initial contract with the production company, Original Productions. The executive producer was present, and there were two cameramen, who were also producers. I met Tony in person for the first time, and the line producer gave us a rundown of a scripted scene they wanted us to shoot together. It was a screen test to see how I looked on camera. I had taken a shot of moonshine to settle my nerves beforehand, but I'm not gonna lie, I was really nervous. I had no clue what to do or what to expect. We shot the scene, and I managed to do alright. I just tried not to look at the cameras, which you're not supposed to do anyways on reality sets unless it's an interview scene. We left Coffman's, and one of the camera crew rode in the truck with me. He filmed me on the way to the farm, while I was talking about my life as a farm girl. The other producers followed behind us in a presidential fleet lookin' Ford Escalade rental.

The farm scenes were all non-scripted. I was supposed to be completely natural and just talk about my life and the land. They wanted me to have a cowgirl persona and had me change wardrobe when we got to my house. I wore cut off Daisy Duke jean shorts, a tank top, and my cowboy boots with my hair in a ponytail and a ballcap. I was playing the part of a badass mountain woman. I wasn't nervous at all for this round of filming. I felt at ease with the crew after hanging out with them casually before the shoot. They were all very nice and laid back. They liked my mini horses and took pictures with them. We spent several hours composing different scenes. They filmed me inside my house taking shots of whiskey, at the barnyard working with the horses, brush hogging the upper field on the tractor, splitting firewood on the hydraulic splitter, walking with my dogs down the driveway, playing my guitar and singing, then blasting tin cans with the 44 revolver. They got some really cool footage, especially of me target shooting. I told the cameraman not to get too close to me since he had no hearing protection. He was trying to film the bullet leaving the gun, and insisted he would be fine. On the first round, I blasted a half-full can of beer and it flew twenty feet up in the air. The cameraman was like, "Dang, you weren't kidding." His ears were ringing for hours afterwards. Overall the crew seemed happy with what we got that day. The purpose of the sizzle reel, was basically for the production company to sell me to the network, History Channel.

Soon after they left, the one in charge started texting me. He was flirting with me and actively pursuing me. And he was a good looker. He looked like a GQ model, with pretty hair and dark brown eyes. He was also an actor in Hollywood. Stupid me started flirting back with him. I had spoken with my sister Haley before I ever started filming. I asked her for advice since she was involved with show business as a singer and a theater stage performer. She was even a professional opera singer for the Florida Grand Opera in Miami. The words of wisdom she gave me were, "Don't date any of the producers." I should have listened. But my stubborn self was going to find out the hard way. Once you learn something the hard way, you never forget it. Next thing I knew he was back at my house, but not to film. And we were kissing. After that, we talked constantly. I quickly became captivated by this man. He was charming in every way. Then he invited me to come to see him in Lewisburg, where the crew was set up with their base camp. One thing led to another, and we became an item. But it was all top secret because it was a big production No-no for him to date me. However, we maintained a professional relationship regarding the show. He was very encouraging and reassured me that I would be a hit as the first female character. I was told that the History Channel loved me based on my sizzle reel. I was given the good to go greenlight as a Season Two character. I was hired to be the original Lady Outlaw, on Appalachians Outlaws. I went to my first big reality star event, where cast members from the first season would be present doing meet and greets. It was held in Van Lear, Kentucky. Although I wasn't on the show yet, I was told it would be a good idea for me to introduce myself to the rest of the characters.

I had seen a few of them earlier that spring when I took J.J. to a shooting range where they were having a skeet competition. And I met a few of them at a smaller gathering at Jackson's Meat Shop, a local business owned by one of my cousins, Charles Jackson. But I drove to Kentucky to get better acquainted with the Outlaws. I met them and spent the day with them. They were all really nice and welcoming to me as the new girl. I met Mike Ross, who I was to be partnered with on the show. There was one in particular at Van Lear that would end up being a main character in my personal life. His name is Chris Carswell, but everyone knows him as "Ewok". I didn't know it then, but he would become one of my very best friends. I went to the childhood homeplace of Loretta Lynn. I took a tour from her Uncle, and talked to him for a long time on the front porch of the "cabin on a hill in Butcher Holler". He had an albino mule. We discussed the mule, the weather, and country music.

I still worked as a bootlegger and at the bank during this time. I paid for a subscription of the first season of the show on YouTube. I was trying to get an idea of the premise of the show. I watched the episodes between customers while I was working at the bank. I informed my boss there that I had been hired as a cast member. He was a fan of the program and even took me out for a drink at the Tractor Bar to celebrate my new role. He also gave me his word that he would allow me to have a flexible schedule, to be freed up for filming days. The thing with Hollywood though, is you are at their mercy and on their watch. It is all very last minute and lots of flying by the seat of your pants. You have to be ready to hurry up and wait, at a moment's notice. There are always last-minute changes and storyboard alterations. You do what they say when they say, and how they say. They don't take special requests or excuses. Most people are just so desperate to get on tv, they will do anything for fifteen minutes of fame. So producers will make you jump through all their many hoops without question. It's all part of a big game.

I was given my first real film date. My storyline was intertwined with Mike Ross, one of the top main characters. He was the "MacGyver" mastermind of booby traps and the designated heartthrob on the show. The female fans loved him. I drove to his farm in Greenbrier County. I was given my official contract for the History Channel. It was a stack of pages about a mile high. I didn't even read it, I just signed the dotted line. I was already invested in the project. I was told to bring a suitcase of clothes for wardrobe selection. I had to use Mike's bedroom to change, which was awkward. Then I did somewhat of a fashion show for the producers, so they could select my filming attire. They chose blue jeans, a khaki-colored tank top, and my cowboy boots for me to wear.. with a low side ponytail for my hair. You are required to wear the same outfit for every day of filming for a reality show, to keep continuity for the season. This film shoot had a crew of about ten men.. camera guys, audio techs, field and line producers. I was overwhelmed when I saw them with all their equipment and black Escalades. It was a full-scale production. They wired me with a microphone, gave Mike and I a rundown of the scenes we were shooting, then they started rolling film. Lights. Camera. Action.

The premise of our storyline basically, was that I played a damsel in distress, with poachers stealing ginseng off my land. And Mike Ross was going to be the hero and come to my rescue. But they had it written in a way that there was some conflict between Mike and I in the beginning. We had to perform some fight scenes. This turned out to be my favorite day of filming. The skies were dark with threatening storms approaching, and the wind was blowing hard. It was a dramatic setting for our initial confrontation. I had to pull up in an old beat-up pickup truck, get out and have a yelling match standoff with Mike, then squall tires leaving his farm when he turned me away. We were fed our lines word for word, which were being dictated by the writers in Hollywood in live time while we were on set. If you don't say what they tell you to, and how they want you to deliver the lines; they will keep doing takes till you get it right. Again, I'm not an actor, so it was hard for me to get in the right mind frame to be hateful to Mike, who was a genuinely good guy. But I finally found it within myself to put my own raw emotion behind a performance. I got to thinking about things that really did make me mad and then channeled my inner Apache into how I directed pretend anger towards Mike. At that point, I made him the target of my rage and lashed out at him like I was on a warpath. Once I accomplished that, the producers took notice and said, "Whatever you just did, keep doing it cause it worked beautifully." They even clapped for me when the fierce "Untamed Tiff" came forward as "Lady Outlaw", and changed the entire tone of the scene.

Part 2

One of the producers stated, "For such a short girl, you carry yourself with a big presence." That comes from working with horses who are ten times bigger than me, and from experiences of being brave in the face of adversity. I may be 5' 3", but I know how to project myself as ten feet tall and bulletproof. I can be intimidating and authoritative when the moment calls for it. My horses recognize me as their alpha, just from reading my body language and feeling my dominant presence.

You don't even have to say a word to exuberate an aura of strength and power. It is something that comes from within and radiates outward through your being. And bringing the Lady Outlaw character to life was a perfect occasion to bring all that to the table. For me, it wasn't a role I was playing, it was a real-life version of who I am. And since I was filming for "Reality TV", I felt like in order to be believable on-screen, I needed to personally believe in who I was portraying. It was an extension of myself. I had to know it like the back of my hand and make it come across in a way that allowed viewers to capture the essence of the character they were watching. Lady Outlaw was me, and I was her. We were one in the same. This is what I kept in mind while the cameras were rolling. I just had to perfect the reflection of all the many moods and traits of Lady Outlaw. She is a compilation of the recurring theme of all the different "Tiffs", together combined and encompassed into one solitary identity.

I did have several serious discussions with production about the "Damsel In Distress" part that they revolved my storyline around. I deeply disagreed with how they were conveying a mountain woman from Appalachia, as someone who would rely solely on seeking the help of a man. Mountain women are historically strong, extremely resilient, and self-sufficient. If someone threatens their family, their home, or their livelihood, they will be the first to take matters into their own hands. They were born and bred that way. They toiled and slaved keeping up the homeplace, harvesting and preparing food, rearing all the children, clothing everyone in hand-sewn garments. Most notably, they were protecting what little they had, because they worked like hell to have it. Their men were almost always off breaking their own backs in the coal mines, the farm fields, or timbering in the forests. Nobody was around to cater to the women. They were on their own and tough as nails. Even modern-day women of the Appalachian region are just an unyielding breed of stock. We have evolved into a hard-working and determined culture of females. I can load a gun and fire it just as fast as any man. If someone means to do me harm, that's between them and I. No man is going to come jump in the middle and save the day. I wouldn't even waste the time asking for assistance. I'm a grown-ass woman, and I can take care of myself. I just felt like if the show wanted to feature the role of a mountain woman, they should paint it in the correct light. I wanted to be a voice for West Virginia women. I wanted to carry the flag for them. But the production company wasn't paying me to hear my ideas. They hired me to mind my own business and do the job I was told to do. I didn't want to be labeled as a diva, so I finally backed down.

Mike Ross and I filmed another scene in the woods on his property. I forgot I was wired with a microphone. After producers would feed me my lines, I would curse about the script to myself once they were out of sight. Some of the shit they instructed me to say was just ridiculous. It was obvious that someone in a suit and tie, in a high-rise office in Hollywood, was writing the content for the show. Someone who had probably never even set foot inside the Appalachians. I almost felt like they were trying to stereotype us as ignorant hillbillies. Well anyways, after cussing up a fit about some such stupid lines, one of the field producers ran back to my solo location to give me a heads up. He whispered to me that the entire crew could overhear everything I was saying since I was on constant audio recording that went directly to their headsets. Oops. I'm sure the History Channel got a kick out of that when it landed on the desk in their L.A. studios. Mike also told me to be careful what I said, because they can take your audio footage and splice it together with other things you say then make it sound like you verbally told something that you never actually did. That's why a lot of reality stars get in hot water. Their words are mixed up and distorted into something controversial.

Mike came to my farm too. They rolled in on a convoy with their Hollywood SUVs. The entire bottom of the driveway was lined with them. Passers-by were slowing down on the highway to see what the big fuss was about. The cameramen with their big video recorders were everywhere. It looked like a movie set. We were scheduled to film the next scene on our storyboard, about Mike finally coming to my rescue. But we had another showdown there to shoot things off. This time I pictured guitar man's head on Mike Ross's body. I reared back and took aim on him. I poured my outrage into that scene, over how I had been done dirty. The producers patted me on the back for my realistic performance. And I apologized to Mike for being so vicious. We went on to film another scene with my children. Part of my story was about me being a single mom, with a farm to take care of. The kids did everything the producers told them to do. I was so proud of J.J. and Faith. And it was exciting for them to have an experience with filming. They saw firsthand what it was like to be behind the scenes and in front of the camera.

Next, Mike and I were to film a scene in the woods on my farm. So when you're watching episodes of the show, they make it look like they are way out deep in the backwoods of the mountains. Well, we were set up maybe two feet inside the wood-line, right beside my house. And guess what I found there when I was scouting the location before the arrival of the crew? Hippy's contraband. He had transplanted his two weeds from my flower box, into a big flower pot. They had grown as tall as palm trees, right near my house in the wood-line. I had to call Hippy and make him come collect his illegal horticultural experiment, and take it off the property. He named the plants appropriately Cheech and

Chong. Shame, shame Hippy. Anyways, while we were filming there, the crewmen got shovels and dug holes where my imaginary ginseng had been stolen by the nonexistent poacher. This is how reality TV works. It's all smoke in mirrors. I kept breaking out in laughter at the crew members. They were all California city boys. They were afraid to get their designer shoes dirty. They were scared to death of spiders and snakes. One of them got a gnat in his eye and flipped the hell out. He was crying like a girl and doing a bug-in-the-eyeball dance. I was literally laughing my ass off at their metropolitan shenanigans. They kept having to cut footage on me and restart from the beginning. Mike and I would cause each other to cut up too. Sometimes we had to do a dozen takes before we could put on a serious face. We had a lot of fun on the set. It was like a bunch of grownups playing pretend in the woods. I became friends with a lot of the crew also. They were mostly really cool and interesting guys.

I was still secretly dating mister producer man. I would sneak into his apartment in downtown Lewisburg late at night, then sneak back out early in the morning before anyone could notice me leaving. Although one time he did take me to a coffee shop, but I was told to act professionally. I knew by now exactly how to be an undercover girlfriend, like I was with guitar man. Same deal, different guy. I had fallen in love with him, in a summer fling sort of way. I knew he would be going back to Los Angeles once the season was wrapped up. But still, I was infatuated with him and attracted to him. He treated me like I was his leading lady. He was

400

gorgeous. And he was so different than any man I had ever been with, so refined and high caliber. Or at least he seemed that way. I should have kept in mind that he was also an actor. He is the single most convincing man I have ever known. He was my biggest cheerleader, always giving me pep talks and encouraging dialogue. He told me that I was awesome, a rock star, and would be a huge hit on the show. At some point, after I had filmed several scenes from my storyline, he said that we were getting too serious. He was worried about getting caught and losing his job since it was clearly bad business for a producer to date a cast member of their show. But since he was the big wig in charge, I felt safe and secure with the role I had landed. And although he wasn't on the film sets with me, the other producers were relaying to him that I was doing well and the post-production was coming along nicely. I thought it was all going to be alright as long as we laid low with our romantic relationship. To be honest, I even started to get a case of the big head thinking I was gonna be a big TV star on the History Channel. One night over the phone, the producer man asked me to choose between him or the show. He said I couldn't have both. I chose him. I didn't have my heart set on being a reality TV personality. I would rather have a real-life experience, with love. He encouraged me to go for the show instead. He said the show needed me and would help me become rich enough to better support my children financially. So based on that, I took his advice. But then we still continued our romantically involved encounters, on his personal command, even against his own advice. We were playing with fire. One or both of us was bound to get burnt.

During film season, I was invited back to Tennessee for a big celebration. The producer man gave me permission to leave the state since it wouldn't conflict with my film schedule. He told me to go and have a good time. This trip was all about the 60th anniversary of the legendary music career of W.S. Fluke Holland. He was Johnny Cash's only drummer and he also played drums for Carl Perkins. The big celebration was to be held in Jackson, TN at the Carl Perkins Civic Center. It was a huge deal. I met with my friend Chuck and we carpooled together from Nashville. My good buddy Chance Martin rode with us there as well and I hung out with him for a good part of the event. Tommy Cash and his wife were also there and I was able to visit with them. Hundreds of other A-list Music City celebrities were present. There were hours of top of the line performances. And again, I was VIP for the whole shebang. I got to go backstage and mingle with all the music industry greats. I had the huge honor of speaking with W.S. Fluke again after his performance that evening and we got our picture made together. I congratulated him on his lifetime achievement. It was amazing.

Chance, Chuck and I rode back to Chuck's house together. We sat and drank moonshine and told stories. I stayed the night there, and the next day after Chuck left for work at the Cash Museum, Chance took me out on the town for some more behind the scenes Nashville fun. He drove me back to Chuck's place that night. I proceeded to go into the house but I pushed the wrong code for the home alarm system. After several more failed attempts, I accidentally set the alarm off. Chuck called me immediately, as 911 had called to notify him of a possible burglary. He was leaving the museum to come home and disengage the alarm. He said the cops were on their way too. I had moonshine. Chance said, "Let's run." So we hightailed it. That was the beginning of mine and Chance's outlaw relationship. He officially became my partner in crime. And sadly, it was the end of my friendship with Chuck. He never forgave me and Chance for running from the law and leaving him in the dust that night after activating his alarm. I don't blame him. It wasn't the nice thing to do, but it was necessary.

Back in WV after that trip, I returned to my bank job, my bootlegging, and my filming for Appalachian Outlaws. I got word that another female was also cast on the show, her name was Jessica Hatfield (of the Hatfield/McCoy Feud). She was partnered with another of the main characters, Obie Bennett. I reached out to her and we became good friends right away. She is a cool chick, and a professional ginseng hunter. We were both Lady Outlaws. By this time, we were being promoted as upcoming cast members for Season 2 of the television series. Jessica was Lady Outlaw Hatfield, and I was Lady Outlaw Sparks. We were a team even though we weren't working directly together. But we thought it would be cool if they would pair us up as a girl duo of badasses. With the promotional campaign underway, it didn't take long before we both started developing haters. Women tend to get all riled up when they see other women becoming successful, which I have never understood. But unfortunately, females were the presidents and members of our hate clubs. There were even entire Facebook pages dedicated to hatred for us, where this group of anonymous women congregated to talk shit. It was immature and pathetic. There was no call for it and no sense in it at all. It was hard not to take it personally, but I tried not to let it bother me. I just let it be the fuel for my fire, to keep me going and keep my head held high. I had no idea it would get much worse before it got any better.

Before the promos for the tv show started, I only had about three hundred Facebook friends and I knew all of them personally. But now, I was having a ton of new friend requests flowing in constantly. Because my relationship status was listed as single, I received a ridiculous amount of private messages from hundreds of guys with every pickup line known to man, marriage proposals, and unwanted nude photographs. I once had a male teacher warn me that he was going to send me a picture of his ass. My mother was standing there and when he sent the attached photograph, I made her reply to him about how that was inappropriate. My poor Mama saw the teacher's hairy buttocks. I ended up having to make an announcement for men not to send me unsolicited naked pictures of themselves. It was a frequent offense.

I was overwhelmed by all the sudden attention in general. I wasn't even on TV yet, but I had all these followers claiming to be fans. It made me uncomfortable, I hadn't done anything to warrant gaining a fan base of any kind. I didn't know how to address this huge wave of people that were following me. Most of them were genuine supporters and have stuck with me to this day. They have cheered me on all this time and become true friends of mine. I value them more than they know.

The producer man called to tell me that the Vice President of the production company was flying into WV. She was to be hosted by him and the other producers in Lewisburg during her visit. He asked me to secure a load of moonshine for the occasion. At the time, the bootlegging business had slacked off. Most state distillers were only making it for self-consumption that season, not for distribution. I had a hard time procuring the order. I finally got it and let him know. He said he would send some of the crew over to pick it up. But I had to work at the bank during the timeframe they were able to stop by for it. I told the producer man that I would leave my back door unlocked, and gave instructions as to where they could locate the moonshine. As soon as I got home that evening, I saw the footprints on the spiral stairs, where they had come down from the back door. I went straight to the hiding place they were to recover the liquor from, and it was gone. I assumed the mission had been successful. A few days later, the producer man called me and said they never found the shine. When I started freaking out about it telling him it was taken the day it was supposed to be picked up, he quickly said that Greg Shook stole it out of my house.

Greg Shook needs no introduction. He is the most recognizable cast member from Appalachian Outlaws. I had never met him, although I wanted to. Our conflicting schedules and the producers prevented us from meeting. But when I was told he stole my liquor, I automatically had a score to settle with him. I was like who is this Greg Shook character? And what makes him think it's okay to walk in someone's house and raid their shine stash? I was really mad. Now he was known as an enemy to Ewok on the show. There was a scene on the first season, where Ewok took Greg boating and left him on the side of the river, stranded. Ewok even got death threats because of that scenario. I took to social media and started blasting Greg Shook, saying that he stole my moonshine and deserved to be left high and dry. After this went on for several weeks, I finally sent him a private message and just asked, "How was the moonshine?" He replied back and said, "It was good, thank you." In trying to get to the bottom of this scandal, I find out directly from Mr. Shook that he was never in my house and he never stole anything from me at all. It was all behind the scenes of a reality TV set-up. Greg and I started talking, and he told me his grandmother was also a Sparks. Immediately, Greg and I hit it off and became friends. When I went back and questioned producer man, he tried to quickly cover up and say that when the crew did the pickup of the jars, it was all filmed as part of the show. Which I knew was total bullshit, but I just let the shine scandal die down. It is was what brought me to one of my very best friends in the whole wide world, the one and only Greg

Shook. He is one of the truest friends I have ever had. The whole thing is funny to us both now, knowing how that all turned out. They tried to pit us against each other for some unknown reason and it went the opposite direction. We still give producer man hell every time we're together.

The other big deal that arose from the shine scandal was a spontaneous connection to the moonshine community around the country. Since the cat was out of the bag about my business as a bootlegger, I had people from high and low flocking to see who I was and to make my acquaintance. It seriously happened overnight. Before I could even bat an eyelash, suddenly I knew all of them, and they all came to know me. It was like the entire underground black market network of shiners came out of the woodworks. They rose up to meet me, and they adopted me as one of their official members. They let me join their tribe and fall in with their pack. As soon as I understood that these were literally some of the best folks around, salt of the earth hard workers, and would literally give you the shirt off their back; I was instantly bonded to them. They opened the door to the industry, welcomed me with open arms, and I, in turn, reciprocated that hospitality. I felt like I finally found my true clan. These would become everlasting ride or die friendships, and my real second family. My brothers and sisters in all parts of the industry always have my respect and support. And because the moonshine market is historically a predominantly male-driven trade, I felt extremely honored to be accepted as a female contributor to the cause. But more on that in the next chapter.

Back to show business. Towards the end of the filming season, I was assigned to a new field producer. I had a briefing with him over the phone before I met him in person. As soon as he arrived in from L.A., I was given orders to meet with him in person at his hotel room, where he had more paperwork from the network for me to sign. I went and did as instructed. He seemed like a nice guy and was excited to work with me. The main field producer who had been my direct supervisor so far was put on assignment with another History Channel series that was being filmed simultaneously in the swamplands of Louisiana. I felt a little hesitant about working with someone I just met. I had grown comfortable with the other producer on set. The new guy must have sensed that. He ended up inviting me to his birthday party a few days later, in Lewisburg. I accepted, only because I hadn't seen my mister producer man for a few weeks, and I was missing him. I thought it would be a chance for me to have time with the man I was secretly in love with. So I got dressed up and made the hour and a half drive to Greenbrier County.

The party was to be held at an Irish pub on Washington Street in downtown Lewisburg. It was the favorite meeting spot of the entire crew while they were stationed in West Virginia. They were regulars there. And it was located directly across the street from producer man's apartment, where I had stayed the night with him. He was there at the pub when I arrived. But he gave me a look to remind me that we had to be professional around the rest of the crew. It was hard for me to not rush at him and give him a hug and kiss. I really had missed him, and he looked so handsome. But I kept my cool and maintained a safe distance, tried to play it off and be a good secret girlfriend. That sucked. I was sick and tired of these type of under the counter relationships. I was happy to see the rest of the guys from the crew though. And they seemed happy to have me there. The new one I was to work with bought me several rounds of drinks. He was also trying to flirt with me. I brushed him off. I kept telling him I had enough, and couldn't drink anymore because I had to sober up for my drive home later on. I was hoping that my producer man would somehow let me know that I could stay with him that night. I assumed that's how the evening would end. I was waiting for him to give me a wink, or send me a text, or give me some sort of sign. None of that happened. The behind the scenes plot twist that unraveled next, I never saw it coming. It became one of the biggest cliff hangers I have ever had a front-row seat to.

The producer man, the one I was really there to see, stood up at the end of the long table where we were seated. He announced that I was to go stay the night with my new field producer, who's lodging was within sight of his own apartment. When he said that, my jaw hit the floor. I was so shocked at his abrupt and ludicrous suggestion, I just sat there with a stupid look on my face. Then I went straight up to him and hugged him in front of everyone. I grabbed hold of him and whispered in his ear, "Why are you doing this?" He pushed me away and told me to go with this other man. He literally tried to pimp me out. I was too drunk to drive home. I didn't know what to do. Next thing I knew, the man I loved was escorting me through the door of the pub and having the other producer lead me down the street, away from him. Luckily that guy ended up being a gentleman when we made it to his place. He could see how upset I was and left me alone. I just laid there in the room with the door shut, crying about being treated like a prostitute by someone I believed actually cared about me. I texted him and told him it wasn't right. He was just full of excuses. The next day, (although I wasn't violated by my new boss), I had to do a walk of shame out of that town. The producer man promised to meet me that morning but he stood me up. It didn't align with his agenda.

I knew as I was driving home, that I had inadvertently ended my role on Appalachian Outlaws. It was over. The romantic relationship, the TV show deal; poof, just like that. Done. The entire episode of the night before was another setup. It was producer man's way of trying to get himself out from under the bus, so his neck wouldn't be cut from his career if our secret status was discovered. If I had slept with the other guy that I was pimped out to, I would have been allowed to continue on with the show. I knew that. But I didn't sleep with him because he was not the man I had feelings for. So because of that, I became an instant liability. I was unofficially blackballed by the production company because the man I had been intimate with was in charge of the entire fucking project. This account of what happened with my rise and fall from fame is the first time I have ever told the truth about it to anyone other than the other cast members on the show and my closest confidants. I tried to save face for the series. It is embarrassing. It is shameful. It's partially my fault because I should have known better. But the truth is the truth no matter how hard it is to tell. There it is. That is the reality about my experience with reality TV.

My first reaction was to report this scandal to the production company and the network. It was a form of sexual harassment. I could have filed charges and had a valid lawsuit. I had proof of all of it on text messages, from the beginning to the end. I didn't give a damn that I lost my fifteen minutes of fame. I never sought to be on TV before all this show shit came about in the first place. I did, however, care about the fact that the only reason I was done dirty was because I am a woman. That alone made my temper rise. I was done being dicked around. All men I gave a chance to, had proven themselves to me as nothing more than narcissistic assholes. Lesson learned. For a while producer man was trying to play it off like I would finish up the film season. He was trying to lead me along so I wouldn't blow the whistle on him. I could have had him by the balls. But I knew when everything went from full production mode to nothing at all, that my character had been killed off.

A few weeks after all this happened, I was still trying to decide on my course of action. I went back to Nashville to hang out with Chance in early November. We were going to work on recording our duet. On my way there I found out that the show had already found my replacement. At the last minute, they shot her scenes, which would take place of everything I had done during four months of filming. They only had a few weeks before the entire season was wrapped. I texted the producer man to let him know that I was aware. He was freaking out, blowing up my phone with relentless calls and texts. I messaged back and told him I couldn't deal with him. I finally answered one of his calls the next morning and got all riled up just hearing his voice. I yelled at him till I blew out my vocal cords and completely lost my voice. I couldn't even talk by the time I was supposed to meet with Chance, let alone sing.

We ended up having a fine time anyways. Chance took me to a private recording studio where I was able to witness the process of one of his singles being mixed. It was a song entitled "Don't Drop Names", about all the legends he knew personally over the course of his impressive career. I was honored to see one of his tracks in the completion stage. That song is played regularly on Sirius XM Outlaw Country. Chance was a rock star in his younger days, one of the best. He also put out a successful country album. He worked with everyone who was anyone in the music and film industries. He started off as the cue card man for the Johnny Cash Show on TV. He ended up being his stage lighting director, tour manager and one of his best friends. He is a professional photographer and has a private collection of Johnny Cash photos that he took himself. He also taught Johnny how to use a camera to take good pictures of his own. He worked on several movies, in front of the camera and behind the scenes. Then he has his longstanding career as the host of his own Alamo Jones Show on Sirius XM Radio. He also announces for the Grand Old Opry and makes announcements on the Willie's Roadhouse channel. Chance is talented and hilarious. He can make me laugh even if I don't want to. He is the funniest person I know. And any time spent with Chance is time well spent.

But my disease crept up on me again and wiped me out. The pressure of everything held me down and beat me like a punching bag. I went back to see the producer one last time, to force him to look me in the eyes and explain himself. He was just beating around the bush in a very dramatic performance of his own. I left crying and even more confused. The producer man arranged a bullshit scene with me and Tony Coffman at my house. It was his last-ditch effort to keep my mouth shut about what happened. I was filmed aiming a shotgun at Tony. I was just pissed, I wasn't in the mood for any of it. It didn't go well at all. That was the final time I ever saw the producer man.

I was the first to film and the last to film for season two of Appalachian Outlaws. I was over it, and too worn out to retaliate for the shit end of the stick I got. I decided to take the high road and keep all of this to myself. I wanted to show my support for the other cast members, instead of turning their show into a Jerry Springer episode. I continued to promote the upcoming season. I did make an announcement of my own, for those who had been following and supporting me. I composed a politically correct vague public statement, informing everyone that the production company was not going to use my scenes for this season after all, but they may carry them over to season three... blah, blah, blah. That's basically what I was told to say. I assumed that the whole Hollywood ordeal would die down as soon as that information was released. I had grown so tired and weary of this adventure gone wrong. I was prepared to go back to the normal and quiet life that I had been within reach of before the fame monster got a hold of me. That's what I truly needed and wanted. I was even thankful and actually relieved that the show for me was all over before it ever really started. Honestly, I was happy to be done. I figured that was the end of the line for Lady Outlaw.

Shine On

My announcement of bowing out for my final curtain call on the big stage of Appalachian Outlaws, well it backfired on me. My role as Lady Outlaw got an unintentional encore presentation. What I thought would allow me to go back into hiding unnoticed, turned out to be a launch into further publicity. I somehow gained even more followers and supporters. It was not the way I predicted it would go, it resulted in the complete opposite outcome. People still recognized me as part of the program, even though I stated otherwise. But I left it open to interpretation. Perhaps I should have been more blunt and specific. But I continued to be a promotional target for the tv show. Either way, there was nothing I could do about it now, short of deactivating my social media and basically seeming ungrateful to the thousands of people around the country and even internationally, who had rallied to my side and backed me 100%. I felt like it would be a direct insult to them on my part if I just fell to the wayside off the face of the planet, and they never heard from me again. So I decided to use this instead as a personal platform, to switch gears and steer Lady Outlaw into the direction that I wanted her to go. A prospect that held profound historical meaning to me. An ongoing endeavor I knew I could be proud of and passionate about. A real-life part to play that I would make my own mark on, with due time and pure dedication. Something that meant a great deal to me, and I held with high respect and regard... the moonshine industry. I flipped the coin and it landed on the side

415

that would determine the fate of my future. Lady Outlaw, the woman shiner from West Virginia.

There are many reasons why not only did I choose moonshine, but it also chose me. The main basis for my true desire to be a part of the current history of the trade was the past significant history of the market. Moonshine was born in the Appalachian Mountain region. Settlers from Scotland and Ireland brought their knowledge of distilling spirits with them when they fled to this country for freedom from persecution.. and found solace in the hills and hollers. Just like they brought their musical instruments, which became their entertainment and the founding sound of Bluegrass music. But they used this form of making homemade whiskey as a secondary source of income. And ever since the initial introduction of spirits, Appalachians have relied on the black market trade to supplement their financial stability in what has been a largely impoverished region. It became a permanent part of our culture and heritage. It turned into a way of life.. because it allowed for poor people to provide a roof over their families' heads, to put clothes on their backs, and place food on their tables. It sustained these households. It helped them meet the basic needs of survival. That is where my true respect lies in the industry. That's why I am so drawn to it. I entered the trade for the same reasons, to provide for my family. It has less to do with the actual alcohol for me, and more to do with the ingenuity of an underprivileged demographic area, and the way they so intelligently created their own system of commerce, to make ends meet.

Anyone who assumes that moonshiners are ignorant hillbillies, you are wrong. They are some of the most brilliant and innovative people around. Not just anyone can set up and distill whiskey. There is an enormous amount of physical labor, science, math and pure art involved in the process from beginning to end. If it is done correctly, you can be assured that whoever made the moonshine, put every ounce of their heart into what came out as the final finished product. True shiners take great pride in what they do and what they deliver for others to consume. They are the farmers of grain spirits. They carefully craft a time-honored tradition and fill Mason jars full of their extensive knowledge and credible skills. They never stop trying to learn or improve on their personal level of craftsmanship. Even moonshiners who have perfected the process, are always aiming to go above and beyond, to outdo what they've already done. To invent new ideas, new recipes, and new methods. They remain as veteran students in the study of the trade. For the most part, they compete more with themselves than with others in the industry. They are known for patting fellow shiners on the back for a job well done. And for giving advice to anyone who falls short on the many skills involved with turning out something of high-quality standards. It is a brotherhood, a union of blue-collar workers, a diverse family of folks who are in it for worthy and respectable reasons. Once you have been invited to join the inner circle of moonshiners, they have your back and you have theirs. That's the way it's supposed to be.

On with the story... I took J.J. and Faith for a trip to Florida during their winter break. We were to celebrate New Year's of 2015 there. I needed quality time with my babies after the recent waste of my time in filming. I wanted to get away from the farm and out of the state. Also, the cold weather makes my arthritis a hundred times worse, so I was looking forward to the warm climate of the South and hoping to catch a break from my pain. Winter is my favorite time to go to Florida. You can leave a blizzard in WV, and arrive to tropical sunshine and flowers in FL. By this time I was calm and happy again for the most part, back in a good groove of life. The kids and I had fun on our road trip, even though we got stuck in bumper to bumper traffic on I-95 for about six hours in South Carolina. But we finally made it safely to our destination of Lakeland, where we stayed as guests at Haley's house. I showed the kids around Polk County. I drove them by my old high school, the house I was mostly raised in, and some of the places I had worked. I took them on a hike in the Green Swamp, where they were scared of gators. We had fun on our trip. It was nice to get away with them. It was our first vacation with just the three of us.

On New Year's Eve, we caravanned with Haley and her family to Bok Tower Gardens, the highest point in Florida. It is one of the most beautiful places in the central region of the state. There is something mysterious and magical about it. We toured the entire grounds, while my sister and I enjoyed watching our children run and play together. There is a wish fountain in front of the tower. I stopped there and pulled a shiny copper penny from my purse. I closed my eyes and said a prayer to God, to please send me the man I was supposed to be with, the right one. I knew he was out there in the universe somewhere, waiting for me too. I tossed the penny into the fountain. The prayer was my wish. That night, I took J.J. and Faith to Downtown Disney for the New Year's Eve celebration. There was live music and fireworks. Disney always does everything in a spectacular way. We had the best time. It was my most favorite ringing in of the New Year on record. 2015 started off with a good vibe for me. There were no two humans I would have rather started it off with than my beautiful children. They are my heart and soul.

We ended up getting gridlocked in the parking lot when the night was over. We were stuck there for four hours, with constant horn honking. But we made the most of it, as I honked out tunes on the horn of the Blue Spark, which is an impressively loud horn for such a tiny car. We spent New Year's Day with our family, and we left late that evening. I drove all throughout the night while the children slept. When we were within sight of the street to our farm, I got pulled over for speeding. I must have looked like a zombie with bloodshot eyes after driving all night and downing gallons of coffee. Before the cop got out of his car, I cued up "Fuck The Police" on J.J.'s iPod. I said if I get a ticket, I'm going to play this song for the lawman. (Bad example of parenting, I know). I was just mad that I got blue lighted on literally the last mile of an 851-mile trip. The cop looked frightened when he came to my window and I rattled off at him yelling, "I've been driving all night on a 14-hour trip and I'm tired. And I'm fixing to pee my pants... and I can see my road sign from here!" Luckily, he told me to have a nice day and let me go.

While I was still working for the bank, I had a run-in with the law. I was on my way home from work one day, and I stopped by the grocery store for some ingredients to make supper and a pie. I was behaving myself, till I wasn't. I had intentions of being a good girl that day. But I accidentally ran through a construction area on the Mountaineer Expressway, about two miles away from the farm. I was doing 80 some in a 55 mph work zone. I didn't even realize it till I saw the undercover cop car and its blue lights in my rearview. Dammit. My registration and inspection stickers were expired, and I didn't have my insurance card. I just knew I was gonna be hauled off to jail. I was completely illegal and flying way above the speed limit. The officer came to my window and asked for my drivers' license. I handed it to him. He read it and asked, "Why were you speeding Miss Sparks?" To which I looked him in the eye and boldly stated, "Because I like to drive fast, and I have groceries in the car, and you're slowing me down." I'm an idiot. I don't know what possessed me to say that, but it just fell out of my mouth before I could catch myself. Then my dumbass proceeded to say, "Oh and by the way, I'm an outlaw." The policeman laughed out loud at me and shook his head. He asked what I did that's against the law. I said, "I'm not telling you, you're a lawman." He told me it was alright, I could tell him. So I went on to confess that I was a bootlegger.

About that time my phone rang on my lap. It was Chance Martin. The picture of him with Johnny Cash popped up and the cop saw it. He asked if I needed to answer the call. I said, "No, it's Johnny Cash's best friend. I will call him back later." (It happened to be Chance's birthday). The officer just looked puzzled, like who the hell is this crazy chick? I was thinking he probably wished he had never pulled me over. He then asked me if I had any moonshine in my vehicle. I responded, "As a matter of fact, yes I do." I was just getting stupider by the minute. I don't know what came over me. I flat out told on myself for no good reason. He asked to see the contents of my haul and opened the driver door for me to step out. We walked around the back of the Blue Spark, and I popped open the hatchback to reveal four cases of illegal liquor. I said, "I just keep this in my vehicle in case I run out of gas, so I can pour it in the tank and get down the road." He insisted that it wasn't strong enough to run an automobile. I replied, "Bullshit, take ya a swig." He laughed and shook his head at me again. We stood on the side of the road and just talked for about twenty minutes. He let me go without even so much as a warning. He told me to have a nice day and sent me on my way.

I don't know why I give lawmen a hard time. I actually do respect them and their line of duty. I don't agree with every law, but I do support the fact that they are just trying to keep peace and uphold the laws they were sworn to enforce. But I find myself being an unintentional smartass to them, every time. It's a bad habit of mine. But again, being an otherwise innocent-looking lady, they let me get away with having inappropriate conduct. It is a good cover for black market activity. Sometimes I think maybe they appreciate my indecent humor, it breaks up their regular monotony of hearing "Yes Sir, No Sir, I promise I won't do it again." I catch them off guard and amuse them I guess. I devised a plan to print off and hand out "Get Out Of Jail Free" cards to hand over when they ask for my license. Just to see what will happen. I also started telling officers that I am the "Zipper Police". They immediately check their flies every time. It's like a magic trick. I once told a cop that I was intentionally going to break the West Virginia law which states that it is illegal to whistle underwater, (this is a legitimate law by the way. A ridiculous one, but real). I said, "I dare you to catch me whistling underwater and issue me a citation for it." I really need to stop myself from carrying on with them. Eventually, I'm going to say the wrong thing to the wrong lawman and land myself in the big house for harassing an officer. I honestly don't mean any harm or disrespect though. It's just the way I am. It's my way of bucking the system.

Being an outlaw to me doesn't mean you are a criminal. It doesn't mean you are out to lie, cheat, or steal...or intend to hurt anyone. Outlaws and criminals are two separate things in my book. Society has tried to corral everyone into a box. It has been set up so that we all resemble carbon copies of one another. We have been programmed like robots to follow suit and be herded around like cattle, tagged with numbers and corralled into designated boundaries. Kids go to school and sit at a desk all day, so they can get a job. Adults go to work and don't even make enough money to pay their bills. You work till you earn the right to retire. When you retire, you are too old to enjoy life anymore, or to spend all the money you saved up in your retirement plan for vacations and adventures you held off on while you were too busy working. You retire, then you die. What was it all for? Were you happy? Were you fulfilled? Did you live life to the fullest? We follow rules. We follow laws. We follow every set procedure in the handbook of how to live life. It is a vicious cycle of what has become the standard way of living for Americans. That's not really living. It is a parade that we march along in because we don't know any different or any better. It's a three-ring circus and we are following a ring leader. To me, being an outlaw means you operate outside that box of society. Color outside the lines. Make your own set of rules. Do things your way and by your terms and conditions. Choose to be the black sheep, on purpose. Separate yourself from the herd, and set yourself apart as your own unique individual. Lead the pack instead of being a follower. Blaze your own trail and stake your own claim. Undo the leash that is attached to your neck, and take back control of your own life. It doesn't necessarily mean breaking the law. But instead outsmarting the law, and finding a way to operate beyond the boundaries of modern-day civilization.

Anyways, as an indirect result of all the time I took off for filming when I was with the show, I subsequently got myself fired from my bank job. My boss there reneged on his word to allow me a flexible schedule, then tried to mask it as a bank policy that I supposedly didn't handle correctly, which was a lie. I did my job well and by procedure. He kicked me out to bring some personal guy friend of his onboard. Oh well. Surprisingly I didn't get fired for all the times I threatened to rob that bank. I lost my full-time job over something lame. But I still had bootlegging going for me. And in the meantime, I started looking for other work. I landed the absolute worst job I have ever had in my life. A hotel maid. Big bad movie star actress Lady Outlaw, had been reduced to changing beds and scrubbing toilets. I am not knocking anyone in this line of work. I give them props. It is one of the most physically demanding occupations I've ever had. Cleaning a dozen or more dirty rooms is no small task. I'm not saying that I thought I was too good to do it. Otherwise, I would have sought employment elsewhere. But I'm saying that at almost 35 years old when I saw my reflection in the bathroom mirror while I was bent over wiping down the toilet bowl, wearing a maid uniform. I was like what the hell have I become? This is really what I'm going to be when I grow up?

My first day on the job, the very first room I was assigned to.. a grown man had downed two cases of beer, and wet the damn bed like a toddler child. But it was a man-sized puddle. And I had to clean it up. So glamorous, huh? After about a few weeks of working there, I made peace with my new role as a housekeeper. I decided that it was honorable in the fact that I was making the rooms tidy for travelers to lay their weary bodies and rest. Being a travelling gypsy myself, I could relate the need for a nice clean room to unwind in after a long day on the road. So I started whistling while I worked. I put my best effort into the new less glitzy role I landed, even though it was taking a toll on my bad back and arthritis. But I ended up quitting that job after about a month and a half because it was the most despicable and discourteous group of women I have ever worked with. All except for one were completely spiteful and vindictive. The boss was the most uppity of them all. I finally got to the point where I couldn't deal with that hen house anymore. So one day I left a note on the manager's desk, that literally said, "Take this job and shove it."

With no job other than bootlegging, which didn't provide a steady income, I started getting behind on my bills. I couldn't keep up with my car payment, and could barely keep the lights and water utilities on. I was having a very hard time finding another full-time job. West Virginia is known for having an almost non-existent job economy. Sadly, that is why natives tend to leave the state and go where there are more career choices. This was during the time when Obama was in office and had every coal mine in the state shut down. Mountaineers were packing up and fleeing like refugees. It was all around one of the worst financial climates for my home state that I have ever seen. I ended up filing with West Virginia Workforce for unemployment, which was granted based on their investigation that proved I was unfairly released from my job as a banker. But I still couldn't make ends meet, so the repo man started coming after my Blue Spark. I would hide it in different locations on the farm, under tarps and behind hay bales. I was prepared to even put it in neutral and push it off a cliff before I let the bank have it. I was sick of having things taken from me. I didn't file for food stamps because I was too proud. So I did without and went hungry for most of this time period. Even with my extremely small rations, I was seriously struggling to put food on the table for my children. That made me feel like a failure.

Desperate times call for desperate measures. I started my own Robin Hood campaign. This is horrible but I'm going to tell it. I had a shopping basket that Jason accidentally took from Walmart. J.J. had brought it down to our house from up the hill. So I put it to use, instead of signing up for welfare and standing in line for government cheese. While Jason was at work, I would go to his house. I would scavenge food items and put them in the grocery basket.. potatoes, ground beef, deer meat, macaroni, butter, eggs, etc. I was shopping at Jason's General Store (Well, more like stealing). I was taking from the rich and giving to the poor. But see if I had claimed the child support the judge tried to award me, I never would have been in this predicament in the first place. I would have been living high on the hog. Hippy was doing renovations to Jason's house at the time, and once caught me thieving a pack of bacon. I always confessed my crimes and told on myself for what I had taken though, it was not a mystery to Jason. When Hippy noticed what an impoverished state I was in, he started making it a point to feed me and the kids. He would bring groceries to my house, or take me out to eat on occasion. He kept us from literal starvation. Hippy saved the day, many times. And I, in turn, would cook for him, or let him shower at my house and do his laundry. It was a win, win situation for us both. We made a good team for a couple of rough customers.

That February, the Season 2 Premiere Party for Appalachian Outlaws was scheduled for the night of Groundhog's Day in Newport, Tennessee, which is the moonshine capital of the world. Since I was still being promoted as a cast member of the show, and the other cast members had become good friends of mine, I was invited to make an appearance for the event. My buddy Ewok was hosting the party in his hometown. He was one of the few who knew the truth of what happened to me behind the scenes. He graciously insisted that I come, and I accepted his invitation. The day that I was to make the journey, a huge snowstorm hit the mountain region. Anyone who knew of my travel plans tried to talk me out of going due to the inclement weather. I made up my mind to stay home and forego my invite. I was very low on funds and really couldn't afford the travel expenses anyways. At the very last minute, my intuition told me to go. I changed my mind and hit the highway. The weather was brutal. I had no business being on the dangerous roadways in my tin can Spark. What should have been a five-hour drive, turned into an eight-hour horrendous voyage in blizzard conditions. I stopped at the Tennessee Welcome Center off of I-81 near Bristol, and changed clothes in the bathroom stall, fixed my hair and threw on some makeup. My gas gauge was flashing on E thirty miles out from my exit. I was running late and didn't have so much as a dime to my name. I had put my last bit of pocket change into the tank at the beginning of my trip, but it wasn't enough. I literally coasted in on fumes to the big Hollywood Premiere Party red carpet event. It was held at a moonshine bar on the outskirts of Newport, called Brandywine Tavern. I barely made it, but I was there. I was stressed out and worn out from the trip. I composed myself anyways and walked in as Lady Outlaw.

I found Ewok and his wife Raven straight away. Cast member Rufus was there, along with a few others. There was a buffet dinner, which I quickly took advantage of since I hadn't eaten all day, and I was starving from my poor girl status. I fixed a big plate and found a table to sit at alone. The local newspaper, The Newport Plain Talk, was there to cover the event. Ewok introduced me to two of the reporters who were there with the paper. I didn't catch their names, but one of them was also a friend of Ewok's. This one didn't say a word to me. He just stared at me all night. Even when the first episode of Season 2 came on screen, I could feel his eyes on me. He was sitting behind me but I sensed his gaze. I would turn to look from the corner of my eye, and he was constantly staring in my direction. He never even watched the tv show we were all there to see. Normally I would have felt like his behavior was stalkerish. But I didn't feel that way for some reason. Later, when I got a better vantage point of this man, I thought he was very handsome with his dark skin, dark hair and even darker eyes. I guessed him to be around the same age as me. I kept feeling a profound overwhelming sense of longing that I wanted to go home with him. I even thought to myself, "That's crazy, why would you want to go home with a complete stranger?" Stop this nonsense Tiff". I honestly didn't feel compelled to go with him to do anything inappropriate, like a one night stand. That wasn't for me anyways. I wasn't that kind of girl. I just felt like I was supposed to go home with him, and I didn't know why. He never did say so much as one word to me. We never spoke at all that night.

The party ended around midnight. There was a hotel close by, and Ewok had arranged for a group discount at these lodgings for anyone in town with the Appalachian Outlaws. I coasted my car over to the parking lot. Then shut it off before the gas fumes ran out. It was freezing cold outside and I couldn't even run the engine for heat. My unemployment funds were supposed to hit right at midnight on my issued bank card. I called the number on the back to check the balance. The money hadn't been deposited. I sat there in a blizzard, in the middle of the night, with no money to pay for the hotel, and no money for gas to get back home. Normally I would have just slept in my vehicle, with the heater full blast. But I was just plain as day up shit creek without a paddle that night. I could have asked Ewok and Raven for help. They are the kind of good people who would be the first to assist a friend in need any way they could, at any hour of the day or night and they lived just a few miles from where I was stranded. But I was too ashamed of my poor girl circumstances to reach out to them. I did the only thing I could think to do. I called my ex-husband and woke him up. I told him of the predicament I had gotten myself in. He had me coast to the nearest truck stop, a Pilot station. He paid over the phone with his credit card to fill my tank and buy me a pack of cigarettes plus a cup of coffee. After all our former battles had died down, we turned out to be good friends. We were even still family in our own way. And he saved the day for me. I drove all throughout the rest of that night with no sleep over a 24-hour-period, on snow and black ice and finally made it home around 8am the next morning.

That day, I got a friend request from the tall, dark and handsome man that kept his eyes on me the night before. His name was Jason Kolar. That immediately let me know that I couldn't get romantically involved with this man, just based on his first name alone. It was an instant strike against him as far as my policy to never be with another Jason. See there is a strange occurrence in my family. My mother married two men named Mark. And my father married two women named Lori. I couldn't fall victim of the family curse. But this Jason sent me a message and said it was nice to meet me. Then sent me a copy of the pictures and write up that was to be published in the newspaper article about the event. He wasn't even trying to flirt with me, although I did check his status and discovered he was single, and he was close in age to me. But it was all innocent, and we became friends. I really didn't need to be in another relationship yet anyways, after the string of failed ones with the three men in the entertainment industry. They all drug my mechanical tin man heart through the mud. And I needed to work on myself as a person before I ever even thought about getting involved in another serious relationship. I needed to get my shit together and pull myself out of the rut I was in financially and emotionally. I had nothing to offer anyone else at the time. But Jason Kolar and I talked as friends, almost daily. We had a lot in common and enjoyed the same outdoor hobbies. He loved animals too and lived on a farm. He would tell me about his pet goats and send me pictures of them. We always had something to talk about. He was a true gentleman.

Ewok kept trying to matchmake me with this guy. He would say "Sparks, I think you should give Kolar a chance." He told me Jason was a good guy, and he had a crush on me. I kept telling Ewok, "No buddy. I can't date a man named Jason that lives two states away. Not happening. We're just friends." Ewok and I had this same conversation at least a hundred times, and it went the same way every time. I was happy to be single anyways. I was finally getting comfortable being on my own without a man to contend with. I was off the market. I had no desire to date anyone, casually or seriously. But I maintained my friendship with Jason Kolar. Even if he secretly had a crush on me, he never let on like he did. He was different than the dozens of other guys who were trying to win me at the time. He didn't have a game plan and pickup lines or attempt to actively pursue me in any way. He was just nice to me, reserved and polite. And because of that, I didn't push him away like I did every other man in my "bound and determined to stay single spree." I was like an elusive doe high tailing it from a herd of bucks in rut season. But I would let Kolar catch up with me because he wasn't chasing me like the others. He was one of the very few guys I would even give the time of day to. What all the other men did wrong, he was doing right. And I took notice of that.

At the end of February, I returned to Nashville to attend Johnny Cash's birthday celebration at the Cash Museum again. This time I was Chance's date since Chuck was still annoyed with us for our running from the law house alarm incident. The last time I was in town to see Chance, he had taken me out and bought me a very fancy beautiful pair of black and rhinestone high heel shoes. So I revolved my entire wardrobe for the Cash event around those prettiest shoes I've ever had. I got all dolled up and Chance got all rock starred up, and we set out on Twang Town together, a pair of misfit Outlaws. Everywhere you go with Chance is as VIP as it gets. And he was to perform on stage that night for Johnny's party. Right before he got on stage, I noticed he had a banana in his pocket, (he keeps one always handy due to dietary reasons, and also keeps a roll of cherry-flavored Life Savers). Anyways I told him to hand the banana over before it fell out of his pocket during his performance. I was thinking back to a story he told me about an incident that happened to Elvis when Chance was working for "The King" on tour. Elvis dropped a loaded chrome derringer, and it spun around on the stage. Chance saved the day for Elvis. And I pictured a similar incident unfolding for Chance with the banana. I was trying to save his day. So I stood there and watched Chance sing live on stage, sounding just like Johnny Cash while I held the banana in my hand, with my sparkly black outfit and fancy high heel shoes.

Chapter 2

Chance and I had a lovely time at the Johnny Cash Museum. I was able to see all the same familiar faces of those that I had met there on my first time to Johnny's birthday party. They welcomed me back again. I had become good friends with many of these fascinating men and women. Chuck even digressed his issue with us that night, and we all ate, drank and had a merry time. Plus more birthday cake. I was especially honored to visit with Mr. Tommy Cash again, my hero.

The next day Chance took me to visit with the daughter of Cowboy Jack Clement, her name is Alison. She is one of the coolest women I have ever met. She showed me artifacts from Cowboy Jack's career with Sun Records. He was one of the major music executives there in Memphis for the record label that launched Elvis, Johnny Cash, Jerry Lee Lewis and more. There is a home movie her father made with Johnny Cash, a comedy. Chance is also featured on the production. It's called, "Shakespeare Was a Big George Jones Fan." In this film, Johnny Cash wears a rubber pig snout and a plastic gold crown, and says, "Pigs can see the wind." Alison let me wear that very same gold crown and pig snout, and I took a selfie with them on. I felt extra VIP while I was wearing the same items Johnny Cash once wore. It was one of my best moments of that entire weekend, and one of the highlights of my life.

In mid-April, I was invited back to the Newport, TN area to attend another event for Appalachian Outlaws. It was a meet and greet at a book store in the town of White Pine. We were also scheduled to have a cookout hosted by a supporter of the show, and do a white water rafting trip on the Pigeon River with Ewok that weekend. Jason Kolar knew I was coming, so he invited me to be a guest in his home, and wanted to take me turkey hunting for spring gobbler season. I thought it was very thoughtful of him to ask, but I declined his invitation at the last minute, because my friend and other cast member, Lady Outlaw Jessica Hatfield, was to travel with me to the event. So I booked her and I a hotel room in Newport. Jessica and I enjoyed our road trip together and talked the whole way to Tennessee. We arrived at the White Pine bookstore just in time for the event. Jason Kolar was waiting for me in the parking lot, he actually spoke to me in person this time, as I was rushing in to find my place at the long line of tables. There were a bunch of other legitimate cast members present, and long lines filing through with fans of the show. Jason stood on the sidelines and kept an eye on me the whole time. He left once to get some copies of *Visiting The Smokies*, a publication that he was the main contributor to with the newspaper he worked for. Ewok had been featured in the latest edition and requested some copies. But when Jason came back, he stayed within close range to me.

I had printed off photographs of myself as Lady Outlaw, with a black leather corset and the 44 on my hip holster. It was my first time ever signing my autograph to anything, and the first time people asked to have their pictures made with me. It was a strange occurrence and a foreign concept to me because I really had no valid reason to be on the publicity side of the table. I had done nothing notable to earn the right to sign autographs. I didn't deserve to be regarded as a celebrity. But I had become well known by that time. And although I was never actually on the Appalachian Outlaws, I had still been accepted by the cast and the fans as one of the characters anyhow. I was there to support my friends on the show. But it surprised me how many in the crowd actually turned out to also meet me. They seemed genuinely happy that I was there. Several of them had been following me and supporting me since the beginning of my reality show journey. I felt humbled and appreciative that they took the time to acknowledge me and speak to me. I knew I was no one special. But they treated me like I was. They were sincere and genuine. I was honored to meet everyone that came there that day.

I was personally excited to meet one cast member in particular at the event. I had never met him before, but I was a huge fan of his from watching Season One of the show on my YouTube subscription. He was a big tall real-life giant of a man, named Tiny. And he was the only moonshiner ever on the series. I knew as soon as I saw him and we got to talking, that he was going to become my big buddy. I would find out later on down the road that our paths were destined to cross for a specific reason.

After the bookstore event wound down, we all proceeded to the cookout prearranged for us by a generous supporter of the show. Her name is Laura Ward, and she was also responsible for setting up the meet and greet in White Pine. We all followed her to her home on the outskirts of town, where she hosted the outdoor gathering. I brought fresh ramps I had dug in WV to contribute to the pot luck dinner. Jessica and I got to work on cleaning them as soon as we arrived at the location. Jason Kolar was also at the cookout. He never said much to me there, but he followed me around like a little lost puppy dog the entire time. Never getting too close, but never straying far away either. I spent a great deal of time talking to Tiny about the moonshine industry. He owns his own legal distillery in Piney Flats, TN, called East Tennessee Distillery. He brought some of his bottles of shine to share with everyone at the cookout. We took turns sampling the different jugs of liquor. I barely took a tiny sip of his 150-proof firewater, and I was instantly drunk. He made his moonshine in the traditional way. It was not the neutral grain spirits that most bigger distilleries offer. It is authentic corn whiskey. He immediately earned two thumbs up and a five-star rating from me on his quality products. We all had a great time at the outdoor social event. It just felt like a big family reunion. Jessica and I left after dark and headed to our room at the Motel 6 in Newport. I didn't realize it then, but we were just a few miles down the road from of Jason Kolar's house. I wasn't far away from the man I had wanted to go home with on Groundhog's Day a few months earlier. And I didn't know it then, but he worked really hard cleaning his house before that weekend, in hopes that I would come there to visit him.

The next day we all went on a white water rafting adventure with Ewok, the master of all river guides. It had been his profession among others for many years. Ewok was also a veteran Army Ranger and a professional actor. He even had a role in "The Last of the Mohicans" as a British redcoat. Ewok is just an all-around badass. And he became one of my closest friends. I had never been rafting before, but I trusted him completely to guide us safely through the river rapids. I am not really a good swimmer, so my main objective was to not go overboard. Jason Kolar was there, in a separate boat with Rufus who was fishing the Pigeon. Jessica and I were the only passengers on Ewok's raft. Jason was documenting the trip for his *Visiting The Smokies* publication. For some reason, I felt safe knowing he was nearby. I knew that if I fell out and needed to be rescued, he would jump in the river and save me. All went well, and we had a blast.

Jessica and I ended up landing on the front cover of the next issue for *Visiting The Smokies*. After we switched to dry clothes, we all took a private tour of the moonshine distillery, Bootlegger's, located in the rafting town of Hartford. I swapped contact info with the master distiller and told him of my bootlegging business. Then the Appalachian Outlaw crew went out to dinner at a pizza place in Newport. Jason sat close to me there. And I kept feeling the urge to hold his hand. But I would quickly coax myself from that desire, and back into the safety of our friend zone. When Jessica and I left, she commented to me that she thought he was cute. I told her he is a really nice guy, and she should go for him. During that time, I was romantically talking to the front man member of the McCoy family. And since Jessica was a Hatfield, and knew the Mr. McCoy

I was interested in her and I had several discussions, and girl talks about the possibility of me having a relationship with him. He was a male version of myself, in the same outlaw category I was in. We hit it off through hours of conversations, and I thought we would wind up dating and become an outlaw couple. But I hadn't met him in person yet. He lived in Pikeville, KY. I kept trying to set up and arrange meetings between us, but it just never worked out. I even told him we could meet on the West Virginia/Kentucky border just to pass a jar of moonshine across the state lines. That never happened. There was always a conflict in our schedules. Mr. McCoy turned out to be the one that got away. But we remained as good friends, and still are to this day. We also became business partners later down the line.

The very next weekend, I was invited back by Ewok to return to Hartford for a river festival. Also, the distiller from Bootlegger's wanted to hold a meeting with me to talk moonshine business. I didn't want to make the long drive to Tennessee again. And I was broke, still without a real job. I had mentioned the festival to Hippy in passing. He jumped on it and was like hell yes, we're going. He offered to pay for the fuel to get there. So Hippy and I set out on our first long-distance road trip together. That was when I initially recognized that Hippy is a pain in the ass to have as a travel buddy. He didn't shut up for so much as two seconds the entire 310-mile drive. And he kept reaching over into my driver's side of the Blue Spark cockpit, just to mess with me. I finally slapped him and told him to stay on his passenger side before he caused me to swerve and wreck. I threatened to leave him on the side of the road. I kept thinking to myself, never again. I will never travel with this talkative immature grown man best friend of mine again. I happily dropped Hippy off at the river party and left him there. I went to the Bootlegger's Distillery and met with the owner Darrell Miller. We discussed business for about two hours…numbers, prospects, marketing, etc. We intended to strike some sort of deal together involving the moonshine industry. I was well known by both legal and illegal shiners at this point in time, as a female contributor to the trade. And I was being sought after by some of the major players in the market. I was carefully weighing out my options and what I refer to as "courting" distilleries, to find the right fit for me.

I went back to the riverside party, and Hippy was nowhere to be found. I thought surely he had gotten drunk on shine and floated on down the river. And then I locked my keys in the car. Jason Kolar was there and came to my assistance. He got my car unlocked after a while of working on it in the dark. A drunk Hippy turned up from whatever festivity rock he crawled out from under, and we got him into the passenger seat where he passed out and took to sawing logs in his sleep. Jason and I went to the bonfire. He brought his own homemade jar of moonshine, and we passed it around. I played my guitar and sang. Then a big thunderstorm came rolling in. Hippy and I never even made any arrangement for lodgings. We were poor bastards. I was just planning to camp in the car where Hippy was already settled. Jason offered to go home and bring us back a tent. Or he said we were welcome to come stay at his place in his guest room. As the storm got drastically worse, I opted to take him up on his offer to host us. With Hippy still passed out, and clueless as to this plan, I followed Jason Kolar home. There was lightning crashing, wind-breaking branches across the road and rain pouring down like Niagara Falls on my windshield. But we arrived safely at our destination. I had, after all, followed this man home. Like my intuition told me to the first time I ever saw him.

We managed to get drunk Hippy to the couch, where he began snoring again before his head even touched the pillow. Jason showed me to his guest room. Then he followed me like a puppy dog when I went into the bathroom to brush my teeth. He just stood there watching me like he was mesmerized by such a mundane daily task. I thought that was odd, but there was something endearing about it. Then on my way to the sleeping quarters I was given next to his room, he mentioned innocently that he would snuggle with me if I wanted him to. Without even thinking, I just said okay. And so we snuggled that night, in a twin-sized bed listening to the pouring rain on the tin roof, watching lightning bolts as they lit up the dark sky and hearing the thunder rolling. It was a dramatic and romantic setting. Also, the sound of his rooster crowing at the street light just outside the bedroom, kept me awake all hours. But I felt like I was where I was meant to be, warm and safe in his arms. All my intentions to keep things in the friend zone with him flew right out the window that night. He became my person. I was home with him. He was the prayer wish I made in the fountain at the turn of the New Year. God sent me to find him, and he was there, waiting for me.

The next morning, Jason Kolar gave me two baby fainting goats. He had promised them to me beforehand after I relayed to him that I had wanted a fainting goat for years. I used to get on YouTube and watch hours of videos of them. I thought the breed was hilarious, the way they kill over with their fainting spells. I couldn't take the two he gave me home that day, (a road trip with a Hippy plus goats would be a noisy nightmare), but he said he would keep them for me till I could get them to my farm. That's how Mr. Kolar really won me over, he gave me baby animals. That's the way to this woman's heart. We visited and drank coffee. I started looking around Jason's house now that it was daylight. It was a complete disastrous bachelor pad. He was 38 at the time, and had never been married or had children. He never even lived with a woman, and it was obvious. But I could also tell that he had the same interests as me since most of his home decor was similar to my own. But I thought, oh Lord help me if I have to be the one to clean up after this man. He was just as messy if not worse than my first Jason. It must be a common thing with men of that name. Hippy and I hit the road back home. Unfortunately, we got some expired crockpot Cajun hot boiled peanuts from a gas station in Hartford when we stopped back by the river before we left town. Things went badly wrong on our return road trip, on account of those boiled peanuts. It took us all day between pullovers, pit stops, and rest areas to make it to West Virginia.

After that weekend, Jason Kolar and I were two states apart, and he was my boyfriend. So we were having a long-distance relationship, talking every night on the phone. I knew this would be tricky, trying to figure out how to spend time together. There was a five-hour drive and 290 miles between us. But I also felt like there was no need to rush anything along. It was a few weeks later before I was able to make the trip back to Newport to see him. Mama told me not to stay the night with him, she said, "He could be a serial killer, and you could wind up in a ditch somewhere." I didn't mind my Mama. When I got to his house, he ran up to me and picked me up off the ground to kiss me. We spent the weekend together, just being with each other. He took me turkey hunting, trout fishing, to the movies, and to meet his parents for dinner at their home. I knew it was serious when he introduced me to his mom and dad. They were welcoming and kind to me. It was so nice for a change just to be with someone normal, in a regular way, doing everyday things. Not being secretive and hiding, and sneaking around like I had done with the men in the entertainment industry. My new man was proud to have me by his side and show me off, to publicly claim me as his woman. Jason Kolar was a breath of fresh air. He was a true gentleman and treated me like a true lady. He liked all the same things as me—westerns, being outdoors, animals, moonshine, etc. I took the baby goats he gave me to my home that time, in the back seat of the Spark. I was so hoping I would get blue-lighted just to see the look on an officer's face when they saw two fainting goats in a compact car. I didn't get pulled over, but I stopped by East Tennessee Distillery on my way, to see Tiny and tour his still house. So he and his woman, Miss Dorothy, saw the goats in my car.

After I got back home, something horrible happened on the farm. My beloved Gandalf dog was struck on the highway while he was crossing to check on the baby goats. He had already survived a bear attack, and he lived through a previous hit on the road. That time I got a call from 911 while I was working at the bank. Whoever ran into him was going to shoot him where he laid on the pavement. He managed to get up and walk away. I rushed home and searched everywhere for him. I was running around the woods in a dress and high heeled boots. I heard a branch break when I was calling for Gandalf. I found him badly injured. I ran and got a snow sled, and pulled the Avalanche up to the roadside. I lifted him onto the sled and drug him down the mountain and through the creek, then lifted him into the truck. He weighed about the same as me at the time, 135 pounds. I sped him to the vet, where they stabilized him. I kept him inside the house till he healed. The farm is on the only straight stretch of the entire two-lane, and vehicles fly through here doing ridiculous speeds. This time, Gandalf did not survive. He managed to crawl to the gate of the horse pasture, where he died. I was crushed with devastation. Sad and crying my heart out. He was one of my best friends and family members. My ex-husband helped me bury him on the hillside behind my house. And I laid a bouquet of fresh Mountain Laurel on his grave. My regal and noble Gandalf was gone. He was one of the best dogs I have ever known.

Jason Kolar wanted to come straight away and comfort me after he saw my post about Gandalf on social media. When I get upset, I shut down and don't speak to anyone. I can't. That's my way of dealing with things in an introvert manner. It took me a while to answer his call. He asked if he could come up to see me. I had never introduced my children to any of the three guys I dated in between the two Jason's. I was adamant that I would not let them get acquainted with a love interest of mine unless I got to the point where I knew for a fact that man was there to stay. I didn't want my kids to get attached to someone who may be temporary. Since Jason Kolar and I established that we were in a long term relationship, I allowed him to come to the farm in Birch River, to comfort me. I was ready for him to meet my children and be a guest in my home. He had never even been to the state of WV before that trip. When he arrived, he first met Faith, who brought a bouquet of flowers and a bag of cookies to greet our guest. Then we went to my brother Andrew's graduation, where he met J.J., my mother, both my brothers, my stepdad Jack, and my ex-husband Jason. We all went out to Pizza Hut for lunch afterwards to celebrate. Jason Kolar and J.J. hit it off and immediately became buddies.

My ex-husband told me before my boyfriend's arrival, that he would take him back in the woods with a loaded gun for a man to man talk as soon as they met. But it didn't go that way. I threatened him not to do that. Instead, after we dined together and went back to the farm, I found the two Jason's working together that evening on fencing for the fainting goats. To my surprise, they were getting along just fine. The following day I took my boyfriend to meet my dad's side of the family, my Aunt Alta, Aunt Brenda and some of my cousins. We took my cousin Sarah who is my best girlfriend and went to another Appalachian Outlaws event on the New River in West Virginia. Sarah knew every detail of everything I had been through with the other men. She lives in Texas, but she held my hand all throughout my failed relationships. Sarah approved of this one and could tell I was happy and settled with him. I was done spinning my wheels, and spinning out of control with bad decisions. There was at least one good man left in this world, and he was mine. I was proud to introduce him to my family. I meant to keep this one.

Jason Kolar seemed to like the farm, my family, my tidy little house, and all my animals. He fit in well with everyone and everything. Most men would have never even dared to step into my strange world like he did, but this man handled everything like a pro. He knew that in order to accept me, he also had to accept my unconventional life. It was all part of my package deal. One of the major aspects of why I chose this man to be mine, was the fact that he didn't try to control me, and he didn't want to change who I am. He wanted me to be just as I was. Jason Kolar said to me when we were just friends, "Your eyes have a wildness to them that I like." I guess he wanted me to keep that and hold onto it, to never lose that spark in my eyes or the wildfire passion within me. That was one of the reasons he fell in love with me to begin with. He said it was the wildness that he was attracted to. I respected him and trusted him, not because he demanded it, but because he earned it. I could let him in and still maintain my own identity. I was unapologetically myself. Jason Kolar recognized that right away. He didn't want to tame me or break me at all. He wanted to run free beside me.

In the meanwhile, I was busy with photo shoots for two different distilleries. I was "courting" them both. Bootlegger's and East Tennessee Distillery. I was working on a moonshine calendar for Bootlegger's, with somewhat racy photos. And I was doing promo shoots for East Tennessee Distillery. Ironically, I had become good friends with the aunt of guitar man, she is known to all as Aunt Frankie. She is a professional photographer and she did a shoot with me on their family farm. We hit it off immediately and she has become one of my best friends. Jason Kolar went with me to do the professional shoot at East Tennessee Distillery with Tiny. I was supposed to be the "bad girl" and they had another lady who portrayed the "good girl". I showed up in a red dress. But they wanted me to wear the merchandise shirt for the distillery, so I ended up doing that first shoot in a t-shirt and my underwear. My boyfriend was okay with it, he respected the fact that it was strictly business. He supported everything I did. He was able to separate Lady Outlaw from Tiff, my work from my personal life. That was another reason I knew he was the right one. Not only did he allow me to do what I needed to and wanted to, but he also backed me and routed for me along the way. He didn't want to hold me back. He wanted me to follow my dreams and be successful in everything I did.

I was struggling with many issues at the time though. The repo man was still after my car and I still hadn't found steady work in West Virginia. Plus my haters who were aware of my bootlegging activity tried to turn me in and the law was after me. Jason Kolar and I nearly broke up one day when the police were at my local post office trying to find out my whereabouts. I think he realized then that I was a handful and had too much scrutiny surrounding me. But we worked through these issues. I decided to find temporary work in Tennessee until I could get everything under control. I was running from the repo man and the lawmen. I already had a deal going on with Bootlegger's Distillery which was supposed to make me money. And Tennessee has a million job opportunities, compared to none that I could find in West Virginia. The hardest part was having to work two states away from my children and only being able to come home on the weekends. But ex Jason wanted to catch up on lost time with them since he hadn't been around much when I was raising them. He assured me that everything would be fine. J.J. and Faith were at more independent stages now at 14 and 12 years old. They seemed okay with this plan when I sat them down and explained to them what I had to do and why I had to do it. I knew this arrangement would kill me. I didn't know how I would ever survive not seeing my babies every day. They were my whole world and my reason for living and breathing. But I had to take care of my issues, so I could take better care of them and have more to offer my kids in the long run. Me and the two Jasons discussed the logistics of me coming home as often as I could and ex Jason bringing the kids to me in Tennessee when I couldn't make it home. I packed one suitcase and nothing else. I left my house as my home. I went to Tennessee to find work and cried the whole way there.

Being in the moonshine capital of the world, Cocke County Tennessee, I decided it was time for me to evolve from a bootlegger to an actual moonshiner. I used a makeshift still and got to work on the science experiment of making corn liquor. Trial and error, over and over. Everything that could go wrong my first few runs, went badly wrong. I almost gave up because I felt like I wasn't smart enough to obtain the skills to master the art. But I didn't give up. I kept trying till I got it right, just like I had done with Grandma's biscuits. Throw out the bad batch, and start all over from scratch. By this point, I knew about everyone there was to know in the market, so I started asking for advice. I had never seen the tv show of Moonshiners. But I was temporarily living in the same town as Mark and Digger from the show. They somehow came to know who I was since my overnight rise in the industry. They contacted me and wanted to meet me in person. I also became great friends with a man I met at the Bootlegger's Distillery grand opening, his name was "Uncle Steve". He lived in Newport too and made the moonshine. He took me under his wing making me his apprentice. He became one of my best buddies ever. Steve was a mandolin player and tenor singer for his own Bluegrass band called, Uncle Steve and the Hurricane Ridge. He played regularly at the Maggie Valley Opry House with world-renowned Native American banjo player, Raymond Fairchild. Uncle Steve performed every weekend at the Sugarlands Distillery in Gatlinburg. He had also worked very closely with Popcorn Sutton in the past, and with Jim Tom Hedrick and Roy Grooms on the Moonshiners show. I ended up going to the local video store and renting the first two seasons of the tv show, so I could get better acquainted with the characters of the cast members that I was becoming friends with.

I attended my first moonshine festival, the Popcorn Sutton Jam in Newport, hosted by Popcorn's lovely wife Pam Sutton. I met many of the big players of the industry there, including finally getting to meet Mark and Digger after a cat and mouse game around town in which we never caught up with each other. I met Mike Peek, (who looks just like Brad Pitt), from Georgia HiProof. He helped me get my foot on the first rung of the ladder to climb to the top of the shine business. I gave him a sip from a jar of my homemade liquor, and he approved. I didn't think it was possible for a woman to be a top dog in the predominantly male trade of moonshine, black market, or legal side. I wasn't sure if I could earn the respect and support of established fellow shiners. Mike is the one who gave me the confidence to keep climbing that ladder. He told me I had what it takes to make it. I was already a flag-waver, spokesperson, promoter and supporter for the shine community. But Mike saw the fact that I had something different to offer than what was mainstream. I wasn't a man in overalls with a coonpecker. I was a woman in a dress with class. That set me apart from everyone else right out of the gate. The innocent-looking Lady side of me, and the rebellious streak Outlaw side of me, came together to make a contender for reaching the top of the trade. It was my launch to blaze a trail and further a career for myself as a professional moonshiner. That one person believing in me changed my perception of what I thought I could be capable of. I saw the open door to walk through, to follow a path that would lead to me making something worthwhile of myself after all the failures I had accumulated. I wanted to be someone my children could look up to and be proud to see that I rose from nothing and became something important.

Part 3

That first moonshine event led to a string of what I refer to as, "hitting the dusty trail". It's similar to the music industry, in the way that new artists pay their dues. They start small and work their way up to bigger venues. My first festival was one of the biggest platforms on the shine festival circuit, so I didn't exactly start from the bottom of the barrel; I sort of butted ahead of the line. But it's like a rodeo. Sometimes you ride and stay on, and sometimes you ride and get bucked off. The next major festival I went to was in Maggie Valley, NC. The Hillbilly Jam was a big deal to be part of. I wasn't a big enough deal to make a formal appearance there myself. But I bought my ticket at the gate and went as a supporter of my friends who were set up for meet and greets and vendors. I also went to support Uncle Steve who was to perform on stage that year. He was the one that invited me to attend. That was the first time I ever saw firsthand just how well known I had become. I had no idea, till I walked into the festival and immediately heard people calling my name, (Lady Outlaw or Tiffany Sparks). They were asking for autographs, asking to have pictures made with me, following me like an entourage. I couldn't believe the overwhelming response to me just being there. It felt like an out of body experience. I didn't even know how to handle all the attention coming my way. So many of these people had been supporting me on social media. But meeting them in person was a huge honor for me. Putting faces to the names of so many, giving them hugs, meeting their families.. it all meant a great deal to me. That kept me returning to every festival I have ever attended, the real-life friendships I formed with this beautiful group of individuals who would become my extended family. I am still on the dusty trail of the moonshine circuit, because of them. I show up to spend my time with so many who have spent their own valuable time supporting me. These festivals aren't just big parties, they are family reunions.

For the most part, now that word was getting out that I wasn't just a bootlegger, but was also a maker of white lightning. I had some lingering die-hard haters, but more importantly, I had a continuation and growing outpour of sincere supporters. I was overwhelmed with how much my followers and other folks within the shine industry were behind me patting me on the back and pushing me forward. I never would have made it anywhere if it wasn't for people who genuinely cared about what I was working so hard for. They kept me going. They still do. I wish I could name every single one of them in this book. But there are so many I could never list them all. I could never repay them or give them the amount of gratitude they deserve. I owe my success to those fine folks that never gave up on me. They have followed my personal journey as well as my professional journey. They have been cheering for me on the sidelines of the marathon I have been running nonstop for seven years now. And I know they will be there whether I trip and fall, or cross the finish line at the end of my long haul. Either way, I could never thank them enough. Every dime I have made from moonshine goes into my travel expenses, so I can afford to show up at these events and personally thank as many of my supporters as I can. The ones I have not had the pleasure to meet yet, thank you. The support I have been given means more to me than I could ever express.

When you see me at these events, I try to step into the character that I believe people expect me to be. Lady Outlaw is an extended version of myself, yes. But I'm also a mom, a farmer, a regular everyday woman with the same kind of insecurities as every other woman. There are things about my appearance that I'm uncomfortable with and self-conscience about, my weight fluctuation, the shape of my nose, the big birthmark on the back of my left arm (which I try to hide with my pocketbook strap because I was made fun of for it in my school days). I'm not as confident as I seem to be. I do what I can to disguise my autoimmune illness because I want people to see me as vibrant and full of life. I have to put a lot of effort into my wardrobe selection, not what I would personally wear, but what my character would come to life wearing. On a normal day, most of my followers wouldn't even recognize me. When I'm in the privacy of my home. I like to have the attire of mismatched comfy clothes, a messy bun and my eyeglasses. I purposefully look like shit if I have nowhere to be but the farm. When I do appearances as Lady Outlaw, I step into her like a costume. And I try to portray her as a mix between three of my idols, Johnny Cash (the legend), the Queen of England (the classy lady) and Chief Sitting Bull (the fierce warrior). They all have attributes I admire. (I know that may sound funny, and any of my haters reading this book just to be nosy are going to laugh about it. Read on and know this, I don't give a flying fuck what my hate club thinks of me.) Anyways, that combination of iconic figures is what I think of and how I attempt to get in character and project the role I feel folks are anticipating when they meet me for the first time. I view it as a performance and don't want to disappoint anyone who is hoping to be entertained by me in some way. Then I have the funny side, which is just me. I love to make people smile and laugh.

Meanwhile, I was perfecting my craft of making moonshine spirits. I had previously done extensive research on flavors and brandies. I was trying to find something floral based for a feminine touch on a liquor I intended to produce specifically for the female population. My role as Lady Outlaw has been inspired by women, and for women. I want every woman to feel like she is the real Lady Outlaw. I believe we all have both sides of that character wired within us on some level. After reading and studying, thinking and prospecting different ideas, then consulting my mom for her opinion, I finally settled on the flower of Honeysuckle. I wanted it to be a nostalgic experience for anyone who drank the beverage, so it would take them back in their mind to a riverbank in the South, with the aroma of fresh blooms filling the air. Honeysuckle just happens to be one of those edible plants that has a flavor exactly the same as it smells. The fragrance factor was as important to me as the sense of taste. Similar to the way perfumes are formulated, you are looking for notes that stand out, or mix well with other notes. I began the development stage of the process once I finished the research. Kolar and I picked every single honeysuckle flower off every vine we could find that season. Ewok even took us rafting on the river to search high and low for them. We ended up with five pounds worth, tightly packed. The blooms themselves are as light as a feather, so it takes an enormous amount of them to add up to that weight.

I took my harvest to Bootlegger's Distillery where the master distiller Darrell Miller helped me formulate the recipe. He first tried to run the honeysuckle through Gin baskets, which blew the cap off his rig and made a hell of a mess in his still house. Then we resorted to another method. That run worked out well, but it still needed fine-tuning. It ended up taking me many months of tweaking the math and science to finally reach the perfect formula, which is still what I currently use today. No one else in the industry made it when I first turned it out. And although I intended it to be a ladies' drink, men tend to love it just as much as women. The burn is on the front end, with the sweetness at the backend. It is the aftertaste that mostly accentuates the floral note. It captivates your taste buds and makes you want more. Honeysuckle became my signature moonshine.

The only family members of mine that dealt in the moonshining business, that I'm aware of, were three of my great grandfather's. The one I mentioned before, whose wife shot up the still, Ephraim Roberts. Another one that was a bootlegger on Grandpa Sparks side, Alonzo Sparks. And my Peepaw's grandfather, James Venable, who made moonshine up on Kimball Mountain in the coal fields and fired shots at the revenue men. These three of my ancestors were all from West Virginia. I am the first one in my family to join the trade since them. I know some of you reading this may not think that's something to be proud of. Well, I am very proud of it. It's not about getting away with something illegal, although that is a by-product of it. To me, it is about carrying on the tradition. It's about something that is passed down throughout the culture of the Appalachian Mountains. Moonshine can be made anywhere. But it was born in the hills and hollers of Appalachia. That is why I feel such a strong connection to the production and distribution of shine. It is part of my heritage. It's a historically significant craft, that is relevant now, and will carry on down the lines of future generations. There is a saying, that you should be a drinker or a maker. It's a bad idea to be both. I've never been much of a drinker, although I do enjoy the social occasion of passing a jar around to enjoy my fellow shiner's hard work. And of course, I taste test what I turn out, to be sure it is worth drinking. But I was proud to be a bootlegger, and I am proud to be a maker of spirits. I hope my forefathers would be proud of me for picking up where they left off and learning the trade.

In between all my work on trying to build a long term career, I found a full-time job in Gatlinburg at the Sugarlands Riding Stables just inside the Smoky Mountain National Park. The boss I had there was the toughest I've ever had. He is a 23-time world champion trainer. He owns both riding stables in Gatlinburg and around 150 horses. His trail horses are the most well trained on earth. They don't miss a beat. Every one of his employees were scared to death of this man. He almost didn't hire me because he said girls can't ride horses as good as men. But I said to him, "Give me a chance, and if you don't like me, you can tell me to hit the road." So he gave me a chance. I wasn't intimidated by him when the other workers would bow down and grovel before him. He would take fits of yelling and putting everyone in their place. It was a big operation, and he ran a tight ship. He had to, in order to uphold his unbeatable safety record of the 300+ tourists that file through their daily. Most of them have never even been on a horse. When he went off on his tangents, I would say to him, "Boss, you're just a hateful old son of a bitch." The other employees would look at me like, "No, shut up. You'll get us all fired." Then they would scatter and duck for cover. But because I stood up to him and held my ground, I earned his full respect. The bossy man came to love me and I came to love him. We formed a mutual understanding. I would call him "Boss Hogg", and say "I can fire you as my boss any time I want to." I got a kick out of getting him riled up. I would walk up behind him and give him the command to lift his boot like a farrier does to lift a horses hoof. He did not find this amusing but he let me get away with it nonetheless.

I fell in love with one lone horse in particular out of his entire large fleet herd, a big black four-year-old Percheron gelding, named Coal Bucket. His head was the size of my entire body. He stood a massive 17 hands high to his withers. He towered over top of me. But despite our size difference, he saw my soul, and I saw his. I had an instant spirit animal connection to this draft horse. Every guide on staff was afraid of him, they said Coal Bucket was nothing but a giant bully and had bucked several passengers off. None of the trail guides would volunteer to ride him for fear of being thrown. For weeks on end, I begged the boss, please let me ride that horse. Every time I asked, he would say, "No way in hell, that horse will get you killed girl." After months of pleading relentlessly, I looked the boss man directly in the eyes one day and I stated, "Boss, I'm riding that damn horse today." He replied, "Well alright then, don't get killed." I climbed up on the tall back of Coal Bucket, I almost needed a ladder to mount him. He immediately went the wrong direction, trying to outwit me. I wasn't going to be proven weak with the boss man looking on in complete skepticism. So I manhandled the enormous beast and steered him to go the right way, then took off in a gallop to catch up to the end of the horse line on the trail. I rode drag for the three-hour tour. It was by far the steepest and roughest of the three riding trails within the Smoky Mountain National Park. Coal Bucket did try to get away with pulling his huge head down to graze along the path for the first half of the ride. But when I enforced my dominant presence to correct him, he finally realized that I was in charge. The Percheron and I became in unison, and he didn't miss a step. He did exactly as I commanded him to do. I proudly held my head high aboard that draft horse as I rode him back into the stables that evening.. showing proof to the boss that not only did I manage to stay on top and firmly in the saddle, but I was in full control of the big beast everyone else was scared to ride. I proved to him that girls can whoop and ride as well as any cowboy.

During the time I worked away from home in West Virginia, I cried every single day, missing my children more than words can even say, and feeling the sting of guilt for being so far from them. I have never wanted to be away from J.J. and Faith, not even for one second. They are my whole world. My illness caught up with me. I crashed and burned at the end of my work hours, then fevered all through the restless nights. My 14 hour long grueling days working at the stable were taking a toll on me too. Besides Jason Kolar, that Coal Bucket horse was the only thing that cheered me up and gave me a sense of purpose. He became my best friend in those dark hours of sadness. He saw me through what was one of the most difficult trials of my life. I never would have survived without that horse. He loved me as much as I loved him. He knew the sound of my step, and his big ears would perk up as soon as I would walk towards him.

It was a strict policy not to give the horses treats. They were fed very well with hay and grain, and the boss didn't want anyone to get bit or for the horses to learn bad habits. But I snuck treats of all sorts to Coal Bucket, several times a day. He especially loved red licorice. Boss man was smart, he didn't miss anything that happened within his stable grounds on his watch. He knew exactly what I was doing. He would give me a sharp scolding sideways glance from the corner of his eye, but didn't say a word. He let me get away with that too. I would also give some of the other horses Pop Rocks candy and tastes of my moonshine, to see the funny faces they would make. The stable manager Dwight, (a tough old true cowboy), would fuss at me for my constant attachment to Coal Bucket. I would just egg Dwight on and laugh at him. I didn't care who thought I was silly for treating such a gigantic beast of an animal like a little spoiled baby brat. It didn't matter to me who actually owned him, he was mine. He belonged to me, and everyone knew that. I rode my draft horse every chance I got. He is the smoothest four-legged ride I have ever been on. He always seemed to feel so proud and sure-footed when he carried me high aboard his back. He made it his personal mission to keep me safe. He was very protective of me. I would sing "Coal Miner's Daughter" and "Big Black Horse and the Cherry Tree" to him on the trails, and he loved it, my singing soothed him. We were inseparable partners. He knew how very much I loved him.

I have always had a major obsession with black bears. They became a real-life daily occurrence of sport for me in the Smoky Mountains. It was one of my main missions to find them and chase after them. It's a wonder that was not the very death of me. I have no fear of the bears and will rush right at them just to get a closer look because I think they are so beautiful. Earlier that same year, Hippy took me to a wildlife preserve in West Virginia. We passed a sleeping game warden in a work truck. Then down the path, we came across a big 400-pound mama bear. I hopped two fences to get to the one she was contained in. I wanted to pet her. I kneeled down on my side of the fence, then she came to me and laid down directly in front of me on her side of the fence. I dug through my purse to find some candy. All I had was a package of Sweet Tarts. I put some on my hand and stuck my hand through the fence. She ate them, licked my hand with her soft tongue, then looked at my purse intently for me to get more. She knew where they were coming from. Bears are smart. I repeated the same sequence till I fed her all that I had. I then held my empty hand up to her mouth, hoping she would lick me again. She impolitely but gently smacked my hand away with her big paw. She was done playing my game since I had no more candy to offer as a token of our short-lived friendship. It was a scene straight out of a Disney Princess movie. There should have been a score of orchestra music playing along with the moment. I was wearing a bear claw necklace at the time, that Hippy made me. I thought maybe it was why she let me get so close. Perhaps she thought I was another bear. Either way, that first close encounter with a black bear caused me to seek subsequent similar encounters in the wild. There was one black bear that I became well acquainted with. Every morning Kolar would buy me a biscuit, and on my way to work, I would roll my car window down and feed my biscuit to this bear. A few times I was bluff charged by some of the bears I approached, but most of the ones I pursued in Tennessee would trust me and let me draw near.

I travelled home to the farm as often as I could, and Kolar would make the trip with me. I spent quality time with the kids every second I was there. It was always the best feeling in the world to be home with my babies, where I belonged. Leaving again to return to work was pure torture. I would cry the entire drive back to Newport. Ex Jason would also bring J.J. and Faith to me on a regular basis. Sometimes he would stay with us too, and we would all do things together and spend time as one big family. Other times he would meet us halfway in Wytheville, Virginia where we did pick-ups and drop-offs of the kids. The children loved to sightsee in Tennessee, as there are so many tourist activities to do in the Eastern part of the state, and it was all new to them. We took them to Pigeon Forge and Gatlinburg. I showed them where I worked, introducing them to Coal Bucket, the boss man, and all my coworkers. Faith took a trail ride with me one day, just the two of us. We took them go-cart racing, to play putt-putt golf, to Ripley's Aquarium, Dollywood, and all the cool places in the area. Faith and I made pottery together at an art studio while the two Jason's took J.J. to do manly things. We all took a white water rafting trip with Ewok. We went swimming on the Pigeon River and in the clubhouse pool at the golf course where Kolar's parents live. We took them hiking in the Smoky Mountains. We made a trip to Asheville so the kids could tour the Biltmore House for the first time. We took them to every fun place we could think of. They liked our temporary setup because it allowed them to go places and do things they otherwise wouldn't have had the opportunities to do. It was an adventure for them. I had discounts on everything in Gatlinburg since I worked there, but I was also making good money and could afford to treat my babies to special outings.

On one of the visits we all had in Tennessee.. the two Jasons, the kids and I, and Kolar's mother Pam were all headed to spend the day together at Dollywood for the kids' first time there. We were caravanning with Kolar, Faith, and I in my car, Jason and J.J. behind us, and Pam behind them. We were crossing an intersection in Sevierville, directly in front of the Tennessee Aviation Museum (which was founded by Meemaw's cousin Bob, who taught Peepaw how to fly airplanes). It was a left-turning lane with no arrow but a green light yield to straight coming traffic. Jason was in a newer red Dodge Dart. Kolar saw in the rearview mirror and we all heard a crash. It was Jason and J.J., they had been hit by an oncoming vehicle. I jumped out of my car and ran flying as fast as my feet could carry me. I was screaming, sobbing and praying the whole distance it took me to get to the scene. The red Dodge was in pieces all over the intersection. My only son was in that car, my precious little boy. I gasped for air and felt my heart racing and pounding out of my chest. J.J. and Jason stepped out of the wreckage before I got to them, and they were alright, thank God. They were both shaken and upset, but neither of them were hurt. Pam also rear-ended Jason in the accident. We all stayed while the first responders checked everyone out for injuries and made reports of the accident. The totaled car was hauled away. It was later determined that the driver who struck them at a high speed, was under the influence of drugs. Needless to say, we never made it to

Dollywood that day. We all traveled back to WV with the kids in the back and Kolar between them on the center plastic console of drink holders. (His ass was bruised for weeks afterwards). Jason sat in the passenger seat, and I drove. I felt like the accident was all my fault. I was responsible for what happened because if I hadn't been working in Tennessee, they never would have been involved in the wreck there. It was a stressful trip all around. I knew I had to return home to West Virginia for good as soon as possible. Kolar would either have to come with me or stay behind. That was his choice to make. I wanted to be with him and I knew he wanted to be with me, so we would have to come to an alternate arrangement.

It was the end of May 2015 when I first went to work and temporarily live in Tennessee. On June 6th, Jason Kolar asked me to be his wife, and I said yes without hesitation. We set the date for October 17th of the same year. That was the year of weddings for women in my family. Aunt Vicki married her husband Carmen on Valentine's Day. And Meemaw married her husband Melvin that summer. My turn was coming in the fall. I was going to continue the family tradition of my parents after all, and marry another Jason. My fiancé's parents Pam and Phil, instantly adopted me as part of their family, from the first time he took me to meet them.

Pam's career work was as an event coordinator for a big cooperation. Since I was working around the clock, and we only had four short months to plan a wedding, Pam took on the role as our wedding planner. She took me to a bridal store to shop for dresses, and the first gown I tried on was the one. It was a beaded corset style ivory dress with a chiffon embroidered chapel length train. I chose my dress based on a style that would fit well with me on horseback since my Coal Bucket was to carry me down the aisle. Pam took care of every detail involving our big day. She knew exactly the kind of feel I wanted the wedding to have, which was a Western-themed outdoor barn wedding. I didn't have to worry about a thing, she had it all covered.

The day before the big day, Ewok and I went on a recon mission to fetch Coal Bucket on a horse trailer from the stable in Gatlinburg. The boss man reluctantly agreed to let me bail him out for a few days. Our rehearsal went smoothly, and Coal Bucket learned that he was to carry me to the tune of a song. He seemed to know exactly what to do and didn't miss a beat. We had an intimate rehearsal dinner that night with family and the wedding party at Brandywine Tavern, the same place Kolar and I first met. Afterwards, I spent time with my best friend Cousin Sarah, we had too much moonshine and I accidentally crashed a golf cart into the rental car of Kolar's out of state friend. There was a lot of buzz and excitement about our event. I extended an open invitation to anyone who wanted to come attend and celebrate our special occasion with us.

On October 17, 2015, High Pastures Farm, where we lived in Tennessee was bustling with activity. That morning I groomed Coal Bucket and painted his hooves turquoise. Faith and her friend Hailey helped me braid his mane and tail. Then before I started to get ready, I dressed him all up with my turquoise saddle, bridle, and rhythm beads. He was so happy to be away from his work as a trail horse and to be doted over by me and the girls. Pam decorated the big red monitor style barn with a rustic design for the ceremony and reception. She nailed exactly the atmosphere I had in mind. Hay bales were set up for the guests to sit on, with delicate lace covers. The colors I chose were lavender and turquoise. We had purple Irises for the bouquets, corsages, and boutonnières (in honor of Kolar's late grandmother Sue. They were her favorite flowers). There were peacock feathers and burlap throughout the decor. Kolar's cousin Mandy made our wedding cake and decorated the cake table with a creative barn wedding shabby chic style. Sarah did my makeup since she is a professional makeup artist. Aunt Frankie was the official photographer. Laura Ward did my hair in braids. I wore a feather headdress instead of a veil. My Aunt Brenda came from Texas and did everything she could to help us prepare. She bought lunch for everyone, picked up the flowers from the florist, and was there ready to iron out any details that required attention. The bluegrass band, Tennessee Borderline, set up their stage to perform for the reception. Brandywine Tavern was hired to cater the food. Hippy was on hand as my best buddy, with his son Mikey. (I considered making Hippy be my maid of honor, but he would have just looked wrong in a dress). Ex Jason helped Kolar all day long setting up the sound system and running errands. He even ran out and bought me a pair of socks at the last minute. He was very helpful in preparing for the event, although it wasn't easy for him to be there witnessing my wedding day as his ex-wife. But he pitched in and worked hard to help out any way he could. J.J. and Faith accepted Kolar as their stepdad before we even tied the knot. We had already evolved into an untraditional family unit.

Moonshiners from all over came pouring in and passing Mason jars around to kick off the festivities. We had Rich and Joann Minnick from "Moonshine Rednecks", Van Fields and Jeff Edwards from "Living Proof", Johnny Chastaine, Chris Golladay, Brad Phillips (Red Fox) and Lesly McAfee, as well as others. All of these people became family to me and Kolar. They have been our brothers and sisters. And our wedding day was the platform where many of them crossed paths with each other for the first time. We had every flavor and proof of homemade moonshine floating around High Pastures Farm. Ewok had just released his own private label with Bootlegger's so there were cases of it everywhere. Then we had mini Mason jars of Bootlegger's Distillery shine all over the tables as party favors for the guests. The jars were being passed around in pre-party fashion before the ceremony even started. Anywhere you looked someone was tipping one back or passing one to the next person.

Before go time, Ewok's wife Raven gave me the gift of a beautiful Native American ivory fur cape. It was one of the nicest gifts I've ever been given. She was one of my bridesmaids, along with Faith's friend Hailey. Sarah was my matron of honor and Faith was my flower girl. Kolar's dad Phil was his best man. His friends Possum, Seth, Spencer plus my son J.J. were his groomsmen. And his dog Pancho was the ring bearer. Everyone wore different Western-themed attire. It looked like a set of a Western movie with a variety of characters. All my attendants had a different dress.. some looked like Native Americans and some looked like prairie ladies or saloon girls. The men were dressed up as either cowboys, Mexicans, or Indians. Pancho dog wore a cowboy hat and turquoise bandana around his neck which held our rings. Ewok, who was our official matchmaker, also stood in as the Reverend to officiate our marriage. He wore a Daniel Boone getup and looked very convincing. I selected a combination of Christian, Cherokee and Apache wedding ceremonies, blessings and prayers. Kolar and I wrote our own wedding vows. My father's best friends, Cherokee brothers Blaine and Mark Purcell arrived from Kentucky and gifted me with a gorgeous silver and turquoise bracelet, which they placed on my wrist with pride. They were dressed in their Native Cherokee regalia and were there to do the honor of walking me down the aisle and giving me away. I relayed to Mark before I even met Kolar, that if I ever remarried, I wished for them to be the ones to perform the duty that Daddy couldn't be there to do. I knew it would make my father proud to have them stand-in. They also brought sage to incorporate into the Native aspects of the ceremony. Mama and Meemaw were present with their husbands Jack and Melvin. They seemed genuinely happy to share in the day, to support me on my next big adventure in uniting with a man they knew would take care of me and treat me with dignity. Everything flowed together seamlessly. It was a sunny warm and breezy crisp fall day with the Smoky Mountains as an impressive and dramatic backdrop.

Part 4

At 3:30 pm, I mounted Coal Bucket in my big dress, with the assistance of Mark and Blaine. The theme song overture from "Wyatt Earp" started playing. The bridal procession began, with my bridesmaids, followed by Faith throwing out flower petals, and me being led down the aisle on horseback with the regal Cherokee brothers leading Coal Bucket. A herd of horses that belonged to the farm were in a nearby field. They galloped and neighed in recognition to my big Percheron steed as we made way to the front of the barn where the ceremony was to take place. Coal Bucket didn't even look their way. He kept his eyes forward and his gate steady. Some calves in the barn stalls began mooing, my cat Hermione peaked her head out from the barn loft, and the goats chimed in with chatter. It was like all the animals were aware that something of special significance was taking place. I was worried that Coal Bucket may make an attempt to graze on the hay bales which seated our guests, but he never even paid notice to them. He carried me as though it was the single most important moment of his entire lifetime; like it meant everything to him and he felt honored to escort me on his back. He walked intently and proud, with his head held high. I kept my eyes ahead on the man who stood patiently waiting for me. He looked so handsome, dressed like the perfect gentleman that he is. When the overture came to an end, I dismounted with help from the Cherokee brothers. They spoke on behalf of my father and handed me over to my groom. Mark led Coal Bucket to a stall in the barn, and the ceremony began. It was a sacred and emotionally charged observance of the holy sacrament of marriage. I couldn't keep from crying when I read my own written vows to the man who was to be my husband. I found my true love and my soulmate, the one God intended for me to share the rest of my life with, and to walk side by side within a new journey together. His vows were almost word for word identical to mine, and we hadn't even shared them with each other until that moment. We joined our lives as one, he kissed the bride and we were introduced as a man and wife to our family and friends. Jason Kolar became my "Husband", which has been his official name since that day.

We had cap gun pistols (instead of bubbles or rice), for guests to fire off as we walked our recessional down the aisle. J.J. especially got a kick out of shooting caps. We greeted our guests and thanked them for being there, then the reception festivities were underway with music and food, moonshine and well wishes. We had pictures taken with the wedding party and our family members, along with all our many friends who were present. Then we slipped away to have photographs made of Husband and I alone together. We shared dinner, cake, toasts and dancing with our company. Everything went as planned, without a hitch. Except for one thing. My ex-husband Jason had a little too much moonshine, (at least three quarts), and caused quite a scene. He had gotten into some of Johnny Chastaine's fine homebrew, which is some of the smoothest on the market. I missed much of what happened, as I was visiting with friends and family inside the barn, where Coal Bucket was the life of the party. Everyone wanted to pet the big giant draft horse and feed him treats. He was the guest of honor and was treated like a King that day. But I did catch Jason kicking his shoe off while he was dancing, and it landed on the stage during the band's performance. At some point, his pants were falling down, and the groomsman Spencer yanked them up giving him a massive wedgie. When Jason turned around to swing a punch at him, Spencer drew a loaded Colt 45 from his gun belt. Luckily that situation was diffused. But Jason also knocked one of the food tables over and began launching cubes of cheese from the ground at the guests. Most of this I wasn't aware of till the next day. I found him with his shirt off swinging it around above his head. He said to me "Farewell Tiffany, I shall never see you again." I told J.J. to do something with his dad when I noticed guests abruptly leaving the reception early because of this behavior. My son and Hippy's son Mikey wrestled Jason up the hill and secured him into a camper, where he hit his head and passed out. Then J.J. got on stage and borrowed the mic from the band. He made a speech, in which he said, "The drunk man has been locked away, you may now party in peace." Husband was the most understanding about Jason's display of emotions. He was sympathetic to the fact that my ex-husband was a man who had lost the woman that was once his wife and tried to see the situation from his perspective. I was understanding too. It was a complex situation, but we all tried to make the best of it. And since it was a Wild West theme, Jason fit in well as the town drunk.

We celebrated into the night. Husband and I danced to our song, "Everything I Do", from the movie Robin Hood. J.J. and Faith were happy that day, to gain new family members of Husband and his parents. The children still say it was one of the best days of their lives. The moonshiners and ginsengers present enjoyed the fellowship of each other, and new friendships were formed. It turned out to be a memorable event in many ways. I was at peace knowing I finally had the partner I was ultimately destined to be with. Every failed relationship I had, led me to this man. I legally kept my daddy's last name this time. Husband was accepting of that decision knowing why it was important to me and stood behind me without question. He didn't want to own me, he just wanted to be by my side. I wanted to belong solely to him, but not be trapped in a cage like a bird. He let me be his and still be free to be myself. We are a perfect match for best friends, companions and lovers. Getting married didn't change the dynamic of our relationship, it only further enhanced what we already had. Before him, I believed it was more important for me to love than to be loved. He showed me that true love consists of both loving and being loved, simultaneously. Some of my family was skeptical of the short dating period and engagement time we held before committing to each other in the bindings of marriage, which was completely understandable given my bad track record. But for me, when you know something is meant to be, you just know. And time is irrelevant when paths are aligned by God. I knew I landed in my safe place. Husband became my harbor and shelter from the wind. He is my protector.

Shortly after our wedding, we set off for our honeymoon. We drove to Lakeland, Florida where we stayed with Haley and Javier the night before heading onto Miami, where we boarded a cruise ship headed for Mexico. We stopped for a port of call at Key West. The only excursion Husband wanted to have there was to pet Hemmingway's cats. So we took the tour of Earnest Hemmingway's house just so Husband could see the kitties. He petted about every one of them and volunteered to feed one named Audrey Hepburn. We went to a little dive bar in Key West too, Sloppy Joe's, which used to be one of Hemmingway's regular hangouts. We sailed past Cuba to Cozumel, Mexico, then took a ferry boat to Playa del Carmen. From there we rode a bus to Tulum, where we dined on authentic Mexican cuisine and margaritas. We toured the Mayan Ruins, which was our entire reason for choosing the destination we did, as we are both huge history nerds. It was well worth the trip. It was more than a vacation, it was an educational experience. Husband bought me a handmade dress from a little old Mayan woman in the town market. I bought him some expensive cigars. We almost missed the departure of our cruise ship when we were deterred at a jewelry store in Playa del Carmen, which doubled as a black market tequila parlor under the counter. We purchased a bottle of almond tequila; the best agave liquor I have ever tasted. It was a gift for my new in-laws, who sent us on our honeymoon. I did some dealings with the Mexican bootlegger and informed him of the black market of American moonshine.

We made it to the ship at the last minute and set sail back to Miami. We had spa treatments, watched flying fish along the boat, saw the sunrise and set over the Gulf of Mexico. Oh, and Husband took advantage of the all you can eat buffet situation. He literally gained ten pounds on our honeymoon. I didn't discover the full-service chocolate bar until the last day at sea, or I would have gained ten pounds too. After we docked in Miami, we made way back up the coast, stopping in Savannah and Tybee Island Georgia, where we went pier fishing and dined on a seafood feast. Then we returned to Tennessee and got right back to the grindstone. I was content with my gentleman Husband, proud to have him as my partner. He is the only man who has ever truly loved me. He is the one who showed me that true love does exist.

My whole experience as a non-TV star on the reality TV show of Appalachian Outlaws had come full circle. I didn't gain fame or fortune. I never even made one appearance on a single episode, and the program was cancelled after Season Two. The lady they chose to take my place, was the right woman who was meant to have that opportunity. Her name is Willow. Although I have yet to formally meet her in person, I admire her from a distance and follow her on social media. We have spoken through messages several times. She is a remarkable and classy West Virginia farmer. I guess we must look very similar, she has long dark hair like me. Many viewers of the show have mistaken her for me and me for her. I have people all the time say that they've seen me on the show. Out of trying to cover up the truth of the shameful circumstances that surrounded me behind the scenes, I don't say anything in response. I just let folks carry on with their personal perception. I don't want to disappoint them by letting them in on what I have managed to keep a secret all this time. However, in the long run, I may have missed out on my fifteen minutes of fame, but I gained something far more valuable and lasting. I found the truest love of my life and some of my most loyal friendships from my experience as the unseen cast member of Lady Outlaw.

As a new wife, on a new path with my new Husband. I was ready to move forward with new endeavors. This was another fresh chapter in the book of my life. But I needed to steer this ship back to West Virginia, to my children. I couldn't stay away for work any longer. The kids loved Tennessee and we even discussed several times having us all relocate there. But that would have invoked a civil war between me and their dad. After seven long months of living out of a suitcase, missing my babies like crazy, and working around the clock to make something worthwhile of myself; I intended to take Husband home with me, to the farm. He was born and raised in his native state of Tennessee, and never lived anywhere else. So packing up his life to join mine was a monumental sacrifice for him. He did it because he knew I could not spend even one more second away from J.J. and Faith. It was literally killing me. Husband always wished for a wife and family of his own, and now he had both. Plus he held my happiness above his own. So he gratefully made the compromise I asked of him. He drove a U-Haul through a snowstorm to relocate. I returned home with the one suitcase I packed when I first left for Tennessee, my Mister Man, a better head on my shoulders, and solid ground under my feet. My restless days were over for good and I was back to being settled. I was never so happy to step foot on the soil of the farm. I could have knelt down and kissed the ground. Walking back through the door of my tiny house was a huge sigh of relief, and I felt the weight of the world fall from my shoulders when I hung my hat where it was supposed to go. Home sweet blessed home. I swore I would never leave like that again. My intentions were to make it as far and as high as I possibly could in the moonshine industry, so I would have the ability to refuse being driven from my children and my homeland ever again. I aimed to be the first lady of the trade representing West Virginia. My mission was to move forward with prosperity and shine on.

It Takes a Village

It was January of 2016 when Husband moved to the farm and I came home from Tennessee. I had recently undergone surgery to have my gallbladder removed, so I was out of commission in helping him pack or unpack. But we slowly started turning my house into our home together. From now on I will refer to ex Jason as Generator (his nickname), and Jason Kolar as Husband. Now that we were all living on the farm, there had to be a way to differentiate between the two Jasons. Luckily my son (whose name is also Jason), goes by J.J., or three Jasons would have been even more complicated. While I had been away working, my cousin Tyler moved in with my ex-husband Generator. This is where it gets even more confusing. Okay so long story short me, my husband, my ex-husband, our kids, and my cousin all lived on the same property. With my cousin up the hill with my ex, my husband down the hill with me, and the children back and forth between the two houses. Tyler came to West Virginia to live on the farm while he attended his senior year of high school. At this time, J.J. was a freshman at the same high school, and Faith was in 7th grade at middle school. So, my cousin, Tyler was like a big brother to my kids, and they were happy to have him as a roommate. Tyler's girlfriend Paige lived up the hill with him. They both relocated from Florida. Hippy was also temporarily living on the farm in his camper at the time too. Plus Generator had a girlfriend with two sons, Amber, Josh and Brayden, who became primary residents. And my brother Andrew was still a regular honorary guest. The land literally became an entire village of a dysfunctional family tribe. We referred to ourselves as "The Villagers".

So now that we have established all that, (and you've probably had to read it three times to get it all straight), I can go on with the rest of the story. It is going to get even more complex. The funny thing is, I once said to Generator while we were still married, that if we ever got divorced and remarried, it would be nice to have more help on the farm. What started off as my family of four on the land with one house, split up and multiplied into a family of ten between two households. I was the common thread that weaved within the entire farm. Other than Amber and her boys, everyone had a direct connection to the place through me. Sometimes we would all gather up the hill, and other times we would all gather down the hill. I became the camp chef, cooking up a feast for the villagers on a frequent basis. Amber would also have us up for cookouts. We would play games, have bonfires, listen to music, etc. It was kind of one big party. But also everyone pitched in to help pull their weight with all the animals and farm duties. When the village set up worked like a well-oiled machine, all was fine and dandy for the most part. When any outside force would throw a wrench into the mechanism of things, it could be a dramatic disaster at times. None of us were in a normal setting with normal circumstances. It was like living in a crazy commune of sorts. I have joked before saying we should call it Bays Insane Asylum instead of Almost Heaven Homestead. But in its own very strange way, the newly formed village became the way of things and evolved into something interesting and original. J.J. was elected as the official Mayor Of Bays. He named every area and every waterway on the farm. Then he implemented projects as well as proper procedures for his jurisdiction. J.J. was also filming original movie productions with his own company called Erbacon Film Productions. His best friend Elijah became another regular fixture at the village and assisted with J.J.'s movies and farm work.

Now I just have to say right here, that it took one hell of a good man to uproot himself and replant onto the farm and become neighbors with his new wife's ex-husband. I am not oblivious to the fact that this is at minimum a very strange and almost cruel request for me to make of Husband. But he didn't even hesitate in granting this demand of mine. I am a bossy woman, and he lets me get away with it. I appreciate a dominant male backing down and allowing me to take the lead when I feel insistent on matters. Not only that, but he wants to do what I ask of him simply out of his love and adoration for me. You know how when you are in the early stages of a relationship, each party puts on the best show they can so as not to scare the other one away? It's part of the dating game. You normally try to hide your flaws until after you have caught your partner on a hook, then slowly reveal your true nature and shortcomings. Well with Husband, I showed him exactly who I was right from the beginning. I never tried to hide my crazy or put up false pretenses. I was upfront and laid it all out for him to decipher. He didn't get the best version of me. I left that part behind in the ashes. I wish he could have known how I once was before life forced me to become a fighter. But I let him know that he could take me or leave me as I was. I even warned him that he could be making a mistake to take on such a damaged woman. He wanted me anyways. This is how I know his love is true. He chose to love me for who I truly am, which should earn him a Nobel Prize in itself. And he walked into life on the farm with the purest of intentions to make the best of our very unusual situation. I am not easy to live with. And Generator is not the nicest neighbor to have. Plus Husband skipped all the early phases with my children and started his parental role with teenagers. Thankfully, the children have been perfect angels even as teens. All I requested from him as a stepdad to them, was to show them how a woman should be treated with honor and dignity. He has gone above and beyond that. He fit in immediately to the bigger family unit of the farm and all its occupants. He quickly became like a brother to Generator as well as my cousin, Tyler.

Tyler had never seen the movie "Walk The Line". When I discovered this, I immediately turned it on for him. During the opening credits he said, "Oh cool, Joaquin Phoenix is on here." But he didn't pronounce Joaquin the Spanish way. He pronounced it as Joe-Quin; with the first part sounding American, and the second part sounding like an Irish name. I looked at Tyler and said, "What did you just say?" Then he pronounced it incorrectly again. I made him say it like five times in a row and rolled laughing at him. And since that day, I changed his name to JoaQuin, but in the same way, he articulated it. And I have called him that ever since. He will be referred by that name from now on in this book. JoaQuin brought laughter and entertainment to the farm. That was his main contribution as a villager. He is seriously one of the funniest people I have ever known. He has an energy that filled the entire farm with nonstop amusement. He once prompted me, Faith, and himself to participate in the longest laugh-fest I've ever taken part in. It should be listed in the Guinness Book of World Records. We literally laughed our asses off for four hours straight, and couldn't get a hold of ourselves. We were choking, gagging, hiccupping, peeing our pants and just completely malfunctioning. We could not settle down. Husband got so annoyed by it that he left in the middle of the night to sleep in his office, which was a local radio station for the West Virginia Radio Network, where he worked as the manager of the station. We finally laughed ourselves to sleep around 2am that next morning. It was all JoaQuin's fault.

On my 36th birthday that spring, I had Husband take me to Cherokee, North Carolina. My Native friends Mark and Blaine Purcell told me about the reservation, and I had been invited there a few times for special ceremonies, but this was the first trip I was able to make to Cherokee. As soon as I arrived I met two of the tribesmen who were doing demonstrations for the public. I had an instant connection to one of them, a holy man of the tribe. We got to talking and he invited Husband and I to join him for lunch at a place where mostly locals go. I had a nice birthday lunch of buffalo steak, my favorite meal. The holy man spoke with wisdom and kindness. He said things to us that he had no way of knowing since we had only just met him. I do a very good job of covering up my illness, which still plagues me chronically to this day. I am a professional at pretending to be well. Unless I tell someone I am sick, they would never know or even guess. This holy man knew it without me ever saying a word about it. He told Husband that the reason he was meant to marry me is because he was sent to take care of me and help to see me through my illness. He told us many other truths that he had no way of knowing about us. I left the reservation that day with an even deeper respect for the Cherokee people. And I have kept in touch with my friend the holy man, Tony Walkingstick. He made a lasting impression on me and I will never forget him. I ran into him recently in downtown Gatlinburg, where he stood with his beautiful white wolf.

On June 23rd of 2016, I laid down midday to take a nap. Before I fell asleep, the creeks that intersected at my home were almost completely dry. I slept soundly as a big storm rolled through. When I woke up two hours later and stepped out onto the balcony, there was an entire lake and two rivers surrounding my house. It qualified by the National Weather Service as a one thousand year flood event. Nine inches of rain dumped down in a short period of time. I thought about moving my Blue Spark to higher ground when I first saw what was happening, but it was already flooded, and the water was moving swiftly. So I just stood by and watched my car fill up with water, which rose above the license plate and glove box. There was no way for me to get out of my front door, so I went out the second story back door and crossed the bridge to the hillside. I ran up to the Generator's house in search of assistance. My cousin JoaQuin was the only one there. He came down to help me, although there was nothing we could even do. But he did tie my vehicle to the front porch so it wouldn't get swept away. There was no access in or out of the farm. The driveway disappeared under a fast current of about four foot deep from the rushing flash flood. It was all the way to the top of my field gates. In all my years, I've never seen anything like that. I have experienced hurricanes, blizzards, ice storms, earthquakes and an intense Derecho straight-line wind storm.. but never anything that caused as much destruction as that flood. The entire town of Birch River was under water. The storm also spawned several tornados nearby. Most of the state of West Virginia was impacted. It was one of the deadliest in the state's history. The hardest-hit parts of WV are still cleaning up and rebuilding after that flood, more than three years later. But I have never witnessed communities coming together to help each other out like they did during that crisis. That was inspiring.

The only thing I lost in the wake, was my totaled Blue Spark. The repo man never got my Chevy, but the flood did. That's why I will never own another brand new vehicle. I had put over 160k miles on it in the two years I owned it. I replaced it with an older model Silver Spark, with less mileage. J.J. went with me to Kentucky to cash the check from the insurance claim, it was ten thousand dollars. He and I wanted to go on a big travel spree with the money once we had that cash in hand. Or I wanted to buy a 40s model Ford pickup truck, which I had wished for ever since I was a little girl. But we went to a dealership and bought the Silver Spark instead. They are not a bad vehicle for the price, and the fuel economy on them goes well with my constant on the road lifestyle. I had some money left over after purchasing my vehicle. So one day, while Husband was at work, I sent him a text message that said, "I'm going to do something bad today." At least I told on myself before my crime. It's better to ask for forgiveness than to ask for permission. My sister Haley taught me that motto. I took the kids and we went on a couple hour-long road trip. We went to a house in the middle of nowhere, to purchase a mini pig. J.J. was smart, he waited in the car. Faith and I went into this house that looked like something off of the movie "Deliverance". I was waiting for the dueling banjos to start playing. We were invited in, and it was by far the dirtiest house I have ever been in. Filthy and disgusting. There were dogs, pigs, and birds everywhere. The talking birds were telling all the barking dogs to shut up. It was a madhouse. The lady of the filth manor told me and Faith to sit down. We both looked at each other with horror, because we didn't want to touch anything in there. She brought every baby pig from the litter in for us to see and hold. I let Faith pick which one we would keep. I forked over two hundred bucks. Then the two of us ran booking it like Hansel and Gretel.

Faith held the little black male piggy on the long ride back home. He was squalling, and the whole time, I was like, "Shit, what have I done?" I intended him to be a house pig. I knew I was going to be in trouble with the Mister. We got home and dressed the pig in a doll-sized t-shirt and shorts. I named him "Boss Hogg". When Husband came home from work and saw a pig running around our home, he kept stating repeatedly, "There's a pig in the house." I told a white lie and said I only paid a hundred dollars for him instead of double that which I actually spent. It was a few years later before I fessed up and told Husband the truth. Boss Hogg potty-trained within the first day and all the dogs took a liking to him. He thought he was a dog. He quickly settled in and became part of the family. Pigs are very intelligent, and I learned that they are also very emotional creatures. Any time I would scold Boss Hogg for getting into the kitchen cabinets or running in my bedroom to see himself in my mirrored closet doors, he would go lay down and pout for a long time. He always made a laughing sound when he would see his reflection in the mirror. He once got a hold of the school lunch I packed for J.J. and ate everything in his lunchbox. He loved to snuggle on the couch and in my bed and give foot massages with his snout, which we all fought over. Having a pig inside was hour's-worth of entertainment. Boss Hogg was one of the best house pets I've ever had. When he was big enough, he started going in and out with the dogs. He ended up being a big potbellied boar instead of a mini pig. After nearly a year of living in the house, he followed us to the top of the hill one day when we were going up for a cookout at Generators. He found a six hundred pound sow up there and fell in love with her. He never wanted to be an indoor pig again after meeting the love of his life. He just wanted to stay with her and be free-ranging. She was hit by a log truck on Christmas Eve in 2017. We got Boss Hogg a new girlfriend, a potbellied pig like him named Sassy, who was also raised in the house. But he was never the same after he lost his big sow. He mourned her until he passed away this past winter. I still miss my Boss Hogg. He was the best pig I ever knew.

Back to 2016.. that summer we took our annual trip to Maggie Valley, North Carolina to attend the Hillbilly Jam festival. This time, Hippy and JoaQuin wanted to go with us. I should have never. We almost got slammed by a semi-truck swerving lanes in the first part of the trip. If I hadn't reacted behind the wheel exactly the way I did, we would have never made it to our destination. But I was shaken up and stressed out for the rest of the trip. And Hippy would not shut up, blah blah blah blah blah. After he downed several beers, he ended up passed out in the backseat on the righthand side of the car. I could finally hear myself think. About thirty minutes later close to sundown, my open door light on the dash flashed red. I knew it wasn't me or Husband, and JoaQuin was also sound asleep. I was doing over eighty mph in the left-hand lane on I-26. I looked in my rear-view mirror, and Hippy had his door open and was stepping out onto the Interstate while the vehicle was rolling at high speeds. I quickly swerved two lanes over and onto the shoulder of the road. Luckily by the time he made his exit, the car was stopped. At the same time, JoaQuin who was in the backseat behind my driver's side, proceeded to step out into oncoming tractor-trailers, thinking we were at a rest area.

Husband reached back and grabbed hold of him just in time to save his life. They both stood there taking a leak facing the traffic. Hippy started yelling at me claiming he had been saying he had to piss for the last thirty minutes, when in fact he was passed out for over an hour. I was more than fed up with Hippy and JoaQuin by the time we made it to Maggie Valley. They made that road-trip completely intolerable. I should have left them on the side of I-26.

We got to our motel around 2am. I was so happy to be out of the car with those clowns and ready to rest before our busy weekend ahead. They royally screwed that up too. Right about the time I started to doze off, I heard Hippy drop his overall drawers. Then I wake Husband up to tattle tale on Hippy who was going potty on the window of the motel room. Apparently, he couldn't find the bathroom. It wasn't just a little tinkle, he was pissing like a racehorse for like five minutes nonstop, splashing the wall and the door which was right beside him. I was fuming mad. I covered my head with the blanket and tried to go back to sleep. Then, JoaQuin jumps up like he'd been shot, and I direct him towards the bathroom. He is having a puke fest in the shower, with the water running. The place smelled like piss and puke. I was so beyond angry that I jerked the covers off mine and Husband's bed, and left to sleep in my car. After over an hour of tossing and turning, I went back in the motel room. JoaQuin and Hippy were sound asleep in one bed, looking so innocent, and Husband was sleeping in the other bed. I heard the shower running. Then I find out it had been on all that time and flooded the entire room. I was furious. I turned on the light. I yelled at all the guys to get up.

They all stood at attention and did not say a single word. I cussed them up one side and down the other like a sailor for twenty minutes. I even invented new cuss words. I blasted them with every ounce of my bad temper. They all looked scared shitless, including Husband who had no wrongdoing in the matter. I told them I would leave them in North Carolina, and never travel with them again. I said they were the worst travelling buddies in history. I was so ferocious and scary that Hippy ran and hid outside behind a bush until I hushed my ranting and raving. The last thing I said to them around 4am was this, "You bitches better have me a new hotel room before the sun comes up."

They did not follow through with my demand. And I even thought the motel ordeal was kind of funny the next morning, when I found Hippy still scared, peeking out from behind a wall at me to see if I was still a danger zone. I secretly like when people are afraid of me. It makes me feel like I have effectively upheld my First Amendment. Anyone who knows me well understands that I don't deal with bullshit. But we all had a great time at the Hillbilly Jam that year anyways. By this time, I had an entire big circle of shiner friends. There are way too many to list. There was a film crew that followed some of us around the festival, for a production called "On Down The Road". The director named Neal James was a really cool guy to hang out with. He is also in the music industry, and I follow him to this day on social media. Hippy told a falsehood and said it was his birthday, just to pick up chicks. Husband got molested by an old lady who snuck up behind him and grabbed his business. And I threatened to steal Hank Williams Jr.'s ice cream cone. Actually, it was Frank Morrow, with "All My Rowdy Friends". But he put on such a convincing show that we all swore up and down he was Hank. I walked up the side of the stage to give him some moonshine. It was hot that night, and the only thing I could think to say was, "I'm gonna steal your ice cream and hide in the bushes with it." Who the hell says that? Sometimes I'm a complete dumbass. Also that night, I hung out and passed moonshine with a guy that turned out to be one of my best friends, master still builder of Tennessee Thumper Stills, the one and only Rick Gibson. It was a successful trip mostly. Then we had the long ride home through the night with Hippy singing along to Willie Nelson songs every mile of the entire 335-mile distance. Any time I have ever travelled with him I have sworn it is the last time. At least until the next time. It's like I am cursed and next thing I know Hippy and I are like a band of gypsies "On The Road Again".

I kept on the dusty trail of hitting every moonshine event I can possibly get to.. festivals, meet and greets, get-togethers. I have filmed for documentaries with some greats in the business.. such as my friends Roy Grooms, Garmer Burchfield and Uncle Steve. Also, I was present for a Bo Cumberland production titled "Down In The Holler", with Rich, Joann, and Mason Minnick from "Moonshine Rednecks". And I took part in another filming for a Jack Stewart production with Tony Seitz and his family, along with several of our friends. Even though I became accustomed to being in front of film cameras during my time with Appalachian Outlaws, I was always shy and reserved in the documentary sets I was on.

Being on-screen is still something that is not a big deal to me. It's just not what I feel I was meant to pursue. I would rather be behind the scenes or in the shadows. I mostly showed up to these gigs to support my moonshiner friends. I also continued my rounds to legal distilleries and events that different one's host. I wanted both the black market and legal industry to know that my full support lies with each end of the spectrum. It is equally important to network with both sides of the fence and be able to bat for both teams. I didn't want to sit on the bench. I wanted to step up to the plate any time I was called upon by any entity of the shine trade. I have different thoughts and feelings pertaining to the legal and illegal realms. I gravitate more towards traditional non-taxed liquor dealings. But I also see the modern-day relevance of the still young legal distillery boom. There is a rush knowing that you are dealing with the underground secret side of the operation. Then again, there is a relief in not having to look over your shoulder for the law when you go to the legal side. It is a definite catch-22.

By this time, I had come a very long way in getting a firm grasp on my proficiency in the moonshine craft. Although I knew there was still a lot for me to learn. You never finish learning, experimenting, trying to perfect each recipe, and every run. That's part of why folks that start making it get hooked and continue to practice the skill. You are only as good as your last run. There is always room for improvement. It becomes a personal competition to try and outdo the best you have to offer. To refine the art and dial into the signature you make on the finished product. Rick Gibson designed and built two stills specifically for me, making Tennessee Thumper Stills my official sponsor. I immediately put the stills to use. I started to gather a broader skillset and a better sense of what I contributed to the cause. I graduated from corn liquor after getting that algorithm down to second nature, perfecting my honeysuckle, and moved on to making brandy. My full respect lies with the black market. That's where I got my start, and where the historical significance of the trade will always remain.

There is the illegal aspect of it, which is a big magnetic pull for me. There is something I admire about basically saying, "fuck the government". The bottom line reason it is such a big deal to make moonshine is because the government is not collecting taxes on it. I like that. But with all that said, I also set my sights on making it in the legal industry. I was just waiting for the right opportunity to present itself. Even for illegal shiners, the pinnacle of the trade is to earn a private label, with the right to mass produce and mass distribute your moonshine. You know you have arrived when your name, your face and your product is sitting on a liquor store shelf for anyone and everyone to buy and drink. If you make it that far, it is proof that what you bring to the table is good enough to garner notoriety on a grander scale. Since the legal market is still fairly young and in its early historical stages, there are not many that have made it that far in the game yet. It has become a significant goal and a bucket list check-off to many, including myself. As a woman among men in a mostly male line of work, I had serious doubts that I would ever reach this accomplishment. I wanted to go for it regardless. Not for the bragging rights, but for the sake of coming full circle in my career as a maker of moonshine. I wanted to be one of the women at the forefront of the industry to blaze a trail for other women to follow. The first two ladies who made it possible for myself and others to join ranks, are Pam Sutton (wife of Popcorn Sutton), and Patti Bryan (lead female from the Moonshiner's show). They are both remarkable women. I am beyond proud to know these fine ladies. They lit the torch for others to find the way.

After years of actively pursuing my own legal label, I finally got the call that would make that dream possible. I became the third woman in the history of the legal industry to claim a private moonshine label. Tiny Roberson, my friend and Master Distiller from East Tennessee Distillery, gave me the chance I had been waiting for. Not only did he offer me my own private label, but he went much further, and offered me my own brand, Outlaw Spirits. I proudly accepted and proceeded to jump the fence to the other side of the market. What I am most proud of from all my achievements in the shine trade, is the fact that I became the first woman from West Virginia to have a legal label and a brand of spirits. That is what I want to be known for in the history books of the moonshine industry. I am honored to wave that flag for my home state, to represent the women of this particular Appalachian region. West Virginia has a long and steady standing in the roots of moonshine. I am proud to have some small role in being a part of that heritage.

The legal side of things does not necessarily mean that the grass is greener on that side of the fence. You don't have to run from the law or risk jail time, but now you have to learn how to navigate and follow the liquor laws. There is a great deal of behind the scenes hard work that is involved with having your own label or brand. It does not happen overnight. Every state operates differently, and there is so much red tape and bureaucracy that makes it very difficult to find a way through it. You start off with getting your label approved and having your formula approved. Both of these can take months depending on several different factors. You have to recruit distributors, which become the middle man between you and the liquor stores. You have to make rounds to the stores and request that they carry your product. Then you have to show up to the ones that put your brand on the shelves and do tastings to help them sell what they've ordered. I learned the hard way that you have to become a door-to-door salesman when you are batting for the legal team. Most of the doors you knock on get slammed in your face. You basically have to harass the system to get your foot in the door.

I have especially had a hard time because I am not widely known. I have never been on tv like many others who have arrived at this level. Although I have a large number of supporters, it's a big world out there and I am just one person trying to make a name for myself among the big dogs. And I have learned that alcohol consumers are extremely loyal customers. They all have their go-to favorites, and that is what they make a beeline for when they walk through the door of their local liquor stores. They aren't usually interested in trying something different. It is a major task to establish a new brand among an endless line of bottles that are household names whether they be vodka, rum, whiskey, brandy, tequila, gin, etc. And when you are fighting for shelf space in the moonshine section, you have the most key players to contend with, which are actually neutral grain spirits that have taken over the market and distorted the public perception of what shine is and how it is supposed to taste.

Part 2

And so I began on a long and winding journey of hell-bent determination to proceed forward with this new endeavor. I won't start something unless I firmly believe I can finish it. My time is more valuable to me than money. I didn't set out on this path to make money in the first place. I did it to have a sense of pride in the hard work I put into something I feel is worthy of my time and effort. I first envisioned how I wanted to portray myself as "Lady Outlaw". I was adamant to have two key elements on my bottle, my horse and the 44 revolver. These things represent the power and independence I wished to convey as a woman. It was sort of an homage to the Wild West cowgirl and Indian that I admire, but I wanted it to have a timeless aspect so that viewers now or a hundred years from now would not know when the picture took place. I set up a photo shoot on the farm. I selected my wardrobe then did my hair and makeup, plus groomed my paint horse, Pocahontas. The two Jasons were on hand to help me produce the whole thing. They both assisted me in climbing aboard my bareback horse. Husband operated the camera. Ironically, I was aiming the 44 magnum at my ex-husband when the picture was taken. (Of course, neither of the Jasons allowed me to have a loaded prop). I designed my first label around this photograph and came up with the name for my clear 80 proof wheat whiskey. I felt like if one word in the English language could capture the essence of my character, it was "Untamed". And this theme fit well with my unsaddled horse. She is wearing a bridle but no reigns, and I am holding on to her mane. I wanted people to question if the horse on the label was untamed, or the lady on the horse was untamed. I hoped they would draw the conclusion that the underlying answer is both. The horse is free and the woman is free. One does not belong to the other. But they choose to ride together.

None of this came about on a whim. There was a tremendous amount of thought process and decision making involved with every aspect of the Outlaw Spirits brand and the Untamed label. There is meaning behind every detail. I searched through catalogs of hundreds of bottles to pick the one I thought was the best. The use of Mason jars on the legal market is heavily prevalent, and I was advised to choose something that would stand out more on the shelves. It was decided that Untamed would be a wheat whiskey instead of corn. Moonshine can be any kind of distilled grains, and wheat would set my product apart from the plethora of corn liquors in circulation. On the label, I used my photo editing skills to place me and my horse in front of a background of a wheat field and a full moon. Husband put his graphic design skills into the production of the Untamed label. I made every call, down to the font, the colors, the use of patina copper for the border and the back label, the positioning of everything and how it would look on the bottle. Then the graphic artist at the distillery, my good friend and fellow WV native Wilbur Hunter, fine-tuned and added his own flair to finish the final label. Most of the time, the first submission of a legal label is rejected. I fully expected that to be the case with mine. The most controversial imagery on my label was the firearm. With the day and age of gun control activists, there was a big chance the government would reject the label just because of that one detail. Tiny advised me that this could be a deterrent. But I insisted on it and we submitted the label for review. Luckily, it was approved in its entirety within one month, which is record-breaking time. I was astonished when I got the word. I thought surely we would have to go back to the drawing board in several attempts for a green light. Again, it took one person believing in me to put my goal in reach. The next step was to mass-produce the Untamed, and bottle it at the distillery. From beginning to end, from conception to delivery, it took about six months to go from the initial offer of my label to the production process. Again, it took one person believing in me to put my goal in reach. This time that person was the giant known as Tiny, my new boss. And it took a village to make it all come together. Behind every successful person is a team of people who push them forward and pitch in to help.

I then set off on a tour to get my Untamed into liquor stores in Tennessee, the first state the Outlaw Spirits brand became available in. It was picked up by a big distributor and three major retailers in the Bristol area. I had done tastings at a few of these stores with Darrell Miller for the Bootlegger's Distillery in the past, so I knew how to conduct the tasting setups. I also coordinated and arranged a launch party for the brand and the Untamed label, to be held at East Tennessee Distillery. Shane McCoy had a private label of rye whiskey with Tiny as well, known as "Underground" from his family recipe. I attended his launch party, so I knew based on that how to go about planning my event. I had live music performed by my friends Julia Ann and Ed Davis. There were still builders and vendors, friends and family present. Outlaw Spirits was up and running. Although it was an entirely new brand, it came out of the gate with good reception from my supporters. My ultimate desire with the line was to get my signature honeysuckle recipe bottled and distributed. If I accomplished that, I would have reached my end goal. It was decided in a meeting after the launch party to have Shane McCoy's label of Underground merge into the Outlaw Spirits brand with the Untamed. And so, he and I became partners in shine. I was relieved to have someone of notoriety to join forces with, to help establish the brand. We changed both of our original labels to make them look more uniform and give the brand a definitive visual concept. The next step was to get Outlaw Spirits and Tennessee Mellowmoon into the state of West Virginia.

I arranged a meeting with the WV ABC board, and they accepted the distillery products into the state warehouse. That was more difficult than it sounds. The process took about a year to pull through. It was not easy. Nothing on the legal side of the spectrum comes easy. So after that, it was on to a statewide tour of pushing both brands. We all attended the state trade show in Charleston, which helped propel our bottles into some of the liquor stores in a few out of 55 counties. We attended that event alongside Tim Smith with his Climax brand, Mark Hatfield (who is the most widely recognized public moonshine figure from WV), and several other representatives and distilleries. We met the owners of the Bondurant Brothers distillery, who Shane has since begun a new label with. I became a licensed state ambassador, allowing me to represent East Tennessee Distillery, deliver to the warehouse, and carry open containers to conduct tastings around WV. I also set up a meeting with the most reputable distributor, to hopefully further our efforts. It is still an ongoing ordeal. The legal business is no joke. It is easier to break one rule on the black market, then it is to fall in line with the hundreds of rules on the legal side.

In the midst of all this, I had some really cool personal life moments take place. In April of 2017, I spent some more time with my dear friend and legend Chance Martin, aka "Alamo Jones". Of course in true Chance fashion, he took me behind the scenes to even more places I had no business being. On one occasion he took me to the former home of Johnny Cash's mother Carrie. It is known as the "Mama Cash Home" and sits across the street from the site of Johnny and June's house site on Old Hickory Lake in Tennessee. The Mama Cash Home was bought by a couple who spent their lives doing missionary work abroad. They became active advocates in acquiring significant places involving the life and career of Johnny Cash, as well as Elvis Presley. Chance introduced me to this couple, who welcomed me into their house where Johnny's mother lived. Johnny and June both spent their final days in this house as well, since it was more manageable than their bigger estate on the lake. I was treated as a guest of honor, given a tour, and heard the many stories that were contained within the walls of the Mama Cash Home. I was handed the personal Bible of Johnny Cash. That was a religious experience in itself, flipping through the pages and reading some of Johnny's personal notes within the chapters. Then I was given a never before published black and white photograph of Johnny Cash and Elvis together (which I proudly keep on display in my home). And as if all that wasn't a big enough deal, Chance then escorted me and Husband onto some more adventures in Bon Aqua, Tennessee.

The same couple who owned the Mama Cash Home (Brian and Sally Oxley), also purchased and restored another special place owned by Johnny Cash. It was once an old general store down the road from Johnny's private farm that he bought and converted into a music hall, with his own personal stage. He performed for his friends and family there, and also hosted an ongoing event tradition known as "Saturday Night In Hickman County". Under its new ownership, the place was respectfully named "The Storyteller's Museum". As soon as we arrived, I was greeted by my friend Mark Cash, nephew of Johnny. He was one of the hosts of the museum. He gave us a tour of the facility, which includes the famous "One Piece At A Time" car. I was thrilled to sit in the driver's seat of the one-of-a-kind original automobile and have my picture taken. Mr. Oxley who is also an author, publisher, and film producer, gave me a few of his books and a big print from a painting of Johnny Cash. I was taken to the private green room of the museum to visit with Mr. Tommy Cash again. His wife Marcy and other Cash family members were also present. I had taken my guitar on this trip for the sole purpose of having it signed by Tommy since he is the one who taught Peepaw to play guitar and handed over the tradition of music to my family. Tommy and I had more in-depth conversations about my grandfather. It was all I could do to not cry when I told this man again what his contribution meant to my family. He signed my guitar, and also gave me a brief lesson before it was time for him to get on stage to perform with his son Mark.

I was so honored just to be there in the audience, to listen to them as they sang and played their guitars. They took requests, in which I quietly said, "Jackson." They didn't hear me so Tommy asked, "What did she say?" Husband spoke up for me and told them. Then the next thing I knew, Tommy invited me to come on stage to sing with him. I froze. I had never sung on a stage. I couldn't possibly. But Husband and Chance urged me to stand up and make way to the stage. I didn't have time to even think or to get nervous. I do recall as I stepped on stage thinking to myself, "Oh great, you've really gotten yourself into a situation this time." But at the same time, I also felt an extreme overwhelming sense that I was supposed to be there and this moment was fated to happen somehow. So I grabbed the microphone, waited for my cue, and started singing. It was an out of body surreal experience. Somehow I managed to remember all the words of June's part, and honestly felt as though she was standing on stage beside me holding my hand. I wouldn't even believe this moment happened, but thankfully Husband captured it on video. When I walked off the stage and heard the applause of the audience, that's when I got nervous and started shaking. Chance made it possible. And I knew my Peepaw also aligned for this to take place. He wanted one of his descendants to come full circle with the man who bestowed music upon him, Tommy Cash. And I was the lucky one who was there to do it.

We went from there to the farmhouse of Johnny Cash. We were given the grand VIP tour of the house and grounds, then Chance showed us his own personal museum next to the house. His contribution of personal Cash keepsakes and private photographs are displayed there within an atmosphere paying tribute to Johnny's home in Jamaica, known as Cinnamon Hill. The farm in its entirety was also bought by the Oxley's, and lovingly established as a museum and music venue known as the Hideaway Farm. That farm was referred to by Johnny Cash as "the center of his universe". It is the place he escaped to in order to find peace and solace away from the fame and everything that entails. It was his refuge to reflect, pray, fish, shoot guns, spend time with his family. My personal take from what I gathered there, is that whoever "The Man In Black" wanted to be behind closed doors, this is where he found that identity. He is quoted as once saying to his friend Waylon Jennings, "You know what getting away from it all is for me? This place right here." He was talking about his farm. It was his sanctuary. We ended the day in the dining room of his farmhouse, having a private dinner around Johnny's table with

Chance and Brian Oxley, among others. We all took turns discussing our sentiments about the farm, and about Johnny Cash. I spoke up and said what came from my heart. I never met Johnny, but through his friends and their stories, I feel like I knew him. If I had five minutes to spend with him, I would want to spend it on his farm, fishing in his pond, talking about life in general. Bon Aqua translates to "Good Water". We couldn't leave the place without collecting some of the renowned spring water. We gathered some from the very source where Johnny Cash would gather his water. I saved it for a special occasion run of moonshine.

In the following year of 2018, Husband sold a property he owned at the golf course in Newport, TN. He knew of my dream to have an antique model truck, and he talked me out of buying one when I had the insurance check from the flood. But since he made a profit off the sale of his land, he and I started searching for a 40s model pickup. In our search, we came across a 1953 Pontiac Chieftain Deluxe. She was a big black beauty, with sexy lines and curves, chrome and character. The Chieftain line has a Native American theme with the hood ornament and tail fin decals, based on Chief Pontiac. I fell in love with this car instantly. I had never seen one before. There weren't many in production back in their hay day. They were Pontiac's version of the Cadillac from that era and weren't highly sought after being a knock off model back then. So upon researching, I found out that because there aren't many around, especially in as good of shape as the one I found, they have become highly desired by classic car enthusiasts in this day and age. But I reminded myself that I initially had my heart set on a classic Ford truck, so I kept looking for one. However, the Chieftain kept coming back to the forefront of my mind. And so I made arrangements for us to go see it in person so we could take it for a test drive. As soon as I saw the Chieftain with my own eyes, I knew she would be mine. I made an offer. The car only had two owners before me. The first was a woman who had the car through her college years and longer, based on the stickers still on the windows. Then it sat in a barn in War, WV for decades. The second owner lowered the car 3 inches, put a new gas tank in the trunk, and installed dual exhaust flame throwers on it (which was one of the biggest selling points for me). Other than those changes the rest of the vehicle was all original. After my first offer, the current owner changed his mind and decided to keep the Pontiac. I was really upset. So I came back with a higher offer. He accepted and she was mine. I became the third owner of this classic beauty. Husband bought me the most awesome gift I've ever been given. He deserves a lifetime supply of Husband-Of-The-Year awards for hooking me up with the coolest car ever. All good automobiles need a name. I initially wanted to name her "War Chief", since she came from War, West Virginia. But after joining Pontiac clubs online, I discovered that was a popular name given by other owners of Chieftains. So I settled on the name of "She Chief", since she was first owned by a woman, and found her forever home with Lady Outlaw. She Chief looks like a gangster mobile.

It's the kind of car that would have hauled moonshine in the '50s, the same type of vehicle that started the sport of NASCAR.

Which leads me to tell about one of the coolest moments of my entire life. Husband procured the She Chief for me before my Untamed launch party. I wanted to have the Chieftain present at the distillery that weekend, for the sake of looking like a badass with my sexy vintage vehicle. So we hauled her down to Piney Flats, TN on a rollback trailer, so as not to rack up miles on She Chief since the odometer was only at 50k on her original straight-8 engine when we first bought her. The day before my launch party I did some tastings at liquor stores in the Bristol area. By chance, and talking to several race fans who were in town for the spring race that weekend, I was informed that I could drive on the Bristol Motor Speedway track. I knew I had to do it. This was a once in a lifetime opportunity. So that Friday night, I rolled towards the racetrack in the Chieftain. I had never even been inside the Bristol coliseum before. But I found myself outside the gates, waiting in line with other drivers who were there to take on the intimidating track for the sake of a children's charity benefit run. She Chief's engine kept overheating while we sat in the bumper to bumper line up. Husband, who was my only passenger and also my crew chief, kept pouring water in the radiator to cool her off. He really wanted to drive, but was a gentleman and allowed me the honor. This was a huge deal to me because my Meemaw and Peepaw's first date was at the Bristol racetrack. This specific place held significant family history, that is why it meant so much to me. I knew my

Peepaw was most assuredly looking down on me in this moment. I felt certain it was another one of those things he orchestrated from Heaven, just for me. There is no other possible explanation of how I came about this chance for the distinguished privilege to drive on the Bristol track. So I called Meemaw minutes before it was time to enter the stadium, to tell her of this grand occasion. She was proud of me, as I knew Peep would be too, being the lifelong loyal NASCAR fan that he was.

When it came time to fire up our engines and make way into the Bristol Motor Speedway, the nerves set in and I had a brief panic attack of "Holy shit, what have I got myself into this time?" I started to second guess if I could drive this big beast on a racetrack. I had never driven on a track before in my life, although I secretly always wanted to. But this was serious business, and I could potentially wreck my beautiful Chieftain and leave there with a pile of metal. Besides the fact, She Chief has no seatbelts, as they came along after her time. So if I did wreck, Husband and I could end up in the hospital or six feet underground. Not to mention the fact that there is no power steering, and the steering wheel is as big as a captain's ship wheel. You literally have to manhandle the Chieftain like a tank. I had previously pulled muscles in my arms from wrestling with the wheel when we first bought the car. So I was seriously concerned about taking those tight curves on the high banks of the track. Only one way to find out if me and She Chief had what it takes to make it round the world's fastest half-mile. It was now or never. I said a prayer, took a deep breath and proceeded to make my grand entrance onto Bristol Motor Speedway.

As soon as I saw the bright lights and the crowd inside the coliseum, adrenaline took over and set my nerves aside. My car was the only classic on the track, and she stood out among the other vehicles like she was transported through time travel. She Chief immediately gained applause from every spectator we passed by on our way to the starting line. Everyone was yelling "Pontiac!", which I didn't realize why at the time. I thought they were just cheering because it was a vintage automobile. Before we got the green light, a bystander who became an immediate fan, asked if he could come along for the ride. I warned him that I could be the world's worst driver and crash us all, then told him to hop in. So here I am with Husband in the passenger seat and a complete random stranger in the back seat. The checkered flag was waved, and it was go time. The first lap was slow as every driver was finding their groove and take their lanes. When you watch NASCAR races and see the banks on the Bristol track, let me just say that tv does not do them justice, they are way steeper in person. Once we started going fast I was becoming increasingly more disoriented. Gravity takes over. The track is so short that by the time you get out of one curve and onto the straightaway, you are already into the next curve. I was starting to get dizzy by the fifth or sixth lap. But I was blasting those dual exhaust flame throwers every chance I got. I mostly kept one hand on the big wheel, and one hand on the button that sets the fire out the tailpipes. I thought

I may even get kicked off the track for my over-use of sparking the flames. The crowd loved it. Random dude in the backseat didn't say two words the whole time. I must have scared the shit out of him. Husband rolled video the entire ride. The track officials let us run about a dozen laps overall. Each one got faster. I stayed on the low side of the banks and on the inside lane of the track most of the time. I have no earthly idea of how real racecar drivers go around that half-mile for 500 laps. I would have been disoriented for a year if I had driven that many circles. But I made it off the track with She Chief intact and the engine more than cooled. My passengers and I survived. And it was by far one of the most epic experiences I have ever had.

I found out afterwards the reason why the Pontiac was such a big deal and garnered so much attention at the Bristol track. The very first car ever on the BMS was a Pontiac. And the first car that won the first official race there, the "Volunteer 500", was a Pontiac. Also ironically, the site of the speedway was originally set to be the exact location where the distillery I work for, East Tennessee Distillery, sits today. But the town of Piney Flats wasn't in agreeance to have the track inside their city limits, and so it ended up 8 miles down the road in Bristol, TN. Also, a giant named "Tiny" (like my boss) was the first driver, in the first Pontiac on the track, for the first practice race.. back when it was known as the Bristol International Raceway. See all this tied in together for me that weekend. I wanted to represent the good ole days of NASCAR, which got its start with moonshiners souping up their automobiles for the sake of running from the law. She Chief is my moonshine hauler, and she represented the origins of the sport with the same class and style that first set wheels on the tracks in what has become internationally recognized stock car racing. My run on the Bristol Motor Speedway will go down as one for the record books in my personal history of amazing things I got to do in my lifetime. Plus I got cool mom points from my son for being a race car driver, even if it was just a temporary status. And I know without a doubt that my Peepaw was along for the ride with me.

Back to the home-front, things are always shifting on the farm. Seasons come and go. Animals come and go. People come and go. I have seen these patterns repeat over and over throughout my many years here. It is always sad for me, to watch all the changes that have occurred on this sacred land that I hold as invaluable. As I've stated before, I never adjust well to change of any sort, even if I know it is ultimately for the best. In the past year, several of the villagers have moved on and left the farm behind, Amber and her sons, who had become part of the farm story, left for good to return to their hometown of Beckley. Amber worked hard while she was here, landscaping and making things pretty. She even painted the gates turquoise. I think of her every time I see flowers she planted and those turquoise gates. JoaQuin went to Florida, then returned again with his fiancé Paige and their baby daughter Ava, who was born while they were away. They settled back into Generator's house. I grew attached to Ava, being her frequent babysitter for a while. Then that family left again to set out on their own in Summersville.

The farm became very quiet after all of these villagers went their separate ways. Things we had all pitched in together to make work, started falling to the wayside. The constant gatherings, village meetings, chaos and drama.. it all came to a sudden slow-down. We were left with me, the kids, and the two Jasons on the 112-acre homestead. But even with my time away, the farm and I seemed as though we had never been separated. What is left of my soul will always be scattered across this land. No matter what changes this place sees in its lifetime, it will remain forever marked with memories of my lifetime.

Turn the Page

I have delayed, postponed and purposefully procrastinated writing the final chapter of this book. All the others flowed out as if they were waiting for release from my mind to the pages. But I am finding that this is the most perplexing one to put into words. Maybe the last one hasn't been written yet because it is still unfolding. Perhaps that is why I find it so difficult to begin the ending. So much has happened just during the process on this journey of spilling my heart out. It has been by far one of the most emotionally draining experiences of my life and to tell about my life in such detail is extremely emotional. I have never worn my heart on my sleeve or bared my thoughts and feelings to anyone to the extent that I have within these chapters. Also to tell about the past, I have had to immerse myself in those parts of my life that are very painful to relive. I have been forced to jump from the past, to the present, to the future during the duration of working on this, which is exhausting in itself. It isn't easy to open yourself up in this way, to expose what and who you truly are and what you have been through, leaving it up for speculation and interpretation of those who will read it. Once I do finally turn the page on this one, and this book is in the hands of anyone that opens it up, for me it will be equivalent to standing naked in front of all of you, waiting for stones to be thrown.

Although there is an aspect that has been therapeutic and even necessary for my soul to heal from old scars that have been reopened, this endeavor has weakened me in many ways, breaking down so many of my defenses. I am displaying myself to be vulnerable and susceptible for outsiders looking in. I hope I am strong enough to withstand whatever feedback, criticism, or ridicule comes my way from the readers. I know ahead of time there will be some backlash concerning certain truths about specific people who have been mentioned, even though I have tried to keep many of those nameless. My theory on that however is.. if you don't want to be a villain in my story, then you shouldn't have been a villain in my real life. Also, I am not a professional writer. I am worried this book may come across as the rantings of a madwoman. And did I mention that I wrote the entire thing on my cellphone; like literally typed it as one giant text message in my Samsung Notes. Who the hell does that? It may be proof that I am indeed insane. But if that is the case, I am not afraid to say that I have earned my crazy, and after reading the entire story you all got at least a glimpse of how and why. It is damn near impossible to fit an entire lifetime in one book. I could have written complete novels just on each subject and each character I have discussed. I basically had to summarize everything to get it all in.

On the other hand, I think one of the reasons it feels so impossible to write the ending, is because this is not really the end for me. I am nearly 40 years old, but hopefully, I still have many years of living ahead. Putting an ending on something that isn't really over is a daunting task. I named this chapter when I was still in the early stages of writing. And now I feel that the title rings even more relevant. Once I reach the last word, in the last paragraph, in the last chapter, I will "turn the page" and continue theoretically writing the rest of my story with whatever time I have left to walk this earth. And when I am gone, my children and their children will keep a continuation of me and who I am through the parts of me that will live on within them. Just as I have been a continuation of the story my parents, grandparents, and all my ancestors before me have written. I am part of all of them, and they are all part of me. That is the circle of life. We live through one another, intertwined and connected to each other in what becomes our own personal history. I have contemplated and questioned whether or not to actually have this book published once it is complete because it is so deeply personal on so many levels. But I keep coming back to the conclusion that since I managed to survive writing this account, the only logical next step is to put it out there. My hopes are that it will find its way to my descendants someday.

Okay, enough about how damn hard it is for me to finish what I started here. I want to catch you up with current times and see where it goes from there. I have to backtrack a little though in order for everything to make sense. So going back to my childhood first, I want to talk about the travels I had with my Peepaw because that is relative to bring you up to date in a prime example of how we are meant to meet certain people at certain times in our lives so that we are led to the paths we are meant to be on. I rode the roads with my grandfather more miles than I can count. Most of our trips were in a familiar trail from Florida to West Virginia, and back again. I have made that voyage so many times I could literally drive it in my sleep. Peepaw had a very particular way that he traveled. As I said before he drove a vehicle like he was flying an airplane because of his career as a pilot. He didn't like to make stops on the highway. He mostly just wanted to get where he was going with as little disruption as possible. When he did stop to fuel up or take a necessary break for food or bathroom facilities, he had very specific pit stop locations that he used every time like clockwork. Sometimes he even required us girls to go potty on the shoulder of the Interstate in plain view of traffic, so as to keep to his strict route schedule. He was a professional traveler if I have ever seen one. To this day, I travel exactly as he did. That was instilled in me through repetition and learned behavior. I do the most cussing and the most praying when I am behind the wheel, as I am certain he did too.

On the occasional whim, Peepaw would detour from our usual map and take us girls on a trip within a trip, to see a sight or visit with someone. He took us to the Biltmore House near Asheville, North Carolina more than once. He took us to see Grandfather Mountain, and along the Blue Ridge Parkway. He took us to visit with his Uncle Estil in Virginia, where we would sit on the front porch and listen to the two of them exchange stories. Sometimes we would go to Uncle Estil's general store for a bag of candy and a soda pop. This is where the past catches up to the present and has an effect on the future. I clearly recall these visits with my grandfather's uncle. But as an adult for some reason, I always thought Estil lived near Fancy Gap, Virginia. I'm not sure why but every time I have driven through that part of the state that's where I assumed those visits took place. It wasn't until recently that I discovered Estil's homeplace and general store were in the towns of Saltville and Glade Spring, Virginia. I will leave this at that for now, and come back around to the significance of it after I explain the next part of this particular story and how it all ties together.

About three years ago, while attending the annual Hillbilly Jam festival where I finally met Greg Shook, I also met someone else who would inadvertently change the course of my direction. Greg and I spotted a man set up as a vendor. I could tell from afar that he was a mountain man, my kind of buddy. So Greg and I walked up to him and introduced ourselves. His name is Jim Bordwine, and he is a salt maker and a moonshiner from Saltville, Virginia. We immediately hit it off, became instant friends, and kept in touch. In the summer of 2018, Jim invited Greg and I to take place in making a formal appearance at an event that he was a part of, the Battles of Saltville Civil War Re-enactment. We gladly accepted and anticipated the event, since we are both history enthusiasts and this was a completely different scene than our usual gigs.

Jim was our official host for the upcoming event and let us know that he would take care of our lodgings, meals, etc. Most of the "Dusty Trail" stops we make for appearances don't provide these amenities for us so we were grateful for the offer to have prearranged accommodations. Months before the event, Jim hinted to me that we would be staying in a historic haunted Antebellum mansion, but he wanted to keep the identity of the location a secret surprise. I took to the internet as a private detective to see if I could figure it out myself. I researched every standing Antebellum style house in the area till I narrowed it down to a place called the Nickerson Snead House in Glade Spring, VA. I called Jim and told him my guess, which he reluctantly revealed was, in fact, the place where we would stay. I totally blew his surprise. Up until the date of the re-enactment, I read everything I could find and watched every video online about the house. I was so beyond excited to be staying at a haunted mansion with one of my best friends, Greg Shook. I was like a kid waiting for Christmas morning. Having a lifelong fascination with the spirit world and the experiences of living in a haunted house and seeing a ghost as a child, my curiosity got the better of me and I couldn't wait to get there and stay as a guest. I was looking forward to a spooky sleepover which undoubtedly would involve moonshine and merriment.

The time finally came, on August 17th I made way towards my destination of the Nickerson Snead House, off of Exit 29 on I-81. I first met up with Jim at the local truck stop and followed him to the house where he would introduce me to the owner. He explained beforehand that the house was a museum. It wasn't a bed and breakfast. We had special permission to stay there for the weekend. So just based on that I already felt indebted to the owner before I even met her. What generous person would allow for complete strangers, let alone known "outlaws", to take up temporary residence in their museum? That's what I was thinking about on the short drive there. Part of the deal with her opening the doors for us was that we would promote the museum on social media during our stay. Now I want to sidestep here and explain that during this time, I was under contract for a TV show with an L.A. based production company called "DNA Films". They were interested in producing a show about East Tennessee Distillery starring my boss Tiny, the graphic artist Wilbur, plus myself. We had already shot a sizzle reel for the show concept which was to be a competition based program between us and another local distillery. So I was somewhat emerged in the television circuit for the second time in my life. I was in regular contact with the executive producer, a female this go-round, luckily after my first bad experience with the show business industry.

We pulled into the driveway of the grand Antebellum manor and I hopped into Jim's vehicle where we passed a jar of moonshine. The owner pulled up and I was introduced to her. I immediately had two reactions come over me. The first, I instantly felt a connection to the owner, Ronda Caudill, and second, I was automatically afraid of the house. Jim left us and we proceeded inside. Ronda gave me the full tour of the haunted house museum, meanwhile telling me the history of the place. I felt safe while she was there, even though there was an unexplained disturbance upstairs during our walk-through. We completed the tour and continued talking amongst ourselves. The more she spoke, the more I caught on to the fact that she is an extremely fascinating woman.

Then she started telling me about a group of lady psychics she was a part of, which I also found very interesting. Just based on the history of the museum itself, I asked her if the Nickerson Snead House had ever been on a paranormal show. She explained that there had been some offers but none that came through. So I told her I would get her in touch with my executive producer and see if they could come up with a project together. At the time, the production company was in close contact with the Discovery Channel which is known to broadcast paranormal series. Ronda was excited about the prospect of talking to the producers. Aside from being generous and welcoming, I learned that Ronda also has a Ph.D. and is an author as well as the owner of a publishing company called Full Moon Publishing. She gave me a copy of the book she wrote about the museum. I thanked her again for letting us stay for the weekend, then she left me there to settle in.

I planned to sit in the parlor and read the book about the house. But alone in the house, suddenly a sense of complete fear came over me. Here I thought I was a big brave girl, but when it came down to being in there by myself I realized I was a complete chicken shit. I went to my car to get my overnight bags. I called Greg Shook and his ETA was still a few hours out. I was scared to go back into the haunted house with no one there to accompany me. So I did something I had never done before, I started a Facebook live video. I thought if I could take my friends in there with me virtually, that may alleviate my nerves; plus promoting the place was part of the deal.

Now you have to realize that to go live also made me very nervous because I didn't want to make a fool of myself in front of an audience should something frighten me in the house. I am supposed to be the badass "Lady Outlaw". But once I pushed that button there was no going back. So I walked back through the door, like a rookie news broadcaster, live on social media. I proceeded to give my viewers a tour of the mansion. Let me pause to give you the back story of the Nickerson Snead House so you know what we're dealing with. It was originally a fort used during the French and Indian War and also during the Revolutionary War. So it was created before the United States was even a country. In the early 1800s the property was purchased by Dr. Nickerson Snead; that's when the rest of the house was built around a log cabin that was part of the original fort. It was used as a field hospital and a morgue during the Civil War. If walls could talk, I'm telling you this place could tell some stories. So on my live stream, I headed towards the basement (which was used as the morgue for Civil War soldiers). Since the theme of the weekend revolved around the Civil War, I wanted to show this historic site to my friends watching the video. The nerdy side of me wanted this to be educational. I walked part way down the stairs and heard something in the basement that startled me. So I took off running all the way through the huge house and outside to the porch, where I realized I had in fact just made a complete ass of myself on live air. So I caught my breath, pulled my big girl panties up and went back inside towards the basement door (which I left wide open as I ran for my life just moments before). But the door was now completely shut. When I went to open it, the doorknob wouldn't budge. It felt like someone had a hold of it on the other side of the door. I fought with it and finally pulled it open, in which case whatever was on the other side, quickly pulled it back shut. That's when I almost pissed my pants and took my second, faster run, back outside to safety. That's when I realized I was not alone in this house. Once I settled down and took a few swigs of my own Untamed shine, I got the courage up to go back in just briefly, while still rolling live video. I wrapped up my broadcast and hightailed it to the local truck stop where I decided to wait it out till Greg Shook arrived. I refused to go back in the haunted house alone.

Greg finally showed up with his girlfriend at the time, Donna, and their friends Paul and Stefanie. They met me at the truck stop and we went to the house. I thought I would be at ease with a house full of other guests. Plus I trust Greg Shook with my life. He would never let anything bad happen to me. He and I made another live video in the house together, for the sake of keeping with our deal to stay there. For a while, everything seemed fine. We drank and laughed and carried on. A few unexplainable incidences occurred, however, and by the time we all went to settle in for the night, I chickened out again. I ended up having to sleep in the bed with Greg and Donna, like a little kid afraid of the dark. The rest of the weekend we went back and forth between the Saltville Civil War Re-enactment and the Nickerson Snead House. We were treated like guests of honor at the event, and I was proud to be a part of an occasion that revolved around history. It was my first time ever witnessing a re-enactment, and I was fascinated by everything that entailed. The people of the town left a lasting impression on me. I was taken with how kind and down to earth they all were. I felt like I somehow fit in and belonged there. Or as though I had been there before.

On the second night in the haunted house, our friends Tony and Christa Seitz along with their daughters Heather and Kylie plus their grandson Carson came to visit with us. They had seen my live video and could tell how shaken I was so they came to be supportive. Tony came in as a total skeptic of the supernatural. But he left singing a completely different tune. The house was even more active than the day before. There were things going on around us constantly, in every room, any direction you turned. We were all on edge, what would have otherwise been a good time with friends turned out to be like something out of a horror film. Here are some examples of what goes on it that house: You can hear footsteps, whistling, whispering. Two pianos play intermittently on their own. Doors open and shut. Donna got grabbed by the leg from something unseen. A big heavy oak door tried to crash into Stefanie. Something tugged Heather's necklace. We saw baby dolls swinging themselves on a swing set in the hallway. The list goes on and on. And all that was just my first weekend there. I have had worse encounters at the house since then. I am not going to tell the story of Tony, Christa and their family, but something horrible happened to them after they left. In other words, something followed them home.

Ronda and I became good friends after our first meeting. She and the executive producer hit it off and began working on projects pertaining to the paranormal as well as the Nickerson Snead House. I got to hang out at the haunted house with the DNA Films crew along with Ronda and the women in her group. Also, Ronda has graciously let me stay there on other occasions where I was travelling to work at the distillery which is an hour from the museum. On many of my trips I don't have enough money for lodging, so the haunted house has of sorts become a second home to me on nights when I had nowhere else to stay. Although I have never once known of a good night's sleep under that roof. As a grown-ass woman, I can honestly say that I am more afraid of that house than any place I have ever been. I have taken my children and Husband to stay over as well. And for some reason, the house is well behaved when my daughter Faith is there with me.

When you experience the paranormal as a child, it just seems like a distant memory. Experiencing it as an adult takes on a whole new meaning. I was so shaken by what happened my first time there, that I couldn't even wrap my mind around it. I remained thoroughly disturbed by it for months after my initial visit. The Nickerson Snead House is not labeled as "haunted" for shits and giggles. There is legitimately something wrong with that place.

You sense it's presence as soon as you open the door and there is an overwhelming feeling that something is trying to chase you out of there while you are inside. It is no joke. Something evil resides within those walls. Something that has been around way longer than me and you. Whatever it is doesn't want intruders. Ever since my first visit there, even just driving past the house (which is visible from I-81), I feel the house taunting me even from afar, trying to lure me in like a spider to its web. I say to it, "Not today you Formidable Bastard." Nonetheless, something kept compelling me back there. And I have somehow become a regular patron of the place. My boss Tiny and his lady Dorothy have come there to hang out with me. They ditched out as soon as Tiny saw a tricycle roll across the floor on its own. I have even done a live public interview from the museum. The house never fails to produce some inexplicable experience that scares the living shit out of me. I have seen one of its spirits on an overnight stay. My family has begged me not to go back. Mama has scolded me for returning. Friends have worried about my well-being when I go there. For a long time, I kept asking myself "Why would I return to a place I was so deathly afraid of?" Now I know the answer.

I said all that, to say all this; coming back to current events, it has become evident to me that my time on my beloved farm is coming to a bitter end. The place I swore I would live till I died. The land I have raised and nurtured my children on, that I intended to pass down to them. The ground that is soaked with my own blood, sweat and tears. It is time for us to go our separate ways. I have bucked this, I have fought against it, I have done my best to stand my ground firm and refuse to be moved. But too many signs have presented themselves, too many arrows have pointed in other directions. I am being forced out of my homeland against my own will, by obvious red flags that continue to rise up despite my death grip on this of my truest homes. A black veil has descended upon the farm. It has been contaminated and tarnished by a few individuals. I could reveal them here, but the truth will reveal itself in time. It is unforgivable. It makes me sick. It makes me angry. Mostly I am sad beyond words. I intend to haunt the very existence of this land once I say my final farewell to it (dead or alive). I am so afraid that when I leave, my memories will not come with me. Since this is where I raised my children, most of my memories of them are embedded in this place. Too many to count, so many to recall. Letting go of something that has ultimately meant everything to me for so much invaluable time of my life; it is unbearable. This has been the center of my universe for fifteen years. But the land has become cursed. It is not what it once was or what I dreamed for it to be. Yet walking away feels impossible. I can't even imagine the last time I see my home in my rear-view mirror. Shutting a door for finality, that I never ever planned to close. I will have to be drug away kicking and screaming, clawing the ground so hard that the dirt remains forever stained upon my hands. It can never be washed off. But I will have to cross that bridge when I get to it and burn that same bridge once I reach the other side.

When I finally realized that I had no choice but to move on, I let it sink in enough to allow the notion to enter my mind that I need to put some plan in action for the future. I began to make myself look at the bigger picture. It is the equivalent to looking at your reflection when you don't like what you see. But there it is in front of you, plain as day. You can't escape it, because it is looking back at you, eye to eye. You have no choice but to face it head-on and confront the untold truth. The first step of this decision-making process was to decide where to go. That is the hardest one. My rebellious side kicked in and said, "If I can't be home on the farm, then I also have to say goodbye to my beloved West Virginia." It would torture me to be within the borders of this state, so close to my home yet so far away. I have to cross the boundaries. That in itself is like ripping the bandage off of a deep wound and exposing it to the elements. So not only am I losing something that is vital and crucial to me, but I am being pushed to forsake a home within a home. This is almost unspeakable for me. It torments me even to write about it now. Tears come easily when I think about what is inevitably coming. I have cried many rivers in my lifetime. This will be one of the biggest floods I have produced. Catastrophic.

I have always thought, in the depths of my mind, that if ever the day came that I should leave the farm, I could see myself living on a river. Because rivers have always had a way of easing my soul. They sing to me and I could listen to that sound of rushing water as long as it is flowing to the sea. So I began a search of property on a river. I first started looking in Tennessee, as that is the homeland of Husband, the location of the distillery I work for, and my little sister Marci's new residents. and I finally reconnected with her last year after ten years of no contact. But Tennessee was throwing up signs that it wasn't meant to be my new home. So I looked to the state of Virginia, a middle ground between WV and TN. I found a listing for a river property in Saltville, Virginia, the sleepy little town where I had been invited to attend the Civil War re-enactment. I recalled the good nature of the people there and the way it somehow felt familiar to me.

On our way back home from the annual Popcorn Sutton Jam, I decided to view the property in person. So on Father's Day of 2019 me, Husband, and J.J. took a detour to the North Fork of the Holston River to see for ourselves if this was a potential candidate to elect for our future. I had prearranged with the current owners to allow for our inspection of the place. To reach it, you either have to cross a swinging bridge over the river or drive through a water ford to get to the other side. Since we were travelling in the Chevy Spark, we opted for access via the swinging bridge. This instantly brought about a vibe of "Swiss Family Robinson". Once we crossed the bridge, we followed an old country road. The road radiated a sense of historical importance. Both Husband and I caught on to that simultaneously and said so to each other. We reached the boundary of the land we were there to see. An open meadow backed by a mountain of woods on one side and flanked by the big river on the other side of the dirt lane. It is landlocked. It feels like you are tucked away on an island. This is the place. It captured my attention and I could envision a new life there. If I had a white flag to stake my claim on this land like a settler, I would have stuck it in the ground-based on my first impression of the property. It was another blank canvas I could paint a new picture on.

After I saw the river property, a sense of peace came over me concerning the subject of leaving the farm in WV. I made an offer on the place. Shortly after, during a visit with Meemaw, I told her about the prospect and showed her pictures of the property. She responded by telling me that Saltville is the town where Uncle Estil lived. This was an immediate sign. But nowhere near what began unfolding rapidly before me. I started researching about Estil and his store. He passed away decades ago, so all I had to go off of was whatever I could find online. I came across information that Peepaw's grandparents also lived, died, and are buried in Saltville. Suddenly I found a bigger link that directly tied me to this place. Husband helped me narrow down the area where Estil's general store used to be. So we made a return trip to Saltville in hopes of finding clues to tracing my family's history there. We drove to the location where we hoped to find Estil's old Venable Grocery store. It seemed to have been a dead-end as there were no remnants of a store there.

So we went to the closest house in proximity and found a couple in the driveway, heading out to town in their car. We pulled up beside them and asked them if they knew Estil Venable. The man got out and started talking. He stated that he had been a lifelong VFW buddy of Estil's. He then pointed directly across the street and said, "Right there is Estill's house." It was the very house I sat on the front porch of many times as a child, while Peepaw and Estil exchanged conversations. I recognized it. We had come to the right place after all. The man went on to say that Estil's first store was beside his house, but was since torn down. But he explained that there was a second store, in the town of Glade Spring, at the current site of the Pizza Plus. He also told us of a Veteran's Memorial wall in downtown Saltville, that Estil helped commission during his leadership of the local VFW. We shook hands with the man and set off to pinpoint the locations he mentioned.

Part 2

Throughout the entire ordeal of finding myself in need of a new home, I prayed relentlessly to God for answers. But also, I needed my Peepaw at this time more than ever. And I kept saying silently over and over, (and sometimes I would even say out loud), "Peepaw I need your advice. I need your help. What should I do? Please show me a sign." We went directly to the Veteran's Memorial wall. I stood there in front of it, scanning the names on the bricks for any soldiers that may be my relations. And there before my eyes, I see a name stand out among all the hundreds of others, Gary Venable. My Peepaw. He couldn't have presented a more clear signal than that. I immediately broke down sobbing. Husband, (not knowing my personal plea for help from Peepaw), had no idea why I was so completely shaken to the core. He kept asking what was wrong. I couldn't even find the words to say, that my cry for help was answered. It was proof to me that my grandfather is still watching over me. He heard me. And he answered me. I was validated. My tears were happy tears, and tears of relief because at that moment I knew I was being led in the right direction. We also found Estil's name on that wall, along with his brothers, Peepaw's father and his grandfather. No one in my family even knew we had a connection to this town so deeply rooted. They knew nothing about the memorial wall or that Peepaw's name was on it. How could this be? [The town of Saltville I visited as a guest the year before, because of a stranger I felt compelled to introduce myself to, who became a friend and invited me to this town, which started at a festival I attended, because of my path down the road of moonshine, and so on, etc., etc.] It all added up. It was a series of dots on an intricately planned map that connected to come full circle. When something happens in this way, there is no doubt that God directed every part of a grand script that played out exactly the way it was destined to be.

Once I pulled myself together from being blown away with a whirlwind of emotions, we went on to find the location of Estil's general store in the neighboring town of Glade Spring. Low and behold, the place where it once stood was directly across the road from none other than the Nickerson Snead House. I was floored again. This haunted house, that I was invited to be a guest in, that I was scared shitless of, that kept compelling me to return, and led to the close friendship I formed with the owner is right beside my families old general store, that I had visited as a child. Seriously? I called my mother at the end of that day and told her everything that had transpired. She too was in complete awe at the alignment of such a string of events. I sent all our family a picture of Peep's name on the wall. The following day, Husband and I returned to West Virginia. I called Ronda to tell her of my discovery, about my family store being next to her museum. I said, "Hey Ronda, my Uncle Estil's general store was right across from your haunted house." She said, "Estil who?" I replied, "Estil Venable." She went on to reveal that she was also related to Estil. Which means, Ronda and I are related as cousins. And we find this out after being good friends for one year, and my many return trips to stay in her haunted house. Also, Estil purchased his general store from the owners of the Nickerson Snead House at the time. It once belonged to the same property. You couldn't make this shit up if you tried to. It is at minimum, mind boggling. To sort it all out and try to make sense of it seems complicated, but it is in essence very plain. The bottom line is, this was all fate written in the stars before it even came into the light of day. I have no question in my mind that I am headed to where I am meant to be in the next journey of my life.

Having said all that, something else came into play. The road that winds along the river and leads to the property we put an offer on, was a path used by soldiers during the Civil War battles of Saltville. Husband did more research and dug up the fact that his great, great-grandfather was a member of the Union Cavalry, and fought in those very battles. We went back and met with the current owners of the river property, a Native American woman, and her husband who is a National Guard soldier. He told us that the Union Cavalry travelled down the old country road of the property, and camped on the land we were going to purchase. That sealed the deal even more indefinitely. Now we both had historical ties to the place we would make our new homestead. My boss Tiny went with us to see the land that day, along with my in-laws. (I was nervous to cross the swinging bridge with Tiny, being the giant of a man that he is. I could just see the whole thing come crashing down and being swept away in the river). Our clan seemed to like the property. But the fact that the land isn't easily accessible would easily deter many buyers. All who joined us there were concerned about this issue. But that very aspect is exactly what made us initially fall in love with it. We want to be secluded and cut off from the rest of civilization to an extent. Besides that, there is a grand old Willow tree standing tall and proud on the land, and I have always wished for such a tree. It means a lot to me to live in a location where I have a connection to family ties. And not only is that true for me with Saltville but knowing that it also applies to Husband with the river land; I can rest assured that we can make a new home for ourselves. Also, my son has been wanting to return to Virginia for many years. So this gives him another place that he can call home.

The next time I returned to the area in mid-August of 2019, was to attend the annual Saltville Civil War Re-enactment as a spectator instead of a special guest and to close on the property. We took Faith on this trip since she hadn't seen the place yet and I couldn't sign my name to the deed without her approval and blessing. Ronda allowed us to stay as guests in her haunted house again for the weekend. We decided to have dinner at the Pizza Plus across the road (the site of Estil's general store). I was again taken back when I walked in and saw an entire wall lined with pictures of the old Venable Grocery. It was memorialized even in the new business that took its place. That weekend we took Faith to enjoy the local culture and places of interest. We visited the Museum of the Middle Appalachia's in Saltville. We took her to the salt wave pool downtown. We went to the re-enactment where we met with Greg Shook and his now-wife, Donna, along with Paul and

Stefanie (who were also married in a dual ceremony with Greg and Donna. And I should mention that Ewok, who married Husband and I, also officiated their wedding as Reverend). We had a picnic on the beautiful grounds of the Palmer Mill in Saltville. We also took Faith to her first drive-in theater experience in the nearby town of Marion. At the end of our trip, we went to Abingdon and officially closed on our property on the North Fork of the Holston River. We could finally stake a flag on our new land.

We ended up only staying two out of three nights in the haunted house. The second night some scary things happened there that caused us to end up on the front porch at 3am in our pajamas and underwear. Not to mention a mirror falling off the wall and the bathroom faucet repeatedly turning on by itself. We hadn't slept at all so we checked into the Econo Lodge directly behind the museum, which sat where the old plantation stables used to sit. I did another live video from the balcony of the motel, so I could tell my friends about the closing of my new property and the related events that unfolded about my family and my newly found relation to Ronda. Jim Bordwine came and hung out with us there for a while also. That night around 2am, Ronda texted me and offered me a deal. She suggested I should write an autobiography, and offered to publish it with her company Full Moon Publishing. After a moment of thought, I accepted her offer. That is how this book came about. All of this is connected on many different levels. I have Ronda to thank for this opportunity to share my story. The closing of the property and the book offer all aligned on the one year anniversary of my first visit to Saltville (as an adult) and my initial introduction to Ronda. I look forward to being neighbors with Jim and Ronda when I relocate to their area.

Also during that trip, we were repeatedly told by different sources that the Palmer Mill was once leased and may be leased out again. After so many people told us this information, it suddenly seemed like more than a coincidence. So before we left town to head back to West Virginia, we stopped by the Saltville City Office to inquire about it. We left our names and numbers at the desk with the secretary. Before we even got out of the parking lot, the mayor called Husband and arranged for the city manager to meet us at the mill to give us a personal tour. The city officials have a vision for the mill. They want to bring it to life and make it the heart of the town. We were offered a potential role to help make that happen. However, we are waiting for Faith to graduate high school next year before we make the official move from the farm to our river property. So hopefully that will still be in the cards for us by the time we get there. Either way, I was impressed with how welcoming the city officials have been to us as new future residents. The mayor and city manager offered to give us a personal tour of the town. They seem genuinely happy to have us join their community. And we, in turn, are looking forward to calling Saltville home.

The town of Saltville is situated in the very center of the Appalachians.. being in Virginia and surrounded geographically on each corner by West Virginia, Kentucky, Tennessee, and North

Carolina. Also, it is geologically unique, since it was once the site of an ocean that receded to reveal salt wells. Coastal birds flock there and spread the seeds of coastal plant species. It has a seaside atmosphere but in the middle of the mountains. It was once the home to woolly mammoths and mastodons who migrated there in pursuit of the salts. Those prehistoric animals were followed by some of the first indigenous tribes who settled the area. The salt works played a major role in the sustenance of Civil War troops who relied on the mineral to preserve their rations, which is what led to the Battles of Saltville in a fight over the salt wells. The rocket fuel for the first trip to the moon was harvested in Saltville. It was once a booming company town for the industrial business of salt and gypsum mining. Modern-day it is a small sleepy town where businesses are closed on Sundays, residents gather for social events, and daily life seems to go on in a peaceful manner for those who make up the population. It is a very interesting yet seemingly simple place. I for one will feel a sense of pride to hang my hat there when the time comes, regardless of my reluctance to leave the farm in West Virginia.

Now to catch up on other current events. It has taken me about five months to write this entire book. In fact, I could write a book about writing this book. During the time I have been working diligently on this, I have experienced a vast array of highs and lows. That has been the case for most of my life anyways, but this round has especially made me an emotional wreck. I have recently lost three of my beloved animals.. our longtime family dog and king of the farm MoMo, our miniature horse Cooper, and Sassy the pig. No matter how many pets I have loved and lost, it kills me every time. They are my adopted children. Losing MoMo was especially hard on Faith. He has been her best friend ever since she was five years old. I always dreaded the day something should happen to him because I knew my daughter would be the saddest girl in the whole world on that day. And she was. Also recently.. our newest family member, a bulldog named "Cattle Annie", has had a litter of eight puppies fathered by Chief Delshay. Faith helped me midwife Annie as we welcomed all her pups into the world.. in the same room where we welcomed MoMo eleven years ago. I am snuggling with my pick of the litter now, the one I decided to keep, "Half Stache". It seems every time a life ends, a new life also begins.

My brothers Andrew and Anthony both recently got engaged. Andrew is expecting his first child with his fiancé Maxanne, who also has a son named Zayden which my brother loves as his own. Many of us gathered at their home this past Christmas. Ironically, Andrew is living in a house in Summersville, WV that Meemaw and Peepaw used to own, where my mom and her sister lived when they were kids. My big sister Haley is busy raising her two boys, Javier and Julian. Although we have lost almost all of our elders, our family continues to grow with children. Haley brought her kids and husband to West Virginia for a visit not long ago. Her boys had never seen where their mother is from. We took them out to our grandparents' old farm in Canvas. It was the first time Haley and I had been there since my kids were just toddlers. It was like taking a stroll down Memory Lane. Although the old house is close to falling in, and the land has been dismantled with logging.. we could see through the ruin of it all, back to its glory days and all our best childhood memories. We rightfully stole Grandpa Sparks' horseshoe that he hung over the front door many moons ago. It was the only thing we had left to take from the place that gave us our best start in life. The place that helped to shape who we are. Haley and I held hands walking across the cattle guards together and down the old gravel road that is now covered with a carpet of grass. We reminisced on the days of our youth. I hope we can walk that same road together as old ladies. It always takes us back to our beginning. It will always hold a place in our hearts and play like a familiar tune.

As I said earlier, I have been reunited with my sister Marci after ten years of separation. The last time we had seen each other was at the Kentucky Derby in 2009. Same for Haley. None of us knew then that we would be apart for so long again. It was unintentional for us to go our separate ways. We all went through some major changes over the course of those ten years, and life got in the way as it sometimes does. But last spring she contacted me and told me that she was moving from Mississippi to Tennessee. It was the best news I had heard in a long time. As soon as I could, I took a trip to see her. It was as if no time had passed between us at all. We talked nonstop all day and late into the night. The last time I had seen her she was only 21. Now she is 32 with a successful career under her belt in the Emergency Services field. She has been a firefighter, a paramedic, and a professor. She is very intelligent and wise beyond her years. I am so proud of the woman Marci has become. She got married during our time away from each other, so I also gained another brother and two nieces which are his daughters. My nephew Anthony had grown so much since I last saw him, and he looks just like our dad did when he was a little boy. I cannot put into words how happy I was to be reconnected with Marci and Anthony.

Since that first visit Marci and I had, we have made a point to get together as often as we possibly can. The three of us sisters recently made a trip to Nashville together. Haley was there on business and invited Marci and I to join her at the end of her trip. That reunion was everything. It was the first time we had all been together in a decade. We stayed in an amazing Air BNB in Franklin, Tennessee. We all played dress-up like little girls, something Haley and I had done together as kids, but never with Marci. I swear it was as though we all stepped back in time and became little girls for a moment. I just knew if I was to catch a reflection of us in a mirror, I would see a glimpse of us all as children together, a glimpse of what should have been. Marci had tears in her eyes as she curled our hair and helped us with our makeup. We zipped each other up in our dresses and helped select each other's jewelry. We took turns admiring one another. Haley and I tried to choke back the tears on something that meant everything to us. Our long lost baby sister was with us where she belonged.

There were no words any of us could say that would do this occasion enough justice. The three of us sisters embraced in a big group hug, and then the moment vanished of us as little girls playing dress-up. Suddenly we were grown women again, and ready to take Nashville by storm in our high heels and pearls. We went out on the town all decked out in 1920's fashion, to the speakeasy below the Johnny Cash Museum, called "House of Cards". Everything about that night was magical. Everyone that passed by us stopped and complimented us as elegant ladies. We had the most expensive dinner I have ever had, and carried on with the most inappropriate dinner table talk. All weekend, we ate and drank, talked and caught up, laughed and cried. I was so emotionally spent by the time I returned Marci to her home near Knoxville, that when I went to leave, I ended up getting lost and driving for four hours straight in a giant triangle.. then ended up back at her house where I stayed for the night with her. We filled in a lot of blanks that visit. We connected dots and found missing pieces to the puzzle of our childhoods and the loss of our father.

Then we all got together again this past Thanksgiving, for what was our first holiday with Marci. She rented a log cabin on Norris Lake near her home in Sharp's Chapel. Marci's mother Lori joined us. It was the first time Haley had seen her since our dad's funeral, and the first time I had seen her since I met Marci when I was seventeen. Lori shared stories about Daddy with us. We were there during the anniversary of the accident which took his life, so that added to the score of emotions we were all feeling. But we had a good time. We drank wine and moonshine, soaked in the hot tub, played games and danced. We had all our families together for the first time, our husbands and kids (except for J.J. who was away on his own important endeavor).

After we worked together preparing our Thanksgiving feast, we gathered and sat at the tables. As I looked around the room and saw our children around the kids' table, and all us adults seated at our own table, I was swept with sudden sadness. I never got to sit at the kids' table with Marci. We never had that chance. We never got to have food fights with her, like Haley and I had done as children. So I started crying, spilling tears onto my dinner plate. Marci, knowing exactly why I was crying, said, "Would it make you feel better if I throw food at you Sister?" I said, "Yes." And so, as grown-ass women, we had our first food fight together. That did my heart and soul good.

Tears turned to laughter. Yet another experience for us to check off the long list of things we have never done together as sisters. Marci has been my support system for the past year. She has seen me through many of my darkest hours and brightest days. She has also been one of my biggest supporters in the writing of this book. And I look forward to making so many more memories with her and filling the pages of our own book as sisters.

Moving onto other current news.. I have had to get a regular job to help pay for the acquired river property. I worked at Hawks

Nest State Park on the New River Gorge for about four months. I was working the second shift from 3pm to 11pm almost every night, and driving two hours a day. Most of this book was written at Hawks Nest in the Lodge during the quiet hours of the evening. The long drive gave me time to think about what to write. I pulled off the road countless times to type notes of things that would pop into my head. Then I would stay up writing until the early morning hours. I got to the point that the commute was wearing me down. My autoimmune illness still very much runs rampant and my body couldn't take the drive anymore. I struggle every day doing even the most simple of tasks. I am worn down after years of suffering from my sickness. So I quit that job and found a new one closer to home. Working a regular full-time job has forced me to put most of my Lady Outlaw business on the back burners for now, and I have been laying low because of that. Hopefully, when this book comes out along with my signature honeysuckle shine which is finally about to be released, I can get back in full swing to everything I have poured into building a career in the moonshine industry.

Recently, my son swore into the military for a six-year term, graduated high school, turned 18, then shipped off to basic training at Fort Leonard Wood, Missouri.. in that order. It all happened so fast I haven't even been able to process the first of these monumental milestones for him, let alone all of them combined. It has left me unraveled. As I watched him being driven away from me at the MEPS station, I had a major meltdown in the parking lot.

I just fell apart. A passing-by soldier tried to comfort me. He said, "It will get easier, I promise." I couldn't even say thank you. All I could do was sit there sobbing uncontrollably. I knew the next time I saw my little boy, he would be a man. I cried for ten days straight when he first left. I couldn't even function. I just wandered around the house feeling lost without my son at home. He has since graduated from basic and is a soldier of the Army National Guard. He is still stationed at Leonard Wood completing his AIT training for 88M Transportation. He is making a career as a professional truck driver, both for the military and civilian realms. On one hand, I am so very proud of J.J. for volunteering to serve our country. On the other hand, ever since he was a baby, I have dreaded the day that he grows up and flies from the nest. I can't even deal with it. I honestly don't know how any parent copes with their children becoming adults and setting out on their own into this big wicked world. It doesn't seem natural to me. Watching my little boy turn into a man is a bittersweet experience, to say the least. Nothing or no one could prepare me for the pure pride and the harsh heartache that coincide together to form such a mix of indescribable feelings all combined in a roller coaster of happiness and sadness. The past four months have been some of the hardest of my entire life, with my son away, and knowing that he could possibly be deployed to war should that become a factor during his six-year term. For the first month, I had no communication with him over the phone. We sent many letters back and forth. J.J. finally got to make calls towards the end of basic training. Hearing his voice and knowing he was okay made me feel much better. Then I finally got to see my soldier when we drove to Missouri for family day and his graduation. I drove back by myself a few weeks later to pick him up for holiday block leave. Having him home for Christmas was the best gift ever. As I am writing this, there are 40 days, 15 hours, 8 minutes, and 45 seconds till he is released to come back home. Obviously, I am counting down the time till I am reunited with my only son.

Faith will be seventeen this spring. She is driving on her own now, which causes me to have a nervous breakdown. (I don't think I will ever get used to my kids driving.) Faith is in the second half of her junior year of high school. She has always been a straight-A student since kindergarten. She is also dual-enrolled as a college student and will have her Associates's degree by the time she graduates high school. Faith is so smart and so kind. She makes me smile and laugh more than anyone else I have ever known. She is the most beautiful sight my eyes have ever seen. Every time I look at Faith, her beauty takes my breath away. Personality-wise, she is more like me every day. We could be twins. I couldn't have had a child any more like me, even if I had cloned myself. Faith is busy making plans for her flight from the nest which I know will be here in the blink of an eye and has me even more distraught than her brother's departure because when her time comes to leave I will have an empty nest. And I am not even remotely okay with that. I just want my children to stay with me forever. I want to always protect them from every danger and any hardships. Losing my first child has had a permanent impact on the way I have parented my other two children. I remain as an overprotective hawk keeping a constant and vigilant watch on them. I pray for them every second of every day for their safety, health, and happiness.

I find myself involuntarily progressing into the next phase of my life. With my children becoming grown-ups, it seems like the time has almost come to pass on the torch to them. I have lived four decades of my life and now it is time for them to live their lives as individuals with their own dreams and goals. I know the time will soon come for me to take the backseat from a full-time role as their mother to more of a support role for them. I want the next chapters of their lives to take center stage of my existence. I want to be there to cheer them on and encourage them to move forward, just as I have done with them as children. But to shed the wisdom of my years with them in a different light as they progress through adulthood. To give them an extended version of myself, depending on whatever they may need along the way. I look forward to seeing which directions they steer their own adventures.. with military, college, careers, relationships, and hopefully someday lots of grandbabies for me. In some regards, I am ready for my hair to turn grey and to transition into the second half of my life. It is my turn to be one of the elders of my tribe. If I die tomorrow, I feel like I have lived a full life up to this point. But I wish to stick around at least long enough to see my children live out most of their own lives. To watch them flourish and follow the paths that will lead them to where ever they are meant to be. I am beyond proud of the children I have raised. They have far exceeded all my greatest hopes and expectations. They will always be my whole world.

Then there is the transition of farm life to river living for me. I am going from 112 acres to only four acres. That is a major downsize. I will take all the animals I have left, of course, and rebuild a much smaller scale farm on the banks of the North Fork of the Holston River. I have plans to make a secret garden around the Willow tree, where I can grow flowers and have my morning coffee, read a book, or swing in a hammock. We also have the undertaking of building a house on the land. As of now, it sits as a blank slate, other than a small barn that stands as the remnants of an old homeplace that once occupied the property. We are in the process now of getting a camper on the land as temporary living quarters until our home is built. I have recruited Hippy to be the master craftsman on the project. Although his response is "I already built you one house, woman!" But I will talk him into one more. If only I could pick up my current house and move it to the river. It is my absolute favorite of all houses I have ever lived in. It has the most character and the most of my personality throughout it. But sometimes it is necessary to start over with nothing, to create something from the ground up that you can be proud of. Once we are settled into our new place, I intend to carry on with a slower-paced existence. I need peace and quiet for a change. I want to live the river life, with boating and fishing, just relax and keep with the pace of the flowing water. Maybe peddle some liquor downstream in a canoe.

Also, there is the issue of my age. I will be forty in less than four months. I know that is still young by some standards. But by other standards, as a woman, it is hard to see your youth or beauty fade and to watch yourself reaching mid-life. Plus it seems as though there is an expiration date on women when it comes to being a public figure. In other words, I can't be Lady Outlaw forever. At some point, I will be silently asked to step down and retire from my role in the moonshine community. I have already seen that gradually beginning to happen. But I will continue to give it all I've got until I have nothing left to offer. Then I will respectfully and quietly bow out into obscurity. All things run their course in due time. And everything must come to an end at some point. I just hope that when I reach that ending, I can always look back and be proud of what I accomplished and thankful for the chance to be a part of something bigger than myself. I will always be grateful to every single person who has supported me along the way. It has been one of the greatest honors of my life to be at the forefront of the industry as a female participant. But this is not a farewell letter. I'm not going anywhere just yet. I still have more work to do before I fade out of sight. I didn't come this far to give up. I will leave no unfinished business behind.

Part 3

Once I relocate, I will only be an hour away from the distillery. So that will allow me to come and go more frequently in pursuit of getting Outlaw Spirits on more shelves. I will most likely slow my roll on the "Dusty Trail" of festivals, however. I have travelled so many countless miles in my time. I don't know how many more miles I have left in me. I am road weary. But the good part is, I will be more centrally located to events once I move to the Southwest region of Virginia. So logistically the trips won't take as much of a toll on me if I do decide to venture out onto the social scene. I have to say that the festivals I have attended over the years have been the catalyst to get me known on a personal level as a public figure. They have connected me in a more intimate way with my followers. I want to thank the ones who host these events, for having me as a guest and allowing me to be a part of festivities with my friends and supporters. They are the reason we have special occasions to get together as a community. The many invaluable friendships I have formed will stand the test of time and stay with me into the next chapters of my life. I wish I could list all my friends, but there are too many to name. You all know who you are.

And now that I have caught you up on what is happening currently with me and my family, I want to talk about why I have written this book. I have left no subject untouched and no issue undiscussed. I have pretty much laid myself out in the context of words, for anyone to read. That is an overwhelming accomplishment for anyone to achieve. But this is so much more than just words. All the history that went into each word, of each line, on every page of this book; they all have every aspect of me engraved in them. They are all a part of me that I will leave behind when I am gone. This ensures that my story will go on. I am leaving my mark in this way as a testament of my life and what made me who I am. I'm not special. I am no different than any other woman out there struggling through life. And I know there are some who have a more harrowing tale than me. But I share my story because although it is uniquely my own, it is also a universal story. It is relatable to others on many different levels. I want other women to know that there are women everywhere and in every walk of life, who endure the same hardships and heartbreaks, and enjoy the same successes and happiness. We all have a story to tell. And everyone's story is worth telling. Everyone is equally important. Hold your head high. Never give up. Keep moving forward. Never let anyone take your worth from you. That's what I want you to gather from what you have read here.

I wish I could say that I have exaggerated my own story within these pages. But sadly a lot of what you have read has actually been downplayed and minimized, as it is not my intention to hurt anyone in the telling of the truth as I know it. But at the same time, I have been as honest and transparent as I can be without becoming brutal to others. Also, I could have easily gotten off into other people's stories here but I have tried my best to stick to my own, only veering off into others where it pertains to me personally. I have had my closest family members read along as I have written this. They have all been extremely supportive and encouraging. I especially need to thank my beautiful and gracious Meemaw, who has diligently been editing this book along the way. She is my only living grandparent, and her approval of this project means the most to me of anyone. Others who have helped to guide me through this are Faith, Mama, Marci, Haley, Aunt Vicki, Aunt Brenda, my mother-in-law Pam and last but not least, Husband, who is my #1 fan and biggest supporter. I couldn't have made it through this ordeal without all their help. I could never thank them all enough.

Now looking ahead to the future, I hope I can only add to what I have written here. This is not the end, but a new beginning. I know where I am headed but I don't know what awaits me there. I intend to keep living life to the fullest of my abilities. I have more adventures to take, more memories to make and more stories to tell down the road. I want to soak in as many sunrises and sunsets as I can. I want to have a life I can look back on and feel a sense of contentment, knowing I have done everything I set out to do on my trip around the sun. In many ways, I am a walking contradiction of myself; I am whole and incomplete. I am a nice person and an asshole. I am a sinner and a religious woman. I am moral and corrupt. I have good manners but curse like a sailor. I am short in stature but I stand tall. I am humbled and proud. I love hard and I hate hard. I play as much as I work. I always have my mind made up but I also change my mind like the weather. I am stubborn and agreeable. I am confident and insecure. I am calm but I have a bad temper. I am a respectful citizen and a rebellious outlaw. I am restless but settled. I am broken yet strong. I am nothing special and something special at the same time. I am everything it takes to make me who I am. And I will keep being myself because I own who I am. I have tripped, fallen and gotten back up over and over. I have fought battles within myself and I have fought wars with outside forces. All the hells I have walked through, all the fires I have started and put out, all the losses I have endured, all the tragedies I have experienced... they are part of what defines me. But the moral of my story is, I survived to tell the tale. I have also experienced life at its best. I have witnessed miracles. I have known true love and pure happiness. I have felt the sunshine upon me. I have breathed and lived and loved with every ounce of my heart and soul, and hopefully, I have left this world a better place than I found it. I will keep moving forward until I come full circle and my ending is told in its own due course. But for now, it is time to turn the page...

ABOUT THE AUTHOR

Tiffany Sparks, also known as "Lady Outlaw", comes from humble beginnings originating in the hills of Kentucky. She is firmly rooted in her Appalachian heritage, where generations of her family have called the mountains of West Virginia home. Tiffany raised her children on a farm near the small town of Birch River, WV. She is a devoted wife and mother. She has a profound love for animals and nature. Her interests include agriculture, music, travel and history.

Rising from obscurity, Tiffany has become a public figure and a well-known female contributor within the moonshine industry. She proudly represents women among the predominantly male trade. She is the first woman from West Virginia, in the history of the legal market, to obtain a private label of moonshine. She is also a licensed WV State Ambassador for East Tennessee Distillery. Her initial product under the brand established as "Outlaw Spirits" is bottled as "Untamed".

Made in the USA
Middletown, DE
26 October 2020

22764642R00333